# On Socialists and
# "the Jewish Question"
# after Marx

REAPPRAISALS IN JEWISH SOCIAL
AND INTELLECTUAL HISTORY

*General Editor: Robert M. Seltzer*

*Martin Buber's Social and Religious Thought:
Alienation and the Quest for Meaning*
LAURENCE J. SILBERSTEIN

*The American Judaism of Mordecai M. Kaplan*
EDITED BY EMANUEL S. GOLDSMITH, MEL SCULT,
AND ROBERT M. SELTZER

*On Socialists and "the Jewish Question" after Marx*
JACK JACOBS

# On Socialists and "the Jewish Question" after Marx

Jack Jacobs

NEW YORK UNIVERSITY PRESS
NEW YORK & LONDON

*Library of Congress Cataloging-in-Publication Data*
Jacobs, Jack Lester, 1953–
On socialists and "the Jewish question" after Marx / Jack Jacobs.
p.   cm. — (Reappraisals in Jewish social and intellectual
history)
Includes bibliographical references and index.
ISBN 0-8147-4178-9 (alk. paper)
1. Jewish socialists.   2. Socialism and antisemitism.   3. Jews—
Europe—Public opinion.   4. Zionism—Public opinion.   I. Title.
II. Series.
HX550.J4J33   1991          91-16630
335'.0089'924—dc20          CIP

New York University Press books are printed on acid-free paper,
and their binding materials are chosen for strength and durability.

*Book design by Ken Venezio*

# Contents

# Acknowledgments

I have received help from a large number of individuals and institutions in the years during which I have been at work on this book. I have benefited enormously from the aid given by staff members of the Bund Archives of the Jewish Labor Movement, including Benjamin Nadel, Director of the Bund Archives, and Leo Greenbaum. I remember with particular gratitude the help I obtained from the late Hillel Kempinsky, who often brought source material stored in the Bund Archives to my attention, and from Jacob Sholem Hertz, with whom I discussed and debated the history of the Jewish socialist and labor movements on many occasions. I also remember the camaraderie of past and present staff members of the Leo Baeck Institute, including, among others, Alan Divack, Frank Mecklenburg, Michael Riff, and Diane Spielmann. Marion Kaplan, whom I first met while she was working at the Leo Baeck Institute, has regularly taken the time to read and comment on my work. I greatly appreciate her help and admire her insight and erudition. Staff members of both the library and the archives of the YIVO Institute for Jewish Research—among whom Dina Abramowicz and Zachary Baker richly deserve to be singled out—have also helped me over a period of years.

I conducted research for this study not only in the three institutions noted above, but also in the Archiv der sozialen Demokratie, Bonn, the British Library, London, the Central Zionist Archives, Jerusalem, the Columbia University Libraries, the Kölner Bibliothek zur Geschichte des deutschen Judentum, Harvard University Libraries, the Hoover Institution on War, Revolution, and Peace, Stanford, the Institute for Labour Research in Memory of P. Lavon, Tel Aviv, the Internationaal Instituut voor Sociale Geschiedenis, Amsterdam, the Jewish National and University Library, Jerusalem, the Jewish Theological Seminary, New York, the New York Academy of Medicine, the New York Public Library, Rosenthaliana Library, Amsterdam, the Tamiment Institute, New York, the É. Vandervelde Archives, Brussels, the Verein für Geschichte der Arbeiterbewegung, Vienna, and the Zionist Library, New York, and would like to thank each of these institutions for allowing me access to their collections. I am especially thankful to all those who helped me during my visits to Amsterdam (including D. E. Devreese and the late Boris Sapir), Bonn (including Karl-Heinz Klär), Vienna (Wolfgang Maderthaner), and Israel. The Bibliothèque Nationale, Paris, the Library of Congress, the Sozialwissenschaftliche Studienbibliothek, Vienna, the Stadtarchiv, Zurich, the Stadt- und Landesbibliothek, Dortmund, the Státní Knihovna České socialistické republiky, Prague, the Weizmann Archives, Rehovot, and the Zivilstandesamt Basel-stadt graciously sent me materials unavailable in the institutions listed above. The Inter-Library Loan Offices of Columbia University, John Jay College, and the New York Public Library assisted me in obtaining books and dissertations from additional locations.

Many people have read earlier versions or portions of the manuscript or both and have made helpful comments, suggestions, and criticisms. The late Alexander Erlich was particularly generous with his time and knowledge. My thanks as well to Chimen Abramsky, Robert Amdur, Abraham Ascher, Herbert Deane, Jonathan Frankel, Julian Franklin, Helmut Gruber, Helmut Hirsch, John Kautsky, Donald Niewyk, Yoav Peled, Anson Rabinbach, Jehuda Reinharz, and Robert Wistrich. I am grateful for the encouragement given to me by Robert Seltzer, who helped arrange for the publication of this book. I wish to thank Ilse Kautsky Calabi, Harriet Freidenreich, Jacques E. Picard, Leo J. van Rossum, Feliks Tych, and Werner G. Zimmerman, all of whom sent me valuable materials or information, and the members of the Government Department of the John Jay College of Criminal Justice, the City University of New York, who have been uniformly supportive of my work.

My work has been facilitated by the receipt of a Dean Harry J.

Carman Fellowship, a Chamberlain Fellowship, a Leo Baeck Institute/German Academic Exchange Service Fellowship, and by grants from the Columbia University Council for Research in the Social Sciences, the National Endowment for the Humanities, and the Memorial Foundation for Jewish Culture.

I appreciate the permission I have received to reprint material from articles by me that first appeared in *International Review of Social History*, *Studies in Contemporary Jewry*, and *The Austrian Socialist Experiment*.

Susan Milamed, finally, has been unfailingly wonderful throughout the last decade. I dedicate this book to her.

# Glossary

*ADAV:* The General German Workers' Association
*Bund:* The General Jewish Workers' Union
*CV:* The Central Association of German Citizens of the Jewish Faith
*ESDRP-PZ:* The Jewish Social Democratic Workers' Party Poalei-Zion
*Faraynigte:* The United Jewish Socialist Workers' Party
*Folkspartay:* The People's Party
*ISB:* The International Socialist Bureau
*PPS:* The Polish Socialist Party
*PPSD:* The Polish Social Democratic Party of Galicia and Upper Silesia
*PSR:* The Party of Socialist Revolutionaries
*RSDRP:* The Russian Social Democratic Workers' Party
*SDAP [D]:* The Social Democratic Workers' Party [of Germany]
*SDAP [Oe]:* The Social Democratic Workers' Party [of Austria]
*SDKP:* The Social Democracy of the Kingdom of Poland
*SDKPiL:* The Social Democracy of the Kingdom of Poland and Lithuania
*SERP:* The Jewish Socialist Workers' Party
*SPD:* The Social Democratic Party of Germany
*SS:* The Zionist Socialist Workers' Party
*USPD:* The Independent Social Democratic Party of Germany
*Vozrozhdeniye:* The Renaissance group
*VSPD:* The United Social Democratic Party of Germany
*ŻPSD:* The Jewish Social Democratic Party in Galicia
*ZVfD:* The Zionist Federation of Germany

xi

# Introduction

Much of the literature on the relationship between socialism and the Jews is marred by political animus or by overgeneralization. This is particularly true of the literature dealing with the attitudes of socialists toward "the Jewish question," that is, with socialist attitudes toward Jews, the future of Jewry, and related matters.[1]

In a well-known article entitled "Was Marx an Anti-Semite?" first published in 1949, Edmund Silberner concluded that if "the pronouncements of Marx are not chosen at random, but are examined as a whole, and if, on the other hand, by anti-Semitism aversion to the Jews is meant, Marx not only can but *must* be regarded as an outspoken anti-Semite."[2] According to Silberner, moreover, "Basically the same contempt for the Jews, though couched in a different language, is to be found in the writings of Karl Kautsky, Victor Adler, Franz Mehring, Otto Bauer, and others."[3] In other works, published over a period of years, Silberner extended this attack in an attempt to demonstrate that there was "an old anti-Semitic tradition within modern Socialism" and that this tradition explained the attitudes of many of the major socialist thinkers, both Marxist and non-Marxist, toward Jews and Jewry.[4]

A study by the German scholar Hans-Helmuth Knütter on the Jews and the German left in the Weimar Republic, published in 1972, echoed relevant portions of Silberner's works. "The left parties and organizations were in no way a force for the defense of Jewry as the anti-Semites claimed," Knütter concluded. "In all groups there were more or less strong reservations about the Jews, which were religiously, historically and sociologically conditioned."[5]

I

Some academics have completely rejected such assertions as tho of Silberner or Knütter, writing as if European socialists were wholly uninfluenced by anti-Semitism or even were by their nature incapable of having anti-Semitic perspectives. Peter Pulzer, for example, in *The Rise of Political Anti-Semitism in Germany and Austria*, wrote that there were "certain points of superficial resemblance" between anti-Semites and Social Democrats, but he also stressed that they "were at opposite poles of the political world and their mutual enmity was deep and lasting."[6] Walter Mohrmann, writing from a Leninist perspective in the early 1970s, made claims similar to those of Pulzer: "The history of the German workers movement is at the same time the history of the most consequential and most successful struggle against anti-Semitism which has ever been led by a political force in Germany."[7] Israeli scholar Shulamit Volkov rejected the notion that socialism was innately immune to anti-Semitism, but she nevertheless concluded that by the middle of the 1890s the German Social Democratic (SPD) leadership had become immunized against anti-Semitism.[8]

Even academics who have avoided identifying themselves with either of these oversimplistic camps have generally failed to emphasize the substantial differences on the Jewish question that existed within the socialist camp or the extent to which certain major socialist thinkers revised their views over the course of time. In *Socialism and the Jews*, for example—the most serious attempt published in recent years to grapple with socialist attitudes toward the issue—Robert Wistrich claims that "assimilationist internationalism with regard to the Jewish national problem was to be the consistent response of the SPD before 1914 . . . socialist theoreticians like Eduard Bernstein, Karl Kautsky and Rosa Luxemburg, though divided on many issues, were unanimous on this point."[9] In making this assertion, Wistrich stresses what was only an apparent unanimity. The three major theoreticians of the German social democratic movement in the era of the Second International (1889–1914) had notably different attitudes toward the issues of Jewish assimilation and Jewish nationalism. The differences in their attitudes are far more revealing than are the similarities.

One of the major points of this book is to demonstrate that there was a rainbow of perspectives within the socialist world on the

Jewish question (as there was on virtually every other question of theory and practice). Socialists were neither naturally inclined toward anti-Semitism, nor immune from anti-Semitic sentiments, nor united in their attitudes toward assimilation and Jewish nationalism. Differing family backgrounds, differing national contexts, and changes in the political world over several decades all help account for the range of attitudes exhibited by socialists toward individual Jews and the future of Jewry.

In the first part of this book I concentrate on the relevant ideas of a handful of prominent socialist thinkers and leaders who were active in the German-speaking world in the period beginning with the final quarter of the nineteenth century and ending with World War II. The views of the socialists on which I focus are not necessarily indicative of the views of the rank and file within the socialist movement, and the thinkers I emphasize do not necessarily represent the full range of socialist attitudes toward the Jewish question. By demonstrating the significant differences on relevant subjects among unusually prominent socialists, however, I hope to highlight the deficiencies in earlier examinations of this subject. Even among the relatively narrow sample of socialists whose views I examine in depth, all of whom were active within a generation of one another, and all of whom were not merely socialists but social democrats, there was no unanimity on the Jewish question any more than there was on the question of the road to socialism or, for that matter, the nature of socialism itself. The generalizations made by Silberner, Mohrmann, Pulzer, and Wistrich do not withstand scrutiny.

The second part of this book focuses on the reactions of Jewish writers to socialist writings on the Jewish question, which could best be characterized as contradictory. Jewish publicists in the Russian Empire, in Germany, and in the Austro-Hungarian Empire published a large number of responses to the writings, pronouncements, and actions of leading socialists touching on the Jewish question. The reactions by Jewish publicists that I survey differ dramatically from one another both within each of the countries I discuss and from country to country. The Jewish responses to socialist writings on the Jewish question, which differ from one another even more than do socialist attitudes toward the Jewish question, reveal more about differences within the Jewish world than they do about Marxism or socialism. On the whole, these Jewish responses tended to mirror their authors more than they clarified the views of the socialists about whom they were written.

The subject of socialists and the Jewish question after Marx is far more complex, and far less open to generalization, than earlier studies would have us believe. There was not a Marxist attitude toward the Jews, but a spectrum of Marxist (and socialist) attitudes toward the Jews. There was never a unified Jewish response to Marxist writings but a broad array of responses. My hope, throughout this book, is to substantiate and demonstrate the significance of these propositions.

# CHAPTER I

# Karl Kautsky: Between Baden and Luxemburg

Karl Kautsky's views on the Jewish question are of great import because of Kautsky's historical stature. In the years following Friedrich Engels's death, Kautsky was the leading orthodox Marxist theoretician, executor of Karl Marx's literary estate, editor of *Die Neue Zeit*, and a prolific author of popular Marxist tracts. Kautsky drafted the theoretical part of the SPD's Erfurt Program of 1891, and he wrote the classic rebuttal to Eduard Bernstein's revisionist works. It is scarcely an exaggeration to say that an entire generation of socialists around the world were taught Marx through Kautsky.

There is a sense in which Kautsky's views on the Jewish question were even more influential than were his views on other matters. For Kautsky was perceived as an authority on the Jewish question, even by many Marxists who were, or eventually became, sharply critical of his views on other matters.

In general, the academic community has neglected the study of Kautsky's views on the Jewish question. Those who have examined Kautsky's writings on this subject have tended to blur the distinctions between Kautsky's views and those of Marx and have also tended to ascribe anti-Semitic views to Kautsky. Edmund Silberner, for example, whose groundbreaking studies influenced many academicians, asserts that Kautsky had a "contempt for Judaism" differing in intensity, but not differing in essence, from that of Marx.[1] George Mosse claims that "for both Marx and Kautsky the Jews' supposed lack of humanity was of crucial concern."[2] Shlomo Avi-

neri, similarly, has allegedly commented that Kautsky's defense of
the Jews in the revised edition of his work *Rasse und Judentum*
"serves to reinforce in the mind of the Socialist reader one of the
fundamental doctrines of anti-Semitism."[3] While there is reason to
accept the view that Marx held anti-Semitic attitudes to some
extent, the evidence put forth by those who make this claim about
Kautsky does not stand up to a close examination.

Kautsky, who was born in Prague, initially spoke German with a
Czech accent. This accent led some of the German-speaking children of Vienna with whom Kautsky had contact when he moved to
that city in 1863 at the age of eight to suspect that he was of Jewish
origin (though that was not in fact the case) and to slight him on
the basis of that suspicion.[4] Though Kautsky never did make a
conscious connection between this early experience and his later
attitudes, it may well be that his early victimization at the hands
of those who thought that he was a Jew can help explain Kautsky's
considerable sympathy for the plight of the Jews throughout his
adult life.

There were no Jews in the first school that Kautsky attended and
no Jews in his father's circle of friends.[5] As a child, however, Kautsky occasionally visited his paternal grandfather, who owned a
house in the Jewish quarter of Prague. These visits provided Kautsky
with his first opportunity to observe Jews. In a memoir written six
decades after his initial exposure to Prague's Jewish quarter, Kautsky described the Jewish tenants of his grandfather's house as "poor,
intimidated, stunted beings who crawled before my grandfather
when he came to collect the rent."[6] Thus Kautsky's first significant
encounter with Jews, which left a lasting impression on him, involved Jews who were exploited. "It was not the Christians who
groaned under the rent-slavery of a Jew," Kautsky pointedly commented, "but the opposite."[7]

Kautsky had more extensive contact with Jews when, at the age
of twelve, he transferred from the Melk Seminary to the Academic
Gymnasium of Vienna.[8] Unlike the Melk Seminary, which was run
by Benedictine monks, the Academic Gymnasium had a substantial
number of Jews in its student body. Kautsky did not, at first, get
along well with his Jewish classmates. By 1870, however, Kautsky's
best friends were Jewish students in the gymnasium.[9]

During his student years, Kautsky tended to stereotype Jews and to poke fun at what he perceived as "Jewish characteristics."[10] As late as January 1880, Kautsky described his patron Karl Höchberg as "a Jew from Frankfurt, who, however, does not look markedly Jewish; his character is not at all Jewish."[11] Nevertheless, Kautsky's attitude toward Jews in general during this period was already far more sympathetic to Jewry than was that of many assimilated Jews. When Kautsky submitted an unsolicited article on the Jewish question to Höchberg's *Jahrbuch für Sozialwissenschaft und Sozialpolitik* in the spring of 1880, for example, Höchberg was unhappy with the piece because it manifested "too good an opinion of the Jews."[12] The manuscript submitted by Kautsky to the *Jahrbuch* is (unfortunately) not extant. Höchberg's letter to Kautsky of August 12, 1880, discussing Kautsky's article, however, allows us to conclude that Kautsky's description of the "Jewish character" was markedly partial to the Jews.[13]

During this same period Kautsky became a Marxist. Though Kautsky had joined the Austrian socialist movement in January 1875, it was not until he had met Eduard Bernstein and studied Engels's *Herrn Eugen Dührings Umwalzung der Wissenschaft*, widely known as *Anti-Dühring*, together with Bernstein that Kautsky became an advocate of Marxist rather than romantic socialism.[14] Both the fact that Kautsky was converted to Marxism by a work of Engels, and the fact that he studied this work together with Bernstein, explain much about Kautsky's philosophy for the rest of his life. For Kautsky's worldview, including his view of the Jewish question, was influenced more by Engels and Bernstein than by Marx.

Kautsky visited London between March and June 1881 and hoped to develop a close relationship with Marx during his visit. Kautsky did not succeed in this effort. He neither spent much time with Marx, nor was he able to impress Marx with his abilities. In fact, Marx's assessment of Kautsky—made after their first encounter—was extremely cutting:

He is a mediocrity with a small-minded outlook, superwise (only twenty-six), very conceited, industrious in a certain sort of way, he busies himself a lot with statistics, but does not read anything clever out of them, belongs by nature to the tribe of philistines but is otherwise a decent fellow in his own way. I turn him over to friend E[ngels] as much as possible.[15]

Since Marx kept his distance from Kautsky throughout Kautsky's 1881 visit and died before Kautsky returned to London in 1884, Kautsky never succeeded in reversing Marx's initial judgment of him. Although Kautsky eventually gained a worldwide reputation as an expert on Marxism, his study of this subject was not conducted under the auspices of Marx himself.

In contrast to his relationship with Marx, Kautsky's relationship with Engels eventually became quite close. Engels's initial opinion of Kautsky was not much higher than Marx's.[16] Engels, however, spent quite a bit of time with Kautsky on Kautsky's visits of 1881 and 1884 and had enormous, direct influence over Kautsky during Kautsky's third trip to London—a trip that extended from January 1885 to June 1888. Kautsky described the development of his relationship with Engels in the following terms: "Our acquaintance became friendship and led to an intimate communion, partly oral, partly maintained through correspondence, which lasted until the death of my great friend, and to which I have an unending debt."[17] In fact, the friendship between Engels and Kautsky actually cooled markedly after Kautsky left London in 1888 and never regained its earlier intensity.[18] The influence that Engels exerted on Kautsky's thought, however, never diminished in the slightest. Kautsky's Marxism bore the stamp of his contact with Engels throughout the rest of Kautsky's life.

Engels was Kautsky's greatest teacher, but Bernstein was clearly Kautsky's closest friend. As such, Bernstein exerted almost as much influence over Kautsky during the 1880s and early 1890s as did Engels. Bernstein was five years older than Kautsky and was a prominent figure in the socialist movement when Kautsky met him in Zurich in January 1880. Bernstein, for example, had been a delegate to the February 1875 conference that had unified the major wings of the German socialist movement. By October 1878, when Bernstein left his native Berlin for Switzerland in order to work as Höchberg's secretary, he had also embarked on the period of ideological transition that was to lead him to Marxism. Bernstein read *Anti-Dühring* in the winter of 1878–79, and in June 1879 entered into a regular correspondence with Engels. Thus, when Kautsky arrived in Zurich on January 23, 1880, at the invitation of Höchberg, Bernstein was in a position to act as his political guide. "I found a powerful leader in Eduard Bernstein," Kautsky wrote. "He was head and shoulders above me."[19] Kautsky and Bernstein lived in the same building during the years in which they were both in Zurich. They collaborated on many projects, agreed on all major political points, and were in fact all but inseparable.

Kautsky's conversion to Marxism was, of course, not contingent on the position of the Marxists in regard to the Jewish question. The deep and lasting influence that Engels and Bernstein had on Kautsky's views, however, is evident in Kautsky's writings on the Jewish question, as well as in his works on both capitalism and the road to socialism.

It is striking that none of Kautsky's writings on the Jewish question discusses—or even mentions—Marx's "Zur Judenfrage." There can be no doubt that Kautsky was familiar with Marx's piece. "Zur Judenfrage" was published in *Der Sozialdemokrat* in 1881, in *Berliner Volksblatt* in 1890, and was quoted in the *Vorwärts* in 1891.[20] Even if it were true, as Massing claims, that "Zur Judenfrage" was "relatively little known" before 1902,[21] it was certainly known to Kautsky long before that date. Why, then, did Kautsky never mention Marx's article?

Though the policy advocated by Marx in "Zur Judenfrage" was less onerous from the perspective of most Jews than the policies advocated by many of Marx's contemporaries (including, notably, Bruno Bauer), Kautsky was well aware that readers could take Marx to be an anti-Semite. Kautsky did not want Marxism to be associated in any way with anti-Semitism, and, above all, did not want himself to be associated with an anti-Jewish perspective. Kautsky, however, was also unwilling to criticize Marx openly unless absolutely necessary. For Kautsky saw his role as interpreter and as defender of the Marxist tradition, and he was unwilling to give ammunition to the opponents of Marxism by attacking Marx himself. Thus Kautsky sidestepped his problem by writing works on the Jewish question wholly different in tone from Marx's "Zur Judenfrage" but written in Marxist terminology and using a Marxist mode of analysis.

In so doing, Kautsky probably comforted himself with the knowledge that Engels and Bernstein had also broken with the tone of Marx's "Zur Judenfrage" in their writings on the Jewish question.

Throughout his career, Kautsky's views on anti-Semitic political movements, on Jewish assimilation, and on the Jewish socialist and labor movements were very similar to the views that Engels and Bernstein had held on these phenomena in the 1880s and 1890s.[22]

But Kautsky ought not to be seen entirely in the shadow of his teachers. The death of Engels, and Bernstein's break with orthodox Marxism, left Kautsky as the most prominent surviving member of what had been a group of Marxist leaders. Whereas before 1895 Kautsky's perspective on the Jewish question was merely one example of a view shared by many of the most renowned Marxists, a decade later Kautsky was the single most authoritative theoretician in the Marxist world, and his views on the Jewish question commanded enormously increased attention and respect. Even when Kautsky did no more than restate earlier opinions, his words were translated and debated in socialist circles.

Kautsky, however, could not and did not solely reiterate his mentor's views. On the contrary, Kautsky confronted aspects of the Jewish question which quite simply had not existed in Engels's day —let alone Marx's. One of these new aspects was the emergence of a mass-based Jewish Marxist movement with a national program— the General Jewish Workers' Union, most often known as the Bund. It was one thing to support the Jewish socialist and labor movements when these movements were cosmopolitan and anti-national, as they generally had been in the 1880s and 1890s, but it was quite another thing to support these movements after they began to demand national rights for Russian Jewry.

Another phenomenon related to the Jewish question that did not emerge until after Engels's death was the rise of Zionism as a mass political movement. Engels never so much as mentioned Zionism in his correspondence or other writings. Bernstein, similarly, did not take a public position on Zionism before the revisionist controversy. It was, therefore, left to Kautsky to set the tone for the orthodox Marxist position on the Bund and on Zionism. In fact, it was Kautsky who set the tone for the orthodox Marxist debate on the Jewish question in general during the period from 1895 to 1914.

The first piece by Kautsky relevant to the Jewish question published after he became a Marxist appeared in *Der Sozialdemokrat* in October 1882. "It is a characteristic sign," Kautsky wrote, "that

*Jew-baiting* breaks out precisely in those lands where 'divine right' rules uncontestedly."[23] Kautsky did claim there is a social "moment" to this baiting, but he also wrote that because the anti-Semites single out Jews, rather than attacking societal parasites without regard to race or religion, the anti-Semitic movement is unhealthy. The appearance of a Jew-baiting movement in Austria-Hungary demonstrates the corrupting influence of the absolutist form of government. In Kautsky's mind, there could be no doubt that the Austrian government was ultimately responsible for the attacks on the Jews that occurred in the Austro-Hungarian Empire. In explaining why the people had participated in anti-Jewish actions, Kautsky noted that in those places where the people are absolutely without rights, they tend to strike where they are least likely to encounter resistance. Thus, in Austria-Hungary, Jews were likely victims precisely because they were weak. "A thing like this" Kautsky concludes, "would not be possible in a free land."[24]

*why Jews were targets in Austria-Hungary*

Kautsky continued to attack anti-Semitism, both in public and in private, in the years following the publication of this article. In September 1883, for example, Kautsky wrote an article for the *Züricher Post* in which he noted the "ominous" magnitude of Jew-baiting in Austria-Hungary.[25] At the end of the same year, Kautsky wrote a manifesto to the workers of Austria in which he stressed the reactionary character of anti-Semitism: "Not the birth cries of a new society, but the death spasms of an old one manifest themselves in Hungarian Jew-baiting."[26] The Jew-baiting, Kautsky prophesied, will and must repeat itself and will ultimately affect not only the Jews, but also all those in the propertied classes.

Just as did Bernstein, Kautsky warned Engels of the power of the anti-Semites. In a letter to Engels written in 1884, Kautsky told his teacher that

we [Austrian Social Democrats] have difficulty in hindering our own people from fraternizing with the anti-Semites. The anti-Semites are now our most dangerous opponents, more dangerous than in Germany, because they pose as oppositional and democratic, thus comply with the instincts of the workers.[27]

Kautsky reiterated this warning in December 1884. The anti-Semitic movement is an enemy of the socialist movement, Kautsky declared, an enemy of "colossal dimensions."[28]

The first article by Kautsky on the Jewish question to appear under Kautsky's name was published in the *Oesterreichischer Arbeiter-Kalender für das Jahr 1885*. Though not many people openly identify themselves as anti-Semites, Kautsky asserted in this piece, nine-tenths of the population of Hungary belong to the anti-Semitic tendency. What, Kautsky asks, are the roots of the anti-Semitic movement? It is, he replies, first and foremost a class struggle. Society is divided into three sorts of classes: a rising class, a ruling class, and declining classes. Anti-Semitism is associated with the last of these three groups. Anti-Semitism, however, does not emerge in all areas in which there are declining classes, but only in those in which Jews "are still nationally separated from the rest of the population."[29] Where this is not the case, as in Western Europe, it could not possibly occur to any one to wage a class struggle against a race.

To Kautsky, the position the social democrats ought to take in regard to anti-Semitism is clear. Though the anti-Semitic movement borrowed socialist slogans, though it thundered against capital, the social democrats must condemn it, for it is "reactionary through and through."[30]

The anti-Semitic movement is also exploitative. The anti-Semites claim to struggle against exploitation, but they actually direct their energy primarily against working Jews. "There is, therefore, nothing more inimical to Social Democracy than anti-Semitism. . . . Anti-Semitism is not misunderstood socialism, but misunderstood feudalism."[31] It is not doing the preparatory work for socialism, but it is, on the contrary, socialism's "most dangerous opponent."[32]

The importance of this article by Kautsky cannot be overstated. It was the first open attack on the anti-Semitic political movements that could be definitely attributed to a major Marxist theoretician. Bernstein, while certainly in agreement with Kautsky's position, had not yet published anything on the issue in his own name by 1885. Engels, similarly, had, in *Anti-Dühring*, paved the way for the position delineated by Kautsky in this article. Engels, however, did not publish a public condemnation of the anti-Semitic political movement until 1890. Not necessarily in theory, but rather in terms of presenting a jointly held analysis to the public, Kautsky led the way.

In his article in the *Oesterreichischer Arbeiter-Kalender* Kautsky makes passing reference to Jewish "racial characteristics", which, he asserts, came into being as a result of historical conditions. Kautsky returned to the theme of Jewish characteristics in an article published in *Die Neue Zeit* in 1890. The modern anti-Semites, Kautsky notes in this article, attack the Jews because they are economic competitors. The anti-Semites do not admit that this is the case but claim that their ideology is grounded in "laws of nature," in a "natural" and "eternal" opposition of races.[33]

Kautsky states that opposition to the Jews is a long standing phenomenon. There were examples of such opposition as early as Roman times. He also says that anti-Semitism is geographically widespread, and can be shown to exist in all the lands of Europe and even in Asia. Nevertheless, he maintains, this opposition ought not to be attributed to a natural feeling, nor ought it to be thought of as eternal. For the supposedly natural characteristics of the Jews are characteristics that are also exhibited by other peoples. These characteristics are not racial, but are "the characteristics of inhabitants of specific localities under specific conditions of production."[34]

In the case of the Jews, the geography of Palestine, and the pressure of overpopulation in ancient Palestine, go a long way toward explaining Jewish traits. When overpopulation led Jews to emigrate in ancient times, Kautsky claims, these emigrants always thought in terms of eventually returning to their homeland. They therefore chose nonagricultural occupations, which, they hoped, would facilitate their eventual return to Palestine. Thus the Jewish people, which had been an agricultural people when it was based in Palestine, became a trading people outside of Palestine.

This tendency was accelerated by the conquest and subjugation of the Jewish state. For, at that point, the peasant component of the Jewish people ceased to exist. Whereas the urban populations of all other nations have been continuously influenced and replenished by the peasants of those nations, Jews, in the second century of the

Christian era, became a purely urban population, with no possibility of replenishment by peasants of their own stock.

In this sense the Jewish case is unique. The Jews are the only nation that has managed to survive under such circumstances. Thus, for historical reasons, the Jews became the people that most strongly exhibited the characteristics, both positive and negative, of city dwellers. In Kautsky's words: "What appears to us as the unbridgeable racial opposition between the "Aryan" and the "Semite" is, in truth, only the opposition between the peasant and the city dweller driven to the extreme by special circumstances."[35] But precisely because the purportedly Jewish characteristics are historical rather than natural, these characteristics will cease to exist in time. Jewry is becoming stratified along class lines. Increasingly, this stratification within the Jewish people will eliminate the unique aspects of the Jewish case.

Kautsky stressed that he did not expect that anti-Semitism would disappear rapidly. In a book review published in *Die Neue Zeit* Kautsky asserted that the modern mode of production tends to efface religious and national differences when these differences are not combined with social differences. When, however, religious and national differences coincide with social differences, the contemporary mode of production tends to strengthen differentiation. "The expectation of bourgeois ideologues, to wit, bourgeois democrats, that the progress of 'culture' within our society must by itself lead to the abolition of all national and religious disputes, is, consequently, only partially substantiated."[36] Anti-Semitism will continue to exist for as long as the petty bourgeoisie and the peasantry continue to consider it possible to "secure a tolerable existence within the framework of modern society."[37] Thus, while the anti-Semitic movement has no ultimate prospects for success, it cannot be wholly eliminated in today's society.

A letter by Kautsky to Emma Adler written in 1895 reveals much about Kautsky's attitude toward the anti-Semites of that era. In Germany, Kautsky wrote, the SPD deals with the anti-Semites too snobbishly, for the Party thinks of the anti-Semites as a negligible quantity. The German socialists do not properly understand Austrian anti-Semitism. "As an element of decomposition, and of nullification of stability of that which exists, anti-Semitism has, in my opinion, great significance."[38]

In sum, Kautsky's position on anti-Semitism in the period before the revisionist controversy was extremely close to that of Engels and Bernstein: Kautsky condemned anti-Semitism as reactionary, believed that it was tied to declining classes, and believed that it could not occur on a large scale "in a free land."[39] It is highly probable that Kautsky developed this view in conjunction with and under the influence of Engels and Bernstein.

Kautsky's view of anti-Semitism, once developed, seems to have remained more or less fixed. In fact, Kautsky never departed from the view that he put forth in the 1880s and 1890s. As his stature in the Marxist movement rose, his pronouncements on issues of the day—including his pronouncements on the Jewish question— were accorded greater respect and attention. The social democrats of Central and Eastern Europe did not always act in accordance with the views expressed by Kautsky, but in the years before World War I, Kautsky's views always received an attentive hearing.

An indication of the kind of role Kautsky played can be seen in an incident that occurred at the time of the Dreyfus Affair. The affair had caused splits within the French socialist movement. Jean Jaurès, leader of one of the French socialist factions, had undergone a transformation and was, by late 1898, fully supportive of Dreyfus's cause. Jaurès's biographer, Harvey Goldberg, notes that "Jaurès, moving beyond the limited confines set by the schematic Socialist approach to the European Jewish question, made the struggle against antisemitism one of the central symbols of socialism."[40]

In 1899, Charles Rappoport, a prominent Russian Jewish émigré active in French socialist affairs, suggested to Jaurès that opinions on the correct handling of the Dreyfus Affair be solicited from the most prominent leaders of the world's socialist movements.[41] Jaurès polled a large handful of individuals—including Kautsky. One of the questions in Jaurès' poll read: "Can the socialist working class, without abandoning the principle of class struggle, take the sides in the conflicts among various bourgeois factions, whether to save political liberty or, as in the Dreyfus Affair, to defend humanity?"[42]

While all of those polled answered "yes" to this question, not all were willing to support Jaurès' stance in the Affair. Liebknecht, for example, maintained that the socialists ought not to involve themselves in the Dreyfus Affair. He did not believe in Dreyfus's innocence, and at one point he went so far as to claim that the affair was of import only insofar as it exposed the dangers inherent in military espionage.[43]

Kautsky disagreed with Liebknecht, and supported the stance taken by Jaurès. He not only endorsed Jaurès's positions in the poll, but also wrote the French socialist leader a strongly worded note in which he declared

I use the opportunity to express to you my deep admiration for the incomparable manner in which you have saved the honor of French socialism in the Dreyfus Affair. I can think of no more disastrous position for a fighting class than to persist in a position of neutrality in a crisis which stirs a whole nation; I can think of no more destructive position for a party of social regeneration than to remain indifferent in a question of law, no mistake which would be more unpardonable than irresolution against soldiery. I wish your noble work full success and shake your hand with friendship.[44]

Another indication of the respect accorded Kautsky's views is evident in a letter to Kautsky by Adolf Warszawski, (a leader of the SDKPiL) in May of 1903.[45] Warszawski's letter was written immediately after the Kishinev pogrom of 1903,[46] and it contains a request that Kautsky write an article on anti-Semitism and the tasks of social democracy for *Przegląd Socjaldemokratyczny*, an SDKPiL organ. Warszawski informed Kautsky that there was reason to believe that pogroms similar to the one in Kishinev would occur in Poland, since representatives of the Czarist government were involved in instigating anti-Jewish actions. He also noted that the SDKPiL was particularly concerned with this question because of the large Jewish population in Russian Poland. Warszawski admits, however, that the SDKPiL was interested in an article by Kautsky on anti-Semitism primarily because the party wanted to use such an article to bolster its position in the ongoing struggle between the Polish social democrats and the Bund.

Warszawski claimed that the Bund was becoming increasingly nationalistic, and that it was increasingly moving toward advocacy of a separate party organization for the Jews. Warszawski wrote of fears that the recent massacres would drive the Bund further in a separatist direction. He wrote that there were already two social democratic organizations in each city—one non-Jewish and the other a national-Jewish organization.

Leaving aside the question of whether the Jews truly form a nation and whether they have a national future in Russia—as the Bund claims—the question of party organization and of the relation of the Jewish worker to the working class as a whole must be solved on the basis of common class interest, and not on the basis of isolating, national, interests.[47]

Thus, Warszawski concludes, precisely because the Bund would consider an article by Kautsky to be of the greatest importance, the SDKPiL hoped that Kautsky would see fit to write on this subject.

Kautsky fulfilled Warszawski's request by writing an article entitled "The Kishinev Massacre and the Jewish Question." His article begins as follows:

The editor of the Przegląd Socyaldemocraticzny [sic] . . . requests me to express my opinion on the Kishinev bloodbath. It is not easy to give an answer to this question which goes beyond that which is self-evident, beyond the self-evident horror of the dreadful brutalities. It is difficult to meditate quietly and dispassionately about events the very reporting of which makes our blood run cold, and which, at the same time, kindles our most furious hatred of those who are responsible . . .[48]

Kautsky continues by analyzing the cause of anti-Semitism from a Marxist perspective. He notes that anti-Semitism in Western Europe is linked to the despair of declining strata, and that it is the history of Jews rather than racial characteristics that explains the concentration of Jews in certain economic categories and occupations.

In Eastern Europe, where Jews are not overwhelmingly affiliated with either the bourgeoisie or the intelligentsia, the antipathy toward them cannot be explained solely in terms of the jealousy of declining strata. It is, however, explicable as a specific example of the general tendency of primitive and traditional peoples to display hostility toward neighbors of another stock. Not only Russian Jewry, but also the Negroes of the United States and the minorities of Turkey and Austria-Hungary suffer from the effects of this phenomenon.

Kautsky maintained that the hostility between the backward East European peoples and the Jews would not be overcome until there were no cultural differences between them. Thus Kautsky "advocated" the assimilation of Jews and non-Jews because he believed that only assimilation could rid the world of the scourge of anti-Semitism. In his article on Kishinev, Kautsky stressed the factors leading to such assimilation. The fact that Jews no longer controlled their original homeland, and thus no longer had the territorial base that had made them a nation, the fact that there were class divisions within Jewry, and the commonality of interests between Jewish and non-Jewish proletarians were all discussed.

So long as assimilation does not occur, however, "there is only one means whereby to counteract the aversion toward the Jewish character: the enlightenment of the masses." Since the Czarist government blocked enlightenment of this kind

There is no doubt that the Russian autocracy is the key guilty party in the Kishinev murders—indirectly through the ignorance, through the isolation from the rest of the world and from all new ideas in which it artificially maintains the masses, directly through its tools who were active as inciters of these masses.[49]

"The Kishinev Massacre and the Jewish Question" appeared in German in *Die Neue Zeit*, was translated into Polish and published by those associated with Rosa Luxemburg, and was published by the *Iskra* in Russian.[50] Those active in the Jewish socialist movement were less pleased with Kautsky's piece. There is no record of its being translated into Yiddish, nor of its Polish or Russian versions being distributed by the Bund. The disagreements that the Bundists had with Kautsky's article, however, did not lead them to break with him. The Bundists believed in the necessity of an autonomous Jewish socialist organization in the Russian Empire. Kautsky's article did not directly make such an assertion, but it implied that autonomous Jewish movements would hinder assimilation and were therefore not desirable. This difference notwithstanding, Kautsky's good will and intentions—not always present in other socialists who wrote about Jewry—were manifest even to those Bundists who disagreed with him.

On the eve of World War I[51] Kautsky wrote a book-length critique of anti-Semitism in which he expanded upon many of the themes mentioned in his article on Kishinev. German anti-Semites had shifted the basis of their attacks on Jews from traditional and religious rationalizations to pseudo-scientific racial ones. Kautsky's *Rasse und Judentum* destroyed the scientific mask of the anti-Semitic propagandists, and it was, in fact, motivated by a desire to do so.

Drawing on his considerable knowledge of Darwinian and other theories of evolution, Kautsky attempted to prove that

The sharpness of race demarcation, which is evident in the case of animals, disappears more and more among men. In the place of sharply distinct races, unchanged for long periods, we find a constant and increasingly rapid process of race disintegration . . .[52]

The Jews, Kautsky maintained, were a classic example of such a process. By presenting scientific data on the color of hair, shape of nose, and form of head of Jews in various parts of the world, Kautsky demonstrated that there were no longer sharply defined physical traits that were both exclusively Jewish and could be considered racial. Having made this point, Kautsky went on to contend that all remaining Jewish traits, whether acquired due to environmental, social, or economic factors, would likewise disappear as Jews assimilated. He provided figures on the steady increases in the number of conversions from Judaism, and of mixed marriages, and concluded that

it is only in the ghetto, in a condition of compulsory exclusion from their environment, and under political pressure, deprived of their rights and surrounded by hostility, that the Jews can maintain themselves among other peoples. They will dissolve, unite with their environment and disappear, where the Jew is regarded and treated as a free man and as an equal.[53]

Thus, just as in his article on Kishinev, Kautsky "advocated" assimilation in *Rasse und Judentum* because he believed that the assimilation of the Jews (and of other small peoples) would be a positive development for the Jews and for their neighbors. It must be stressed, however, that Kautsky was absolutely opposed to forcing Jews to assimilate by denying them the right to educate their children and use their own language or by other means. One of the reasons for which Kautsky was opposed to forced assimilation was that he believed that it would backfire. Referring to the case of the

Czechs, for example, Kautsky noted in 1917 that the attempt to force them to assimilate had actually hindered assimilation.[54]

Similarly, in Die Befreiung der Nationen, Kautsky remarked that the assimilation of Jews had been hindered by an era of persecutions.[55] Kautsky was well aware that policies designed to pressure Jews into assimilating or a general increase in anti-Semitism might prevent assimilation from occurring. While he believed and even hoped that Jewish assimilation would occur, his theory was neither mechanistic or fatalistic.

Kautsky's views on the desirability of assimilation help explain his principled opposition to Zionism. When Kautsky first concretized his position on Zionism, the Zionist movement, while growing in strength, represented a small minority of Jewish opinion, and was especially weak among Jewish workers and artisans. Several different socialist-Zionist movements emerged in Eastern Europe in the first few years of the twentieth century. The mainstream of the Zionist movement, however, was essentially antisocialist.[56]

In Germany, Kautsky's home at the turn of the century, the official newspaper of the German Zionists, the Jüdische Rundschau, cautioned Jews not to vote for the SPD in 1903, claiming that anti-Semitism was evident in the socialist ranks and insisting that Jews were deluding themselves if they believed that the political situation of the Jews would improve under socialism.[57]

This animosity on the part of the general Zionists toward the SPD probably contributed to Kautsky's strong condemnation of Zionism.[58] In the course of his article on Kishinev, Kautsky declared that

The Zionist movement . . . can only strengthen the anti-Semitic feelings of the masses in that it increases the isolation of Jewry from the rest of the population and thus stamps Jewry even more than hitherto as a foreign tribe, which must not look out for its own notions on foreign soil. Against its will, it thereby looks after the business of Czardom, by which it was hitherto only tolerated. The Zionists should be cured of the hopes which most of them now place in the Czar.[59]

In 1909, after a piece critical of the Labor Zionists had been published in Die Neue Zeit, Leon Chasanowitsch (a prominent Labor Zionist writer) decided to interview Kautsky.[60] Chasanowitsch hoped that Kautsky's position on Zionism was based on ignorance and that Kautsky could be convinced to change his opinion of the Labor Zionist movement. The interview disappointed Chasanowitsch and led him to characterize Kautsky's positions as outmoded and naive.[61] Kautsky's answers to the questions posed by Chasanowitsch, far from demonstrating naiveté, actually demonstrated a principled commitment to the positions delineated in the articles on the Labor Zionist movement that Kautsky had allowed to be published in *Die Neue Zeit*. During the interview, Kautsky explained that he was not opposed to Jewish colonization per se, and that no one should be opposed to such colonization, but that he feared that the Zionist movement was interfering with the activity of the Bund. By encouraging Jewish workers to believe that a Jewish state would solve all their problems, Kautsky said, the Zionist movement was undermining the zeal of the Jewish proletariat to work toward a socialist revolution. Jewish colonization projects ought to be left to philanthropy, not undertaken as the major goal of the Jewish socialist movement.

The revised edition of *Rasse und Judentum*, published in 1921, contained two chapters specifically devoted to Zionism. Because Kautsky believed that only assimilation would bring an end to anti-Semitism, and that Zionism hindered assimilation, he was led to conclude that Zionism was "a reactionary movement. Zionism aims not at following the line of necessary evolution, but of putting a spoke in the wheel of progress."[62] Kautsky was also skeptical of the practical possibility of realizing the Zionist goal. He noted the lack of a solid economic infrastructure in Palestine, the absence of a large body of experienced Jewish farmers, and he predicted that the lack of economic opportunities would induce young Jews to emigrate from rather than immigrate to Palestine. Again, in 1927, Kautsky claimed that the restoration of a diminutive Jewish state in Palestine would not change much for world Jewry, and he pointed to the hostility of the Arabs to such a state.[63]

The prediction of Arab hostility was confirmed by the pogrom in Hebron in 1929. Writing in the wake of this pogrom, Kautsky explained his long-term and continued opposition to Zionism in the following words:

Its goal is one which we like very much: to create a home for tormented Jewry, in which it would freely control itself, secured against every type of maltreatment. Only unwillingly did we come to the conviction—the "we" being almost all of social democracy up to the First World War—that Palestine is not the best basis on which to collect the Jews as a nation and in which to unite them in a national state. For that purpose Palestine is much too small.[64]

Kautsky also pointed to the problems that "Europeanized" Jews would have living in an Islamic area, and he did not find the argument of Jewish historical rights to Palestine convincing. He believed that the Jews already in Palestine could live there only under the protection of the British, and he predicted a rise in Arab nationalism followed by a catastrophe for the Jewish settlers.

Far from gloating over the confirmation of his prophecies of 1921 and 1927, Kautsky very much regretted their fulfillment:

It is rather astonishing how many of the expectations which Marx and the Marxists expressed have come about. We were not always enthusiastic about the correctness of the prophecy. For it not rarely consisted in predicting a failure for enterprises which we would rather have wished success. Who had not wished that Lenin's bold enterprise would have succeeded and that it would have brought Russia, and, from there, the world, socialism! That our fear that the Leninist method must end in disaster was realized did not by any means fill us with satisfaction. And the situation with Zionism is the same.[65]

Kautsky's writings on Zionism in 1929 provoked rejoinders from other prominent social democrats, including Émile Vandervelde, Camille Huysmans, and Eduard Bernstein.[66] In a letter to Vandervelde dated November 26, 1929, Kautsky commented on Vandervelde's rejoinder, and clarified his own position. "I am entirely in agreement with you in your sympathy for the Zionists, particularly the socialists among them."[67] But this sympathy, Kautsky immediately added, was comparable to the feeling that he had for utopian socialist experiments based on the ideas of Owen, Fourier, or Cabet. Kautsky said that there is another similarity between the utopian socialists and the Zionists. The Zionists have no better chance of success than did the utopians. There are also differences between the conditions under which the Zionists work and those that confronted the utopians. The Zionists, for one thing, have access to capital. But the Zionists also confront great obstacles. "There is not one country at this time where the Jews are more menaced by pogroms than Palestine."[68] Encouraging Jews to migrate from Europe to Palestine, therefore, creates great danger for the Jews themselves.

Kautsky also replied to Bernstein's rejoinder. Bernstein's comments, Kautsky claimed, can be so "construed as to imply that I denied Zionism any justification. This is in no way correct. . . . I objected not to the *justification* of Zionism, but to its *prospects*."[69] These prospects, Kautsky continued, remain dim, and the expectation of inducing harmony between an increasingly large Jewish population in Palestine and the Arabs living there remains chimerical. "On this point my critics have not produced anything which could shake my views."[70] Kautsky also rebuts the charge made by Bernstein that his remarks were similar in tone to those made by Nazis. Kautsky insists that he did not and would not charge the Zionist movement with consciously acting as an agent of British imperialism. Nevertheless

Whatever intentions the Zionists may have, the basis of the home which is offered to them in Palestine is to be found exclusively in the military might which England has unfolded there, not for the sake of Jewry, but for its own imperialistic aspirations.[71]

Thus, whether or not they so desire, the Zionists are in fact tied to English colonial policies. In sum, Kautsky declares that his view is "not a *reproach*, and it is also not a *disparagement* of Zionism, but a warning . . . I wrote my article in the interests of Jewry."[72]

Referring to Kautsky's articles of 1929, George Mosse has suggested that "Kautsky seemed to be weakening in his polemics" with Zionism, and that there is "scattered evidence of a certain new ambivalence" in Kautksy's attitude toward Zionism during that period.[73] But the evidence brought to bear by Mosse in support of these suggestions is not convincing. It is true that Labor Zionists such as Berl Locker, Marc Jarblum, and David Ben-Gurion wrote to Kautsky in the 1920s.[74] Kautsky, however, did not encourage these men to do so, and he did not answer their requests for support affirmatively.[75] The tone of Kautsky's articles on Zionism is neither surprising nor indicative of a substantial change. Through all of Kautsky's writings on Zionism the same spirit is evident. He was, and always remained, an opponent of the Zionist movement, but he was an opponent who was sympathetic to Jewry's plight. The fact that this was the case is manifest in Kautsky's relationship with the anti-Zionist and non-Zionist Jewish socialist and labor movements.

The non-Zionist Jewish socialists—a sizable portion of the Jewish community in Kautsky's day and the portion of the Jewish community with the greatest knowledge of Kautsky's ideas—considered Kautsky to be an ally and teacher. The leaders of the Jewish socialist movements around the world considered it a great honor to meet with Kautsky. Abe Cahan, Morris Hillquit, and Raphael Abramovitch were among the socialists of Jewish origin who made the pilgrimage to Kautsky's home.[76] Discussing the impact of Kautsky on his own thought, Abramovitch comments that "the first socialist brochure which I saw in my life was, after all, Kautsky's *Erfurt Program.*"[77] When the Bund began to disseminate socialist materials, Kautsky's works were amid the first items thought worthy of translation and distribution.[78] The respect that many Jewish socialists had for Kautsky, and his import as a filter of Marx's ideas to the Jewish proletariat, is also demonstrated by the request made to Kautsky by the Bund that he write a special foreword for its Yiddish translation of the *Communist Manifesto.*[79]

The unmistakable esteem in which Jewish socialists held Kautsky was reciprocated. In a congratulatory greeting written by Kautsky in 1901 for the twenty-fifth issue of *Di arbeyter shtimme*, A Bundist organ, Kautsky described the intolerable conditions of the Russian Jewish worker.

"It is bad enough," Kautsky proclaimed, "to be a Russian," worse to be a proletarian, and even worse to be a Russian proletarian.[80] It is bad enough to be a Jew, and thereby belong to a stock that is despised. But to be at the same time a Russian, a proletarian, and a Jew is to unite all afflictions. The Russian Jewish proletariat is the pariah among pariahs, and is subjected to all of the abuses of a hard-hearted, all-powerful, greedy, murderous regime.

But therefore it is even more marvelous and lofty that the Jewish proletariat in Russia, which has to struggle even harder than all others, has been successful, this need to struggle harder notwithstanding, in raising itself from its degradation and in developing a movement which has already become a powerful factor in the international social democratic movement and also in Russia's inner politics.[81]

At the Socialist International's Amsterdam congress of 1904, Kautsky, as a member of the International Socialist Bureau (ISB), the executive committee of the International, helped to adjudicate a dispute on the seating of the Russian delegation that revolved around the Bund's voting rights. In the course of this dispute Kautsky noted that "I feel very warm sympathies" for the Bund "and stand for the same principled point of view as it does."[82] Kautsky also exhibited his support for the Bund by sending a congratulatory letter to its seventh congress in 1906,[83] and another public letter of support to the *Tsayt* (an organ of the Bund) in May of 1914.[84] Kautsky's letters of support were of enormous propaganda value to the Bund in its battles with other East European political movements.

These letters, however, were only one of the ways in which Kautsky demonstrated his sympathy for the Bund. For Kautsky also gave the Bund access to the international socialist movement by regularly printing articles by Bundist leaders in *Die Neue Zeit*. Among those whose works were published in the pages of Kautsky's journal were Boris Frumkin,[85] M. Nachimson,[86] Vladimir Medem,[87] Lippe Rosenmann,[88] J. Pistiner,[89] and Vladimir Kossovsky.[90]

Significantly, Kautsky did not publish articles by the Bund's socialist opponents in the Jewish world.[91] The publicists of the SERP, the SS, and the ESDRP-PZ were, therefore, virtually forced to publish in the revisionist-oriented *Sozialistische Monatshefte* (the only significant alternative to *Die Neue Zeit*) when they wanted to reach a West European socialist audience.[92]

Independently of the pros and cons of their proposed solutions to the Jewish question, these Jewish socialist rivals of the Bund were thus associated with revisionism in the minds of the West European socialists, and they were unable to gain support in orthodox Marxist circles, precisely because of Kautsky's editorial policy.

Kautsky did publish articles critical of the Bund written by activists in the Russian and Polish socialist movements. These activists were themselves frequently of Jewish origin, and they attacked the Bund from an assimilationist perspective. Kautsky was hesitant about allowing himself or his journal to be drawn into internecine struggles. Nevertheless, on at least one occasion he allowed the Bundists to state their objection to a charge that had been made against them in the pages of *Die Neue Zeit*. On the occasion in question, Kautsky had received a number of such objections. The Bund was the only group given space to respond.[93]

Though Kautsky did publish articles in *Die Neue Zeit* that were critical of Jewry, there was a line beyond which he would not go. In the early 1890s, for example, Max Zetterbaum, an assimilationist of Jewish origin active in the Galician Workers' Party, submitted an article to *Die Neue Zeit* in which he suggested that the capital of all Jews who possessed more than 100,000 fl. be confiscated. Kautsky rejected the article, and wrote to Zetterbaum that this suggestion "stands in the sharpest contradiction to the principles for which our party stands. We ought be least likely to demand exclusionary laws against any particular stratum of the population."[94]

Kautsky had words of support not only for the Bund, but also for the Jewish socialist and labor movements of England and America. He contributed an article to a Yiddish-language socialist periodical published in London (and named after his own journal),[95] greeted the New York-based United Hebrew Trades on its fortieth anniversary,[96] and sent fraternal messages to the *Forverts*[97] and to *Der veker*[98] on several of the anniversaries of these American Jewish social democratic periodicals.

Kautsky's messages to the Jewish socialists frequently had the same theme: that Jewish socialists have a specific role to play in furthering the socialist cause. Addressing himself to the Jewish socialist workers of England, for example, Kautsky noted that each nationality displays a specific psychic character. The English have been characterized by the love of freedom. They have, however, not prominently displayed some of the characteristics needed by the proletariat in order fully to liberate itself from bourgeois thought, that is, the ability to think in the abstract and the ability to think critically. It is, however, precisely these latter qualities that have predominated among the Jews. Thus

the Jewish proletariat possesses this capacity which the English proletariat lacks . . . The Jewish worker . . . through his example, shows the Anglo-Saxon worker that the theory of socialism . . . not only does not hinder a real, practical, class politics, but, on the contrary, that it is the socialist view which first affords the possibility of such a politics.

In that they give the Anglo-Saxon worker such a practical lesson in socialism—as comrades not as tutors—the Jewish workers pursue a more productive propaganda than theoretical speeches and writings are in a position to
achieve.[99]

Kautsky made similar observations about the tasks of the American Jewish labor movement. Whereas in an earlier day German
immigrants to America had had the task of "fertilizing" the class
struggle of the American proletariat movements, this had now become the task of the Jewish immigrant workers. "The Jewish worker
ought to form the bridge between the labor movement of America
and that of Europe."[100] Kautsky saw the English and American
Jewish socialist and labor movements not merely as branches of the
international movement of the proletariat, but as branches capable
of playing a key and distinctive role.[101]

Kautsky received—and answered—requests for endorsements from
socialist movements and periodicals throughout the world. The fact
that Kautsky's statements on the Jewish socialist and labor movements were not merely standard "comradely greetings" but indicative of a more deeply rooted concern with the Jewish question is
attested to by those Jewish socialists who met with Kautsky. John
Mill, a leading representative of the Bund, reports that he visited
Kautsky in Friedenau-Berlin at the end of 1903 to discuss the possibility of Kautsky's writing a special introduction to the Yiddish
edition of the *Erfurt Program*. Mill expected that the meeting would
take no more than fifteen minutes but found, to his surprise, that
Kautsky was very interested in discussing the form and content of
the Jewish socialist movement. For several hours Kautsky ques-
tioned Mill about these matters, about the pogroms in Russia, and
about the relationship of the Bund to the other socialist groups in
the Russian Empire.[102] Kautsky was aware of the differences among
the various Jewish political movements, endorsed only those with
which he agreed, and displayed an unusually strong interest in the
Jewish socialists and their problems.

It is, true, of course, that Kautsky's strong support for the *Der
veker*, for the *Forverts*, and for *Tsukunft* (a literary journal published in New York by Jewish social democrats) cannot be explained entirely on the basis of his position on the Jewish question.
In the wake of the Bolshevik Revolution, virtually every Marxist-

oriented organization in the world split into pro- and anti-communist factions. When the dust settled, the *Der veker*, the *Forverts*, *Tsukunft*, and Kautsky were all firmly in the camp of the anticommunist wing of the social democratic movement. The Jewish socialists in America associated with these institutions were supported by Kautsky *primarily* because they supported his anti-communist stance.

On a more mundane level, Kautsky also fostered good relations with the Jewish social democrats in the United States because he was partially dependent on the income he received from writing for their periodicals. Kautsky moved to Vienna in 1924. His strong condemnations of the Soviet Union, however, made it relatively difficult for him to publish his work in the Austrian socialist press, whose editors tended to disagree with Kautsky's view on this critical issue. Kautsky therefore needed the anticommunist social democratic Jewish periodicals both for monetary reasons and because he had few other outlets for his literary work during the 1920s and 1930s.[103]

None of these factors, however, explains Kautsky's continued support for the Bund. Kautsky was well aware that much of the Bund was substantially to his left during the Weimar years. In January of 1920 the Menshevik Martov wrote to Kautsky that the Bund "which, during the War and Kerensky periods, stood on the right wing of the Party," was supporting the system of Soviets, and was threatening to split from the party.[104] "The split," Martov wrote, "appears in any event to be unavoidable."[105] The Bundists "speak an altogether 'communistic' prose without noticing it."[106] Similarly, the editor of the *Forverts*, Abe Cahan, wrote to Kautsky at the end of 1931 that "the Bund in Poland has very few followers among our people" in New York.[107]

Still, some of the old time Bundists living in America are apt to confuse what is practically the Bolshevist theory of the present Bund with the glorious doings of the old Bund during the first years of the present century. This Bund teaches the children of the Jewish workingmen in Poland to celebrate and hold sacred the October Revolution of 1917.[108]

Cahan refers to a purportedly "Bolshevist" speech by H. Erlich, a leader of the Bund in Poland, that Erlich had made at the International in Vienna, and he concludes by requesting from Kautsky that "if you do write the article for us . . . please don't mention the Bund."[109]

In light of these criticisms of the Bund by men with whom Kautsky was allied, Kautsky's continued support for the Bund is especially striking. Kautsky manifested this support in no uncertain terms in an article written in 1937 on the occasion of the fortieth anniversary of the founding of the Bund. Kautsky's article was entitled "From a Glorious Past to a Magnificent Future" and specifically noted the Bund's "courageousness and intelligence and its solidarity with the entire non-Jewish working class of Poland and the world."[110]

Just as he did in attacking anti-Semitism, Kautsky was following in the tradition of Engels when he supported the Jewish socialist and labor movements of the early twentieth century. Engels encouraged his supporters to work among the East European Jews living in London, spoke highly of the work of the Jewish socialists, and even wrote for them. There is, therefore, nothing surprising about Kautsky's support for the Bund during the early years of its existence.

The dominant ideology of the Jewish socialist movement, however, changed markedly between the time of Engels's death and the beginning of World War I. Whereas the early Jewish socialists (including all of those supported by Engels) had been cosmopolitan, and had organized as Jews solely in order to facilitate the work of the movement as a whole, the Bund and its supporters gradually became more nationally conscious, and eventually they began to demand national rights for Russian Jewry. During the period between the world wars, the Bundists living in independent Poland would actively foster and encourage the development of a secular and progressive Jewish culture in the Yiddish language.

Kautsky's words of praise for the Bund thus raise the important questions: Did Kautsky think of the Jews as a nation? And did Kautsky's support for the Bund include support for its national program? During the first part of his career, Kautsky tended to think of the Jews as a race with the vestiges of national characteristics. In 1885, for example, Kautsky wrote:

The uneasiness, indeed, the despair, of declining classes could make the Jew out to be a scapegoat only where he is still *nationally* separated from the rest of the population. Where he has merged into the rest of the population, as in Western Europe, it could not occur to anyone to start a class struggle against a *race*.[111]

Again, in his article on the Jewish question written in 1890, Kautsky described the Jews as a race on one page and as a nation on another.[112]

The single most important statement by Kautsky on this issue is contained in his letter to the seventh congress of the Bund and was written on August 31, 1906.[113] The nation, Kautsky wrote at that time, is not something that is fixed by nature once and for all. It is, rather, a historical organism and thus changes and takes on various forms at various times. Nations that exist at the same time, moreover, have somewhat different characteristics because they have different paths of development and because they exist at different levels of development. There are, Kautsky continued, at least three types of nations in existence at the present time.

In the West European type, the state and the nation are one and the same. This is true, for example, in the case of the Swiss nation, despite the existence of distinct language groups within that nation.

The East European type of nation is characterized first and foremost by language. In Eastern Europe, those who speak the same language normally live within a given territory, but do not necessarily live within the same state. In every state of Eastern Europe, more than one nation inhabits a given state.

The third major type of nation is best exemplified by the Anglo-Saxon world. Here, Kautsky claimed, one finds one nation broken up into a number of states. Are the Australians a nation or a part of the English nation? In the Anglo-Saxon world, it seems, the Australians may not be a nation despite having a state of their own.

However difficult it may be to answer the question of whether the Australians are a nation

it is even more difficult to answer the question of whether the Jews form a nation of their own. To be sure, the Jews are not a nation like the other nations which we have mentioned here. Jewry differentiates itself in that we do not find in commensurate proportion among the Jews all the classes which make up modern society, as we do among the other nations. Moreover we frequently do not find among the Jews a common language. The Holy Tongue has ceased to be a living language. Jews in various lands have adopted the language of the people among whom they live, or speak a German which has been slightly altered. From the other side, one can manifestly not deny that Jewry is a distinct societal unity with a culture which is peculiar to itself, and that it differentiates itself from the nations of Eastern Europe among which it lives. There is no great difference between saying to us that Jewry forms a separate type of nation, which differentiates itself from all other types, or saying to us that Jewry has ceased to be a nation in the sense of the other nations.[114]

A similar discussion appears in Kautsky's article "The Question of Nationalities in Russia," first published in April 1905. "The French, the Irish, the Austrian, the Jewish, the Armenian nation each signify something altogether different from the others," Kautsky proclaimed in this piece.[115] In general, the capitalist mode of production calls forth national strivings among individual nations that are divided between different, adjoining, countries. Economic development leads such nations to strive to unite their people in one country.

Where such national tendencies still have to struggle for recognition, every modern party, including the representative of the proletariat, the Social Democratic Party, must take this necessity into account. Just as it must support the striving for a democratic configuration of the state, so must it support the striving for concentration of the state and the striving for self-determination of the individual nation in which it works. In this sense it must therefore be just as national as it is democratic.[116]

It, however, may not be necessary for nations such as the Poles and the Ukrainians to form self-governing states wholly separate from Russia—if certain changes can be made in the structure of the Russian state. If Russia can be democratized, then the striving of these nations for self-determination can be satisfied by a transformation of the Russian empire into a "United States of Russia." Much depends on the extent to which the proletariat participates in the Russian revolution. The greater the extent of proletarian participation, the more likely will it be that the nations which now make up the empire will be willing to remain in a free league with each other.

These articles imply that Kautsky thought of *Russian* Jewry as having nationlike characteristics and as being fully worthy of the same national rights as were nations such as the Poles and the Ukrainians. They thus also imply that Kautsky was willing to accept the national program of the Bund.[117] For the Bundists did not make claims on behalf of a world-wide Jewish nation, but restricted their demands to the Jews of the Russian Empire.

If Kautsky had any doubts about the program of the Bund, these doubts were probably connected to the question of party organization rather than to the national question. Kautsky believed that the unity of the proletariat was of the greatest importance. Insofar as he feared that the position of the Bund on the question of the organization of the RSDRP isolated Jewish workers from non-Jewish workers, Kautsky probably opposed the position of the Bund. In fact, Kautsky's article on Kishinev was written at least in part in order to discourage the Bund from isolating itself. Kautsky, however, never condemned or directly criticized the Bund. He merely stressed the importance of diminishing isolation—and reiterated this stance in many of his messages to the Jewish socialists. Thus, in sum, Kautsky's position may be said to have revolved around consistent support for the work of the Bund, tacit support for its national program, and gentle prodding on those occasions when he feared that the Jewish socialists were isolating the Jewish proletariat.

Kautsky's apparent tacit support for the Bund's national program might, on the face of it, appear to contradict his "support" for the assimilation of the Jews. The superficial contradiction between these points, however, is easily reconciled. Kautsky believed that only after the Jews had gained the freedom to develop their culture, only after they were treated like other people, would assimilation set in.

The productions and resources of an active national life on the part of the Russian Jews will become progressively greater and stronger as long as the struggle for Jewish freedom advances. But that which we call the Jewish nation can achieve the victory only in order then to disappear.[118]

In this important sense, Kautsky's view of the Jewish question was a logical extension of the view first presented by Marx in "Zur Judenfrage."

Marx had insisted that the Jews must be granted equal civil rights. Whereas Bauer maintained that Jews ought not be granted political rights equal to those of Christians until and unless they ceased to be Jews, Marx argued that the Jews would only cease to be Jews once they had been granted such rights.[119]

Kautsky, stripping Marx's argument of its anti-Semitic terminology, and extending it from the realm of civil rights to that of national rights, followed in Marx's footsteps insofar as he argued that assimilation was a result of equal treatment. He sincerely supported the Jewish socialist movement, and thought of it as a necessary phenomenon, but he also believed it to be a transitional phenomenon. Kautsky hoped for the success of the Bund, fully recognizing that such a success would have entailed the flowering of a secular Jewish culture. But he also hoped and believed that over a long period of time Jewish socialist institutions, including those of the Bund, would disappear as the conditions that had brought them into being themselves disappeared.

### Kautsky and the Czechs

Kautsky's position on the Jewish question can be profitably compared to his position on "the Czech question." Johann Kautsky, Karl's father, was of Czech origin and was sympathetic to the Czech national movement. Though Johann was "not a fanatic Czech nationalist," he "had a predilection toward cultivating Czech acquaintances."[120]

Despite Johann's political orientation, Karl reports that he did not think of himself as a Czech when he lived in Prague as a young boy. Karl's self-identification, however, underwent a change in the mid-1860s, and, for a period of several years, he thought of himself as a "pronounced Czech nationalist."[121] In fact, Czech nationalism was the first political ideology to which Kautsky was attracted.[122]

Unlike certain other Czech nationalists of the mid-nineteenth century, Kautsky did not link his ideology to hatred of Germans—a hatred that he could not share with these others in light of his love for his mother, who was partially of German origin and who spoke German rather than Czech with her children.[123] Even during his Czech nationalist period, Kautsky recognized the legitimate claims of other nationalities, and he maintained that his Czech nationalism required that he demand the same rights for other nations that he demanded for his own.

The Paris Commune of 1871 led Kautsky to reject Czech nationalism as too narrow a worldview. In the period immediately following his rejection of Czech nationalism, Kautsky made an almost complete about face and began to denounce nationalist ideologies of all kinds. As early as 1873, Kautsky referred to the idea of nationality as "probably the most lamentable" idea that has ever existed. Nationality, Kautsky wrote, is a "product of innumerable coincidences," it is an "arrogance" that is "foolish and supercilious." "The idea of nationality is pernicious because it weakens the cause of freedom . . . freedom makes the idea of nationality superfluous."[124] Again, in 1874, Kautsky wrote an essay in which he maintained that the national feeling is not deeply rooted in human nature and is artificial.[125] It is, he thought, a feeling that has already reached the highest point of its power. Commenting on these articles in his memoirs, Kautsky notes that though he still had much to learn, the position that he took on nationalism and internationalism in the mid-1870s was essentially what he continued to propound for the rest of his life.[126]

Kautsky's position on nationalism during the period of his greatest influence was not one that dismissed it as superfluous and shallow, but one that admitted its validity and power. In 1887, Kautsky still insisted that capitalism would condemn to extinction the languages of less developed nations—including the Czech nation. By the late 1890s, however, Kautsky had once again adopted a somewhat different view of the national question. In a letter to V. Adler written in November 1896, Kautsky proclaimed that "I am in the Eastern question as in the Polish question of the opinion that the old position of Marx has become untenable, as has, indeed, his position as to the Czechs."[127]

An introduction by Kautsky written in 1896 to *Revolution and Counter-Revolution in Germany* contains objections to the anti-Czech and anti-Croatian attitude maintained by Marx (and by Engels).[128] Given the antirevolutionary position of the Southern Slavs during the upheavals of 1848, Kautsky admitted, Marx's position was not surprising.

But didn't Marx allow himself to be carried too far by his righteous wrath, and didn't he make an assertion which he could not justify, when he downright denied these Slavic stocks, and above all the Czechs, the possibility of a national existence? Haven't the facts belied his words? Isn't it the case that the capacity for existence of the Czech nation is no longer denied today even by its most embittered enemies?[129]

Kautsky discusses the development of the Czechs from 1848 to 1896 and concludes that "the Czech nation possesses . . . today all of the ingredients of a modern people of culture."[130]

There were hardly any matters on which Kautsky disagreed with the legacy of Marx and Engels during the 1890s and even fewer matters on which he was willing to publicly criticize the founders of Marxism. Kautsky's explicit criticism of the traditional Marxist position on the Slavs is therefore extremely unusual and important. It represents, moreover, yet another transitional position on Kautsky's part. In his introduction, despite his recognition of Marx's mistakes on the future of the Czechs, Kautsky still asserted that the national struggle was ceasing to be of great importance in Austria-Hungary. A national movement for which the most important question is the language in which the street signs are written, Kautsky mocked, need not disturb a truly revolutionary party.[131]

But 1897—the year following the publication of Kautsky's introduction—was a troubled period in the Czech-speaking lands and a period in which national tensions were high in Austria-Hungary. Victor Adler, leader of the SDAP [Oe], wrote to Kautsky that the Party was not prepared for these troubles, and that it had "no positive program" with which it proposed to deal with the problem of national tension in Austria.[132]

Kautsky answered Adler on August 5, 1897. "The situation," Kautsky wrote, "shows that the masses can only be filled with a durable enthusiasm for socialism where and insofar as the national question is solved."[133] Kautsky explicitly differentiates himself from those, such as W. Liebknecht, who continued to think that the era of the national question had passed. Kautsky, however, also admitted in this letter that he had no better idea than did Adler as to how the Austrian language problem could be solved.

Despite the uncertainty that he had revealed to Adler, Kautsky soon thereafter wrote a significant work on the national question in Austria-Hungary.[134] In an article entitled "Der Kampf der Nationalitäten und der Staatsrecht in Oesterreich," Kautsky noted that a number of factors, including the needs of the bourgeoisie and an increase in levels of education, had led to an increase in national sentiments. To Kautsky, this was a positive sign, indicating that society was continuing to develop. Kautsky proclaimed that the proletariat is not an enemy of national movements, and that it has a strong interest in the continued development of such movements. The fact that the proletariat upholds the tradition of international-ism does not mean that it withdraws itself from every nation, but that it stands for the freedom and equality of all nations. Addressing himself to the problems of multinational countries, Kautsky main-tained that in such countries each nation, defined by language, ought to be made self-determining. Kautsky saw the program of national self-determination for each nation living in a multina-tional country as progressive, but he did not view the demand for territorial independence for each nation in a similar way. As Kaut-sky pointed out, no matter how the territorial boundries were drawn in a country such as Austria-Hungary, there would always be lin-guistic minorities within the confines of any given territory, and these minorities would continue to feel and be oppressed even if the majority nation in that territory had an independent nation-state. The only just answer to the national question was therefore the self-determination of nations, defined by language, not inde-pendence for territories inhabited mostly by members of a given nation.

The national troubles in the Austro-Hungarian Empire in 1897 contributed to the decision of Austrian socialists to reorganize their party. At a congress held in Vienna in early June of that year, the socialists agreed to a federal plan under which socialist groups working within six of the nations in the empire acccepted a com-mon program and the authority of an "all-Austrian" executive committee, also agreeing that each of these groups would have autonomy within its own sphere of operation. German, Czech, Pol-ish, Ruthenian, Slovenian, and Italian socialist groups active within the empire were all recognized as legitimate, and each of the groups recognized accepted the new organizational proposal.[135]

The first congress of the All-Austrian Social Democratic party to meet after the adoption of this reorganization plan was convened in Brünn in September of 1899. After considerable discussion and debate, those attending this congress adopted a resolution sketching the party's position on the national question. The Brünn Resolution, which clearly reflected the influence of Kautsky's argument in "Der Kampf der Nationalitäten," declared that:

1. Austria shall be transformed into a democratic federation of nationalities.
2. The historic provinces (crown lands) shall be replaced by nationally delimited self-governing areas in each of which legislation shall be entrusted to national chambers . . .
3. All the self-governing regions of one and the same nation shall jointly form a single national union which shall manage its national affairs on the basis of complete autonomy.
4. The rights of national minorities shall be protected by a special law to be adopted by the parliament of the empire.
5. We do not recognize any national privilege and therefore we reject the demand for an official language.[136]

Kautsky wholly supported the Brünn Resolution. In a letter to the Czech socialist F. Modráček in October 1899, Kautsky went so far as to declare that he could "not conceive of another policy on nationalities for the Social Democratic Party in Austria than the one which is embodied in the resolution."[137] The ideas expressed by Kautsky in "Der Kampf der Nationalitäten," and the fact that he backed the Brünn Resolution, demonstrate the extent to which Kautsky had broken with his perspective of the mid-1870s. In the period following the Paris Commune and his own entry into the socialist movement, Kautsky wholly rejected national sentiment and had no sympathy for national movements. By the turn of the century, however, Kautsky was generally sympathetic to the desire of the smaller nations of Austria-Hungary for national rights. In answer to a poll conducted by the editor of La Vie Socialiste in 1905, Kautsky clarified his stance by declaring, "Proletarians of a nation which is oppressed, exploited or simply threatened in its independence by another must fight against this oppression."[138]

It is important to recognize, however, that despite his support for movements struggling for the right of their nations to self-determination, Kautsky continued to oppose the Czech independence movement and the "separatist" tendency among Czech socialists (which supported the formation of Czech trade unions and which ultimately justified the formation of an independent rather than autonomous Czech socialist party).

In 1899 Kautsky condemned the movement for Bohemian *Staatsrecht*. He insisted that the success of this movement would result in a strengthening of clericalism in the Austrian Alps, of feudalism in Galicia, and of absolutism in all of Austria. In Kautsky's mind, the Czech nationalists were the twins of the German anti-semites.

The classes which support the Young Czech movement are the same ones which flock to anti-Semitism—the petty bourgeoisie and the peasantry. And the allies of the young Czechs are also anti-Semites, the German-national deportment of the latter notwithstanding. . . . We must struggle against Bohemian *Staatsrecht* as a product of and a means to advance reaction; we must struggle against it as a means of splitting the Austrian proletariat. The road from capitalism to socialism does not go through feudalism. Bohemian *Staatsrecht* is just as little a precursor of the autonomy of peoples as anti-Semitism, the one-sided struggle against Jewish capitalism, is a precursor of Social Democracy.[139]

The overwhelming majority of the Czechs within the All-Austrian Social Democratic Party disagreed with Kautsky's perspective and believed that the Austrian party leadership was insensitive to Czech needs. Animosity between the Czech and German socialist workers eventually resulted in a split of the Austrian Metalworkers' Union along national lines. Because of Kautsky's enormous authority, the Czech separatists attempted to use quotes from Kautsky to justify themselves. It was claimed by the separatists, for example, that Kautsky's "Nationalität und Internationalität" provided arguments that would be used to support actions such as the division of the Austrian Metalworkers' Union.[140]

When Kautsky became cognizant of the way in which his work was being used, he disavowed the separatists in no uncertain terms. Kautsky insisted that he did not justify a "national dismemberment of the organizations" in "Nationalität und Internationalität," but merely a "certain national autonomy" that "must be created for purposes of propaganda."[141] It is ruinous, he believed, for the proletariat of a given state to be split along national lines for "action purposes." "If the attempt is made to use me as an advocate of a national dismemberment of the union movement, then I must decidedly protest against it."[142] The proletariat of a given land, he thought, has a need for propaganda in its own language, and this need ought to be filled insofar as it is practical to do so. A loosening of the relations of proletarians of a given nation living in a multinational country to the country-wide union organization of that country, however, must be energetically condemned. The bitter struggle between the Czech separatists and the leadership of the SDAP [Oe] intensified yet again in the period immediately following the above-cited letter by Kautsky. In response to urging from the German-speaking leadership of the All-Austrian Social Democratic party, the International, during its congress in Copenhagen in the summer of 1910, adopted a resolution condemning the separatist ideology. The resolution contributed to the decision of the Czech separatists to leave the Austrian party, and to form an independent socialist party of their own. The Czech Social Democratic Workers' Party in Austria was officially constituted at a conference held in Brünn on May 13 and 14, 1911.

Even after this split, Kautsky continued to urge the Czechs to unite with the German-speaking socialists of Austria, but he was unwilling to temper his criticism of the Czechs even if this would bring about a rapprochement. In August of 1911, for example, an article by Kautsky was published in *Der Kampf,* an organ of the Austrian Marxists, in which Kautsky proclaimed, "Separatism is no less pernicious and reprehensible than is anarchism," and that it must be fought just as strongly.[143]

Kautsky addressed the issues raised by Czech separatism in greater detail in an article that appeared under the title "Separatismus, Nationalismus und Sozialismus." The victory of Czech separatism, Kautsky proclaimed in this article, would not only deeply damage the Austrian socialist movement, but would also undermine internationalism elsewhere. Kautsky noted, for example, that the Czech Social Democratic party had established ties with certain Ukrainian socialists who were seeking greater independence from the RSDRP. To allow a victory of Czech separatism, Kautsky warns, is to encourage separatist movements elsewhere in the socialist world. Kautsky quotes a statement printed in the Czech separatist organ *Právo Lidu* condemning the International for taking a purportedly anti-Czech stance and remarks, "With this [statement] the summit of nationalistic megalomania and persecution mania is surely revealed."[144] In the same article, Kautsky goes so far as to suggest that the Czech separatists ought to be expelled from the International.

Thus a brief review of Kautsky's writings on the national question in general and the Czech question in particular reveals a number of parallels between the positions that Kautsky took in these writings and the position that he took on the Jewish question. By the 1890s, Kautsky realized that the workers of oppressed nations would not wholeheartedly work for the socialist cause unless and until the socialist movement acknowledged and worked against national oppression. Thus Kautsky advocated support for Czech national rights within the context of the Austro-Hungarian Empire, and he came to believe that a decrease in national tensions was a necessary prelude to socialism. But socialism could no more be realized in the Russian Empire without a solution to the national problems of the Russian Empire than it could in Austria-Hungary without an answer to the Austrian national question. Kautsky believed that the Russian economic and political systems, precisely because they were backward, had fostered the retention of certain national characteristics among the Russian Jews. Thus just as he thought that the Czechs ought to be granted national rights in Austria-Hungary because this was a pre-condition of socialism in that country, so he thought that Russian Jewry ought to be granted certain national rights in accord with their national characteristics, because he feared that without these rights there would continue to be tension between Jewish and non-Jewish workers, and that continued tension of that kind would seriously weaken the socialist movement.

Kautsky's attitude toward the Czech separatists paralleled his attitude toward the Zionists. While he acknowledged the right of the Czechs to national self-determination, Kautsky believed that the creation of an independent Czech state would strengthen reactionary forces within the Czech people and within Austria-Hungary as a whole. Kautsky therefore condemned the call for an independent Czech state. Similarly, Kautsky condemned the movement working for the establishment of an independent Jewish state as reactionary and unworthy of support by social democrats. In both the Russian and Austro-Hungarian empires, Kautsky was perfectly willing to support social democrats working within minority peoples and demanding national rights for their people if those social democrats also worked closely with the overarching social democratic movement of the empire in which they lived. Thus Kautsky supported the Brünn Resolution of the Austrian movement, and he supported the Bund, because and insofar as the Bund was willing to cooperate with non-Jewish socialists. When the Czech socialists broke from the all-Austrian movement, and when they split the Austrian trade union movement, Kautsky harshly criticized the Czechs. When Kautsky feared that the Bund was isolating Jewish workers, he wrote an article that contained veiled and indirect criticism of this purported isolationist tendency. The Bund, however, did not take positions as extreme as those taken by the Czech separatists, and thus they were never subjected to the kinds of criticisms that Kautsky directed against the latter.

The parallels between Kautsky's position on the Czech question and his position on the Jewish question are important in that they indicate that Kautsky asked neither more nor less of the Jews than he asked of the Czechs. Kautsky's strong criticisms of Zionism, and his advocacy of the assimilation of Jewry, were not motivated by anti-Semitism of any sort, but were, rather, similar to the stance that Kautsky took toward small nations in the Austro-Hungarian Empire—including the nation of his father.

Kautsky's influence and reputation diminished dramatically during World War I, and continued to diminish after the victory of the Bolsheviks. At one time, his works were read throughout the world. Today, his works are rarely read and even more rarely praised. For several decades, Kautsky has been seen—when he has been seen at all—primarily through the eyes of Lenin, Trotsky, Luxemburg, and Bernstein and has suffered accordingly.

It has frequently been contended that Kautsky's ideas are overly deterministic.[145] Kautsky certainly had his failings—including, notably, an uninspiring writing style and a tendency to write too much. His writings on the Jewish question, however, were by no means mechanistic or deterministic. Kautsky hoped that anti-Semitism would decrease. He did not believe that it must necessarily do so. Similarly, Kautsky hoped that the Jews would eventually assimilate, but he also recognized that they might not do so under certain circumstances. In this sense, a study of Kautsky's writings on the Jewish question raises doubts as to criticisms that have been made about his general theory. It may well be that Kautsky's democratic Marxism, which has been all but squeezed out of existence, retains more validity than is currently recognized.

The decline of Kautsky's reputation in the world at large has been mirrored by the decline of his reputation in the Jewish community. The decline of the anti-Zionist Jewish socialist and labor movements, assimilation, the Holocaust, and the rise of Zionism have virtually eliminated Kautsky's base of support within the Jewish world and have also greatly diminished interest in his ideas. Just as Kautsky's works on capitalism and socialism have come to be seen primarily through the eyes of his opponents in the socialist world, so his works on the Jewish question have come to be seen through the eyes of his Jewish opponents. In the post-Holocaust world, Kautsky's anti-Zionist, proassimilationist perspective has been misinterpreted even by scholars of enormous erudition.

Kautsky's own lineage, a mixture of many nationalities, seems to have been a major factor leading Kautsky to conclude that the future would bring a general mixing of nations and a decrease in nationalism.[146] To Kautsky, the answer to *both* the national and Jewish questions was assimilation. Kautsky's support for Jewish assimilationism, and his opposition to those Jewish nationalists who advocated the creation of an independent Jewish state, were a specific case of his general position on small people, and were intimately tied to his perception of the needs of the socialist movement.

In his own day a number of factors—including the fact that Kautsky's grandfather had owned a house in the Jewish ghetto in Prague, that Kautsky repeatedly attacked anti-Semitism, that he was manifestly interested in the Jewish question and devoted considerable time to the study of it, that both of the women he married were Jews,[147] and that two of his three sons married Jewish women[148]—contributed to the widely held impression that Kautsky was himself Jewish. An indication of just how widespread this erroneous impression was may be inferred from the fact that Eduard David, a prominent figure in the SPD, thought that Kautsky was Jewish as late as

1915.[149] In the post-World War I era, Kautsky was often assumed to be Jewish, and often attacked, by anti-Semitic propagandists.[150]

Kautsky was well aware of this mistake and mentions it in a memoir written in 1936: "Not in order to prettify myself, but only in order to pay due tribute to the truth, I must confirm my purely Catholic descent."[151] Kautsky refers explicitly to the reports that he was a "child of the ghetto of Prague" and responds, "If that were the case, it would not particularly trouble me."[152] In so doing, Kautsky neatly summarized his own attitude toward the Jews. Kautsky identified with the plight of the Jews and fought their enemies throughout his career. He believed that it was the task of the social democratic movement to be "the most tireless champion of the freedom of all who [are] oppressed, not merely [of] the wage-earner, but also of women, persecuted religions and races, the Jews, Negroes and Chinese."[153] He asked of the social-democratic movement only what he asked of himself.

In a classic piece written in 1910, Kautsky described his position within the socialist camp using a geographic analogy.[154] Examine a map of Central Europe, Kautsky suggested, and you'll find that the Duchy of Luxemburg is to the left of Trier—the city of Marx's birth—and that the Duchy of Baden, a revisionist stronghold, is on Trier's right. Kautsky, in other words, saw himself as an orthodox Marxist, "between Baden and Luxemburg." Kautsky's position on the Jewish question during the twentieth century was also between Baden and Luxemburg. It was distinct from that of both Eduard Bernstein, foremost theoretician of the revisionists, and Rosa Luxemburg, foremost theoretician of the left wing of the German social democratic movement.

# CHAPTER 2

# Eduard Bernstein: After All, a German Jew

Eduard Bernstein was brought up in surroundings that encouraged assimilation. His mother, born Johanna Rosenberg, was raised and educated in the home of the legal historian Eduard Gans, who had been converted from Judaism to Christianity in 1825.[1] Eduard's father, Jakob Bernstein, though descended from rabbis and scholars,[2] worked as a tinsmith and later as a locomotive engineer—occupations that were atypical for German Jews and that gave him few opportunities to develop close relationships with Jews. Jakob's opportunities to develop such relationships were further diminished by the fact that he chose to live, and raise his family, in a primarily non-Jewish neighborhood.[3]

Both Johanna and Jakob were openly Jewish. Jakob, according to Eduard, knew quite a bit about Jewry and was able to explain Jewish customs to his children.[4] Eduard's parents sent him to the reform Jewish school for religious instruction, attended the reform temple on major Jewish holidays, and were members of the reform community.[5] In fact, Jakob's older brother, Aron Bernstein, with whom Jakob maintained a close relationship,[6] was one of the leading figures in the reform community.[7]

This community, however, was itself made up largely of Jews anxious to integrate themselves into German society.[8] In the first half of the nineteenth century German Jews had been the victims of pervasive discrimination. They had responded to this discrimination in part by altering many of the institutions of Judaism that had been criticized by non-Jews, including institutions that had previously been thought to be fundamental and unalterable. Though German Jewish intellectuals associated with the reform movement formulated religious rationalizations for the changes that they advocated and instituted in Jewish law and practice, these changes were motivated to a significant extent by the demands of the non-Jewish world and by the desire of German Jews to be accepted in that world. By the time Eduard Bernstein was old enough to have had contact with the reform community, the members of that community had considerably lessened the gap between their own lifestyles and those of their Christian neighbors. In one of his memoirs, for example, Bernstein mentions that the Jews in the reform community observed Sunday as the day of rest and did not observe traditional Jewish dietary laws.[9] Bernstein also noted that Christmas was his father's favorite holiday, and that his parents had a favorable opinion of liberal Christianity.[10]

Given this family background, it is far from surprising that Eduard Bernstein, as a child, had a greater interest in the New Testament than in the Hebrew Bible or that his parents did not object when he attended Protestant rather than Jewish services in his childhood years.[11] For Bernstein had little contact with Jews or with orthodox Judaism. There were few Jews in the school he attended, and none in his class.[12] Moreover, all of Eduard's closest childhood friends were Christians.[13] In fact, until his older brother was subjected to anti-Semitic taunting, Eduard apparently did not even know that his family was Jewish.[14] When, as a gymnasium student, Eduard once attended an orthodox Jewish service, he found it to be "everything but inspiring."[15]

Eduard Bernstein was raised in a time and a place where assimilation was the natural course. Though he had brushes with anti-Semitism, these brushes were minor.[16] "He did not fight for assimilation and did not have to fight for it,"[17] for the battle had been fought and, to a considerable extent, won by his parents' generation.

But the processes of emancipation and assimilation were accompanied by psychological scarring. Many German Jews—including much of the reform Jewish community—internalized and accepted the anti-Jewish prejudices maintained (to one extent or another) by a large number of Christians in Germany.[18] Bernstein himself noted that "no Christian could have felt stronger disdain for . . . manifestations of orthodoxy than I felt" as a youth.[19]

Many of the attitudes that he absorbed as a child and youth remained with Bernstein long after he became a socialist. In the 1870s Bernstein reacted to the role that certain unscrupulous Jews played on the stock exchange and to the role that certain Jewish journalists played in drumming up public opinion against socialists in precisely the same manner as did part of the Christian population. He became, as he himself admitted, anti-Jewish. "The first indications of anti-Semitism which manifested themselves in Germany in the second half of the seventies," Bernstein once wrote, "appeared to me to be a comprehensible reaction to unseemly forwardness to such a degree that [these indications] disturbed me [only] a little."[20]

Bernstein also reported that he was very attracted to the work of Eugen Dühring, and that, in 1873, he recommended Dühring's *Kursus der Nationalökonomie und des Socialismus* to August Bebel.[21] Bernstein was willing to overlook Dühring's anti-Semitism, "since at the time certain strata of Jewry in Germany in fact pushed themselves to the fore in a way which very much repelled even many Jews—including myself."[22]

Thus when, in 1877, Johann Most, a leader of the social democrats in Berlin, called on his comrades to leave the churches, Bernstein responded by renouncing his formal membership in the Jewish community.[23] In his own eyes he no longer had any significant ties to Judaism, Jewry, or to individual Jews as Jews. On a conscious level, Bernstein was not at all attracted to people because they were Jewish.

And yet even during this period, Bernstein maintained unusually close ties to other assimilated Jews, and he was particularly close to socialists of Jewish descent active in the Russian revolutionary movement and living in Germany. The fact that Bernstein was acquainted with many of the most important early Russian Jewish socialists is most dramatically confirmed by a letter to Bernstein from Moses Aronson.[24]

In 1928 Bernstein sent Aronson a copy of his newly published book, *Sozialdemokratische Lehrjahre*, in which Bernstein discusses his contacts with the Russian exile community in Berlin in the period from 1874 to 1878.[25] Aronson responded to this gift by mailing Bernstein a thank-you note, in the course of which he made some critical comments on the contents of Bernstein's memoir. "Strange," Aronson wrote, "that of all the Russian comrades of our circle you mentioned only Efron,[26] Grischa[27] and, in another passage, in passing, me. Of Sundel[e]vitch,[28] Jochelson,[29] Klemenz,[30] Zuckerman,[31] Lieberman—no word.[32] You were certainly our strongest link."[33]

Collectively, the Russian Jews mentioned by Aronson were the heart and soul of the so-called Jewish Section.[34] The claim that Bernstein knew *all* of these men implies that he was well aware of their ties to one another. In fact, Aronson's letter suggests that Bernstein was not merely aware of the existence of the Russian Jewish socialist group in Berlin, but was closer to it than any other German social democrat.

The memoirs of Grigori Gurevitch tend to corroborate the impression given by Aronson. According to Gurevitch, Bernstein

introduced me to his circle and family. . . . We frequently got together with Eduard and his comrades in the cafes and beer halls. . . . I used to visit all the gatherings and meetings together with Ed. Bernstein; in short, I became his shadow. He used to not make a move without me, and we used to see each other every day, or, more correctly every evening.[35]

Kautsky also confirms Aronson's claim: "Bernstein was one of the first German Social Democrats to recognize the importance of Russian socialism, and to draw nearer to the Russian students living in Berlin in the 1870s. He became friends with several of them."[36]

Bernstein's contacts with the Russian socialists of Jewish origin continued unabated after he left Berlin for Switzerland.[37] With the passing of the antisocialist law on October 19, 1878, many of these Russian Jews themselves moved to Switzerland, joining the Russian colonies already in existence there. Of the members of the Jewish Section, Zuckerman lived in Switzerland in 1879, Efron in 1880, and Gurevitch in 1880–81.[38] During this period Bernstein became particularly close to Aronson,[39] to yet another former member of the Jewish Section, Maxim Romm,[40] and also became friends with several Russian socialists of Jewish descent who had not been members of the Jewish Section, including Pavel Axelrod and Leo Deich.[41]

Given the evidence of extensive contact between Bernstein and the Russian Jewish radicals, what was the attitude of Bernstein's Russian Jewish friends toward the Jewish question? And to what extent did Bernstein agree with this attitude?

The memoirs and works of the Russian Jewish radicals all give similar accounts of their attitude toward the Jewish question during the 1870s and early 1880s. Vladimir Jochelson reports that "we" (the members of the Vilna revolutionarty circle to which Jochelson, Sundelevitch, and Lieberman had belonged before escaping to Germany)

> reckoned that the liberation of the Russian people from the reign of despotism and from the oppression of the ruling classes would also bring about the political and economic liberation of all the peoples of Russia, including the Jewish people. One must, however, admit that Russian literature, which implanted within us a love for education and for the Russian peasant, also implanted in us, to a certain extent, a conception of Jewry not as a people but as a class of parasites. It was also not rare for the radical Russian writers to express opinions such as this one, and this was one of the reasons which led us to turn away from the Jewish people.[42]

Aron Sundelevitch described the attitude of the Russian Jewish radicals in the following terms:

> For us Jewry as a national organism did not present a phenomenon worthy of support. Jewish nationalism, it seemed to us, had no *raison d'être*. As for religion, that cement which combined the Jews into one unit, it represented to us complete retrogression . . .

> For a Jewish *Narodnik* the motto . . . "Go to the people"—meant go to the Russian people.[43]

The question of whether or not Bernstein was *influenced* by his Russian Jewish friends is impossible to answer. The question of the extent to which he agreed with them, however, is more easily dealt with. Bernstein undoubtedly was fully in agreement with the general stance expressed by Jochelson and Sundelevitch. The members of the Jewish Section and the other radicals of Jewish origin with whom Bernstein came into contact were almost certainly Bernstein's major source of information on the state of Russian Jewry. Before the pogroms of 1881, however, these Russians were not particularly interested in the Jewish question. They considered themselves to be part of the Russian revolutionary community rather than the Jewish community and related to Bernstein as a fellow revolutionary, not as a fellow Jew. It is no accident that Bernstein's descriptions of Efron, Gurevitch, Zuckerman, Lieberman, Romm, and Aronson in *Sozialdemokratische Lehrjahre* do not mention that any of these individuals was Jewish.[44] To Bernstein these men were *Gesinnungsgenosse* (comrades), "Russian acquaintances and friends"[45]—and they most certainly preferred that he think of them in this way. Bernstein, however, was perfectly aware of his friends' backgrounds.[46] The fact that he described them as Russians rather than as Jews is rooted in the fact that he agreed with their general attitude toward the Jewish question.

As his parents had before him, Bernstein rejected the notion of Jewish national identity.[47] In a description of his attitude during the 1870s written almost half a century later, Bernstein wrote, "To think of the Jewish question as a question of a separate national right of Jews or as one of a national Jewish interest—such a thing did not enter my mind."[48] Thus Bernstein's contacts with the Russian Jewish revolutionaries would have confirmed his preexisting notion of the proper answer to the Jewish question. Just as the experience of his family led Bernstein to believe in the desirability and relative ease of assimilation of Western Jewry, so his contact with the Russians most probably led him to conclude that East European Jewry would undergo a similar process. Both Bernstein's hope that the Jews would assimilate, and his tendency to see the Jews as a religious group rather than as a nation, were strengthened by his encounters with Russian Jews who concurred with him wholeheartedly on these issues.

Even the pogroms of 1881–82 did not alter Bernstein's beliefs. The assumption that Bernstein remained an assimilationist during this period is given credence by an examination of articles printed in *Der Sozialdemokrat*.[49] Bernstein became editor of *Der Sozialdemokrat* in January 1881, and continued to edit it until its demise in 1890. Though Bernstein ought not be considered to have been in agreement with every piece published in his paper, he solicited articles, rejected others, wrote copy when space had to be filled, and thereby strongly influenced the paper's political stance. Thus

the fact that *Der Sozialdemokrat* supported an assimilationist perspective on the Jewish question suggests that its editor in chief held
a similar position.

The policy of *Der Sozialdemokrat* was most clearly indicated by
an article published in the issue of May 22, 1881. The article, which
is unsigned, discusses a proposal that had been recently advocated
by the non-Jewish Ukrainian socialist, M. Dragomanow.[50] In 1880
Dragomanow, acting in pursuit of his own Ukrainian nationalist
ends, had become the moving spirit behind an effort to spark the
publication of Yiddish-language socialist propaganda.[51] In a proclamation disseminated by a Jewish socialist group and endorsed by
Dragomanow, the argument was made that many Yiddish-speaking
Jews did not know the language of their non-Jewish neighbors, and
that there was a large number of exploited workers among these
Yiddish speakers. The time had come, the authors of this proclamation announced, to advocate socialism among the exploited elements of East European Jewry by disseminating socialist literature
among them in their own language.

The proclamation was met with hostility by many of the East
European revolutionaries living in Switzerland at the time of its
publication and particularly by the revolutionaries of Jewish descent.[52] It therefore failed in its goal. As late as mid-1881, however,
Dragomanow remained committed to this plan and described it in
an article published first in French and later in *Der Sozialdemokrat.*[53]

The commentary on Dragomanow's article that appeared in
Bernstein's paper is very telling. This commentary notes that radical and religious problems might be sharpened rather than weakened by a separate Jewish socialist movement. Thus, while the
commentator admits the necessity of propaganda directed at Jewish
workers, he insists that this propaganda aim at the "immediate
joining of the Jewish workers to the Russian or Polish revolutionary
party." The sole purpose of socialist propaganda in a Jewish language, in the eyes of the commentator, would be to "tear" the
Jewish workers "out of their separate sphere."[54]

While the author of this commentary is unknown, a scholarly
discussion of the debates among East European revolutionaries living in Switzerland at the time suggests that Pavel Axelrod and Leo

Deich were among those vigorously opposed to Dragomanow's position.[55]

The Jews active in the Russian revolutionary movement were not all equally cosmopolitan. The differences among them became especially manifest during the pogrom wave beginning in 1881.[56] The pogroms, however, did not fundamentally alter the beliefs of the majority of Russian Jewish radicals *with whom Bernstein had contact.* Though shaken and disturbed by the events in the Russian Empire, they retained their beliefs in the desirability and inevitability of assimilation—as did their friend and comrade, Eduard Bernstein.

In 1881 Bernstein left Switzerland and took up residence in London, where he once again had occasion to meet Russian Jewish socialists. Whereas in Berlin and Zurich the Russian Jewish socialists had been primarily intellectuals, the movement in England in the late 1880s and 1890s was based in the Jewish working-class community living in London's East End.[57]

The institutions of the Jewish socialist community were reaching their peak when Bernstein arrived in England. On March 16, 1889, for example, the Jewish socialists sponsored a demonstration for "work, bread, and the eight hour day" that attracted three thousand people.[58] In December of that same year, four thousand Jewish workers gathered in London and proclaimed the establishment of the Federation of East London Labor Unions.[59] Though these successes were followed by fragmentation of the Jewish movement into anarchist and socialist wings, and by the eventual defeat of the socialists by the anarchists, the Jewish socialists retained a sizable presence in London through the 1890s.

Bernstein did not play a prominent role in this movement. As a close friend of Eleanor Marx,[60] however, Bernstein had access to information on activities among the Jewish socialists and was fully aware both of Engels's and of Eleanor Marx's interest in and sympathy for the Jewish workers.

Bernstein commented on Eleanor Marx's attitude toward the Jewish question in an obituary published in *Die Neue Zeit.* Bernstein's comments are revealing:

A noteworthy characteristic of Eleanor Marx was her strong sympathy with the Jews. At every opportunity she declared her descent with a certain defiance. "I am a Jewess"—how often I heard her—who was neither Jewishly religious, nor in any contact whatsoever with the official representatives of Jewry—shout this with pride to the crowd from the rostrum. She felt herself drawn to the Jewish proletarians of the East End with all the greater sympathy. But her opposition to every sort of anti-Semitism did not exhaust itself with this. Where the Jew as Jew was oppressed, she did not allow herself to be misled by the feelings of the proletarian class which lay deeply stamped on her soul, and took a lively interest in the oppressed without regard to class position. . . . However [the Jewish question] was for her a so-to-say more theoretical question. She did not have a practical interest [in it].[61]

Bernstein's comments on Eleanor Marx are interesting for at least three reasons. First, they document the extent to which Bernstein was aware of her perspective. Second, they imply that Bernstein himself frequently accompanied Eleanor on her trips to the East End. Third, and most important, the comments are also written in a tone that suggests that Bernstein was sympathetic to her stance. There is, however, very little in the way of additional evidence to document this impression. Neither Bernstein's letters to Eleanor Marx nor her letters to him are extant.

Bernstein discussed his own relationship with the Jews in London in only one article. "Despite close to thirteen years residence in London," Bernstein wrote,

I had very little opportunity to acquaint myself in a detailed manner with the condition of the Jewish proletariat living there. To be sure, I repeatedly visited the quarter of the East End, which was inhabited especially by Jewish proletarians. To be sure, I also held lectures from time to time in the Jewish workers' unions there, or in the unions there which were composed chiefly of Jews. But through such occasional visits one doesn't gain any knowledge of conditions beyond the knowledge gained from official publications and from the material made known by the press. My time, which was taken up by other work, geographical separation (I lived, almost always, in parts of London quite far from the East End), and very inadaquate knowledge of the dialect or jargon which is spoken by the Jewish workers and petty bourgeois who immigrated from Eastern Europe, prevented a more intimate acquaintance with their lives and way of living. . . . Still, I frequently met with the leaders of the Jewish labor movement of the East End. But our conversations touched more on party questions and on questions of union organization than on the precise details of the life of the Jewish worker. Besides, the political friends in question were either already strongly assimilated themselves, or well on the way to being assimilated.[62]

Thus Bernstein's stay in London does not seem to have had a strong impact on his perspective. He does not seem to have been impressed by the growing national consciousness among the Jewish socialists evident in the years immediately preceding the publication of his article or by the enormous development of Yiddish culture that had occurred by that time.

Though there are virtually no records of the conversations of Bernstein with the Jewish socialist and labor leaders that he mentioned in his article (above), there is at least one published account of Bernstein's reactions to his encounters with the organized Jewish workers of London. When, in late December 1894, the Russian radical Sergei Stepniak[63] died, Bernstein spoke at Stepniak's funeral as a representative of the SPD.[64] The Russian Jewish radicals also turned out to pay their respects to the departed. Up to a thousand people marched behind a wreath on which was inscribed "in memory of Sergei Stepniak from the Russian-Jewish Unions."

According to the Bundist Franz Kursky, who became a close friend of Bernstein's in the 1920s and writes as though he had discussed this incident with Bernstein, the procession at Stepniak's funeral was the first and only time in Bernstein's life that Bernstein was to see a march of Jewish workers, and "it made an immense impression on him."[65] When, Kursky claims, the first news of the founding of the Bund reached Bernstein (in 1897–98), Bernstein connected this news in his mind to the "exemplary" march of the organized Jewish workers of London that he had witnessed several years earlier.

Kursky's view of the impact of the march of the Jewish workers, however, differs from the impression left by Bernstein's description of this march in the volume of reminiscences that he published under the title *Aus den Jahren meines Exils. Erinnerungen eines Sozialisten* in 1917. In this volume, Bernstein comments in passing that "it was a gloomy day on which the burial took place, and only about a thousand mourners, the great majority of whom were Russo-Jewish workers, took part in the procession."[66] Far from emphasizing the extent to which he was impressed by the procession, Bernstein's wording suggests that he thought the turnout was rather small.

Just as Aronson and Gurevitch give a different impression of the intensity of their contacts with Bernstein than does Bernstein's account of his relationship with them, so Kursky's assessment of the impact of the march of the Jewish workers on Bernstein suggests a stronger impact than does Bernstein's description of the march.

In the period beginning with 1874 and ending in 1896 with the revisionist controversy, Bernstein had numerous contacts with Jewish socialists. He was more closely tied to the Russian Jewish radicals living in Berlin in the mid-1870s than were his German contemporaries, and he was an important liaison person to the SDAP[D] in the eyes of these Russians. Bernstein also evidenced more of a preference for the company of assimilated Jews than he was prepared to admit. On a conscious level, however, Bernstein displayed little interest in the Jewish question as such during this era. The hints of a growing sympathy for the Jews evident in his article on Eleanor Marx did not fully manifest themselves until after Bernstein's break with orthodox Marxism.

The distance that Bernstein put between himself and the organized Jewish community in the 1870s did not prevent him from being the target of anti-Semitic attacks. When Bernstein became a member of the SDAP[D], which was led by Wilhelm Liebknecht and August Bebel, the party was engaged in a bitter struggle with the ADAV—the General German Workers' Association. The ADAV frequently resorted to anti-Semitism in an attempt to undercut the influence of its rivals.[67] Soon after Bernstein became active in the SDAP[D], he became a subject of ADAV attacks. On January 23, 1873, C. W. Tölcke,[68] one of the most prominent leaders of the ADAV, referred to Bernstein in the *Neuer Sozialdemokrat* as an "honest-to-God little Jew."[69] Similarly, when Bernstein addressed a workers' meeting in Bernau, Wilhelm Hasselmann,[70] another prominent ADAV member, who attended the meeting in order to heckle the SDAP[D] speakers, took the floor and attempted to discredit Bernstein by referring repeatedly to his Jewish origins. In his memoirs, Bernstein notes that Hasselmann "skillfully created an anti-Jewish mood," and that Hasselmann portrayed the SDAP[D] as the "window-dressing for Jewish wire-pullers."[71]

Bernstein's response to Hasselmann's attack is unknown. Bernstein, however, responded to Tölcke in the pages of the *Volksstaat*, party paper of the SDAP[D]. While Bernstein's response deals primarily with other charges made by Tölcke, it does refer to Tölcke's use of anti-Semitism. "The epithet 'little Jew' with which Mr. Tölcke honors me," Bernstein wrote, "is too vulgar to go into."[72] Bernstein's experiences with anti-Semitism did not deeply affect him at that point. He thought of the attacks made by the ADAV as political ploys, did not identify with the Jewish community, and to some extent even agreed with the ADAV when its anti-Semitic attacks were directed against Liberals rather than against members of the SDAP[D].[73]

The rise of Adolf Stöcker's anti-Semitic movement in the 1880s, however, led Bernstein to reassess his stance. At that time, Bernstein began to speak out in public and in private against anti-Semitism. In fact, Bernstein became both more sensitive to the Jewish question than was Engels and, at least initially, took anti-Semites more seriously than did his teacher. In a letter to Engels dated July 23, 1881, Bernstein wrote

I sent you the anti-Semitica so that you could get to know this movement —which one ought not underestimate, at least not in practical struggles— somewhat better. If you want, I will pass on to you some of this material more frequently. In Berlin alone there are now published several of these newspapers—not counting the conservative and ultramontane papers— and in the provinces their number is growing with every passing day. I also do not believe that the movement will attain its end with the elections. All of government officialdom (including the judges), the higher body of teachers, the petty bourgeosie and the peasants sympathize with it, the former *mala*, the latter *bona fide*.[74]

When Engels responded to this letter by dismissing the anti-Semites as a transient phenomenon, Bernstein changed his tone to some extent. In a letter to Engels written in 1882, Bernstein admits that Stöcker had been unable to seize control of the unions, "all of his fawning to the contrary notwithstanding."[75] Bernstein, however, also made another attempt at that time to convince Engels to follow the anti-Semitic movement more closely by suggesting that Engels might want to read the reports on this movement in the *Berliner Volkszeitung*.[76]

In addition, Bernstein repeatedly warned Engels of the prevalence of anti-Semitism within the SDAP[D]. In 1883, for example, Bernstein commented, "You must know that just as are on the

whole *the majority of the "intelligentsia" in our party* the gentlemen in Stuttgart are also anti-Semites. This is in accord with their
petty-bourgeois attitude."[77]

Bernstein was known to be particularly interested in anti-Semitism.
This is demonstrated by the request made by Eleanor Marx to Bernstein in 1884 that he write an article on anti-Semitism (which she
probably intended to publish in the English socialist press). Bernstein did not write the article, both because he was too busy and
because he did not think that the time was right to do so, but, in
explaining his decision, he indicated that he expected that the
problem of anti-Semitism would become acute at the time of the
next elections, and that he would speak out against it at that
time.[78]

    Bernstein's position was markedly different from that of many
other Jews active in the German socialist movement. This difference between him and his party comrades was noted by Bernstein
on several occasions. In August 1884, Bernstein had a long discussion with Paul Singer and came away from this discussion with the
impression that Singer's attitude toward the conservative parties
was warped by psychological factors. Singer, Bernstein wrote, "did
not want to see" why the socialists and the workers in general
ought to care how the conservatives fared in the coming elections.[79]

It is for him a conflict with his emotions, for at bottom, I have noticed,
anti-Semitism—and in particular the anti-Semitism among our "intelligentsia"—aggrieves him greatly. He believes, out of an exaggerated scru-
pulousness, that he himself must play the anti-Semite and the state socialist.[80]

A month later, Bernstein made a similar comment about Abraham
Grumbel and others in the socialist movement: "Just like most of
the Jews in the Party, he considers himself to be obliged to accom-
modate himself to anti-Semitism. This is, for example, also the case
with Kayser, Höchberg, Singer, and many others."[81]

    In the 1890s, while living in England, Bernstein wrote a number
of articles in which he attacked anti-Semitism, and published these
articles in *Die Neue Zeit*. The first and most important of these
articles, "Das Schlagwort und der Antisemitismus," was published

in May 1893. In the course of this article, Bernstein once again singled out "the comrades of Jewish descent who, precisely because they are of Jewish origin, consider it to be their special duty to keep *interesting* the Party free of every suspicion of promoting Jewish interests."[82] While respecting their concern, Bernstein advised these comrades not to condemn philo-Semitism. For, Bernstein points out, the anti-Semites also engaged in attacks on philo-Semitism. According to Bernstein, philo-Semitism can mean several things. It can mean "a certain sympathy for the Jews which excludes neither a condemnation of their notorious mistakes nor repudiation of possible over-encouragement of them," or alternatively, it can mean "obsequiousness before capitalist money-Jewry, support of . . . Jewish chauvinism, excusing of injustices perpetrated by Jews and of loathsome characteristics developed by Jews."[83] If philo-Semitism is defined in the first of these ways, Bernstein comments, then it is "very legitimate."[84]

Bernstein was not opposed to condemning philo-Semitism in the latter sense, but feared the *blanket* condemnations of certain of his party comrades, which, he was afraid, might play into the hands of the anti-Semites. Wouldn't it be better, Bernstein suggests, for socialists to distinguish their positions more clearly from those of the anti-Semites by using a different terminology? Socialists ought to attack not philo-Semitism, Bernstein proposes, but rather *pan-Semitism*—by which he apparently meant philo-Semitism in the second sense delineated above. The correct social democratic position, Bernstein concludes, is one that opposes anti-Semitism and pan-Semitism equally.[85]

Though Bernstein does not explicitly say so, his wording implies that he was a philo-Semite in the first sense of the term. What was it that caused Bernstein to develop this "certain sympathy for the Jews" that he clearly had not had when he first entered the socialist movement? As we have seen, Bernstein, unlike Engels, took the anti-Semitic movement seriously. Whereas Engels believed that the anti-Semitic movement would rapidly disappear, Bernstein was concerned with the fact that it had not already done so. Thus it may be that Bernstein's sympathy was rooted in his assessment of the threat posed by the anti-Semites.

This explanation, however, merely raises the question of why

Bernstein took the anti-Semitic threat more seriously than did Engels. One possible explanation revolves around Bernstein's geographic vantage point. Bernstein lived in Switzerland in 1878–88 and was closer to the centers of anti-Semitic agitation than was Engels. Hence Bernstein's geographical position may have given him access to more and perhaps to better information than was available to Engels.[86]

While this suggestion is plausible, another explanation is more compelling. The fact that Bernstein took the anti-Semitic movement more seriously than did Engels, and that he seemed to have a "certain sympathy" for the Jews, may have been due to his Jewish origins and, thereby, to a subconscious identification on Bernstein's part with European Jewry. It is certainly true that Bernstein claimed that he had no such identification.[87] As we have seen, however, Bernstein actually had closer and earlier ties to the Russian Jewish radicals than did any other important social democrat in Germany and had himself been the target of anti-Semitic attacks. It may also be significant that he chose to marry a Jewish woman and that he maintained ties with his (Jewish) family. Bernstein, it would appear, identified with other Jews more closely than he was prepared to admit in 1892.

The differences that existed between Engels and Bernstein on the Jewish question in the 1890s may also have been early harbingers of the revisionist controversy. Insofar as Bernstein took petty bourgeois-based anti-Semitism more seriously than did Engels, Bernstein's position implies a greater willingness to acknowledge the importance of the petty bourgeoisie than does Engels's position. Bernstein also seems to have been more concerned than was Engels with the question of what socialists ought to do about the Jewish question before the revolution. In both of these ways, Bernstein's position on the Jewish question in the years immediately before Engels's death hints at the differences between Bernstein's Marxism and the Marxism of Engels (and of Kautsky) —differences that ultimately led to a serious theoretical and practical breach within the Marxist world.[88] Thus the possibility ought to be raised that it was Bernstein's psychological identification with the Jews that first led him to reassess an orthodox Marxist position, and that, in this way,

Bernstein's Jewish origins ultimately contributed to the development of revisionism.

It is important to emphasize, however, that these underlying factors were in no way manifest to Engels, Bernstein, or Kautsky in the early 1890s. There were in fact differences between Bernstein's view of the Jewish question and Engels's view, but these differences were relatively subtle, never became a point of contention between Engels and Bernstein, and were overwhelmingly outweighed by the similarities between Engels's view and the view that Bernstein maintained.

An examination of Bernstein's writings of the early 1890s reveals, for example, that he thought of the anti-Semitic movement as a "connecting link" between the reactionary parties and the socialists, and that he described the anti-Semitic movement as a "first stage" on the road to socialism—very much in the same way as did Engels and Bebel during this same period.[89]

Again, just like Engels, Bernstein could not conceive of a lasting victory by the anti-Semites over the socialists. The anti-Semites, Bernstein believed, could win only where the social democrats had "not yet" enlightened the masses.[90] Just like Engels, Bernstein insisted that anti-Semitism did not have a mass following in the West or even in Central Europe. For more than half a generation, Benstein proclaimed, anti-Semitism has been preached to the masses in Western and Central Europe. Appeal has been made to all possible prejudices. Nevertheless, anti-Semitism has been able to win adherents only in "very isolated points."[91]

Thus Bernstein's position on the Jewish question during this period could be said to have complemented Engels's position. Bernstein exhibited the same friendliness toward the Jewish socialists and willingness to speak out against political anti-Semitism evident in Engels's letters and other works. He added to it an open advocacy of Jewish assimilation, which Engels certainly agreed with, though he never actually wrote about this issue. Whatever differences hindsight allows us to uncover between the views of Engels and Bernstein on the Jewish question before 1895, these differences were extremely subtle and not of great significance.

Bernstein dramatically revised his views on the Jewish question after he began to question orthodox Marxism. As early as 1898, Bernstein demonstrated that his position—which he had earlier described as neither anti-Semitic nor "pan-Semitic"—was now somewhat different. For the first time he openly declared, "It is for me a categorical imperative under the present conditions to be a philo-Semite in the face of any anti-Semitism."[92]

In November 1899, Bernstein reiterated this statement in the course of an interview with a nonsocialist Jewish periodical, *The Jewish Chronicle*.[93] The fact that Bernstein allowed himself to be interviewed by a representative of this periodical was in itself a political act, because it meant cooperating with a nonsocialist organ even though there were Jewish socialist periodicals in existence at that time.[94]

Several prominent Zionists, sensing that Bernstein had begun to change his stance on Jewish issues (and possibly encouraged by Bernstein's affiliation with the *Sozialistische Monatshefte*, the editor of which was open to Zionist ideas),[95] attempted to establish relations with Bernstein during the first years of the twentieth century.[96] In 1902 Chaim Weizmann reported that he

had a long talk with Bernstein . . . in Berlin. I took him to task for taking up the cause of the Armenians and not taking up the Jewish cause. He declared: "Wenn ich jüdisches Gefuehl haette, ich waere Zionist. Vielleicht kommt es." Together with him we cursed the assimilationists. In the journal we shall be publishing Bernstein will write against the assimilationists: he is on the road to Zionism, and his daughter has paid her shekel.[97]

But Weizmann, it appears, allowed his hopes to cloud his assessment of Bernstein's views. Weizmann's comments on Bernstein's views of both assimilationists and Zionists could more correctly be described as an indication of the positions toward which Bernstein was moving than as accurate descriptions of Bernstein's perspective on these issues during the first decade and a half of the twentieth century. In response to a questionnaire circulated by a Jewish periodical, for example, Bernstein asserted in 1907 that "the solution of the Jewish question can consist only of the denationalization of Jewry."[98]

Bernstein's perspective on the Jewish question during this middle period of his career is clearly revealed by an interview with Bernstein conducted in his home in August 1907 by Karl Fornberg, editor of the New York *Varhayt*.[99] Upon entering Bernstein's place of residence, Fornberg reports, he was immediately struck by the feeling that "I find myself in a Jewish home"—a feeling that did not disappear over the course of his two-hour conversation with Bernstein.[100] At the beginning of their conversation, Bernstein in a somewhat apologetic tone, explained that he did not read Yiddish. "I did learn Hebrew in my younger years," Bernstein added, "but I have now forgotten how to read Hebrew" as well.[101] After making these polite introductory remarks, Bernstein asserted that assimilation was the only historically correct solution to the Jewish question in Western Europe. He noted that he believed in the possibility of assimilation in that geographic area and also thought that the Jews were in fact assimilating. Contemporary Jewry, Bernstein maintained, did not have a distinctive cultural mission. Bernstein did add, when pressed by his interviewer, that every people has a right to exist. Historical development, however, demands certain sacrifices. It demands the elimination *(fernikhtung)* of small groups and peoples and the unification and mixing of these groups and peoples into greater unities.

Fornberg thought it a bit heartless to preach assimilation when the Jews were so beaten and persecuted. "Everything that I have said," Bernstein replied, "applies only to the advanced lands of culture, such as Germany, France, England."[102] Russian and Rumanian Jewry are in a different category. In these lands Jews constitute the higher cultural mass. There can, therefore, be no talk of assimilation between Russian or Rumanian Jewry and the non-Jewish peoples among which they live. The Jews in these countries ought to emigrate—"as much as possible"—to culturally elevated countries. Organized emigration and eventual assimilation would ultimately eliminate the problems confronting Jewry. Jews certainly do not need a state of their own.[103]

Despite occasional friendly contact with prominent Zionists, this middle period of Bernstein's career—that is, the period extending roughly from the revisionist controversy to World War I—was also characterized by publicly expressed antipathy to Zionism. Shortly before the beginning of World War I, in the midst of a controversy over the language of instruction of schools in Palestine, for example, Bernstein described Zionism as a kind of intoxication which acts like an epidemic. Like an epidemic, it may, and presumably will, once more blow over. But not overnight. For it is, ultimately, only part of the great wave of nationalistic reaction which has poured over the bourgeois world and which is also seeking an entrance into the socialist world. Like that wave, it too can have only a retarding effect. And that is reason enough for Social Democracy to take it seriously and to criticize it from the bottom up.[104]

Bernstein, however, showed more interest in Jewish matters, and had more contact with individuals active in Jewish affairs, between 1898 and 1914 than he had earlier in his career.[105] During World War I, moreover, Bernstein began to reassess some aspects of the position on the Jewish question that he had accepted as correct up until that point in time. Bernstein changed his mind, for example, on the issue of whether or not Jewry had a distinctive role to play in public affairs. In 1907, Bernstein had specifically denied that Jewry had such a role. In 1916, however, Bernstein argued that the history of their people had made the Jews "born pacifists. Their history assigns them the task of attending to that which binds peoples together and of working against that which separates peoples and which sows hatred among them."[106] Similarly, in an article written at the request of Der yidisher kempfer (a Labor Zionist periodical published in New York), Bernstein asserted that Jews ought to act as mediators among the peoples of the world.[107]

Bernstein's willingness to write for Der yidisher kempfer was in itself noteworthy. The Labor Zionist movement had cultivated a relationship with Bernstein over a period of years. Bernstein corresponded with Leon Chasanowitsch in 1913 and 1914, met with Berl Locker and Shloyme Kaplansky in February 1916, and wrote to Locker later that year.[108] These tentative contacts began to bear fruit when, in the first half of 1917, Bernstein published a booklet entitled Von den Aufgaben der Juden im Weltkriege in which he declared that there were points on which he and the Labor Zionists were in agreement. Though he explicitly denied that he was himself a Zionist, and pointedly noted that the attainment of the goal of the Zionists would be a regression for Western European Jewry, he also noted that the Zionist goal could have a "liberating effect" on Russian Jewry, and that he admired the idealism of the Zionists.[109]

In the years following the publication of Von den Aufgaben der

*Juden,* Bernstein displayed even greater sympathy for the Labor Zionist movement. When, in early January 1918, Bernstein was invited by Leon Chasanowitsch to submit a piece to an anthology on the Jewish question, he agreed to do so and proposed that he write on the democratic idea of the state and its relation to the Jewish national idea.[110]

Bernstein begins the piece that he wrote for this anthology by giving qualified approval to the goal of the Labor Zionist movement: "Zionism in the narrower sense of the term," that is, as a movement striving to establish a Jewish nation-state "does not . . . now present a problem for democracy."[111] Bernstein indicates that he still does not think of himself as a Zionist. "My entire way of thinking and of feeling contradicts the national separation of the Jews from the peoples in whose midst they live. The cosmopolitan spirit of the German classical writers of the 18th century lives within me."[112] Nevertheless, in Eastern Europe

> Where the Jews often live together compactly in great masses and where their colloquial language, Yiddish, differentiates itself from the language of the country in which they live in its roots and grammar (and is not merely retained, as in Germany, as a jargon or dialect), one can also understand the strivings of the Jews to be recognized as a separate nationality and their strivings to be furnished with the rights of a nationality.[113]

Though Jewry as a whole is neither a self-contained nation nor, on an international level, a coherent nationality, "but only a very loose community of descent *[Stammesgemeinschaft],*" in certain states the Jews form such strong minorities that they ought not to be refused the right to national organization.[114]

Bernstein's sympathetic approach to the Labor Zionist movement during and after World War I is generally consistent with his long-standing attitude toward the national question. Even before World War I, as one recent commentator has noted, Bernstein "treated the question of national self-determination more from a cultural, humanitarian vantage-point, as an ethically desirable, generally valid principle, and less in terms of its relevance to the attainment of socialism."[115] He distinguished between bourgeois nationalism (which he condemned) and what he described as the "noble patriotism" of Fichte and of Lassalle, which, in Bernstein's words, "strives for a respected position in the republic of the peoples for its own people, but never lets out of sight the thought of this greater republic and its unity."[116] Since Bernstein eventually came to believe that the Labor Zionist movement stood for precisely this kind of patriotism, he warmly endorsed the work of the Poalei-Zion.

By 1919, Bernstein was willing to speak at events organized by the Poalei-Zion.[117] The first meeting of this kind that Bernstein addressed took place in Berlin on May 7, 1919, and was held in order to celebrate the achievements of the Labor Zionist movement at the recently concluded international socialist conference that had been held in Amsterdam.[118] In his comments at this meeting, Bernstein pointed out that the socialist movement had, in the past, thought of Jewry solely as a religious community, and that it had, therefore, not conceived of a Jewish party as a suitable candidate for a role in the International. "I do not want to conceal from you," Bernstein continued,

that I still stand today completely on the international standpoint. I do not know any French socialists, and I do not know any English socialists and I also do not know any specifically Jewish socialists. But I recognize that there is a specific Jewish movement in socialism that is today necessary. The union of peoples will first come into being when peoples have ceased to think in states and to haggle over states. The Jews as well, who have developed a national life, must be recognized as a nationality, in the union of the other peoples of the earth. The Jewish national movement, insofar as I understand it, and insofar as it especially documents itself in the Poalei-Zion, does not want to divide but to combine with the new union of peoples and to help the new union to organize itself, and to this extent I too cannot argue with its legitimacy. In this sense, I can only congratulate it on having been accepted as a fully entitled member of the International.[119]

Bernstein's relationship with the Labor Zionist movement grew stronger and warmer in the Weimar years. In 1924, for example, Bernstein joined the Komitee für das arbeitende Palästina and the Deutsches Komitee Pro Palästina zur Förderung der jüdischen Palastinasiedlung.[120] However, Bernstein's sympathy for Labor Zionism during these final years of his life was expressed not merely by paper membership in organizations, but also in a wide variety of other ways. He wrote for Der Neue Weg,[121] and for the bulletin of the International Socialist Committee for the Organized Jewish Workers in Palestine,[122] contributed funds on several occasions to the

Keren Kajemeth Lijisrael,[123] spoke at a number of conferences and
meetings organized by groups affiliated with or sympathetic to the
Zionist movement,[124] and attempted to use his influence to have
pro-Zionist material published in the German social democratic
press.[125]

An examination of the talks that Bernstein delivered beginning
with the mid-1920s documents and clarifies Bernstein's change of
heart. Typical of these talks was a speech that he delivered on
March 10, 1924 in Leipzig.[126] Bernstein began his lecture by remi-
niscing about his childhood years and his early hopes that the
peoples of the world would be brought closer to one another. These
fantasies, Bernstein remarked, had been disappointed. Reaction
marches and anti-Semitism followed every step. He himself had
long seen assimilation as the only possible solution to the Jewish
question, and he had been convinced that with the disappearance
of capitalism, the Jewish question too would come to an end. He
had, however, recently become convinced that Marx too had erred
on this issue. The new phenomena in Jewish life, Bernstein asserted,
compel all who are honest enough to own up to them to change
their positions. When the Zionist movement began, with its dream
of a Jewish empire, he continued, he had assessed it as reactionary
and regressive. But by 1924, according to Bernstein, the movement
of the workers of Palestine stood at the focal point of the Zionist
movement and linked its national success with international strivings. Though he could not be a Zionist, since he lived in a too
assimilated circle, Bernstein concludes, it is everyone's "most holy
duty" to support a movement that is striving to make Jews into a
working people within a world based on equality and justice. Bernstein reiterated these and similar points—the dangers of anti-Semitism and of the reactionary movements, his respect for the idealism
of the Jewish workers of Palestine, and his belief that the program
of the Poalei-Zion could and ought to be consistent with an
internationalist stance—on numerous occasions.[127]

Bernstein did not actually consider himself to be a Zionist in the
generally understood sense of that term during World War I or in
the 1920s. In 1916 Bernstein declared, "I cannot bring myself to join
any specifically Jewish association, and would consider myself a
stranger in relation to such groups, of whatever kind they may be,

*evolved view of Zionism*

purely social or political, General Zionist or socialist Zionist."[128] As late as 1929, Bernstein published an article in *Tsukunft* in which he stressed that he was a supporter rather than a member of the Zionist movement, and that, though he was a member of the Pro-Palestine Committee, he was a member "in a limited sense."[129] The long, slow progression on Bernstein's part toward an all-but-full identification with the goals of the Labor Zionist movement, however, did in fact reach its culmination with a declaration by Bernstein of membership in that movement. In January 1930, in a speech given at a conference of the German Poalei-Zion organization, Bernstein proclaimed, "I consider it to be my duty to be a member of the movement of the Poalei-Zion."[130]

Both in Bernstein's day and in our own the extent and depth of Bernstein's commitments to Zionism have been seriously underestimated. Franz Kursky, for example, who first met Bernstein in 1901 and who became quite friendly with him during the 1920s, acknowledged Bernstein's activities on behalf of the Zionist movement, but insisted that these activities were in no way a "result of a serious inner interest. Everyone who was close to him could see that this was simply submissiveness, an expression of trust in certain persons whom he found very genial."[131] It is true that Bernstein had several Bundist friends, and that he wrote for the same New York-based non-Zionist Jewish socialist periodicals as did Kautsky.[132] Nevertheless, Bernstein's ties to the Zionist movement ought not to be belittled. In the final years of his life, Bernstein's activities on behalf of the Zionists seem to have been limited by advanced age and poor health rather than by lingering ideological doubts of any kind.

The changes in Bernstein's perspective on the Jewish question in the first few years of the Weimar Republic were not limited to his view of the mission of the Jews or to his attitude toward Zionism, but also included revisions in his view of Jewish assimilation and an interest in Jewish cultural and educational institutions. Significantly, Bernstein once contributed a piece for the *Jüdisch-liberale Zeitung*,[133] accepted invitations to address a Jewish students' association[134] and the Scholem Alechemklub of Berlin,[135] and endorsed the work of ORT[136] and of the Hilfsverein der Deutschen Juden.[137]

By the end of his life, Bernstein had significantly altered his earlier proassimilationist attitude. Writing to the *Forverts* in 1922 on the occasion of that newspaper's twenty-fifth anniversary, Bernstein confessed that he had originally been among those who had doubted the wisdom of publishing a Yiddish socialist newspaper. At the time that the *Forverts* was founded, Bernstein wrote, he had feared that the use of Yiddish would hinder Jews from learning the languages of the "great culture-nations" and would thereby hinder them from becoming citizens in fact as well as by the law.[138] In 1897, Bernstein had seen the *Forverts* as, at best, a tool with which to educate the Yiddish-speaking population until such time as this population grew comfortable with more important languages. He had, moreover, believed that this process of linguistic assimilation would not take long. By 1922, however, Bernstein frankly admitted that he had made a mistake. The fact that the *Forverts* had survived for twenty-five years

demonstrates that the need for a newspaper of this kind was much deeper and more durable than it had appeared to me and to other socialists. Now we must evaluate the Yiddish language altogether differently than earlier, even if it is only a temporary language. A language spoken by millions is a living language and has the right to live.[139]

Bernstein's new perspective on the Yiddish language led him to become a member of the honorary presidium of the board of trustees of the Yiddish Scientific Institute (YIVO),[140] and to heartily endorse the work of the Central Jewish School Organization (TSYSHO), the secular Yiddishist school system run by Jewish socialists in interwar Poland.[141] In response to an invitation from the leaders of TSYSHO to attend one of their conferences, Bernstein wrote

I have a great interest in the schools. . . . I would, on my part, like to help maintain the life of these worthy institutions . . . on another occasion I will happily do everything in my power, by speaking or by writing, for the schools mentioned above.[142]

Bernstein's encouragement of the YIVO and the TSYSHO indicate that he supported their efforts to foster and develop Yiddish culture. Bernstein seems to have reached the conclusion that there was no inherent contradiction between the goal of fostering secular Jewish culture and that of working for a socialist society.

To a significant degree, the changes in Bernstein's attitude toward

Zionism were sparked by his concern over the severity of anti-Semitism during the latter part of World War I and in Weimar Germany. Whereas many other German social democrats, including social democrats of Jewish origin, tended to underestimate the political significance of anti-Semitism in the Weimar years,[143] Bernstein repeatedly (and with notable prescience) insisted that the anti-Semitic movement of the 1920s was quite different from earlier anti-Jewish movements. According to Bernstein, the ranks of those receptive to anti-Semitic lies during the Weimar years were drawn primarily from among those who had believed the lies told to the German people by the German government and leadership during World War I.[144] Since the Germans had not been given accurate information concerning the military defeats suffered by the German armed forces as these defeats occurred, Bernstein noted in 1924, the loss of the war came as a shock to most Germans and led them to search for those responsible. In this environment, the allegation that Jewry had "stabbed Germany in the back" was readily believed by many Germans. "We are living in a time of the blackest of reactions," Bernstein warned in 1925, "a reaction that is still on a constant upswing."[145] Such a development, Bernstein continued, was never before considered possible:

> the reaction of the present time is by far more evil than that in the middle of the last century. For our time is a time of intellectual reaction, while at that time, political oppression notwithstanding, intellects were free. Anti-Semitism at that time was also a purely intuitive phenomenon. . . . Even exceptions, such as de la Garde, were far from leading the struggle with the viciousness and sharpness of today.[146]

In Bernstein's eyes, the Zionist movement of the Weimar years was a natural product of the reactionary forces that were advancing through Europe.[147] As Bernstein put it in 1930, in the course of an interview with a Jewish correspondent that was widely noted in the German Jewish press, "the anti-Semitic wave, which is becoming ever larger," compels the Jews to vigorously advocate the idea of a national homeland in a more unified manner than in earlier days.[148]

In this same interview, Bernstein also declared that, though he had formally left the Jewish community in the 1870s, he had "always remained a Jew" and was proud of his Jewish origins.[149] If he had to make the same decision in 1930 that he had had to make in the 1870s (that is, the decision as to whether or not to remain a formal member of the organized Jewish community), Bernstein continued, he would not choose the option he had chosen more than half a century earlier. "For now," Bernstein declared

a Jew who leaves the community can be interpreted to be acting out of cowardice. Whoever leaves a harried and oppressed religion is cowardly. The anti-Semitic wave of today is more poisonous than ever. And therefore I would never take the step [of renouncing my membership in the Jewish community] in the present. . . . You see . . . that I stand positively vis-à-vis Jewry, the outward renunciation of membership notwithstanding.[150]

Though Kautsky and Bernstein engaged in a published debate on the prospects of Zionism in 1929,[151] they tended to belittle the differences that existed between their respective views of the Jewish question during the Weimar years. Kautsky referred to the difference between their views on Zionism as a "small difference" that "does not disturb our friendship."[152] Similarly, Bernstein, referring to Kautsky's article "Die Aussichten des Zionismus" commented, "I cannot subscribe to everything which you say in its second part, but in the question which matters it says, nevertheless, precisely the correct thing, and can, therefore, only work splendidly."[153] By the late 1920s, Bernstein and Kautsky had lost most of their oldest friends. The fact that they still had each other was of great importance to both of them. Neither Bernstein nor Kautsky had any interest whatsoever in harming a friendship that stretched back fifty years. They therefore underplayed the significant difference that existed between them on this issue, and on other aspects of the Jewish question, for the sake of their friendship.

Nevertheless, there was a gulf between Kautsky's position on the Jewish question during the Weimar years and the position maintained by Eduard Bernstein. Bernstein was highly sympathetic to Labor Zionism. Kautsky was highly critical of the Zionist movement. Bernstein was willing to associate with nonsocialist Jewish organizations. Kautsky never did so. Eduard Bernstein, finally, actively supported Jewish cultural institutions committed to the nurturing of a secular Jewish culture in the Yiddish language. Karl Kautsky, on the other hand, while tacitly supporting the right of Jews to maintain Jewish cultural institutions, never directly endorsed or fostered the work of such institutions.

*[margin handwritten note: views of Kautsky v. Bernstein]*

In the final years of his life, Bernstein revealed a quite different perspective on the Jewish question than he had displayed during the first part of his career. Before the revisionist controversy, Bernstein was sympathetic to assimilationism and displayed no interest in Jewish affairs per se. Between 1895 and 1914, Bernstein became somewhat more interested in the Jewish question and manifested scattered evidence of changes in his point of view, but he did not decisively break from his earlier positions. From approximately midway through World War I to the end of his life, however, Bernstein became ever more closely tied to the Zionist movement, explicitly rejected his earlier assimilationist stance, and provided aid to Jewish cultural institutions. It was, above all, the rise of anti-Semitism that precipitated these changes.

The obituary for Bernstein published in the *C. V. Zeitung*—the organ of the most powerful and most representative of the Jewish organizations in Germany—was entitled "Trotz allem Jude," a description with which I fully concur.[154] His long years of noninvolvement in Jewish affairs notwithstanding, Bernstein died thinking of himself as a Jew, and he was so regarded by much of non-Jewish Germany as well as by the Jewish community.[155]

*[handwritten notes:]*
- Went from assimilationist ⇒ zionist sympathizer ⇒ zionist supporter, supporter of Jewish & cultural preservation in face of increasingly strong wave of anti-semitism

# A Familial Resemblance: Rosa Luxemburg, Polish *Maskilim*, and the Origins of Her Perspective

Many of Rosa Luxemburg's biographers have described her family as uninterested and uninvolved in Jewish affairs. J. P. Nettl, for example, asserts that the family (which used the name Luksenburg or Luxenburg during the period of Rosa's childhood) had "little or no part" in the life of the Jewish community, and also claims that the family "did not lead a consciously Jewish life."[1] It is almost certainly true that Rosa Luxemburg's parents and siblings were sympathetic to assimilationism and absolutely true that they were far more acculturated than were most East European Jews of their day. It is, however, simply not true that the Luksenburgs were either uninvolved or uninterested in Jewish affairs. Eliasz Luksenburg, Rosa's father, was closely associated with Polish *maskilim* (adherents of the Jewish Enlightenment) and played an active role in the life of the Jewish community of Zamość (the town in which Rosa was born and in which her family lived during her infancy). The ideology of the maskilim with whom Eliasz was associated, moreover, bears a marked resemblance to Rosa Luxemburg's views on the Jewish question, and may even be a source of her views on that question.

Zamość was the cradle of the *Haskala* (the Jewish Enlightenment movement) in Poland and the homebase of a number of maskilim.[2] Aryeh Leib Kinderfreund, Solomon Ettinger, and Alexander

Tsederbaum were all natives of the district of Zamość. Samson Halevi Bloch, Jacob Eichenbaum, Feivel Schiffer and Ephraim Fischel Fischelsohn all lived in the district at various points in their careers. By the end of the second decade of the nineteenth century, Zamość, which had a relatively small Jewish population, had the second largest concentration of so-called enlightened Jews in Poland. The Luksenburgs were by no means divorced from this "enlightened" part of the Jewish community but were an intrinsic part of it.

There is a fair amount of evidence attesting to the views and affiliations of the Luksenburg family. There is documentary evidence, for example, indicating that Eliasz Luksenburg was at one time a student in the Warsaw Rabbinical School.[3] The Warsaw Rabbinical School was established in 1826 by ideological assimilationists who were intent on polenizing the Jewish population.[4] Most classes in the school were taught in Polish. Many of the instructors in general subjects were non-Jewish Poles. Excerpts from a textbook published in 1850 by an instructor in Jewish history at the rabbinical school, Abraham Paprocki, give a sense of the school's orientation. In the introduction to his textbook, Paprocki asserts, "Only in their obligations to God do Jews constitute one body, but with respect to society they constitute neither a nation nor a particular social group."[5] At another point in his work, referring to Jewish suffering during the Middle Ages, Paprocki concludes

The sorrowful annals of our forebears were in the main a consequence of ignorance, of a lone and isolated posture among the nations, and of their way of earning a living which was directed solely toward trade and the acquisition of wealth and not toward labor and creative work.[6]

Those most closely associated with the Warsaw Rabbinical School were committed to breaking down the barriers between Poles and Jews, rejected the notion that Jewry was a nation, had strong emotional ties to the Polish language, and disdained both the Yiddish language and East European Jewish mannerisms. They continued to accept certain Jewish religious tenets as valid, but they believed that Jews ought to practice a modernized form of the Jewish religion. It is highly likely that Eliasz Luksenburg agreed with most or all of the ideological stance outlined above. He all but certainly came out of his experience at the rabbinical school with a Jewish identity, but one very unlike that of most Polish Jews of his era.

In a brief article on Jewish assimilation in the Polish lands, Ezra Mendelsohn once distinguished between two types of Jewish assimilationists, that is, the idealistic-romantic type, who was ideologically committed to assimilationism and who supported the revolutionary movement for Polish independence on the one hand, and the "Poles of the Mosaic persuasion," who were often members of the bourgeoisie, "law-abiding citizens and good Jews as well as good Poles," on the other hand. Mendelsohn's description of this latter type follows:

> The 'Poles of the Mosaic persuasion' were less inclined to make an ideology of their assimilation. They did not proclaim that Jewish history had played itself out, nor did they always identify with Poland's holy struggle. They had left behind the confines of the ghetto and now regarded themselves as Poles just as their German coreligionists regarded themselves as Germans. Strongly opposed to Jewish nationalism and hostile toward Yiddish, they had no clear program as to the future of the Jewish people. Nonetheless, the 'Poles of the Mosaic persuasion' played a prominent role in Jewish life. They could be found, both in Congress Poland and in Galicia, in dominant positions in the official Jewish community, where they cooperated with the Orthodox and represented the Jews vis-à-vis the Gentile authorities. They supported the Jewish-Polish press, which from the 1860s on waged the struggle for Jewish enlightenment and for the polonization of Polish Jewry. It was largely from their ranks that the secular leadership of the Polish and Galician Jewish communities was drawn during the pre-World War I period.[7]

Whereas Anton Eisenbaum and other leading figures of the Warsaw Rabbinical School could best be described as idealistic-romantics, in Mendelsohn's sense of the term, the information available on Eliasz Luksenburg suggests that he was a Pole of the Mosaic persuasion. Luksenburg repeatedly contributed to the publication of Hebrew-language works written by maskilim,[8] and, in 1850, he was among those proposing that a progressive congregation be established in Warsaw.[9] Even more revealing is the fact that Luksenburg was an elected official, a *parnes*, of the Jewish community of Zamość.[10]

In many towns in the Pale of Settlement, men like Eliasz Luksenburg were ostracized by their Jewish neighbors and likely to be uninvolved in Jewish communal affairs. But Zamość differed from other towns in Poland in the number of maskilim who lived there, in the widespread use of German and Polish,[11] and in the lack of a deep chasm between maskilim and traditionalists in the middle of the nineteenth century.[12] This relatively good relationship between maskilim and non-maskilim may help explain Eliasz Luksenburg's active participation in the affairs of the Jewish community. An article on Zamość published in the Polish-language Jewish periodical *Jutrzenka* in 1861, for example, reveals that Luksenburg (and several other Jewish men) had recently raised money within the Jewish community and donated this money to needy Christians.[13] Eliasz's ability to raise money from other Jews living in his native town suggests that he was on good terms with them.[14] Again, in 1870—the year of Rosa's birth—Eliasz was allegedly involved in an attempt to save eight Jews who had been unjustly accused of committing a crime.[15]

Unfortunately—but not surprisingly—there is scarcely any information available on the activities of Rosa's mother, Lina. It has been reported, however, that she was an avid reader of both Schiller and Mickiewicz[16]—which suggests that she, like her husband, may have had sympathy for the ideas of the maskilim. It may also be significant that Lina's brother, Bernhard Löwenstein, served as preacher of the nonorthodox congregation in Lemberg beginning in 1862.[17] The extent to which Lina differed from her contemporaries, however, remains unclear. One source reports that Lina wrote to Rosa in Yiddish[18] (which suggests that she was less assimilated than has hitherto been generally assumed). Anna (Khana) Luksenburg, Rosa's sister, noted that during Lina's final illness, though she was in great pain, Lina had figured out when the Jewish New Year would be, and had insisted that Anna bake blintzes and send them to Rosa.[19] In the same letter Anna also wrote to Rosa, "I often saw her praying." In her recent book on Rosa Luxemburg, moreover, Elżbieta Ettinger claims that Lina was a faithful observer of Jewish holidays.[20]

The Luksenburgs left Zamość three years after Rosa's birth. Ettinger suggests that this move was undertaken first of all for economic reasons and then adds, "[t]here may have been other reasons for the family's move to Warsaw. The Luksenburgs, it seems, formed no lasting friendships among the Zamość Jews, many of them Orthodox and Hasidim, who shunned the assimilationists. . . . [T]he Enlightenment (Haskalah) . . . made serious inroads in the Jewish world. But in Zamość it was fiercely opposed by the Hasidim and the strong Orthodox rabbinical center."[21] This explanation in and of itself strikes me as misleading. It seems likely that the Luksenburgs' decision to leave Zamość in 1873 was precipitated by the cholera epidemic in the province of Lublin that year, which led many families to leave the area at that time.[22] It is also likely that the Luksenburgs had had friends in Zamość, but that changes within the Jewish community of Zamość contributed to the decision of the Luksenburg family to leave for Warsaw in the early 1870s. By the early 1870s, virtually all of the prominent maskilim who had been living in the district of Zamość had either died or moved away. Kinderfreund died in 1837, Bloch, in 1845, Ettinger in 1856, Eichenbaum in 1863, and Schiffer in 1871. Yitzhok Leybush Peretz, who was of a much younger generation than this group, also left town around 1873.[23] With the passing of these writers, the heyday of the Haskala in Zamość came to an end. The Luksenburgs's decision to move from Zamość was in all likelihood strengthened by their desire to escape from the tightening cultural constraints in their hometown. From their perspective, Warsaw—which was far more amenable to maskilim than was the Zamość of the 1870s—would have appeared to be highly appealing. According to Ettinger, "Warsaw represented a step toward assimilation for the Luksenburgs."[24] This may well be the case. But it is also the case, I believe, that the move to Warsaw represented an attempt to find a maskilish environment comparable to what had existed in Zamość at an earlier time.[25]

Did Eliasz Luksenburg continue his involvement in Jewish affairs after moving to Warsaw? Available sources do not allow us to answer this question. Letters from Rosa's siblings to Rosa written in the 1890s and later, however, reveal that the family continued to observe a number of Jewish religious traditions at the turn of the century. In a letter written to Rosa by her sister Anna in 1897, Anna noted that from her deathbed Lina had insisted that Anna prepare a traditional meal in honor of Rosh Hashana "for Papa to know this is a home and this is a holiday."[26] Later letters to Rosa describe her siblings' actions at the time of their father's death: "her family sitting *shiva*, her brothers intoning the Jewish prayer for the dead day after day in the *shul*, and her family at the Jewish cemetery in Warsaw, at *shloyshyim* . . . singing *Kaddish* 'naturally in your name too.' "[27]

Luxemburg's family *was* highly acculturated. Her parents did not observe certain orthodox rituals, they probably conversed in Polish, and they gave their children secular educations. The family, however, was by no means divorced from Jewish life. It was, rather, a family deeply affected by maskilish thought, and involved in efforts to promote ideas associated with the Jewish Enlightenment.[28]

Eliasz Luksenburg undoubtedly attempted to pass his attitudes on to his children. He almost certainly taught them (as he had himself been taught) that the barriers between Poles and Jews ought to be broken down, that the culture of the Luksenburg family was the Polish culture, that West European mannerisms were more refined than were those of East European Jewry, that Yiddish was a jargon or mutilated dialect unfit for use in civilized company, and that Jews were a religious group, not a nation or nationality. He may also have expressed skepticism as to the desirability of Polish independence.

Rosa Luxemburg's own views on the Jewish question bear a marked familial resemblance to those of Polish maskilim of her father's era. Major aspects of Luxemburg's attitude toward Jews and Jewry may best be explained not so much by the concept of Jewish self-hatred, nor by her commitment to Marxism, but rather by keeping in mind the ideas of the mid-nineteenth century Polish maskilim with whom her family seems to have been rather closely associated.[29]

Rosa Luxemburg understood Yiddish. Yiddish words occasionally appear in her correspondence—frequently as insults.[30] She was willing to concede the necessity of work in Yiddish by Jewish socialists attempting to mobilize Jewish workers. The Bundist John Mill reports, however, that "she hated Yiddish as only a Polish-Jewish assimilationist can hate," and that she thought of the language as a "barbaric jargon."[31] Tadeusz Radwanski, an activist in the SDKPiL, of which Luxemburg was, during certain periods of her life, a leading figure, confirms Mill's account.

I remember one of my conversations with [Leo Jogiches, Rosa's long-term lover and comrade, and Luxemburg] about the literature in the Yiddish language [Radwanski reports]. Both of them were totally unwilling to recognize Yiddish as a language. They used the expression 'jargon' with obstinacy.[32]

Radwanski told Luxemburg and Jogiches about a Polish translation of a Yiddish classic, asserted that he had read Yiddish works in the original and remarked that it wouldn't hurt them to do the same. "This is the second crazy person in our ranks," Luxemburg then said, "who, though non-Jewish, has learned the Jewish jargon. Literature in jargon . . . how ridiculous!"[33]

⌐Luxemburg was in contact with the Jewish socialist movement beginning around 1890.⌐ Her original source of information on this movement, Jogiches, had actually been a leader of Jewish workers in Vilna in the 1880s.[34] As late as 1893, when he was already living in Switzerland, Jogiches was involved in publishing a transcription of speeches that had been given at the May Day celebration in Vilna in 1892 and may have had some help from Luxemburg on this project.[35]

*Jewish*
*socialist*
*from a speech*
*1890*

Mill, who knew Luxemburg relatively well, reports that she was somewhat sympathetic to the Jewish workers' movement in the early 1890s.[36] Similarly, Franz Kursky, who, as a member of the SDKPiL and of the Bund, was at one time also on friendly terms with Luxemburg, asserts that Luxemburg did not have a strong enmity for the Bund at the turn of the century.[37] Shortly after the turn of the century, Luxemburg was still sufficiently sympathetic to the Jewish socialist movement to solicit an article on this movement from Mill.[38] During the same time, the Bund's representatives to the Paris Congress of the Socialist International attempted to obtain help from Luxemburg—thereby indicating that they were not on hostile terms with her.[39]

As the national program of the Jewish socialist movement crystallized, however, Luxemburg grew increasingly more critical of that movement. She was willing to support work among the Jews by socialists of Jewish origin. She was not willing to support Jewish socialists making demands for Jewish national rights.

In August 1894 a meeting of Jewish social democrats active in

Vilna concluded that they must "increasingly stress all forms of national oppression," and also concluded that "closer cooperation with Jewish workers' organizations in other cities" was their "logical next step."[40] When Mill, who attended the meeting in Vilna, told Luxemburg about the conclusions that those who had been in attendance had reached, she labeled the position taken in Vilna "hundred percent separatism . . . a type of PPSism among the Jewish workers, a step which would logically bring [the Jewish socialists] closer to the ideology of the petty bourgeoisie."[41] According to Mill, Luxemburg declared that the Jewish socialists needed

not the Yiddish language, and not separate Jewish workers' organizations, but the language of the population around them and blending with the Christian working class. Every other road would only lead [the Jewish socialists] into a nationalistic swamp.[42]

Though Mill continued to maintain contact with Luxemburg, his relationship with her was further strained by the decision made by the Jewish social democrats of Warsaw to give their mandate to the 1896 London Congress of the Socialist International to Plekhanov's Group for the Liberation of Labor rather than to Luxemburg's SDKP.[43] Luxemburg reacted with mounting rage to the general course of action chosen by Mill and his comrades. The intensity of her rage is apparent in a letter to the SDKPiL activist Cezaryna Wanda Wojnarowska, which was written in 1901 on the eve of a visit by Mill and Kursky to Wojnarowska. "These people," Luxemburg wrote

are composed of two elements: idiocy and perfidy. They are simply incapable of exchanging two words with you, of looking at you, without having the hidden intention of stealing something from you (I speak figuratively, of course). All the politics of the Bund rests on the same system. I advise you therefore to administer a kick on the spot on which they sit, and to break off all relations with them, because they will implicate you in a situation which you will bitterly regret.[44]

Roughly two years after writing this letter, Luxemburg outlined her criticisms of Bundist ideology in a book review of a Bundist publication. "In addition to the general demands of the proletariat among which it lives," the Bund had argued in this publication, the Jewish worker "also has his own national desires, his own historical tasks, as, for example, fighting for equal civil rights for Jews in Russia."[45]

The comrades of the Bund, Luxemburg replied, are incorrect in regarding the attainment of equal civil rights for Jews as a special task of Jewish socialists. The elimination of exceptional laws against Jews, Luxemburg pointed out, was included in the programs of both the SDKPiL and the RSDRP. National characteristics, she continued, do not justify the necessity of a Jewish party. National psychology and characteristics require the assurance of a special form of agitation, they do not, however, demand a special party.[46]

In 1905, the SDKPiL and the Bund began to explore the feasibility of cooperation between their parties.[47] Luxemburg was hostile to this tactic. "I do not agree to any alliance with the Jews," she wrote to Jogiches, "this rabble needs us, we don't need them."[48]

At the conference of the RSDRP held in in May 1907, Luxemburg, in her capacity as a representative of the SDKPiL, made a speech on tactics.[49] Her speech was then criticized by both Raphael Abramovitch, a Bundist delegate, and by G. Plekhanov. Luxemburg responded to these criticisms with a sharp attack on Abramovitch, in the middle of which she asserted that Abramovitch and those like him were similar to sugar speculators who figure out whether the price of sugar is going up or going down.

The delegates to this conference were momentarily stunned. All present were familiar with the oft-repeated slur that Jews were speculators (and not real workers). Though used to sharp attacks in the course of political debates, the delegates were not used to hearing language with anti-Jewish connotations used by social democrats against party comrades. A tumult broke out on the conference floor, and Luxemburg was shouted down. Luxemburg, however, was unrepentant. She described this incident to her friend Clara Zetkin, for example, by noting that

The Jews of the Bund revealed themselves to be the shabbiest political hagglers, who, after many prevarications and radical phrases, always stood by Plekhanovistic opportunism. I nailed them for this with lashing words, and brought them to a state of blazing fury.[50]

The gulf between Luxemburg and the Bund was clearly manifested by a series of articles entitled "The National Question and Autonomy," written by Luxemburg and published in *Przeglqd Socjaldemokratyczny* in 1908 and 1909. "Jewish national autonomy," Luxemburg wrote in one of these articles not in the sense of freedom of school, religion, place of residence and equal civil rights, but in the sense of the political self-government of the Jewish population with its own legislation and administration, as it were parallel to the autonomy of the Congress Kingdom, is an entirely utopian idea. . . . Obviously any efforts toward 'developing Jewish culture' at the initiative of a handful of Yiddish publicists and translators cannot be taken seriously. The only manifestations of genuine modern culture in the Russian frame-work is the Social Democratic movement of the Russian proletariat.[51]

Luxemburg scarcely ever so much as mentioned the Jewish terri-torialist or Zionist movement. At the Socialist International's Stutt-gart congress in 1907, Luxemburg, despite lobbying by individuals opposed to the Jewish territorialist and Zionist movements, did not vote on the issue of whether the SS ought to be given consultative status in the International.[52] Luxemburg never wrote about her reasons for failing to vote. A contemporary Bundist newspaper pub-lished in Vilna, however, commented that Luxemburg was moti-vated purely by party considerations in this matter and thereby suggested that her failure to vote ought not to be read as indicative of even a passive sympathy for the SS.[53]

One of the handful of passages in which Luxemburg remarks on Zionism reads as follows:

From all sides nations and nationlets [natioenchen] give notice of their rights to form states. Rotting corpses climb up out of hundred year old graves filled with new spring, and people 'without history,' which never before formed self-determining commonwealths, feel a passionate urge to form states. Poles, Ukrainians, Lithuanians, Czechs, Yugoslavs, ten new nations of the Caucasus. Zionists are already establishing their Palestine-ghetto, for the present in Philadelphia.[54]

Luxemburg's derision is self-evident. What is also self-evident is that her attitude toward Zionism paralleled her attitude toward many other contemporary European nationalist movements. Lux-emburg insisted that Marxists ought to favor self-determination for a given nation only if such a stance was beneficial to the socialist cause. Her attempts to apply this standard consistently led her to support separatist movements in the Ottoman Empire and to oppose such movements in the Russian Empire.[55]

Marx and Engels had supported the Turks because they had be-lieved that the Ottoman Empire acted as an important bulwark against Russian expansion. By 1896, however, Luxemburg thought that Marx's stance had become outdated. The Ottoman Empire, she maintained, would—and should—collapse. The factors tending to undermine the Ottoman Empire, Luxemburg pointed out, were structural in nature. "What we are dealing with here," she reminded her readers, is a "historical process," a "mit Natur notwendigkeit sich ergebender Prozeß."[56] The continued existence of the Ottoman Empire, moreover, itself played into the hands of Russian diplomacy. "So long as a land remains under Turkish domination," Luxemburg believed, "there can be no talk of a modern· capitalist development" in that land.[57] Once freed of Turkey, however, the formerly subservient Christian nations (that is, the Armenians, the Serbs, and the Bulgarians) would gradually be drawn into the general current of capitalist development and would, thereby, create the preconditions for the emergence of class-conscious proletarians. Thus, Luxemburg believed that social democrats ought to support the national movements of the Christian peoples of the Ottoman Empire seeking independence from that empire. She believed, for example, that support for the Armenians against the Turks would both strengthen anti-Russian forces in Asia Minor and ultimately contribute to the social and economic development of that part of the world.

Her analysis of Russian conditions, however, led her to oppose movements seeking independence for national minorities in the Russian Empire, including the Polish minority. Luxemburg first stated the reasons for her opposition to Polish independence in a series of articles published in the latter half of the 1890s.[58] Among the key arguments that Luxemburg made then was that commitment by Polish socialists to the demand for national self-determination would result in a subordination of socialist aspirations to the aspirations of bourgeois nationalism, and that the restoration of an independent Poland would in no way improve the chances of defeating Czardom. In fact, Luxemburg maintained, the struggle for the recreation of Poland was a struggle that undermined the struggle of the Russian proletariat to obtain a constitution.

Luxemburg elaborated on yet another argument in her doctoral dissertation, in which she attempted to demonstrate that those areas of Poland that were part of the Czarist Empire had already been economically integrated into the empire.[59] Since that was the case, Luxemburg argued, the movement for Polish independence was wholly utopian insofar as there was no economic basis for such independence. Moreover, an attempt to artifically sever Polish industry from Russian markets would result in the retardation of the industrial development of Poland and would, therefore, have a negative impact on the continuing development of a class-conscious proletariat on Polish soil.

Luxemburg's fullest exposition of her position on the national question was published in *Przegląd Socjaldemokratyczny* in 1908 and 1909. In the articles she wrote at that time, Luxemburg criticized the slogan "the right of nations to self-determination" as a vague cliché and as meaningless as the right to eat off gold plates.[60] "Historical development, especially the modern development of capitalism," Luxemburg concluded, "does not tend to return to each nation its independent existence, but moves rather in the opposite direction."[61] The fastest and only secure way to end oppression of the Poles—or of the Jews, for that matter—was to help bring about a socialist revolution.

To say that Luxemburg's attitude toward the Zionist movement paralleled her attitude toward the movement for Polish independence is not to say that her attitude toward Jews and Jewish culture paralleled her attitude toward Poles and Polish culture. Luxemburg, raised in a Polish-speaking milieu, always felt most at home in the Polish language. "Your Russian scares me out of my wits," she wrote Jogiches in 1900. "My Leo should speak Polish with me."[62] Very shortly after first arriving in Germany, Luxemburg toured Silesia. "What a delight," Luxemburg reported, "cornfields, meadows, woods . . . the Polish language and Polish peasants . . . a barefoot little cowherd and our magnificent pinetrees. True, the peasants are starved and filthy, but what a beautiful race!"[63] These quotes suggest that Luxemburg thought of herself as a Pole and had emotional ties to the Polish language. She rejected Polish nationalism as wholly reactionary, but remained attached to Polish culture throughout her life.

Luxemburg's sympathy for the Polish peasants of Silesia contrasts sharply with her attitude toward unassimilated East European Jews. Her emotional reaction to Jews is revealed not in her published writings, but in her correspondence with her lovers (with whom, it would appear, Luxemburg felt free to write candidly). In a letter written to Jogiches in 1902 in which Luxemburg describes a meeting at which she had spoken, for example, Luxemburg commented, "Half the hall, and *comme de raison* the best places in front, were naturally taken by Russians or rather by Jewboys from Russia— they were sickening to look at."[64] A casual encounter in 1907 provoked Luxemburg to write Konstantin Zetkin, with whom she was romantically involved at that time

Eine jüdische Bourgeoisfamilie aus Rußland mit zwei Kinderchen macht das Schiff unsicher, ich habe innerlich manches abgebeten den 'echtrussischen Leuten,' die in Odessa und Kischinjow die Judenkrawalle veranstalten.[65]

Here, and in a small handful of comparable passages, Luxemburg seems to reveal that she found unassimilated East European Jews distasteful, and that she was uncomfortable in the presence of such people.

Luxemburg's prejudices, I hasten to add, were not as strong or as blatant as were those of some other socialists of Jewish origin. Luxemburg did not try to hide the fact that she was of Jewish origin (as others tried to do by adopting party names and by others means) and never converted (as did, for example, the Austrian Social Democratic party leader Victor Adler). In fact, a document dating from the turn of the century—that is, a form registering her residency in Zurich—indicates that Luxemburg publicly identified herself as Jewish rather than "konfessionslos" or "dissident" at that time.[66] Unlike an earlier socialist of Jewish origin, Ferdinand Lassalle, who pointedly remarked to the woman he loved that he had no Jewish friends, *most* of Luxemburg's closest friends and trusted comrades— that is, Jogiches, Paul Levi, Kurt Rosenfeld, Adolf Warszawski, Luise Kautsky, Sonja Liebknecht, Marta Rosenbaum, and Mathilde Wurm —were of Jewish origin. Luxemburg generally felt far more at ease with people with backgrounds comparable to her own, that is, with socialists who had grown up in Jewish families but who were not themselves directly tied to the Jewish community, than she did with the non-Jewish leading lights of the German and Russian social democratic movements, who were her intellectual peers and colleagues.

Luxemburg's relatively rare snide remarks about East European Jews, moreover, ought not to be taken as indicative of sympathy for political anti-Semites. No such sympathy, expressed or implied, ever existed—if for no other reason than simply because Luxemburg understood that political anti-Semites were her enemies as well as the enemies of the organized Jewish community. When sufficiently provoked by anti-Semitic attacks aimed directly at her, Luxemburg—unlike Karl Marx—responded vigorously (albeit anonymously).[67] Her comment about "jewboys" notwithstanding, the label "self-hating Jew" does not seem to fully fit her case.[68]

Attempts to explain Luxemburg's perspective on "the Jewish question" as a natural result of her commitment to Marxism are also not very convincing. If we compare Luxemburg's position with that of Karl Kautsky, we find that they disagreed with each other on many salient points. Kautsky showed great understanding for the needs of the Bundists, including their need to work for national rights. Luxemburg criticized such work. Kautsky was particularly concerned about the Jewish condition. Luxemburg exhibited an exaggerated indifference to that condition. Kautsky, finally, betrayed no trace of personal anti-Semitism in his adult years. Luxemburg, however, seems to have disdained nonassimilated East European Jews. These differences suggest that adherence to Marxism per se did not necessarily imply adherence to a specific approach to Jewish affairs. It may well be that the differences between Kautsky's position and that of Luxemburg are owed to the differences in their family background and upbringing.

Elżbieta Ettinger recently claimed that Luxemburg "was torn by conflicting feelings, at one time determined to rid herself of the burden of her Jewish origin, at another filled with doubts and guilt."[69] I see no such conflict within Luxemburg. Rosa Luxemburg favored assimilationism, opposed Jewish nationalism, disdained Yiddish and the mannerisms of East European Jewry, and admired Polish culture throughout her adult life. She never expressed any guilt or hesitancy about any of these positions. Ettinger's assertion that "Luxemburg's attitude toward the Jews became more complex" in her adult years is also questionable.[70] Luxemburg's statements on the Jewish question during those years are no more complex and in essence no different than feelings that she expressed earlier in her life. Neither psychological turmoil nor increasing complexity can explain or be used to characterize Luxemburg's perspective.

There is a strong familial resemblance between Rosa Luxemburg's attitudes toward assimilation, Yiddish, Jewish nationalism, and Polish culture, and the positions taken by the mid-nineteenth century Polish maskilish writers with whom her father was associated and toward whom her family exhibited sympathy. Major components of Luxemburg's position on the Jewish question may well have their roots neither in Marxism nor in self-hatred, but in a specifically Polish variant of maskilish ideology to which Luxemburg was first exposed in her childhood home.[71]

— Polish maskilim through + through

— steadfast assimilationist, disdain for zionism, unassimilated Russian Jews

# CHAPTER 4

# Austrian Social Democrats and the Jews: A Study in Ambivalence

The leading figures in the Austrian Social Democratic Party tended to have somewhat ambivalent positions on the Jewish question both in the Habsburg era and in the very different circumstances of the Austrian First Republic. The SDAP[Oe] was far less influenced by anti-Semitism than any of its major competitors and was the most important opponent of anti-Semitic political movements. The SDAP[Oe], moreover, allowed a large number of individuals of Jewish origin to take highly visible roles within the party itself. It ought also to be noted that the SDAP[Oe] provided both material and moral support for those East European Jewish refugees who continued to live in Vienna during the later years of the First Republic. These facts notwithstanding, the party publicly claimed that so-called philo-Semitism was every bit as noxious to social democrats as was anti-Semitism, declined opportunities to defend individuals who had been the victims of anti-Semitic attack, and used anti-Semitic stereotypes in its publications and counterpropaganda. In so doing, Austrian social democracy allowed its enemies to define the field of battle and, thereby, contributed substantially to its own defeat.

Victor Adler's perspective on the Jewish question set the tone for the party leadership as a whole. Adler's outlook on this question can best be explained by stressing the anti-Semitism to which he was subjected during his formative years and that he found, to his great distress, was present to some extent even in such close personal friends as Engelbert Pernerstorfer (who later became, along with Adler, a major figure in Austrian socialist circles) and Max von Gruber.[1] In fact, one of the earliest pieces by Adler to have survived, which dates from his student days, was written in response to what Adler perceived as an anti-Jewish proposal made by Pernerstorfer.[2]

Approximately a decade after writing this response, when Adler was enrolled in medical school in Vienna, he felt obliged to respond publicly to published comments on Jewry made by Theodor Billroth, who was a member of the faculty of the University of Vienna. In his lengthy work on the teaching and studying of medicine in German-speaking universities, Billroth argued that Jews from Hungary and Galicia were "for the most part lacking the talent for the natural sciences, and . . . absolutely unsuitable to become physicians."[3] According to Billroth, the Jews from the eastern parts of the Austro-Hungarian Empire who immigrated to Vienna in order to take advantage of the University of Vienna's open admissions policy did not have the educational and cultural background that would make it possible for them to become first-class doctors and had no hope of overcoming these deficiencies. To allow students of this kind into the medical school of the university, therefore, would threaten the standards of that school. Though Billroth distanced himself from "the fashionable abuses against Jews which now appear so popular,"[4] he suggested that a *numerus clausus* be used by the school when dealing with Jewish applicants from the east. In a footnote to his text, Billroth attempted to justify his proposal by noting that

the Jews are a well-defined nation. . . . [A] Jew . . . can never become a German. Whatever is meant by Jewish German, it is only coincidental that they are speaking German, only coincidental that they are educated in Germany. . . . It is thus neither expected nor desirable that the Jews ever become German-nationalists or participate in the national struggles like the Germans themselves. Above all, they cannot possibly be sensitive to the accumulated influence of medieval romanticism, upon which our German sensibilities—more than we want to admit—are based . . . in spite of . . . individual sympathy, I deeply feel the cleavage between pure German and pure Jewish blood.[5]

Though Billroth may very well have had sympathy for Jewish students, his comments touched off anti-Semitic protests by students at the University of Vienna. Several days after the appearance of Billroth's book, anti-Jewish comments made in his work were repeated throughout the Viennese Medical School. On December 10, 1875, Jews demonstrating against Billroth were thrown out of his class by counterdemonstrators. Clashes between Jewish and non-Jewish students took place in other medical school courses throughout the week following this incident.[6]

At the time that these incidents occurred, Adler was a long-term and leading member of the *Leseverein der deutschen Studenten Wiens* (Leseverein), a student organization founded in 1871 "to adhere to and represent the German character of the University of Vienna at every opportunity."[7] Adler and Pernerstorfer were active in the Leseverein as early as the second year of its existence, at which time they helped organize a discussion group within it. During the first semester of the next academic year, Adler and Pernerstorfer were the librarians of the Leseverein, and, in that capacity, helped set the intellectual tone of the organization.[8] Billroth's assertion that it was undesirable that "Jews ever become German-nationalists or participate in the national struggles like the Germans themselves" thus must have struck Adler quite deeply. Though Billroth's argument was directed first and foremost against Jews from the eastern components of the empire, it also had profound implications for Adler (and for all of the other rather large number of individuals of Jewish origin actively involved in the German nationalist movement).

Adler replied to Billroth in a talk, evidently delivered before the Leseverein,[9] in which he attempted to rebut Billroth's criticisms of the viability and desirability of Jewish assimilation.[10] Adler grants, in this lecture, that Jews had not, in the past, played a major role in the history of Germany. He points out, however, that two generations of Jews had already been influenced by the German spirit, and that Jewish blood had been shed in German battles. While this shedding of blood did not entitle Jews to thanks from the German nation—"the gift of German culture is not so lightly repaid"—it formed a cement that bound the next generation of Jews more tightly to the German nation. To Billroth's assertion that Jewish assimilation was undesirable, Adler replied that the Jews were an "important factor in the cultural development of the [German] nation." The Germans, Adler suggests, would have to choose between two possibilities—allowing the Jews to be a thorn in their side or assimilating the "remnants" of the Jews.

Significantly, Adler did not attempt to refute Billroth's contentions concerning Eastern Jews. Moreover, Adler had respect for Billroth, and agreed with the general tenor of Billroth's German nationalist approach. Though there is no proof as to how Adler voted, it is quite likely that he supported the executive committee of the Leseverein (of which he was a member) when it published a resolution expressing disapproval of the agitation by Jews against Billroth.[11] In any event, Adler apparently remained a member of the Leseverein well after this resolution was adopted.[12]

The atmosphere in which Adler grew to adulthood was laced with anti-Semitism. This had a great impact on his self-image and on his image of other Jews.[13] It was primarily in order to escape anti-Semitic attacks that Adler, in 1878, converted to Protestantism.[14] As Emma (Braun) Adler (to whom Victor had been married in a Jewish religious ceremony shortly before his conversion)[15] wrote in a biographical study of her husband decades after Victor officially left the Jewish community, Adler's Jewishness "oppressed" him during his years in gymnasium and in the university.[16] He felt no connection with ardent Jews. Judaism, at the time of his conversion, appeared to him as an insurmountable wall that was preventing him from assimilating with people of culture.[17] Though the description ought not to be taken too literally, the fact that the young Adler has been characterized as a most strictly observing anti-Semite *(Antisemit der strengsten Observanz)* by a member of his own family is worth noting.[18]

It is indicative of both Adler's and Pernerstorfer's views during the early 1880s that they cooperated very closely with Georg Ritter von Schönerer,[19] who, though not accenting political anti-Semitism at that time, had already made widely known anti-Jewish comments in the *Reichsrat.*[20] Adler, for example, was among Schönerer's collaborators in the compiling of the so-called Linz Program, which called for a closer alliance between Austria and Germany, nationalization of both railways and insurance, and universal suffrage. The demands made in the Linz program were of far greater significance to Adler and Pernerstorfer than Schönerer's attitude toward Jews. When anti-Semitism began to play a manifestly important role in Schönerer's political program, however, both Adler and Pernerstorfer broke with Schönerer.[21] Their personal opinions of Jews notwithstanding, neither Adler nor Pernerstorfer were ever sympathetic in any way to political anti-Semitism, nor were they willing to work with those who advocated it. They were, however, willing to associate with Schönerer before his anti-Semitism began to take a clearly political form. Peter Pulzer asks how Jews such as Adler and Heinrich Friedjung, who played an even greater role in the writing of the Linz Program than had Adler,

could become the collaborators of a known anti-Semite. . . . But we have to understand that neither Friedjung nor Adler was conscious of being primarily a Jew . . . ; they were Germans, and as Liberals were indifferent to religion. Moreover, Schönerer's occasional anti-Semitic utterances assume a bigger importance if his career is viewed in retrospect. In the context of 1880 they were no more than regrettable.[22]

William McGrath, similarly, has pointed out that even though a number of the members of "the Pernerstorfer circle" were Jewish, "they had long accepted a form of cultural anti-Semitism as part of their völkisch reaction against the bourgeois liberalism of their parents."[23]

Pulzer's comments, and Adler's reply to Billroth, underscore a source of Adler's hostility in later years to Zionism and to non-Zionist Jewish nationalism—a hostility that Adler shared with a large percentage of the German-speaking Jews of his own generation.[24] Because Adler, like most Jews in Germany and German-speaking Austria, believed himself to be a member of the German nation, and first encountered the notion that Jews were a separate nation from individuals who wanted to block equal civil rights for Jews, he was inclined to link advocacy of the existence of a Jewish nation with reactionary politics and continued to do so long after many East European Jewish social democrats had embraced the struggle for Jewish national rights.

Adler had respect for the accomplishments of the Russian Bund (and spoke favorably about it at a meeting of the ISB in the summer of 1904).[25] Nevertheless, he did not manifest any sympathy for the notion that Austrian Jews were entitled to national rights.[26] When, in 1910, Adler proposed a bill that was meant to provide schools for all of the national minorities of the Austro-Hungarian Empire, he did not include Jews in his list of the minorities to which the bill would apply.[27]

Adler's advocacy of assimilationism contributed to his hostility toward the Zionist movement.[28] At a meeting of the ISB held in Stuttgart in 1907, for example, Adler expressed his animosity toward Austrian Zionists in the course of opposing a motion to grant the SS a formal affiliation with the International. "I do not want to criticize the Zionist-Socialists of Russia," Adler noted,

I do not know them; in this matter we must rely on our Russian comrades. . . . In any event, I know the Zionists in Austria—and that is enough for me. They too have workers. But, worthy comrades, they are not only nationalists, they are—although I do not stress this—*clericals*. . . . I express my respect for the sacrifices which the Zionist-Socialists have made, but the National Democrats of Poland have also made sacrifices, and continue to make them. You know, comrades, that I have always been for keeping the doors of the international congress open. But if we now allow a Jewish-social party to enter, we thereby create a precedent and Catholic-social and Christian-social parties will come to us. No, comrades, we must not do this, and I therefore ask you to vote against the proposal.[29]

Adler's hostility to the idea that the Jews ought to be granted national rights also contributed toward his inclination to give a cold shoulder to the anti-Zionist ŻPSD.[30] This inclination was fostered by Adler's desire to maintain good relations with the PPSD, which was the Polish affiliate of the All-Austrian Social Democratic Party and which strongly opposed the formation of the ŻPSD. Adler's attitude toward the ŻPSD may also have been influenced by the difficult relationship between Adler and the Czech-speaking socialists (whose "separatist" tendencies struck Adler as deeply destructive). Adler, it would appear, believed the ŻPSD to be a "separatist" organization, and he may well have feared that the allegedly devisive precedent set by the ŻPSD would be followed by the Czechs.

Adler was aware of the tension between certain Jewish social democrats active in Galicia and the PPSD considerably before the formal formation of the ŻPSD. In a letter from Pernerstorfer to Adler written in 1904, for example, Pernerstorfer pointed out that there appeared to be an inconsistency in Adler's stance. Adler seemed to be sympathetic to the Bund in Russia, but critical of those advocating a Bundist approach to the problems of Galician Jewry. "Are you for the Bund?" Pernerstorfer wrote, "I am very much so, but it would surprise me very much if you were. In Galicia for the PPS[D] and against a Jewish-national organization, and in Russian-Poland for the Bund and against the PPS?!"[31] Emil Häcker (1875–1934), a leading figure in the PPSD, an editor of the Polish socialist organ *Naprzód* beginning with 1894,[32] and a long-term opponent of the idea that the Jewish socialists of Galicia should form a Jewish social democratic organization as a federative part of the party,[33] informed Adler in April of 1905 that "the Jewish 'separatists' in Galicia, who want to form a separate 'Jewish Social Democracy' in Austria" had been "spreading a rumor" that Adler had nothing against the formation of a separate Jewish social democratic party in Austria and that the All-Austrian Social Democratic Party *(Gesamtpartei)* would recognize such a party. Obviously believing that this rumor was a false one, Häcker told Adler that the PPSD was cherishing the thought of inviting him to deliver a public lecture in Cracow on "the Jewish question and Social Democracy." A lecture of this kind, Häcker continued, "would have an enormous significance against the zionist endeavors."[34]

Very shortly after Häcker wrote this letter to Adler, and on the eve of the official formation of the ŻPSD, Henryk Grossmann and seven other members of the organizing committee of the Jewish group informed the executive committee of the Gesamtpartei of the step that they were about to take and invited the executive to the founding congress of the Jewish social democratic organization.[35] The executive—on which Adler exerted considerable influence— replied by passing a unanimous resolution in which it indicated: first, that it was "not in a position to recognize the independent 'Jewish Social Democratic Party of Galicia' because it contradicts our Brünn Program and the organization of our party"; and second, that the executive would not accept an invitation to a congress "from people who have in fact placed themselves outside the Party." The Gesamtpartei executive also endorsed a resolution of the executive committee of the PPSD that was harshly critical of those responsible for the formation of the ŻPSD. In their report on this issue to the conference of the Gesamtpartei held in the fall of 1905, the secretaries of the Gesamtpartei executive added that since the Jewish social democrats had proceeded, despite the resolution of the executive committee, to constitute themselves as an "independent Jewish workers' party" at the the founding congress of the ŻPSD, the members of the ŻPSD had formally carried out the step of leaving the Gesamtpartei.[36] In explaining this part of the executive's report to the social democrats assembled for the party congress, Ferdinand Skaret added that the executive had met with a delegate of "the Jewish separatists," but that the executive could by no means come to the conclusion that an organizational or any other necessity existed for the creation of such a group. The executive had therefore denied the request of the Jewish socialists for recognition, "Naturally in the belief that they would then turn around once again and continue to work with the other Galician comrades."[37] It may be reasonably assumed that Adler agreed with the resolution of the Gesamtpartei executive and with the relevant portion of the executive's report.

The rebuke of the Gesamtpartei executive notwithstanding, the first congress of the ŻPSD, which was held on June 9 and 10, 1905, proclaimed that the Jewish party considered itself to be "a part of Austrian Social Democracy" and that it therefore considered itself obliged to abide by the Austrian party program and general tactics.[38] The ŻPSD, therefore, decided to appeal the decision of the Gesamtpartei executive and asked in September 1905 that its request for recognition by the party be placed on the agenda of the next Austrian social democratic party conference.[39] September through November, however, was highly charged. Events in Russia, as well as the quickening of the movement in Austria-Hungary for universal, equal, and direct sufferage, made a calm party conference devoted to matters of internal organization all but impossible. Thus, when the all-Austrian party conference was finally convened, it became clear to the representatives of the ŻPSD that it would be inappropriate (and counterproductive) for them to demand that the status of the ŻPSD be reconsidered at that time. The ŻPSD therefore chose to withdraw its request for reconsideration of the decision of the executive.[40] As if to hammer home the implication

of this move by the ŻPSD, Adler then noted to the assembled delegates that the party had no reason to depart from the resolution
that "this group stands outside the Party."[41]

The only other known comments by Adler on the ŻPSD were
made in 1912 in the course of a conversation with the labor Zionist
Moyshe Nakhman Silberroth.[42] Adler's conversation with Silberroth
took place shortly after a critical juncture in the history of the
ŻPSD. In the spring of 1911, the leadership of the PPSD, recognizing
that the ŻPSD had succeeded in attracting significant numbers of
Jewish workers, and worried by the prospect of losing seats in the
upcoming parliamentary elections, began to negotiate with the ŻPSD
in an attempt to work out an electoral agreement. The ŻPSD leaders
understood that the PPSD needed their support and used their lever-
age to extract a series of promises from the Polish party. According
to sources affiliated with the ŻPSD, the PPSD grudgingly agreed that
the ŻPSD ought to be recognized as a full member of the Gesamtpartei (alongside the PPSD and the socialist parties representing the
other nations living in the Austro-Hungarian Empire).[43] The PPSD
also agreed to a formal merger between the ŻPSD and the relatively
small group of Jewish socialists who were affiliated with the so-
called Jewish Section of the PPSD (which, in practice, meant the
absorption of the Jewish Section by the ŻPSD).[44] Despite opposition
within the ranks of the ŻPSD to concessions made by the ŻPSD
leaders in the course of their negotiations with the PPSD,[45] a unification conference was held in mid-October 1911, to which the Austrian social democratic executive sent a congratulatory greeting.[46]
At this unification conference, a resolution was adopted asserting
that "the Jewish Social Democratic Party struggles against assimilation, because assimilation contradicts the developmental tendencies of the Jewish proletariat."[47] From the viewpoint of the ŻPSD
leadership, the unification agreement was a major victory and a
justification of its policies.

At the time of Silberroth's encounter with Adler, the ŻPSD was
still basking in the glow of the unification conference, and it still
believed that the telegram sent by the Gesamtpartei to that conference meant that it was only a matter of time until the ŻPSD was
formally granted status as an equal member of the all-Austrian
social democratic movement. From their perspective, therefore, Sil-

berroth's conversation with Adler must have been highly disturbing. For, when asked by Silberroth whether the ŻPSD would be represented at the congress of the German-speaking social democrats of Austria-Hungary, Adler first made a sarcastic comment, then replied, "Yes, as a section, through the Polish S. D." (that is, the PPSD).[48] Again, when the journalist pressed the point by asking specifically about recognition of the ŻPSD by Austrian social democracy, Adler interrupted him and said: "You believe that the old section [the Jewish section of the PPSD] has moved closer to the separatists [the members of the ŻPSD] and we know that exactly the opposite is the case!" Silberroth replied to Adler by pointing out that the telegram sent by Austrian social democracy to the unification conference had been interpreted as a "document of independence"—that is, as a recognition by the all-Austrian party of the independent status of the ŻPSD. "Well," says Adler, "it should interpret that which is inferred!" When Silberroth protests—"But you did not contradict them!"—Adler, with obvious sarcasm, pointedly comments:

I want to tell you something. I am the only one in Vienna who reads Jargon. When Zionists come to see me, I read out loud to them in Yiddish, which they do not know, but you know, I am a busy man and therefore . . . excuse me if I, heaven forbid, accidently skipped one issue of the separatist organ.[49]

Austrian labor Zionists sharply criticized Victor Adler's lack of sympathy for Zionism and Jewish nationalism (as well as other aspects of his approach to the Jewish question) at several points in his career. In 1898, for example, Saul Raphael Landau's organ, Der jüdische Arbeiter, which appeared in Vienna, published an attack on Adler in its second issue after Adler had allegedly allowed a piece critical of Zionism to appear in the Arbeiter-Zeitung. According to the article in Landau's periodical, it was precisely Der jüdische Arbeiter that had pushed the Arbeiter-Zeitung into writing about Zionism after having ignored that subject for years. It did not surprise him, the author of the piece in Der jüdische Arbeiter commented, that the Arbeiter-Zeitung responded to Der jüdische Arbeiter with "swear words" rather than with "pertinent arguments" and that the Arbeiter-Zeitung was content to rely on "disdainful comments," for "we never expected anything else" from "the Jewish leaders of the *Arbeiter-Zeitung.*"[50]

The labor Zionist response to Adler, however, was not uniformly condemnatory. In 1912 Berl Locker, who was editor of the organ of the Galician Poalei-Zion (the Jewish Socialist Workers' Party Poalei-Zion in Austria),[51] published a quite supportive portrait of Adler on the occasion of Adler's sixtieth birthday.[52] After praising Adler's accomplishments in the political arena, Locker turns to the aspect of Adler's career likely to be of most interest to his readers. Locker begins this portion of his article by proclaiming that "Victor Adler is a child of the Jewish people, and there is no doubt whatsoever that one can find many Jewish moments in his personality"—that is, his "clear analytic intellect," his enthusiasm, and his sarcasm.[53] But

Victor Adler is, after all, not ours. He grew up in the lap of a foreign culture, which he imbibed in the long years of his rich life. . . . Victor Adler is a German—and who can have a complaint about that! History is stronger than even the strongest personality.[54]

What, Locker rhetorically inquires, is it which is not genial about the well-known type of assimilationist, of whom there are not a small number of examples—including, unfortunately, within the ranks of the social democratic party? It is, he answers, "their *negative relation* to Jewry."[55] "But," Locker adds, "there is a certain portion of assimilated Jews who do not have this negative relation."[56] While "we cannot like those assimilated Jews in whom the process of assimilation has not yet entirely ended," those whom "history has already reshaped, among whom Jewry has already sunk altogether beneath the threshhold of consciousness . . . are for us no more and no less genial than other non-Jews with their merits and with their defects."[57] Adler, Locker insists, is in this latter category. Thus, Locker comments, though Adler fought against the creation of a Jewish section in the Socialist International,[58] and did not include the Jews in his list of nations who ought to have schools in their own languages, it would "beyond doubt" be a great injustice to attribute his positions to "assimilationist motives."[59] "Adler would not have been an opponent of the Jewish section" in the Socialist International, "Adler would certainly be the first not to begrudge the Jewish people a school of its own," if not for our own negative Jews, who grew up out of our mass, who continue to move among us and who even are often our official representatives. Adler stands vis-à-vis the Jewish revival-movement like every other German social democrat who, unfortunately, receives information from the worst source, the socialist assimilationists.[60]

In any event, "the Jewish proletariat can not relate to a man like Victor Adler with the same feelings as do our bourgeois hyper-nationalists. In the final analysis, Adler's work is of the greatest significance for us as well."[61]

But Locker's positive interpretation of Adler had no impact on Adler's stance. Victor Adler remained hostile to labor Zionism for the rest of his life.

Adler's attitudes toward both the ŻPSD and Zionism are clarified by comparison of those attitudes with those of Pernerstorfer, who displayed sympathy for both Bundist and Zionist ideas at various points. At the time of the Kishinev pogrom, Pernerstorfer addressed a large meeting in Vienna and made positive comments concerning the national goals and hopes of Russian Jews.[62] An article published on the occasion of Pernerstorfer's sixtieth birthday in the organ of the ŻPSD notes that when, in 1905, that party applied for admission in the Gesamtpartei, "no one" on the all-Austrian executive committee "understood the Jewish worker as deeply as did Pernerstorfer."[63] During World War I, Pernerstorfer, who retained a German nationalist orientation long after Adler's youthful German nationalism had somewhat cooled, asserted that Jewry was a nation, that it "had a right to national existence," and that the creation of a Jewish commonwealth in "Asiatic Turkey" would be very much in accord with the interests of the Central European powers.[64]

But Pernerstorfer, unlike Adler, was not of Jewish origin. The differences between Pernerstorfer's sympathies for labor Zionism and Galician Bundism and Adler's hostility to these movements is almost certainly due to this key difference in their backgrounds. Precisely because Adler was of Jewish origin, he had become sensitized at an early age to the ways in which declaration of Jewish national distinctiveness could be useful to anti-Semites of various kinds, and he had become firmly opposed to ideologies stressing such distinctiveness. Adler's dyed-in-the-wool assimilationism, which explains his hostility to both Austrian Zionists and Austrian Bundists, was itself a result of his Jewish family background and of the anti-Semitism to which he was exposed during his formative years.

Particularly after Adler, who joined the socialist movement in 1886, became the acknowledged leader of Austrian social democracy, he believed that it was necessary to take anti-Semitic sentiment into account when setting the course of the party. Adler was convinced that the Austrian socialist movement could not succeed if its enemies were successful in painting Austrian social democracy as a protector of Jews or as a Jewish party. He therefore consistently declined opportunities to defend either the Jewish community per se or individual nonsocialists persecuted because of their Jewishness. Adler repeatedly equated anti-Semitism with philo-Semitism, and insisted that the SDAP[Oe] was equally opposed to both. In an article published in 1887, for example, Adler declared that Austrian social democracy had to be careful not to allow itself to be used either by the Jews or by the anti-Semites.[65] In practice, this stance often led Adler to remain silent in the face of anti-Semitism even when leading non-Austrian socialists (or non-Jewish Austrian socialists) did not.[66] When, in 1891, the Jewish socialist Abraham Cahan requested that the delegates to the Brussels congress of the Socialist International address themselves to the question, "How should the organized workers of all lands relate to the Jewish question?" and proposed that the congress adopt a resolution greeting the organized Jewish workers of America and condemning anti-Semitism, Victor Adler was among those who tried to dissuade Cahan from pressing this issue.[67] In an article for the Austrian social democratic press on the events of the congress, Adler suggests that his opposition to Cahan was grounded in the notion that the International ought not to spend its time considering a question on which each of the parties represented at the congress had already taken a position and also indicates that he was satisfied with the resolution ultimately adopted by the congress, which condemned both "anti-Semitic and philo-Semitic excitations."[68] In private, however, Adler had argued to Cahan that a discussion by the International of the kind proposed by Cahan was tactless. Both Adler and the German social democrat Paul Singer contended that Cahan's resolution would play into the hands of anti-Semites by giving them an opportunity to identify the Socialist International with the

defense of Jews.[69] The enemies of socialism, Adler and Singer as- *combating*
serted, claim that socialism is a Jewish product. These enemies *asserthen*
point out that Marx, Lassalle, Adler, and Singer were Jews. The *that socialism*
anti-Semites also claim that the whole socialist movement is main- *is Jewish*
tained by Jewish money. Thus, Adler and Singer concluded in their *product*
private discussion with Cahan, if Cahan's proposed resolution were
to be adopted the enemies of socialism would seize the opportunity
to proclaim that the Socialist International had defended the Jews,
and that the congress was a parochial Jewish group. "In Vienna,"
Adler reasoned, "the anti-Semites are powerful, and we, socialists,
are the most dangerous force against them. . . . If we adopt your
resolution, they will meet us with cries that their contentions have
been confirmed, that the entire socialist congress is no more than a
Jewish market."[70] Adler's attempt to dissuade Cahan does not by
any means demonstrate that Adler was anti-Semitic (as certain
scholars who have commented on this incident have insinuated).
Significantly, shortly before Adler had met with Cahan, a prominent reform rabbi had also argued that Cahan's proposed resolution
would "provoke the anti-Semites" and had urged Cahan to keep the
danger in mind and to be as cautious as possible.[71] Although Adler's
actions do not suggest that Adler was anti-Semitic or sympathetic
to anti-Semitism, they do suggest that he was affected by anti-
Semitism, in that he believed that it was necessary to take anti-
Semitism into account when making political decisions.

It is also significant in assessing Adler's stance to note that he
remained on friendly terms with Cahan (a Yiddish-speaking Jew
born and raised in Eastern Europe) after the incident at the Brussels
congress. When, in 1893, Cahan made another trip to Europe in
order to attend the Zurich congress of the International, he called
on Adler and was received by the Austrian leader in a friendly
manner. Adler immediately turned to the topic of their conversations in Brussels and attempted once again to demonstrate to Cahan
that the question of anti-Semitism should not be raised in the context of the International. If, Adler assured Cahan, the American
Jewish socialist was considering bringing up the topic at the Zurich
congress, "there is no hope that it would be allowed."[72] Their
differences on this matter notwithstanding, Adler was manifestly
cordial in his treatment of Cahan and even asked "one of the most

important Viennese comrades" to accompany Cahan on a tour of the city.[73]

Adler provided additional information concerning his response to Cahan's proposal at the Brussels congress on one additional occasion. At the Sixth Party Congress of the Austrian Social Democratic party, which was held in 1897, a Moravian delegate, Jakob Brod, criticized the way in which his party comrades tended to deal with anti-Semitism, mentioned that Adler had been opposed to placing the issue of anti-Semitism before the Brussels congress, and suggested that Adler was pursuing the same policy in the Austrian context as he had in the context of the International.[74]

Adler replied:

Comrade Brod spoke of the International Congress in Brussels. It is true that I was not in agreement with the way in which the question was brought up there. But despite the danger of being considered an anti-Semite by Comrade Brod, I must award myself the right to express my point of view as to whether it is opportune to debate a question or not. I must also say this to Comrade Brod: I at any rate take the point of view that the Jewish question is exaggerated. And it is the greatest crime of the anti-Semites that they have given this question such a turn, that the rich Jews appear as poor Lazaruses; but I would like to know which Jewish proletarian was ever repulsed from our Party. The Jewish question has its specific form from the fact that the capitalist bourgeoisie here in Vienna has a Jewish coloration. That the Jews must endure this is sad, but that we on this occasion find the Jews again and again in our soup bowl is too wearisome to me and others as well. A displacement is thereby brought into being. Every discussion is distorted by it.[75]

To Adler, "just as laughable and absurd as fear of the Jews is fear of the anti-Semites."[76] Adler's highly revealing response to Brod suggests, first of all, that he underestimated both the significance of the Jewish question and the long-term strength of the anti-Semites. His response also suggests that his attitude toward these issues was influenced by his (mistaken) sense of the class-structure of Viennese Jewry.[77] Moreover, Adler's reply gives the impression that the attempt by Brod to spark a reconsideration of the Jewish question by Austrian social democracy only irritated Adler and led him to reaffirm his earlier position.

In Adler's eyes, Jewish family background was an unfortunate burden for a socialist leader. He expressed himself on this issue in

1897, when Benno Karpeles, who was of Jewish origin, informed Adler that he was prepared to take a position in the party. Adler attempted to dissuade Karpeles. "Auf Jahre hinaus," Adler wrote, "ist ein 'Jüdischer Doctor' in der Partei eine Verlegenheit, soweit er nicht blos diskret sich schinden, sondern auch öffentlich anerkannt sein will."[78] It is highly likely that major non-Jewish party leaders agreed with Adler on this point. According to Hendrik de Man, who lived in Vienna during the winter of 1907–08 and who was in contact with key figures in the Austrian socialist movement, non-Jewish leaders such as Renner and Schuhmeier complained in private conversations of what they perceived as a preference on Adler's part to surround himself with Jews.[79] Though there is no evidence that the non-Jews in his party complained directly to Adler about this matter, Adler is known to have asserted that because of his Jewish family background, even he was a burden for the party.[80]

Eminent individuals in France, the United States, Germany, and England protested vehemently when Mendel Beilis, an obscure Jew living in Kiev, was charged by the Russian authorities, on the basis of manifestly false evidence, with having ritually murdered a Christian child. At the time of the Beilis trial, the ISB sent a special circular to all the member parties of the International calling on them to organize special protest meetings and to devote the greatest possible amount of attention to Beilis's trial in their party publications. A leader of the Bund (which was affiliated with the International and which had had contact with Adler through the International)[81] attempted to persuade Adler of the importance of this matter and to convince him that the Austrian party ought to organize a meeting per the circular distributed by the ISB. Adler, however, was not convinced by the Bundist's arguments and made disparaging comments about the trial.[82] According to another source, when asked for his opinion of the Beilis affair, Adler reportedly exclaimed, "Jews and more Jews. As if the entire world revolved around the Jewish question!"[83] Again, when asked by Camille Huysmans for his views of anti-Semitism, Adler is said to have replied, in what was clearly meant to be a witty retort, "My dear comrade! One must have Jews, but not too many."[84] Adler's reaction to the Beilis trial and his comment to Huysmans, it is worth noting, took place during a period when blood libels and other

manifestations of crude anti-Semitism were by no means limited to
the Russian Empire. The case of Leopold Hilsner, who was sentenced to life in 1901, could not have escaped Adler's attention. As
one scholar of Austrian Jewish defense activities recently noted,
referring to the period ending with 1910, "Blood allegations re-
appeared almost every year, all over the realm, generally in spring-
time on the eve of Passover."[85]

*When Adler was willing to speak out against anti-semitism*

Adler was ready and willing to speak out against anti-Semitic
political movements when these movements attacked him or other
Austrian socialists. On one occasion, during World War I, Adler
even condemned Pernerstorfer when the latter published a critique
of certain Austrian socialists that underscored the Jewish origins of
these men. In this critique Pernerstorfer proclaimed, "I am a declared philo-Semite. I am, and have since my youth been, on the
friendliest of terms with Jews. I greatly admire the talent of this
race," but went on to criticize the "internationalistic" perspective
of Danneberg and other left-wing Austrian social democrats of Jewish origin.[86] According to Pernerstorfer, it was not merely coincidental that Danneberg was Jewish. Danneberg, Pernserstorfer, declared, is representative of a certain "type"—that is, Jews of a
particular generation who are also academics and in the socialist
party—and among the characteristics of this type is a notable lack
of warmth toward the Germans among whom they live. "Only we
German social democrats have to put up with it," Pernserstorfer
complained, "when Jews in influential positions such as these strive
zealously to make German workers think of Germanness with dis-
gust."[87] In replying to Pernerstorfer, Adler pointed out that Danneberg was by no means representative of a type and that there were
Jews on both sides of the issue at hand.[88]

But Adler rarely took nonsocialists who made anti-Semitic statements as seriously as he felt obliged to take Pernerstorfer. In general, Adler attempted to undercut the force of anti-Semitic attacks
on Austrian social democracy primarily by pointing to Jews who
supported the anti-Semitic movements. In 1897, for example, Adler
proclaimed, "Although the anti-Semites recently invited just the
richest Jews to the ball of the city of Vienna, they claim that Social
Democracy is led by Jews."[89] Several weeks later a German nationalist, Dr. Mayreder, expressed the desire that the workers would

pick a leader from their own ranks rather than someone like Adler "who owes his whole position of power to the activities of his forefathers."[90] Adler replied:

Dr. Mayreder takes the position that the Social Democratic workers are excellent, worthy people, but their leaders are devilish fellows. Here the gentlemen always speak however only of the 'Jewish' leaders (as an aside, there are among the anti-Semites more Jews than among us) but they never speak of the great mass of leading Aryan comrades. . . . My parents were Jews, but my parents were thereby no worse than yours, Doctor.[91]

Adler's decision to fight anti-Semitic attacks on him and on other Austrian social democrats in this manner did not succeed. His political opponents continued to refer deprecatingly to Adler's Jewish family background, and to the number of Jews in the socialist party, throughout Adler's career. "Although Adler's subjective relationship to Judaism was emphatically negative, he could not escape being regarded as a Jew, and his career and destiny was in some respect overshadowed by his Jewish origin."[92] More serious, however, Adler's use of phrases such as "Aryan comrades," and his mocking comments on the activities of wealthy Jews, may actually have helped legitimate the perspective of his opponents.

Victor Adler's stance toward the Jewish question seems to have been heavily influenced by the recognition that anti-Jewish prejudice was widespread in the Austrian context, and by the fear that social democracy would be identified with Jewry. It arose, as the Austrian social democrat Julius Braunthal once noted, from a mix of political, psychological, and tactical factors.[93] The large number of bourgeois Jews in highly visible positions in Vienna, the hostility of many Jews to Marxism, flirtations between the mainstream Zionist movement and reactionary political movements, and the political realities of Austrian politics all played roles in the development of Adler's perspective. But Adler's family background and early encounters with anti-Semitism seem likely to have provided the major stimuli and help explain the distinctions between his views and those of Kautsky. In a highly revealing letter to his son Fritz, in which Adler discusses his feelings about Fritz's future wife Kathia (who was born and raised in a Russian Jewish family),[94] Victor notes, "She has . . . absolutely no antipathy to Jewishness, which—namely the antipathy—has become one of the foundations of our whole essence."[95] Though Adler's anti-Zionism and assimilationism bear a resemblance to Kautsky's positions, Adler's stance toward the Jewish question manifested none of the profound sympathy for the plight of oppressed Jewry repeatedly expressed by Kautsky, a non-Jewish Marxist theoretician.

During Adler's lifetime and in the period following his death, Austrian social democrats tended to agree with his position on the Jewish question. True, Otto Bauer, Adler's political heir, took a notably different approach from Victor Adler's toward several aspects of this issue. Unlike Adler, for example, Bauer remained a formal member of the official Jewish community.[96] Whereas Adler had chosen to respond to anti-Semitism by converting, anti-Semitism led Bauer to affirm his origins by paying dues to the Jewish community. "How could you possibly understand?" Bauer once commented bitterly, "You've never heard anyone muttering 'dirty Yid' behind your back."[97] Bauer did not participate in Jewish communal affairs. But his decision to continue his membership in the Jewish community (though he was in no way religiously observant and did not think of himself as being a member of a Jewish nation or nationality) seems to be evidence of the searing impact that anti-Semitism had had on him.

It also seems to have been the case that, at least in private, Bauer was less hostile to Zionism during the 1920s and 1930s than Adler had been before World War I. N. Gelber, who was active in Austrian Zionist affairs, asked Josiah C. Wedgwood during a visit by Wedgwood to Vienna in 1926 if Wedgwood would be willing to meet with Austrian social democratic leaders in order to discuss their attitudes toward Zionism.[98] Though Wedgwood agreed, the proposed meeting could not be held at that time. In February 1927, however, Wedgwood was in Vienna once again, and, on this second visit, did in fact meet with Bauer. In the wake of this meeting Wedgwood reported to Gelber that he had

had a good talk with Herr Otto Bauer about the attitude of the Social-Democrat Party to Zionism. He made it clear to me that the Party was not antagonistic to Zionism, that in particulars it sympathised with the Eastern Jews of the pale and approved of the work of Poale Zion. But the Party as a whole has no policy on the subject. While the leaders of the Party could in no case join the Committee of Pro-Palestine (any more than they can join any other Committee in which non-Socialists take part) other members of the Party are perfectly free to do so.[99]

Despite Bauer's continuing membership in the *Israelitische Kultusgemeinde* (the official body of the Jewish community) and an apparent softening in later years in his attitude toward Zionism, Bauer agreed with much of Victor Adler's stance on the Jewish question, and did not alter the outlines of the party's response to anti-Semitism when he inherited Adler's mantle. Bauer went beyond Adler only in that Bauer provided a theoretical defense for the assimilationism that Adler advocated by his personal practice.

Bauer devoted a chapter to the Jewish question in his brilliant work, *Die Nationalitätenfrage und die Sozialdemokratie*, which was published in 1907. Bauer summarizes the argument made by the ŻPSD in support of its quest for recognition by Austrian social democracy: the Jews are a nation; Austrian social democracy supports national autonomy for all of the nations living in the Austro-Hungarian Empire and national autonomy within the Gesamtpartei for the socialist movements of each of these nations; and the Jews are entitled to the same rights as are these other nations. In response to these contentions, Bauer notes that during the Middle Ages Jews were doubtless a nation. But, he continues, "the position of the Jews in society changes with the advance of the capitalist mode of production."[100] As Jews enter into other lines of work, and become geographically dispersed, they have ever greater contact with the non-Jewish nations among whom they live, and begin to assimilate with these nations. This process, Bauer comments, has not yet ended. "Today, even in Western and Central Europe, it would probably be an exaggeration to claim that the Jews are not a nation. But one certainly may claim that they are ceasing to be a nation."[101] In those lands in which capitalism has already taken hold, the process of assimilation is proceeding rapidly. It proceeds at a slower pace in those areas—that is, Galicia and Bukovina—that are less economically developed. But however different the rate of assimilation may be in various locations, the process of assimilation is underway everywhere, even in the Russian Empire.

The process of assimilation not only occurs at different rates in different locations, but also occurs at different rates in different classes. The bourgeoisie and the intelligentsia assimilate first. In Western Europe, the other classes have also assimilated. Thus the Jewish nation, Bauer concludes, is made up of the Jewish workers and petty bourgeoisie in Russia, Poland, Lithuania, Galicia, Bukovina, and so forth. Even among these workers, however, the process of assimilation can be lengthened, but it cannot be halted. "With the progressive development of capitalism and of the modern state the Jews of the East will also cease being a nation, will also merge among the nations, just as the Jews of the West have long ago merged among them."[102]

Since this is the case, Bauer insists, it is not in the interests of the remaining segments of the Jewish nation in Galicia and Bukovina to demand autonomy for their people. "The question of the national autonomy of the Jews is essentially a question of schools"[103]—and Jewish children in Galicia are already in the public schools, where they are learning the language of the nation in whose midst they live. Moreover, the separation of the Jewish children of Galicia from non-Jewish children would contradict the economic interests of the Jewish worker. According to Bauer, "the Jewish school signifies for the Jews first of all artificial maintenance" of their cultural specificity,[104] and is therefore not desirable from the point of view of the workers' movement. Since, in sum, the only thing that would be accomplished by the granting of national autonomy to the Jews of Galicia by the state would be the creation of segregated Jewish schools, and since these schools are not desirable from the workers' standpoint, "national autonomy can not be the demand of the Jewish worker."[105]

Bauer's failure to attack labor Zionism in *Die Nationalitätenfrage und die Sozialdemokratie* explains why the Austrian Poalei-Zion seems not to have published a full-scale response to Bauer in the pages of their major organ, *Der yudisher arbeyter*. Under the circumstances, the labor Zionists probably reasoned, it made most sense to leave well enough alone. The ŻPSD, however, apparently believed that it must reply to Bauer and did so in a three-part article by L. Waynshtayn that appeared in early 1909.[106] Waynshtayn notes that the chapter in Bauer's book dealing with the Jews is the only chapter of *Die Nationalitätenfrage* that has a subjective and polemical character to it. Instead of utilizing the scientific method that he had used when dealing with the Czech question, Bauer puts forth assertions that he then attempts to substantiate by means of purely abstract pieces of evidence, and not, as he ought to have done, by means of "facts of life."[107] Bauer, Waynshtayn insists, had made methodological errors. The most important of these is Bauer's failure to devote sustained attention to the special aspects of the Jewish situation, that is, the fact that Jews live almost exclusively in cities, do not have a "closed national territory," and yet still do not assimilate.[108] Whereas Bauer stressed that there were no large geographic areas in which Jews formed a majority of the population, Waynshtayn counters that Jews formed a majority or at least a plurality in a number of cities in both the Russian and Austro-Hungarian Empires. In both Kolomay [Kolomea] and Brod [Brody], for example (both of which were in Galicia), Jews formed an absolute majority of the population. To Bauer's contention that the lack of a "closed territory" undermined the continued viability of the Jewish nation, Waynshtayn replies that the development of capitalism is removing the significance of territory for the nation. Bauer, moreover, is alleged by Waynshtayn to have inappropriately taken the history of the West European Jewish bourgeoisie to be indicative of the future of the East European Jewish proletariat. Whereas the former could assimilate easily because it was not "tied to the masses of the Jewish people," this is not the case for Galician and Russian Jewish workers. "The same capitalist development which makes the Viennese factory owner into an assimilationist, awakens the national consciousness of the merchant in Brod and of the worker in Lemberg and creates thereby a secure basis for the development of Jewish culture."[109] The national revival taking place among Jews in Eastern Europe is not a transitional phenomenon. It has a secure future. Bauer argued that if separate Jewish schools were created, these schools would be dominated by a traditional, reactionary spirit. Waynshtayn, however, insists that it is far more likely that if there were separate Jewish schools in Galicia, these would be molded by the new Jewish culture which was in the process of coming into existence. Waynshtayn, in sum, is strongly condemnatory of Bauer:

"Bauer, in writing on the Jewish question, was unable to free himself from bourgeois, assimilatory prejudices, and therefore the thoughts which he expresses are superficial and false."[110]

There is no evidence that Bauer ever knew of Waynshtayn's critique. Nonetheless, Bauer stepped up his criticism of the ŻPSD in a piece published roughly four years after *Die Nationalitätenfrage und die Sozialdemokratie.* "Every attempt to artifically hinder assimilation and to cultivate in Jewry an ideology opposed to assimilation" Bauer asserted in January 1912, when the elections that had led the PPSD to enter into its agreement with the ŻPSD were safely over, "is inimical to development, reactionary."[111] The danger exists, Bauer continued, "that Jewish Social Democracy could become the center of a nationalistic agitation, an agitation inimical to assimilation. . . . The danger exists that the existence of an autonomous Jewish Social Democratic party will splinter the forces of the workers movement in Galicia even more" than is now the case.[112] Because the Jews are not territorially concentrated in a compact area of settlement of their own,

a fully independent Jewish workers politics is . . . unthinkable; the Jewish proletariat can only conduct its struggle in the framework of the united Galician workers' movement. The unity of this struggle can not be assured if the Jewish party is completely independent of the Polish one. . . . The unity of the class struggle in a common territory demands the organizational knotting of all proletarian forces, their collection in common organizations, their representation through common organs.[113]

While this is the case for all national minorities, it is particularly true for the Jews, because they lack their own area of settlement. Thus, Bauer concludes, the German-speaking social democrats of Austria "can only recognize Jewish Social Democracy when it becomes an organizational component of the overarching socialist movement in Galicia, when it is guaranteed that Jewish Social Democracy will not become a center of nationalistic agitation.[114]

Given the precedent set by Adler, it should come as no surprise to discover that Bauer never published a direct rebuttal of the arguments made by Austrian anti-Semites during either the Habsburg era or the era of the First Republic. In fact, Bauer's best known piece on anti-Semitism, which was published in 1910 at the request of the SDKPiL in order to disavow the use of Bauer's name by the

Polish anti-Semite Andrzej Niemojewski,[115] while implicitly critical of positions taken by Emil Häcker,[116] a leader of the PPSD and an editor of *Naprzód*, did not so much as mention the power of the anti-Semites in Vienna during that time.

Bauer begins his article by noting that the restrictions on geographic mobility imposed on the Jews of the Russian Empire by the Czars had led to a concentration of the Jewish population, and that this concentration had sharpened the competition between the Jews and the Slavs, and had made more difficult the economic and cultural adaptation of the Jews to their Slavic surroundings. The conditions in the Russian Empire strengthened anti-Semitism on the one hand and Jewish nationalism on the other. Later in this article, Bauer also notes that in the East European context anti-Semitism functions not as anticapitalism, but as nationalism "which splits the workers."[117] If, therefore, the proletarians of the East European nations are to be unified, Bauer adds, both East European anti-Semitism and Jewish nationalism ought to be combatted. "For that reason," Bauer concludes, "I consider it to be dangerous when the struggles within the socialist movement of Russian-Poland are also poisoned by an anti-Semitic phraseology, which on the one hand fills the Polish proletariat with mistrust of the Jewish worker, and which, on the other hand, must drive the Jewish worker into the arms of Jewish nationalism."[118] This danger, Bauer notes, is also great in Galicia.

But Bauer is careful to distinguish his condemnation of anti-Semitism in the East from the situation in Western and Central Europe. In those areas, Bauer claims, the Jews are very strongly represented in the capitalist classes. It is "very often" the case in those areas, Bauer asserts, that the "Aryan worker" stands opposite the Jewish factory owner, the Aryan artisan stands opposite the Jewish middleman, and the Aryan peasant stands opposite the Jewish usurer. "Anti-Semitism," Bauer proclaims

was here nothing other than the first naive expression of anti-capitalism. Social Democracy does not have the task here of defending Jewish capital against its opponents, but only of teaching the masses that Jewish capital must be fought against not because it is Jewish, but because it is capital. Marx's 'Judenfrage' already separated us harshly from liberal philo-Semitism. Social Democracy has never been a 'Jewish protective troop.'[119]

The *Jüdische Zeitung*, a Zionist weekly published in Vienna, replied to Bauer immediately. Bauer "forgets completely," the Zionists noted, that even in the West there was an enormous Jewish proletariat and artisan class.[120] Seventy percent of the Jews who died in Vienna were buried at the expense of the community (presumably because their survivors could not afford private burial). It is "terribly sad" to see how even the most educated and most capable theoretician of social democracy loses his sense when it comes to the Jewish question, "because he is himself a Jew and therefore not capable of scientific objectivity in these things."[121]

Bauer was directly and intensely interested in countering the political influence of the anti-Semitic parties of Austria, but, like Adler before him, was prepared to use weapons from the anti-Semites' arsenal when necessary.[122] Bauer's use of such weapons during the 1920s and early 1930s was far from unique. The Austrian social democrats of the First Republic consistently attempted to protect their party by drawing attention to Jewish influence on other parties. A booklet entitled *Der Judenschwindel*, published in the 1920s by the Wiener Volksbuchhandlung, argued, "The Christian Social Party under Seipel's leadership defended . . . the citadel of Jewish capital," and Seipel was one of "the darlings of the Jewish press."[123] Another pamphlet published by the Wiener Volksbuchhandlung, *Wenn Judenblut vom Messer spritzt*, pointed out that the anti-Semites "take money from Rothschild," and discussed a "Verjudete Hakenkreuzblatt."[124] A third such pamphlet, *Der Jud ist schuld*, condemned the *Protocols of the Elders of Zion*, and the vandalizing of Jewish cemeteries in Germany, but also endeavored to demonstrate the hypocrisy of the anti-Semites by unmasking a Jewish journalist employed by a pro-Nazi periodical and the Jewish origins of a National Socialist writer.[125] Just weeks before the events that culminated in the collapse of the social democratic Party, *Das Kleine Blatt* reported (with appparent delight) that though Einstein was hounded out of his home, the Nazi party maintained a close friendship with Jewish bankers and industrialists. "Jewish bankers who are important for the financial policies of the Third Reich are . . . named Aryans!"[126]

The best known example of Social Democratic use of this tactic occurred in July 1926 when Robert Danneberg—who was himself of

Jewish origin—attacked the "Aryan" banks of Vienna by publicly revealing their economic ties to individual Jewish businessmen and to so-called Jewish banks. In a speech delivered before parliament, which was well received by his Social Democratic colleagues, Danneberg provoked laughter by commenting, "If I know these Jewish banks," they did not engage in business dealings with their "Aryan" counterparts because of "Christian charity," but rather for "jingling coins."[127] The social democrats were so pleased with Danneberg's speech that they had it published in pamphlet form.

The intent of the social democrats in pointing to the "Verjudung" of other parties was to turn the tables on their opponents. By using such arguments in their own propaganda, however, the social democrats unwittingly undercut their own political viability.[128]

Throughout the years of the First Republic, Austrian social democracy remained consistently opposed to political anti-Semitism. Max Adler, Friedrich Austerlitz, Julius Braunthal, Julius Deutsch, and Wilhelm Ellenbogen—to name just a few of the most prominent Austrian socialists—were all born into Jewish families. The prominence of Jews within the leadership of the SDAP[Oe], however, did not immunize that party against anti-Semitic sentiment. In truth, many of the leading Austrian socialists of Jewish origin were themselves somewhat prejudiced in their view of Jews and Jewry (and were denounced by both Labor Zionists and Bundists living in Vienna in the period following World War I).[129]

Stereotypes with anti-Semitic overtones seem to have been rather widely accepted in socialist ranks. When, in the early 1920s, Julius Deutsch sued an individual who had slandered him (by making a claim that was often made by anti-Semites), the *Arbeiter-Zeitung* criticized the tactics of the defendant's attorney by referring to "the Jewish trick of an Aryan lawyer."[130] The *Arbeiter-Zeitung* indirectly referred to another stereotype in 1925 when it published a cartoon with the following caption:

Nach Hitlers Verlobung mit einer Juedin und nach der Gruendung der juedisch-hakenkreuzlerischen Wechselstube an den Wiener Hochschulen wird ein neues Wappen fuer die Hakenkreuzpartei geschaffen: eine sinnige Verschmelzung von Hakennase und Hakenkreuz.[131]

The use of terms like "the Jewish trick" and *Hakennase* (hooked nose) by socialists almost certainly did more long-term damage to the socialists than to those against whom these terms were directed. Though these terms were meant to ridicule anti-Semites, their use in the Austrian context by socialists tended to reinforce widespread stereotypes and prejudices. These terms were double-edged, but they cut the socialists more deeply than the anti-Semites because of the power dynamics that existed within the republic.

Most Austrian social democrats continued to believe that assimilation (and socialism) would eventually answer the Jewish question. Before World War I, Bauer had delineated the factors that he believed would lead toward the assimilation of the Jews.[132] He neither retracted nor altered his stance on this issue between 1918 and 1934. Friedrich Adler was also a confirmed assimilationist. When, in 1902, Friedrich was wrestling with the issue of whether or not to accede to the demand made by the family of Kathia Germanischskaja that he and Kathia be married in a Jewish ceremony or not at all, Victor Adler advised that Friedrich give in on this point, suggesting, " 'Principle' is not important in ceremonies."[133] Friedrich (who had dropped the formal affiliation with Protestantism that he had inherited from his father, and who was officially konfessionslos —unaffiliated with any religious community)[134] responded by proclaiming

Gar so einfach ist das mit dem "Princip" bei Ceremonien in dem Fall doch nicht, denn durch die Ceremonie *tut* man etwas Tatsächliches. Führt man sie nicht aus, so ist ein Keil—wenn auch nur ein ganz kleiner—in die Barbarei des Judentums getrieben, der vielen, die in ähnlichen Conflikten sind, den Weg zur Civilisation erleichtern kann. Führt man sie aber aus, so bedeutet es einen ganz direkten Gewinn für das Judentum, das darauf hinweisen kann, daß Leute, die doch tatsächlich zur Cultur gehören und bei denen, wie bei mir, schon vom Vater der Schutt wegeräumt worden ist, es doch für möglich erklären, in Beziehung zu bleiben mit den alten Sitten. In Wirklichkeit sind ja das alles mikroskopisch kleine Kräfte, aber auch solche darf man nicht übersehen *wollen*, wenn man sie tatsächlich sieht. Es sind so viele Compliziertheiten in dem Fall, daß ich noch immer nicht weiß, wie daraus herauskommen."[135]

Unlike Eduard Bernstein, the rise of anti-Semitism during World War I did not lead Friedrich Adler to reconsider his position.[136] Somewhat more surprisingly, World War II also did not shake Adler's commitment to the assimilationist perspective. In an article published in the Swiss socialist newspaper *Volksrecht* in 1949, Adler declared:

I, like my father, always considered the complete assimilation of the Jews not only desirable but also possible, and even the bestialities of Hitler have not shaken my view that Jewish nationalism is bound to lead to reactionary tendencies—namely, to the resurrection of a language which has been dead for almost two thousand years and to the rebirth of an antiquated religion.[137]

Friedrich Adler, and most other Austrian socialists active during the First Republic, coupled their proassimilationist views with an anti-Zionist standpoint.[138] At the Congress of the Labor and Socialist International (LSI) held in the summer of 1928, for example, Adler very sharply attacked the leaders of the Poalei-Zion, charging that they were obstructing the international workers movement and bringing chaos into the Jewish workers movement.[139] Jacques Hannak, writing in *Der Kampf* in 1919 (when only a small minority of Jews were affiliated with the Zionist movement and when Zionism was bitterly opposed by several different tendencies in Jewish political life), characterized Zionism as "not more than an economic category of specifically Jewish capitalism" and as a "reactionary phenomenon" that ought to be fought.[140] Hannak reiterated his charges against Zionism in another article in *Der Kampf*, which appeared in 1927. In this article, Hannak described Zionism as a "petty-bourgeois Utopia" and as an "illusion."[141]

Friedrich Adler's hostility toward Zionism contributed to his sympathetic attitude toward the non-Zionist Jewish socialist movement in the United States and toward the anti-Zionist Bund (which was centered in Poland in the 1920s and 1930s). He followed up on a feeler from the *Forverts*, for example, by writing Abraham Cahan in 1920 that he was tentatively interested in contributing articles every two weeks or so to that periodical.[142] In a letter to the Bundist leader H. Erlich dated October 15, 1929, Adler urged the Bund to enter the LSI, arguing that "it should be your own special task to represent in the LSI the interests of the great masses of the Jewish proletariat outside of Palestine."[143] Friedrich Adler also demonstrated his sympathy for the Bund in 1937 (after the fall of the First Republic) by sending it a greeting on the fortieth anniversary of its founding. Adler's greeting, which was published in the Bundist

*Naye folkstsaytung*, stressed the "historical merit" of the pioneers of the Bund and praised both the fighting spirit of the Jewish organization and its accomplishments.[144]

Of course not all Austrian socialists active during the First Republic agreed with Bauer's assimilationism and F. Adler's anti-Zionism, as evidenced by the fact that representatives of the labor Zionist movement were invited to attend a congress of the Austrian social democratic party in 1923.[145] Following the precedent set by Pernerstorfer during World War I, a small percentage of First Republic social democrats expressed sympathy for socialist Zionism and skepticism concerning Jewish assimilation. Max Adler (whose politics were considerably to the left of Pernerstorfer's, and who, unlike Pernerstorfer, was of Jewish origin) was the most prominent of those who adopted this stance. In 1928 Adler delivered an address on the theme "national and international" before a meeting of young Jewish socialists. In the course of this speech Adler noted:

Viele meinten frueher, dass mit dem Eindringen des Kapitalismus in die osteuropaeische Wirtschaft das Judentum sich assimilieren werde. Das ist nicht eingetreten. Das Judentum lebt und will nicht untergehen; da kann es doch keine Frage sein ob man eine juedischnationale Arbeiterschaft unterstuetzen soll![146]

In that same year, the World Bureau of the Poalei-Zion Confederation undertook to organize a conference for the purpose of creating an international committee that would support the organized Jewish workers' movement of Palestine. Max Adler expressed his regrets at being unable to attend this conference, indicating that he was "deeply interested" in the cause.[147] Two years later, Adler sent a message to a labor Zionist-oriented conference in which he expressed his sympathy for and interest in the efforts made by socialist Zionists to establish a Jewish home in Palestine, declaring that he was "filled with admiration for the idealism and abnegation" of the labor Zionist pioneers.[148] Again, in 1931, Adler demonstrated his goodwill by writing a foreword to a work published by the radical socialist Zionist youth movement Schomer Hazair. There can be various opinions within the Socialist International about the necessity of creating a Jewish national home, and about the necessity of creating such a home precisely in Palestine, Adler wrote in this foreword:

doch kann man die Tatsache der nationalen Wiedergeburt der Juden und ihres Willens zur nationalen Konzentration als historische Faktoren nicht uebersehen. Man darf sie auch nicht bekaempfen. Denn der marxistische Sozialismus ist absolut kein Gegner des Nationalismus.[149]

Adler's fullest published discussion of his attitude toward Zionism appeared under the title *Das Verhaeltnis der nationalen zur sozialistischen Idee. Bemerkungen zum Poale-Zionismus.* It is based on a speech that he delivered on January 22, 1933, at a celebration held in Vienna. In this speech, Adler argued that it was incorrect to consider Zionism only from the West European assimilationist perspective. The assimilationist viewpoint, Adler maintained, is actually the least capable of comprehending the sociological and psychological reality of the national problem. According to Adler, the Poalei-Zion had played an important role by transforming a sector of the Zionist movement into a part and means of the Socialist International. The Poalei-Zion, Adler believed, had used its influence to deemphasize the national idea (without, however, excluding it) and to emphasize the socialist idea. It is because he saw the labor Zionist movement in this way that Adler referred to the work of the Jewish socialists in Palestine as one of the few bright spots in the otherwise dreary situation of contemporary socialism.[150]

Julius Braunthal agreed with M. Adler's view of the labor Zionist movement. In 1930 he too saluted the work of the "pioneers" in Palestine.[151] But Braunthal went beyond M. Adler in that he explicitly identified himself with the Jewish community. "I certainly felt Jewishness," Braunthal once wrote

and I felt that this added something of an imponderable feature to my individuality which differentiated me slightly from my Gentile comrades. I also felt a sense of belonging to the Jewish community all over the world. . . . I was never a conscientious "assimilationist."[152]

Both *Der Kampf* and the *Arbeiter-Zeitung* occasionally published articles that were sympathetic to labor Zionist efforts.[153] According to one informed source, it was above all Braunthal (who had served at one time on the staff of the *Arbeiter-Zeitung*, was for many years an editor of *Der Kampf* and was also on the central committee of the social democratic party) who made it possible for articles of this kind to be published.[154] The views of Braunthal, who came from a background that was markedly different from and more religious than that of the other prominent Jews in the Austrian Social Democratic party, were, however, clearly exceptional. Neither Max Adler's views on Zionism nor Braunthal's views on assimilationism had a major impact on the theory, policies, or propaganda of the party.[155] The attitudes toward the Jewish question of Bauer and Friedrich Adler, however, were rather typical of those of the party leadership as a whole.

Though this dominant attitude had been initially adopted partly in order to protect the Austrian socialist movement from the charges of being "Judaized" and a "protective troop" for the Jewish community, it did not succeed in achieving that goal. For despite the attempts made by Bauer, Robert Danneberg, and others to distance Austrian social democracy from the Jewish community in the minds of the public, Austrian anti-Semites repeatedly attacked the socialist leaders of Jewish origin precisely because of their origin. "The brown shirts bellowed 'Saujud' whenever Danneberg began to speak."[156] Julius Deutsch was subjected to similar treatment.[157] The term "Judensozi" was widely used throughout the period of the First Republic.[158]

It could be argued that the Austrian socialists had no feasible alternative to the policy that they adopted. In the face of overwhelming anti-Semitism Austrian socialists may have been forced to dissociate their party from the Jewish community in order to protect the party itself. Such a line of reasoning, however, would appear to be undercut by a comparison of the record of the SDAP[Oe] with that of the SPD. For, when faced with a rise of anti-Semitic sentiment during the Weimar years, the SPD regularly defended Jewish rights to an extent far beyond that of its sister party in Austria. There were, of course, lapses on the part of the German socialists, and significant differences between the Austrian and German parties and between the contexts in which they operated.[159] But the SPD cooperated (albeit discretely) with the Centralverein deutscher Staatsbuerger judischen Glaubens (CV—the most important German-Jewish organization) in order to combat their common enemy.[160] There is little evidence of comparable cooperation between Austrian social democracy and Austrian Jewry.

The Austrian social democratic party had no desire to cater in any way to Jews and did not do so. There were concentrations of Jewish voters, particularly in Vienna, that were useful to social democratic candidates. In 1927, the Zionists and the social democrats agreed to a secret electoral pact under which the Zionists would only put up candidates in certain specified districts.[161] The social democrats of the First Republic, however, were well aware that the collapse of the liberal parties left an overwhelming majority of Austrian Jews, both Zionists and non-Zionists, with the sense that they had little choice but to vote social democratic.[162] By the final years of the First Republic, the social democrats were receiving approximately three quarters of the Viennese Jewish vote.[163] But precisely because the social democrats understood that they could count on the Jewish vote, the Austrian social democratic party did not engage in strenuous efforts to solicit Jewish support, nor did it feel a need to adapt its program or its propaganda to appeal to the Jewish community.[164] In fact, the confidence engendered by the belief that Jewish voters had nowhere else to turn probably encouraged the party to continue to adhere to its traditional perspective on the Jewish question.

There is no doubt that Austrian social democracy was less infected by anti-Semitism than was any other major political party in the First Republic. But there can also be no doubt that the anti-Semitic prejudices that were so widespread in Austria during the Habsburg and First Republic years had an impact on Austrian socialists, including socialist leaders of Jewish origin. The Austrian social democratic perspective on the Jewish question bore similarities to that of other socialist parties. There were, however, distinctive aspects to the Austrian social democratic perspective that may be attributed to the Austrian context within which it operated, a context characterized by anti-Semitic prejudices. By accepting the premise that Jewish origin was a burden to the party, by allowing unflattering stereotypes to be used in socialist literature, and by refusing to defend Jews per se, Austrian social democrats allowed themselves to be put on the defensive. Precisely because there were so many Jews prominent in Austrian socialist ranks, the defensive policy on the Jewish question followed by the party ultimately tended to undercut the party itself.

CHAPTER 5

# Each Took in Accord with His Needs: The Reception of Socialist Ideas on "the Jewish Question" by the Jewish Intelligentsia of the Russian Empire

*1. Russian Jewish Politics, 1897–1914*

The three major ideological orientations dominant in Russian Jewish life immediately before and after the turn of the century were orthodoxy, Zionism, and Bundism. The adherents of the first of these orientations were wholly inattentive to and uninterested in social democratic writings. Those in the mainstream of the Zionist movement were only minimally interested in Marxist or even in socialist works. The Bundists, however, thought of themselves as Marxists, and were, therefore, part of the attentive public for works on the Jewish question by socialist theorists living in the West.

The Bund was the first modern Jewish political party and was the largest Jewish working-class party in the first years of the twentieth century.[1] Nine years after its founding in Vilna in 1897, the Bund claimed a membership of 33,000. Its founders, rejecting the tactics of earlier, cosmopolitan Russian Jewish radicals who had attempted to organize the Russian peasantry, hoped to organize the Russian Jewish working class and aid in the efforts to overthrow the Czar. As the Bund evolved, it became increasingly receptive to recogni-

tion of Jewish national identity, and defended its positions by referring to the works of Marxist theoreticians and, above all, to the
works of Karl Kautsky.

The Bundists also paid considerable attention, of course, to the
works of such other Marxists as Otto Bauer. There were, however,
at least three reasons why the members of the Russian Jewish intelligentsia in general and those of the Bund in particular devoted
more attention—at least initially—to the works of Kautsky than
to those of Bauer. First, Bauer was only in his mid twenties when
he published *Die Nationalitätenfrage und die Sozialdemokratie.*
Thus, however important his work may have been, Bauer had not
yet established a reputation great enough to allow the members of
the Russian Jewish intelligentsia to rest their arguments primarily
on his work. Second, Bauer's book was not published until 1907, by
which time the debate over the Jewish question had already been
long under way. Third, in *Die Nationalitätenfrage* Bauer had explicitly and directly criticized the ideology of the ŻPSD and had
unambiguously denounced that party's advocacy of national cultural autonomy for Galician Jewry. Bauer's criticisms of the ŻPSD
made it more difficult to use Bauer's writings to support the position of the Bund than to use Kautsky's writings. Nevertheless,
Bundists did attempt to make use of certain aspects of Bauer's work,
just as they made use of Kautsky's name, reputation, and arguments.

The Bund's opponents, Jewish and non-Jewish, did not allow the
Bund's use of Kautsky, Bauer, and other socialist theorists to go
unchallenged. The debate over the meaning of these theorists was
especially pronounced after 1904, when a number of Jewish work-
ing-class-oriented groups that had generally worked within the Zionist orbit crystallized into distinct parties and therefore emerged
as direct competitors with the Bund.

The first of these competitors to emerge as a party was the Zionist
Socialist Workers' party, often known as the SS (the initials of the
name in Russian).[2] The SS, founded in Odessa in February 1905,
maintained that the overthrow of capitalism could be accomplished
only by a class-conscious proletariat and that the conditions of the
diaspora did not allow for the formation of such a proletariat among

the Jews. The SS therefore argued that the Jews needed a territory of their own. Only in such a territory could Jewry satisfy its national needs. More important, only with a territory of its own could Jewry spawn a Jewish proletariat that could organize for socialist goals.

Unlike the Zionist mainstream, the SS was not particularly interested in Palestine. To the SS it was the fact of territorial concentration rather than the place in which this concentration would occur that was of paramount importance.

During this period, the Bund advocated national cultural autonomy for Russian Jewry. The SS believed this program to be unrealistic, and therefore called not for autonomy but merely for equal rights for the Jewish nation and language. "The Jewish proletariat in the countries of the Diaspora can satisfy only those of its national needs which relate to education in its own language," proclaimed the SS, "Institutions generally necessary for the fulfillment of national needs cannot, however, acquire effective binding force under the present realities of Jewish life."[3] The program of the SS attracted a significant number of workers. The party claimed 27,000 adherents around 1906.

The Jewish Socialist Workers' Party (SERP), the followers of which were known as *sejmistn*, was based on a slightly different synthesis of socialist and territorialist ideas. SERP had its origins in the small intellectual grouping *Vozrozhdeniye* (Renaissance), which had been formed in 1903 in Kiev.[4] Unlike the Bund, which was instrumental in organizing the RSDRP, several of the leading members of Vozrozhdeniye were open to the possibility of cooperation with the Party of Socialist Revolutionaries (PSR).[5]

Vozrozhdeniye believed that under certain conditions diaspora communities would blossom, thus differentiating itself from the Zionist movement. Vozrozhdeniye, however, favored in principle the territorial concentration of the Jewish people, either in Palestine or elsewhere, at some point in the future.

Whereas the SS considered the Bund's demand for Jewish national cultural autonomy to be unrealistically ambitious, Vozrozhdeniye considered the Bund's platform to be too timid. National *political* autonomy, not merely national cultural autonomy, was necessary to assure Russian Jewry of its rights.

Despite its advocacy of territorialism, Vozrozhdeniye did not in fact engage in active territorialist work. It increasingly emphasized the need for a revolutionary overthrow of the Czarist regime—the precondition of socialism, of Jewish national political autonomy, of Jewish territorial concentration, and of its ultimate goal, a national renaissance of the Jewish people.

Though leaders of Vozrozhdeniye participated in the founding of the SS,[6] several of them were never wholly satisfied with the Zionist-Socialist platform. These leaders, therefore, held a conference in Kiev in April 1906 at which they proclaimed the founding of SERP.

SERP, while larger and more broadly based than Vozrozhdeniye, had a similar ideological orientation. The SERP differentiated itself from the SS by, among other matters, placing far greater emphasis on work in Russia than did the Zionist-Socialist Party and by placing far less emphasis on territorialism in its day-to-day work.

The SERP differentiated itself from the Bund in its vision of the road to socialism—the Bund supporting a Marxist vision, the SERP having leaders who were more open to the social revolutionary perspective.[7] It also insisted that part of its ultimate goal was territorial autonomy for Jews, and it demanded national *political* autonomy for Russian Jewry. Whereas the Bund seemed to believe that political autonomy might weaken the class consciousness of Jewish workers,[8] and believed that the Jewish community ought to have control only over a relatively narrow sphere,[9] the SERP called for the establishment of an extraterritorial Jewish diet for all of Russian Jewry. The Jewish diet, as conceived by the SERP, would have had authority not only over Jewish educational and cultural matters, but would also have had the right to tax, control over matters relating to the public health of the Jewish population, and other functions, including the organization of mass emigration to a future Jewish territory. According to the SERP, territorial concentration could only be the result of work in the diaspora. The membership of the party in the year of its formation was approximately half that of the SS.

Those socialist Zionists who believed that Jewish territorial concentration could and ought to be realized only in Palestine organized a party of their own in 1906. Their party, the Jewish Social Democratic Workers' Party Poalei-Zion (ESDRP-PZ), claimed to have

16,000 members and considered itself to be in the Marxist tradition.[10] It advocated continuous work toward the obtaining of Palestine as a Jewish territory, but it believed that there was an indivisible connection between this work and the class struggle of the Jewish workers in the diaspora.

In 1906, the platform of the Zionist organization was itself dramatically altered. The Zionist organization had been founded in 1897 in Basel, at which point it had endorsed a program calling for the establishment of a "publically and legally assured home in Palestine" for the Jewish people.[11] In the period following the Basel congress, the Zionist organization concentrated its efforts on diplomatic maneuvers designed to secure a charter from the Turkish government that would permit the settlement of a mass of Jews in Palestine. Though it claimed a membership of 200,000 in 1905, of which about two-thirds lived in Russia, the organization's impact was diminished by bitter internal disputes over the advisability of creating a Jewish home in a territory other than Palestine and over Herzl's willingness to engage in a dialogue with officials in the Russian government universally acknowledged to have been involved in pogroms. Herzl's death in 1904 consolidated the victory of the pro-Palestine and antidialogue factions. The rise of these factions, and the pressures caused by the emergence of the SS, SERP, and the ESDRP-PZ, were among the factors that led the Zionist organization to endorse a revised program at its November 1906 congress in Helsingfors, Finland.

The Helsingfors Program endorsed the participation of Russian Zionists in efforts to liberalize the Russian government, advocated the introduction of universal, equal, and secret ballots for the election of Russian government officials, and demanded the recognition by the Russian government of the Jewish nation and of the right of the Jews to self-administration "in all matters of Jewish life."[12] In addition, the program advocated the calling of a Russian Jewish national assembly, spoke of the right of Jews to use Hebrew and Yiddish in schools, courts, and public life, and called for the recognition of the right of Jews to take Saturday as their day of rest.

The Helsingfors Program, however, also prohibited the members of the Zionist organization from being members of any other Jewish political parties. Since Russian Zionists had, in the period immediately proceeding the adoption of this program, cooperated with Russian Jewish liberals, the Helsingfors Program led to the collapse of the most notable Jewish liberal group in the Russian Empire.

This hole in the Jewish political spectrum was filled by the creation of the Folkspartay (People's Party), a small but influential Jewish party that was neither Zionist, nor socialist, nor orthodox, nor territorialist.[13]

The Folkspartay appealed to the Jewish middle classes. It considered all of world Jewry to be members of the Jewish nation, and opposed the intensification of class struggle within Jewry. At the same time, the Folkspartay thought the Zionist aim of concentration of Jewry in Palestine to be unrealizable. The general political program of the party was similar in tone to that of the Russian Constitutional Democratic Party (Cadets), and called for democratization of the Russian state and equal rights for all peoples living within the Russian Empire. The program also demanded that Jews be granted the right to use Yiddish in public life and the right to organize their own schools. The Folkspartay hoped that Russian Jewry would obtain and secure its national rights via government recognition of a union of democratic, self-governing, Jewish community councils.

Thus by 1907 the political map of Russian Jewry had become quite complex. Orthodox Jewry, a large part of the Jewish population, was not organized in a political party but relied instead on the influence of its most prominent members. The Zionist and liberal organizations were working within the Jewish middle classes—the former as a large movement that had not traditionally been active in Russian politics, the latter as a small group whose influence was based on the respect accorded its initiators. The Jewish working class, finally, had four major parties of its own: the Bund, the SS, SERP, and the ESDRP-PZ. Theoreticians associated with each of the secular movements debated the Jewish and national questions in the course of working out their own positions and of appealing for support from the Jewish masses. The extent to which these theoreticians made reference to Kautsky, Bauer, and other Marxist writers, the degree to which they supported the ideas of these writers, and the use they made of Marxist writings are explicable given the party platforms of the movements with which each of these theoreticians was associated.

## 2. Kautsky's Impact on the Development of the Bund's Approach to the National Question

An early and prominent Bundist writer, Franz Kursky, has noted that "in the pioneer group" of the Bund "there was no special interest in the national question."[14] There was, however, one prominent exception to this generalizaton. John Mill, one of the thirteen founders of the Bund, was profoundly interested in the national question, if not at the time of the Bund's formation than at least shortly thereafter.

Mill's interest in the national question was sparked by the attacks of the Polish Socialist Party (PPS) on the Bund in 1898. The PPS advocated Polish independence and considered the areas in which the Bund initially conducted much of its work to be, historically, part of Poland. The PPS maintained that the Bund's platform was inadequate insofar as it did not call for the independence of Poland. The Jews of Poland, the PPS argued, would best be served by struggling together with the Poles for independence from the Russian Empire. After the victory of the Polish independence movement, the PPS maintained, the Jews of Poland would be granted civil rights equal to those of the Poles by the new regime.

The criticism leveled at the Bund by the PPS led Mill, who was more closely attuned to Polish affairs than were the other founders of the Bund, to reconsider the Bund's position. The platform of the Bund, Mill soon came to believe, was in fact inadequately suited to Polish conditions. The PPS's platform, however, was similarly inadequate. "We sought a solution," Mill writes in his memoirs.

The national question became a perpetual theme at practically all meetings, at all Bundist gatherings and debates. We were against the historic-territorial strivings of the PPS, but we also could not see the correct answer in bourgeois equal rights and in the right of nations to self-determination.[15]

In the beginning of 1898 Celina Dowgierd brought the leaders of the Bund the issues of *Die Neue Zeit* containing Kautsky's article

"Der Kampf der Nationalitäten und das Staatsrecht in Oester-reich."[16] In "Der Kampf der Nationalitäten" Kautsky argued that the "modern national idea" is founded deep in the needs of peoples.[17] The proletariat, Kautsky maintained, not only need not be hostile to modern national movements, but is "most ardently interested" in their unhindered continuation.[18] Referring to the national problem in Austria-Hungary, Kautsky proclaimed that only one possible solution remained: "Federalism of nationalities, the smashing of the territorial borders of the provinces, Austria's reorganization on the basis of language borders."[19]

Mill reports that Kautsky's article made a tremendously strong impression on the early Bundists. "We used all of his arguments in the struggle against the territorial solution of the national question. We supposed that finally that for which we had so passionately looked had been found."[20]

It has often been claimed that the theoretical roots of the Bund's answer to the national question lie in the ideas of the Austro-Marxists. Those who make this claim point to the work entitled *Staat und Nation. Zur österreichischen Nationalitätenfrage*, written by Karl Renner and published in Vienna under the psuedonym Synopticus in 1899, and to the resolution on the national question adopted by the Austrian social democrats on September 28, 1899, at their party congress in Brünn as being especially influential.[21] Koppel Pinson, for example, among the first academics in the English-speaking world to write on the history of the Bund's ideology, has claimed that the leaders of the RSDRP all adopted a negative stance toward the national question in the pre-World War I era, and justified this stance by referring to Kautsky's works. The Bundists, however, are said by Pinson to have opposed the Russian social democrats by adapting the arguments of the Austro-Marxists.[22]

In reality, however, the situation was considerably more complex. The dichotomy between the the supporters of Kautsky and the supporters of the Austro-Marxists did not exist when the Bund was beginning to formulate its national program. The first steps toward the development of a national program on the part of the Bund were taken before the publication of Renner's work and well before the publication of the Brünn Resolution. The initial impetus for this development was not an attack by the RSDRP, but the necessity of

answering the PPS, and the kernel of the Bund's platform was derived from Kautsky's article on Austria-Hungary.[23]

Moreover the Austro-Marxists were themselves heavily indebted
to Kautsky. Kautsky was one of the coauthors of the Hainfeld Program of the SDAP [Oe] and had thus helped provide the basis for the
party's unification. In the 1890s, the Austrian social democrats were,
to a considerable degree, intellectually dependent on Kautsky's
ideas.[24] More specifically, the Brünn Resolution on the national
question followed Kautsky's formulation and was wholeheartedly
endorsed by him.[25] Since the Bund's program on the national question was strongly influenced by the Austro-Marxists in the first few
years of the twentieth century,[26] Kautsky's influence on the Bund
was felt in two ways: directly and through the impact of Kautsky's
ideas on the Austrian social democrats.

When, in 1899, John Mill became editor of Der yidisher arbeyter,
the official organ of the Foreign Committee of the Bund, he had an
abridged and edited version of "Der Kampf der Nationalitäten"
published in it, thereby making Kautsky's views on the national
question more widely known to the Yiddish-speaking rank and file.[27]
At the third congress of the Bund, in December 1899, Mill, clearly
using Kautsky's reasoning, proposed that the organization demand
not only equal civil rights for Jews, but also equal national rights.
Many Bundists at the third congress were worried that a demand of
this sort could divert the attention of Jewish workers from the task
at hand—the overthrow of the Czar. Mill's proposal, was, therefore, not accepted.[28] But by the time the Bundists convened their
fourth congress, in late May 1901, the tenor of opinion within the
organization had changed. Echoing the argument Kautsky had made
about Austria-Hungary in "Der Kampf der Nationalitäten," the
congress declared

> That a state such as Russia, which consists of a multitude of various types
> of nationalities, ought, in the future, to transform itself into a federation
> of nationalities with full national autonomy for each of them, independent
> of the territory on which it lives.[29]

Another resolution of the Bund's fourth congress proclaimed that
the Bund intended issue number 25 of Di arbeyter shtimme, the
organ of the Bund's Central Committee, to be expanded into a

jubilee issue. Fulfilling this mandate, the editors of *Di arbeyter shtimme* solicited greetings from socialist leaders, including Karl Kautsky. The message sent by Kautsky to *Di arbeyter shtimme*, which was published under the title "Der 'paria' unter di proletarier," contained strong praise for the Jewish socialist movement of the Russian Empire and outlined with great sympathy the state of the Russian Jewish worker.[30] In the eyes of the Bund, Kautsky's message was an endorsement of its work. Given Kautsky's prominence in the socialist world, the propaganda value of such an endorsement was tremendous. Thus the Bund gave Kautsky's greeting the widest possible publicity. It not only published the greeting in *Di arbeyter shtimme*, but also published it twice in pamphlet form —once in Yiddish, once in Russian.[31] But, precisely because of Kautsky's prestige, which was particularly high among the Russian Jewish Marxists, the opponents of the Bund could not and did not allow the Bund's use of Kautsky to go uncontested.

### 3. Lenin vs. the Bund on Kautsky and the Jewish Question

By 1903 the Bund claimed that it was the sole representative of the Jewish proletariat in the Russian Empire, that it had the right to conduct its work throughout the empire, and that it was a federative part of the RSDRP. The Russian social democrats associated with *Iskra* rejected the first two claims out of hand and maintained that a federative party structure would be detrimental to the revolutionary cause. Lenin first began to make use of Kautsky's works on the Jewish question in the course of his polemical debates with the Bund over these issues.

In an article entitled "Does the Jewish Proletariat Need an 'Independent Political Party'?" Lenin responded to the Bund's critique of a manifesto by the Ekaterinoslav Committee of the RSDRP. The Ekaterinoslav Committee's manifesto, which dealt with both anti-Semitism and Zionism, had noted that the anti-Semitic movement had "everywhere found adherents among the bourgeoisie, and not among the working-class sections of the population." The Bund's critique of this manifesto provided specific examples of anti-Semitic behavior by workers in the Russian Empire. Lenin, in turn, answered the Bund by claiming that:

If, instead of flying into a foolish and comical rage at the Ekaterinoslav Committee, the Bundists had pondered a bit over this question and had consulted, let us say, Kautsky's pamphlet on the social revolution, a Yiddish edition of which they themselves have published recently, they would have understood the link which *undoubtedly* exists between anti-Semitism and the interests of the bourgeois, and not of the working-class sections of the population. If they had given it a little more thought they might have realized that the social character of anti-Semitism today is not changed by the fact that dozens or even hundreds of unorganized workers, nine-tenths of whom are still quite ignorant, take part in a pogrom.[32]

The Bund had in fact published a Yiddish translation of Kautsky's *Die Soziale Revolution*, but neither this edition nor the German original contains an extended discussion by Kautsky of the Jewish question.[33] True, Kautsky made a passing reference in this work to the fact that splits in the petty bourgeoisie lead parts of this class to anti-Semitism, but there was nothing in Kautsky's work that was relevant to the Bund's critique of the Ekaterinoslav Committee's manifesto.[34] Lenin's reference is, at best, misleading. Clearly, Lenin hoped to use Kautsky's authority to attack the Bund, thus undermining the impression that the "foremost living Marxist theoretician" endorsed the Bundist position.

If, however, *Die Soziale Revolution* was inadequate for this task, Kautsky's work "Das Massaker von Kischeneff und die Judenfrage" was better suited to Lenin's purpose. In this article Kautsky gives a thumbnail sketch of Jewish history and proclaims, "In its ancestral land Jewry was eradicated . . . With this the Jews ceased to be a nation, for a nation without a territory is inconceivable."[35] Moreover, in describing his proposed solution to East European anti-Semitism, Kautsky writes:

By what means can this hostility be overcome? Most radically by those parts of the population which exhibit a foreign character ceasing to be foreign, by those parts of the population mixing in with the mass of the population. This is ultimately the only possible solution to the Jewish question, and all which can help bring to an end Jewish isolation must by supported.[36]

On the face of it, this analysis differed from that of the Bund in at least two ways. First, the Bund, using criteria similar to those delineated in "Der Kampf der Nationalitäten," considered the Jews of the Russian Empire to be a nation. Second, Kautsky's statement that "all which can bring to an end Jewish isolation must be supported" could be read as supporting a fusing of the Russian and Jewish socialist movements rather than the existence of an autonomous or independent Jewish socialist movement.

Just as the Bund had disseminated Kautsky's greeting to Di arbeyter shtimme for its own purposes in 1901 and 1902, the RSDRP disseminated Kautsky's article on the Kishinev pogrom in 1903. It was published on the first page of issue number 42 of Iskra in June 1903 and was also distributed as a pamphlet.[37]

The Bundists reacted quickly to this chain of events. At the fifth congress of the Bund, held in Zurich in mid-June 1903, Boris Frumkin, a prominent Bundist originally active in Minsk and later abroad, claimed, "Kautsky approaches the standpoint of the Zionists" insofar as Kautsky thinks that the Jews cannot be a nation if they do not have a certain territory of their own—a strong charge in a context in which Zionism was frequently disparaged as reactionary.[38] Neither Frumkin's comment, however, nor any of the other debates on the national question held at the Bund's fifth congress, was made known at that time.[39]

Moreover, Frumkin's comment was atypical of the Bundist response to Lenin's use of Kautsky. Consistently, from 1903 onward, the Bundists, while willing to criticize Kautsky on some points, perceived him as sympathetic to the Bund and as an authority on the national question. They simply did not accept the interpretation of Kautsky's views on the Jewish question advanced by Lenin and his followers.

Mark Liber, for example, speaking for the Bund at the fateful second congress of the RSDRP (July 1903), rather than attacking the views Kautsky had maintained in his article on Kishinev, harked back to Kautsky's earlier work. He answered the Russian social democrats' criticisms of the Bund by noting that:

One wants to create an international socialism without an international movement, and one forgets that we—the representatives of the proletariat of the Jewish nation—have, according to Kautsky's expression, transformed the Jews, the pariah among the other nations, into a powerful revolutionary force.[40]

The Bund walked out of the second congress of the RSDRP in protest when its minimal conditions for adherence to the party were rejected. Lenin, no longer maintaining the minimal proprieties that had to be used when speaking to party comrades, was now able to speak in even harsher language in his polemics with the Bund than he had before. In his article "The Position of the Bund in the Party" (*Iskra*, number 51 [October 22, 1903]), Lenin branded the idea of a Jewish nation as inherently Zionist, "absolutely false and essentially reactionary"—and frequently cited Kautsky as an authority on the subject.[41] Lenin quoted from "The Kishinev Massacre" the phrase that "the Jews have ceased to be a nation" and the phrases calling for support of all that will help end Jewish isolation.[42] He also referred to a recent work by Kautsky, "Die Krisis in Österreich," stating that Kautsky "endeavored to give a scientific definition of the concept of nationality and established two principal critieria of nationality: language and territory."[43] Lenin manifestly believed that the Jews did not fit within Kautsky's definition and mockingly concluded: "All that remains for the Bundists is to develop the theory of a separate Russian-Jewish nation, whose language is Yiddish and their territory the Pale of Settlement."[44]

There were at least two direct responses on the part of the Bund to Lenin's sally. One, published in *Vestnik Bunda*, the Russian-language theoretical organ of the Bund, was signed with the pseudonym L. Bassin, appearing under the heading "Are the Jews a Nation? (A Letter to the Editor)." The other, though unsigned, is known to have been written by Vladimir Kossovsky and was published both in *Vestnik Bunda* and in *Der yidisher arbeyter*.[45]

The article by Bassin directly confronts the assertion that language and territory are the two principal characteristics of a nation. To assert that territiory is an inalienable feature of the phenomenon of the nation, Bassin writes, is to assert either that a nation must be a state as well as a nation or that a nation must live in a cohesive area rather than in scattered areas. The first possibility, that a nation must live in one compact area, is shown to be incorrect by the fact that neither the Austrian Germans nor the English live in such areas. Thus, Bassin concludes, territory is not a necessary feature of the nation.[46]

Bassin next turns to the claim that language is such a feature, and he uses the example of the Irish to show that this is not always the case. Bassin concludes:

But if neither language nor territory can be regarded as the distinctive feature of a nation then what can? There is only one answer to that question—a certain sense of group unity. Nationality is a psychological phenomenon.[47]

Bassin, however, does not direct this argument against Kautsky but against Lenin. It is, Bassin claims, Lenin and only Lenin who asserts that language and territory are the two principal characteristics of the nation:

A closer scrutiny of the Kautsky article cited by *Iskra* will reveal that he was not, in effect, looking into the question of what basic attributes make a nation, but rather exploring the conditions that favor the creation of national unity. Language, territory, blood, kinship and historic tradition—all these are for him not attributes pertaining to nationality but circumstances condusive to the emergence thereof. If the *Iskra* lead writer had paid attention to more than the italics, he would have realized that Kautsky's "territory" and "language" somewhat differ from his own. True, Kautsky himself deviates from reality, and his reasoning on the question of nationality does not stand up to serious criticism, but still he displays in that article much sounder logic and knowledge than one would imagine after reading the *Iskra* editorial.[48]

Vladimir Kossovsky, one of the foremost theoreticians in the Bund, made a similar argument.[49] According to Kossovsky, Kautsky, in the article "The Crisis in Austria," had not given two principal criteria of the concept of nation, as *Iskra* claimed, but had attempted to describe the historic trend of nationalities. This trend can lead one to pick out several different combinations of principal criteria. *Iskra* chose from among these combinations the one that was necessary to its polemic. He wrote, however, that "it has not yet gotten away with it: it has ascribed its own speculations to Kautsky, in order to be able to rely with more authority on 'one of the most prominent of Marxist theoreticians.' "[50] Kossovsky reminded his readers that Kautsky had described several kinds of nations, that is, West European and East European varieties, and that, even within these kinds, Kautsky had noted that the principal characteristics of the nation had changed over the course of time. West European nations, for example, had passed through three levels of development: the nation-race level, the nation-territory level, and the nation-state level. Kossovsky summarizes the lessons of "The Crisis in Austria" in the following words:

There are nations and there are nations . . . One cannot encompass all these different types in one rule, whether this be the rule of *Iskra* (language and territory are the principal criteria of a nation), or any other. Moreover, whether we accept one rule of principal criteria for nations or several . . . we have no right to say, as *Iskra* does, that this or that nation does not exist only on the basis that it lacks this or that principal criterion.[51]

If "Die Krisis in Österreich" was unobjectionable to Kossovsky, "Das Massaker von Kischeneff" remained problematic. Kossovsky attempted to refute Lenin's use of "Das Massaker von Kischeneff" in two ways. First, he offered an interpretation of Kautsky's article that differed sharply from that of Lenin. Second, he rebuked Kautsky himself, offering evidence from other works by Kautsky that contradicted the controversial statements in Kautsky's Kishinev article. Kossovsky comments, for example, that Kautsky's claim in the Kishinev article that it is impossible to imagine a nation without a territory is unsubstantiated and contradicts Kautsky's argument in "Die Krisis in Österreich." Kossovsky also cites Kautsky's "Der Kampf der Nationalitäten" in order to counter the notion that the socialist movement must favor Jewish assimilation. Having summarized those parts of "Der Kampf der Nationalitäten" that suggest that national sentiments are grounded in material conditions and that call for proletarian support of modern national movements, Kossovsky proclaims that the recent history of the Jews in Russia "shows to what an extent Kautsky is right."[52] Kossovsky, however, admits that Kautsky, although "a serious . . . prudent, knowledgeable person," advocates Jewish assimilation in his Kishinev article and that this advocacy is indicative of Kautsky's lack of knowledge of contemporary East European Jewry.[53] Despite his strong admiration for Kautsky, Kossovsky criticizes him in no uncertain terms:

Before his eyes still hovers the old Jewry, from which there arose Spinoza, Marx, Lassalle; of the contemporary Jews he knows only the "reformed" German Jews. . . . [W]hoever wants to show that the Jews must assimilate must first of all demonstrate that the new Jewry, as we see it in Russia, stands in contradiction to the "general-European cultural development."

Kautsky did not even attempt to do this, and he could not have attempted it. . . . The new Jewry is for him a closed book.[54]

As though to take the edge off the criticism of Kautsky in Kossovsky's article, the Bund published Kautsky's foreword to the fifth German edition of the Erfurt Program in the same issue of Der yidisher arbeyter in which Kossovsky's article appeared. Kossovsky's article ends on page 26 of this issue. Kautsky's foreword begins on page 27. Similarly, Kautsky's words of praise for the Jewish socialist movement of England, first published in London in a Yiddish social democratic paper on April 1, 1904, were translated by the Bund and published in Vestnik Bunda in June 1904.[55]

Thus, as early as 1904 the Bund's attitude toward Kautsky was neither wholly supportive nor wholly condemnatory. The Bundists had enormous respect for Kautsky's accomplishments in elucidating, disseminating, and expanding on Marxist theory. They were influenced by Kautsky's interpretations of Marxist theory, including Kautsky's views on the national question. Moreover, the Bundists recognized that Kautsky's opinions carried great weight in socialist circles, and thus reprinted works whenever these works buttressed the Bundist perspective. At the same time, however, the Bund was critical of the assimilationist solution to the Jewish question offered by Kautsky, a solution that it attributed to Kautsky's acquaintance with German rather than East European Jewry. In general, the tone of the Bundists when dealing with Kautsky's views on Jewish assimilation can best be described as one of comradely reproach.[56]

### 4. Kautsky's Reception by the Russian Jewish Intelligentsia

The emergence of the SS, SERP, and the ESDRP-PZ was accompanied by a full scale debate on the Jewish and national questions within the ranks of the left wing of the Russian Jewish intelligentsia. Frequent reference was made to Kautsky's views throughout the course of this debate.

One of the most censorious reactions to Kautsky's views on the Jewish question to appear in the first decade of the twentieth century was written by Avrom Rozin (1878–1942), editor in chief of Vozrozhdeniye's periodical and later a member of the central committee of SERP.[57]

In an article written many years after SERP had ceased to exist, Rozin explained why it had been necessary to respond to Kautsky. The members of Vozrozhdeniye and SERP maintained that the blossoming of national cultures was characteristic of the capitalist epoch. Kautsky, according to Rozin, had recently written that capitalism abolishes national barriers, pours all of humanity together, and thus leads inevitably to a sort of cosmopolitan amalgam of peoples. Social democratic ideas had a great influence on the minds of the Jewish socialists, and Kautsky was one of the most authoritative commentators on Marxist theory. Thus, as Rozin saw it, Kautsky, a powerful force, had directly contradicted one of the basic principles of Vozrozhdeniye—and therefore had to be sharply refuted.[58]

Writing under the pseudonym Ben Ader, Rozin published a long booklet in 1906 entitled *Evreiskii vopros' v osveshchenii K. Kautskago i S. N. Yuzhakova* (The Jewish Question as Seen by K. Kautsky and S. N. Yuzhakov). Rozin rages against the "amateurism bordering on ignorance" that permeates statements on the Jewish question by both anti- and philo-Semites.[59] He condemns their "smug complacency," "trivial cant," and charges that the failures of the philo-Semites constitute "in effect, one of the variations of that 'specific attitude' to the Jews which they do not, of course, suspect in themselves."[60]

In his critique of Kautsky's article on Kishinev, Rozin complains that Kautsky writes as though the Jews were a passive element. Even when writing on the Jewish question, Kautsky was concerned with anti-Semitism, the actions of non-Jews, but not with the actions of the Jews themselves. This, Rozin implies, is indicative of a deeply rooted attitude: to Kautsky, the Christian nations are the real makers of history, the Jews merely affected by it. Seeking an explanation as to why Kautsky would have such an attitude, Rozin suggests that it is based in ignorance. Jewry is "terra incognita" for Kautsky and others like him. Thus Kautsky's analysis and his sketch of Jewish history are oversimplified and superficial. The conclusion that Kautsky reaches as to the causes of West European anti-Semitism parallels "the way the anti-Semites themselves explain anti-Semitism."[61] Kautsky's conclusions as to the causes of anti-Semitism in Eastern Europe are characterized as a return both to "the radical theory of the anti-Semites," and to "the mystic point of view of liberal anti-Semitism"—both of which Kautsky had directly criticized.[62]

From Rozin's perspective, the roots of anti-Semitism ought to be sought in "phenomena of a non-class character."[63] Rozin's alternative theory of anti-Semitism rests on the premise that social antagonism tends to be released along the line of weakest resistance. Since the Jews are a negligible minority in the empire, Rozin reasoned, and since they stand out in contrast to their environment, they constitute this weakest line and therefore become the victims of social antagonism. Since anti-Semitism is not rooted in class antagonism, however, the elimination of class antagonism will not eliminate anti-Semitism. Anti-Semitism will continue to exist in society, as long as the Jews in that society continue to be a weak, small, and easily distinguishable part of that society's population.

Rozin sarcastically interprets Kautsky's suggestion that the Jews assimilate with their neighbors in the following terms:

They beat you, they mash you up. . . . I do not exhort you to defend to the last your right to be yourselves, but on the contrary, I want you to bow your head, whose only fault is that it dares to be unlike the heads of those whose hands command a savage strength and clutch an executioner's knife.[64]

The course of Russian Jewish history, Rozin insists, is unfolding toward the exact opposite of assimilation. The development of Hebrew and Yiddish literature, and the growth of the Zionist and Bundist movements, are all evidence in support of this claim. Rozin concludes: "We cannot resist the temptation to address all well-meaning Judophiles with the following words: less high-flowing phraseology, sirs, less liberal pathos, more serious thought to a theme you are trying to rob."[65]

This terse comment is highly indicative of Rozin's attitude toward Kautsky's views on the Jewish question. To Rozin, a socialist but not a social democrat, a Jew but not a Zionist, Kautsky was manifestly friendly toward the Jews, but nevertheless deeply mistaken in his premises, analysis, and conclusions.[66]

The differences in tone between these responses to Kautsky are attributable to the fact that Bassin and Kossovsky perceived Kautsky as sympathetic to their program, while Rozin perceived Kautsky as an influential opponent of SERP's perspective.

Jacob Lestchinsky (1876–1966), a founder and leader of the SS, also wrote a lengthy response to Kautsky.[67] Lestchinsky's work, *Marks i Kautskii o evreiskom vopros'* (Marx and Kautsky on the Jewish Question), was published in 1907.[68] The problem with both Marx and Kautsky, Lestchinsky begins, is that their opinions are based on reason rather than experience. Precisely by the mistakes that Marx and Kautsky make, however, they demonstrate the general validity of Marxist methodology. Lestchinsky deals in great detail with Marx's famous essay on the Jewish question before turning to Kautsky, whose views "have an immediate influence on the masses."[69]

Kautsky's assumption that the fundamental cause of the Jewish question is economic is incorrect. It is the national "moment," which explains the oppressed position of the Jews. Kautsky "saw an oppressed class where, in reality, there was only an oppressed people."[70] Moreover, Kautsky is mistaken both in his claim that European Jewry has always been part of the oppressed classes and in the claim that the Jews have always been attracted to revolutionary ideologies. It is of great importance to Lestchinsky to disprove Kautsky's second claim, for the fundamental thesis of the SS was that diaspora Jewry could not produce a revolutionary proletariat.

Lestchinsky, therefore, attempts to prove that "The Jewish proletariat . . . remained at the tail of the [Russian] revolution [of 1905]. . . . [D]uring the entire course of the revolution there was not a single independent Jewish proletarian action worthy of mention."[71] In explaining why this was so, Lestchinsky emphasized that the dispersion of Jewry was linked to the abnormal class structure of Russian Jewry and concluded by implying that only the concentration of the Jewish masses in one territory could correct this abnormality and lead to the emergence of a class-conscious and revolutionary Jewish proletariat.

Interestingly, Lestchinsky, relying on Kautsky's message to the seventh congress of the Bund (which had been published in the Bundist *Folkstsaytung* in late September 1906),[72] denies that Kautsky calls for Jewish assimilation. "It is," moreover, "clear that Kautsky is on the road to the comprehension of the particular problems which confront the unique life of the Jewish proletariat."[73]

Maks-Aryeh Z. Shats (1885–1975), who had organized the SS in Saint Petersburg, took note of the views of both Kautsky and Bauer in 1907.[74] Using the pseudonym M. Anin, Shats published an article in the Vilna SS organ *Unzer veg* entitled "The National Question—or National Questions?"[75]

Shats mocks the Bundist and sejmist theoreticians for their tendencies to find and seek "laws" and "regulatory principles."[76] To Shats, there is no simple national question. The phenomena usually grouped under this rubric are varied and often have little to do with one another. Some of these phenomena are necessary results of the capitalist order and cannot be dealt with within the context of the present society. Others, while results of capitalism, are not *necessary* results and are, therefore, treatable even before the revolution. The political and cultural oppression of one people by another is an example of the latter type of result. Thus Shats praises the fact that members of the proletariat struggle against the political and cultural oppression of the nations to which they belong—and cites Kautsky as an expert who supports this perspective. The time when social democrats, including Kautsky, thought of nationalism as essentially bourgeois belongs to the past. Kautsky himself had written that "capitalist development calls forth in the parts of a nation which live in different territories (territories which border on one another but which belong to different states) the need to separate from those states and unite in one state."[77] Kautsky had also urged social democrats to support these strivings for state unity and independence on the part of the nations among which they lived and worked.

In Shats's eyes, the fact that Kautsky had made this argument demonstrated that Kautsky had become sympathetic to territorialism—that is, that Kautsky's position was parallel to that of the SS: "Kautsky commits himself not only in support of a national liberation movement, but recommends to the proletariat that it support national territorialism as well."[78] Thus, alongside the Bundist, Leninist, and sejmist perspectives, we now find another distinct interpretation of Kautsky's views: Kautsky is a supporter neither of national cultural autonomy, nor of assimilation, but rather of territorialism and can be used to support the program of the SS.

*In a limited sense, yes*

The question of why those in the SS arrived at such a different interpretation of Kautsky than had the SERP's theoretician may be answered by referring to the general orientations of these parties. Those in the SERP leadership were generally more sympathetic to the PSR worldview, and more critical of Marxism, than were those in the leadership of the SS. Thus the sejmist leaders differed from Kautsky not only on the national and Jewish questions, but also on such matters as the road to and the nature of socialism. Since the SS was closer to Kautsky on these latter questions than was the SERP, Lestchinsky and Shats were more inclined to search for a positive interpretation of Kautsky's works on nationalism and Jewry.

Not only the SS but also the SERP, however, attempted to use ideas put forth by Bauer to buttress their own perspectives. Shats, for example, published a review of Bauer's chapter on "the Jewish question" in *Unzer veg* in 1907. Shats begins by noting that every person who is familiar with socialist literature on the Jewish question knows that even the best representatives of the historical materialist perspective have often stumbled when it comes to the Jewish question. In so far as they remained true to their Marxist principles, Shats writes, the theorists of historical materialism— that is, Marx and Kautsky—used to altogether ignore the peculiarities of Jewish life. Insofar as they attempted to explain these peculiarities, moreover, they had gone astray because "practically all West European Marxists who have concerned themselves with the Jewish question" believe that conclusions reached through the study of West European Jews can be applied to the entire Jewish people.[79] Bauer's work, Shats, insists, is the best example of this tendency. Shats criticizes the assimilationist aspect of Bauer's work, for example, and stresses that Bauer failed to see from afar the whole of Jewish life.

But, from Shats's perspective, there is much that is praiseworthy in Bauer's work. Shats describes Bauer's description of the role of the Jews in the Middle Ages, for example, as leading Bauer to what Shats describes as a "pure 'SSish' conclusion."[80] He also points, apparently approvingly, to Bauer's conclusion that Jewish workers ought not demand national cultural autonomy and to those passages in which Bauer attempted to document the factors hindering the geographic and economic dispersion of the Jewish proletariat; for example, after quoting a few lines from Bauer concerning the reasons for the slow pace of industrialization among the Jews, Shats proclaims, "This is said not by a Zionist-Socialist, but by the orthodox Marxist Otto Bauer . . . a useful lesson for our political radicals of the social democratic Bund."[81] — apparently meaning to suggest that Bauer's work supported the SS contentions concerning the inability of Russian Jewry to form an industrial proletariat under then-existing conditions.

Mark Borisovich Ratner,[82] writing on behalf of the SERP, also attempted to use Bauer's work to critique the Bund's perspective. Mark Ratner summarized the SERP's criticisms of the Bundist— and, for that matter, of the SS—perspectives in an article published in the German-language journal, Sozialistische Monatshefte. In his article, which appeared in 1908, Ratner quotes the key points of the resolution adopted by the Bund in which that organization had formally endorsed national cultural autonomy, commenting that the portion of the resolution in which the Bund attempted to define national cultural autonomy was not clear. What is the nature of the institutions to which cultural questions will be transferred? Ratner asks. What will be the relationship of these institutions to the organs of the state? "Ferner" Ratner continues

ist von einer nationalkulturellen Autonomie die Rede. Aber eine klare soziologische Auffassung der Kulturgrundlagen des sozialen Lebens führt zu der Überzeugung, dass keine Kultur als etwas Isoliertes existiert. Das Sprach- und Bildungsgebeiet gehört zu den Elementen des Kulturlebens wie die Technik, die wirtschaftliche Tätigkeit, die Rechstinstitutionen, die politische und soziale Ordnung. . . . Bei einer solchen Sachlage ist eine nationale Autonomie, wenn das jüdische Volk sie wünscht, nicht nur für die Regelung von Bildungs-, Wissenschafts- und Kunstfragen nötig sondern auch für die Lösung der Not des jüdischen Volkslebens, der brennenden Interessen des jüdischen Proletariats.[83]

According to Ratner, moreover, support for the perspective that he was putting forth could be found in the argumentation of contemporary socialists on the national question—and the first socialist quoted in this context by Ratner is none other than Otto Bauer!

After quoting a passage from a work by Bauer, as well as passages from works by Kautsky and Renner, Ratner triumphantly concludes that the Bund had written of the nation as if it were merely a community of language and that it had therefore failed to take into account the new socialist perspectives, such as those of Bauer. "And this" Ratner proclaims "is a great error of this party."[84]

The major theoretician of the ESDRP-PZ, Ber Borochov (1881–1917), virtually ignored Kautsky.[85] There can be no question that Borochov was aware of Kautsky's works. Indeed, Borochov refers in passing to those works in "Our Platform" and in "The Role of the Working Class in the Realization of Territorialism."[86] Even during the period from 1903 to 1907, however, when Jewish radicals of other tendencies hotly debated Kautsky's intent, there are only a handful of such passing references to Kautsky in Borochov's works.

The paucity of references to Kautsky may be explained precisely by Borochov's sympathies for Marxism. Zvi Gitelman has noted that the Poalei-Zion "was more . . . strictly Marxist than either the S.S. or the Y.S. [sejmistn]."[87] Thus the fact that Kautsky disagreed completely with Borochov's politics was probably a source of great embarrassment to those in the ESDRP-PZ. Rather than highlight the fact that the world's leading Marxist theoretician was anti-Zionist, Borochov sidestepped the issue by not dealing with Kautsky's works. There is, however, one tantalizing reference to Kautsky in Borochov's most famous essay, "The Class Interests and the National Question,":

How is it possible that at the same time as societies are becoming economically closer to one another and as their comparative isolation is disintegrating, the national question is becoming sharper and the national movements are developing? . . . Kautsky has already attempted to solve this problem several times, but in the process of doing so he has constantly betrayed his materialistic world-view. One must, however, acknowledge that in a series of articles which he wrote on the national question, Kautsky is slowly moving closer to the theory which we are developing here.[88]

In this statement Borochov all but echoes the claims made by the SS. Just as Lestchinsky claimed that Marxist methodology was correct, but Kautsky wrong on this issue, so Borochov claimed that Kautsky "betrayed his materialistic world-view." Similarly, Borochov's claim that Kautsky "is slowly moving closer" to the theory that formed the basis for the program of the Poalei-Zion parallels the claim made by Shats that Kautsky supported territorialism.

There are even fewer references to Kautsky in the works of Simon Dubnow, leading theoretician of the Folkspartay, than in those of

Borochov. The sole mention of Kautsky's work in Dubnow's world famous "Letters on Old and New Judaism," in the revised edition of the third letter, however, ought to be noted for its resemblance to Borochov's comment in "The Class Interests and the National Question."

Dubnow's third letter, which originally appeared in the Russian-language Jewish journal *Voskhod* in May 1899, was rewritten by Dubnow when he was preparing to issue a collection of his *Voskhod* articles in book form. During the period in which Dubnow was preparing this collection, he read the volume entitled *The National Question as Judged by the Social Democracy*, which contained answers by Bebel, Plekhanov, Kautsky, and others to a poll on nationalism and patriotism. The poll, which had been conducted in 1905, asked such questions as: "Is it possible for patriotism to exist together with internationalism?"[89]

Dubnow was very pleased with Bebel's reply, which he characterized as "close to our theses to such a degree that I cannot deny myself the joy of bringing a quote from it."[90] Though apparently less pleased with Kautsky's reply, Dubnow comments that "K. Kautsky is beginning, (true, with an evident distaste), to incline toward nationalism."[91]

Like the blind men and the elephant, a cynic might say, the publicists of the Russian Jewish intelligentsia examined the same works but were led by the limits of their respective visions to wildly different prognoses—all of which missed the mark. With apologies to Karl Marx, I summarize by noting that when it came to Marxist works on the national and Jewish questions, many members of the Russian Jewish intelligentisa jumped the gun. Even in Czarist times, each already took according to his needs.

# CHAPTER 6

# Cooperation without Agreement:
# On German Socialists and
# German Jews

Relations between German socialists and German Jews were very much in flux from the beginning of World War I through the era of the German revolution. Most German socialists agreed with the anti-Zionist and proassimilationist perspective on the Jewish question propounded by Kautsky in *Rasse und Judentum* (which first appeared in the fall of 1914). As I have already indicated, however, Eduard Bernstein (and a small number of other German socialists) began to question this traditional Social Democratic perspective during the course of World War I.[1]

Significantly, much of the German Jewish community was highly critical both of Kautsky's book and of the alternative view suggested by the work of Bernstein. A majority of Kautsky's contemporaries within the German Jewish community were themselves assimilationists and were opposed to Zionism. Kautsky, however, was sixty years old when the first edition of *Rasse und Judentum* appeared, and sixty-seven when the second edition of his work was published. Parts of Kautsky's perspective on the Jewish question may well have been at least somewhat acceptable to German Jews of Kautsky's generation, but this generation was passing away. The autumn of 1914 marked the falling of dusk, not only for the Second International and for the Second Reich, but also for a widely held view of Jewry. Kautsky published his study as the owl of Minerva spread its wings.

But German Jews were as critical of Bernstein's alternative perspective as they were of Kautsky's viewpoint. A deeply felt sense of Germanness, and fear of fanning anti-Semitic sentiments, led the majority of German Jews to reject Bernstein's arguments on the mission of Jewry and to disagree with his expressions of sympathy for the labor Zionist movement.

During the period from 1879 to 1914, a majority of German Jews voted for the Progressive and similar left-liberal parties rather than for the socialists.[2] From the mid-nineteenth century through the final years of the Weimar Republic, however, there was a slow increase in electoral support by German Jews for the SPD. This tendency almost certainly continued during and immediately after World War I. But the apparent increase in support for the SPD by German Jews during that period occurred despite serious misgivings by German Jewry as to socialist views on the Jewish question.

The economic, political, religious, and ideological configuration of German Jewry explains its failure to react to Kautsky's articles on the national and Jewish questions before 1914. Whereas the East European Zionist, Jewish, liberal, territorialist, and Jewish socialist parties, representing a substantial part of Russian Jewry, all maintained that Jewry, or at least Russian Jewry, constituted a nation and were seeking ideological justifications for their positions, German Jews were generally hostile to theories of Jewish nationalism. Kautsky's articles on the national question in Austria-Hungary, which sparked the debate in Russia as to Kautsky's position on the Jewish question, did not spark a debate among German Jews because German Jewry did not consider the national question as relevant to its own situation.

A second major spark to the Russian debate likewise did not exist in Germany before World War I. A large part of the Russian Jewish intelligentsia was socialist and thought of the German socialists as their teachers and guides. Both before and during World War I, much of German Jewry was as hostile to socialism as it was to Jewish nationalism. The Russian Jewish radicals eagerly awaited news from Germany on Kautsky's pronouncements. Much of the German Jewish intelligensia probably did not even read *Die Neue Zeit*. This intelligentsia, moreover, was as alienated by Bernstein's perspective as it was by that of Kautsky.

While Kautsky's pre-World War I writings on the Jewish question did not receive much attention in the German Jewish world, the publication of *Rasse und Judentum* in 1914, and, to an even greater extent, the publication of the revised edition of *Rasse und Judentum* in 1921, provoked a number of responses from German Jews—precisely because the ideological configuration of German Jewry was changing markedly. True, a plurality of Jewish voters continued to support middle-road liberal parties during the early years of the Weimar Republic. The percentage of Jews associated with the parties of the left, however, increased during these years. When the depression and the rise of Nazism led to the collapse of the Democratic and People's parties, the SPD captured much of the Jewish vote.[3] Older German Jews who voted for the SPD tended to do so because they saw it as the lesser of evils rather than because of a genuine agreement with SPD policies. A large number of younger German Jews, however, became genuinely committed to the SPD during the Weimar years. The increase in the percentage of voters for the SPD in the latter part of the Weimar era was to some extent owed to a generational shift.

The Zionist Federation of Germany (ZVfD) was also larger during the Weimar years than it had been during the Wilhelmine era. Approximately 9,000 of the more than half a million Jews in Germany in 1914 were members of the ZVfD.[4] The ZVfD had 20,000 members in 1920–21, however, and 33,000 members in 1922–23. It decreased in strength from 1923 to 1933, but then rapidly increased its membership to 44,000 in 1933–34 and 57,000 in 1934–35.[5] Once again, this change in the ideological proclivities of German Jewry, which is mostly attributable to the rise of the Nazis, is at least partially attributable to a generational shift. In general, the younger generation of Weimar Jewry was less hostile to Zionism than was the older generation of German Jewry. Thus, both an increased attentiveness to socialist thought on the part of one wing of German Jewry and an increased sympathy for Zionism on the part of another help explain the large number of reviews of Kautsky's *Rasse und Judentum* by German Jews.[6]

The strongest organization of German Jewry at the time of the publication of *Rasse und Judentum* was the Central Verein deutscher Staatsbürger jüdischen Glaubens (The Central Association of German Citizens of the Jewish Faith). The Central Verein (CV), whose name was deliberately designed to stress that its members thought of themselves as members of the German (rather than a Jewish) nation, was founded in 1893 and grew rapidly thereafter. By 1924 the CV proudly claimed that 85 to 90 percent of German Jews were affiliated with it.[7] *Im deutschen Reich*, the official organ of the CV, was by far the most widely distributed German Jewish periodical.[8]

A review of the second edition of *Rasse und Judentum* appeared in *Im deutschen Reich* during the summer of 1921. The author of the review, Paul Nathan (1857–1927), was a founder and leader of the Hilfsverein der deutschen Juden and a leading member of the Verband der deutschen Juden.[9] In the course of his review, Nathan wholeheartedly embraced Kautsky's perspective on racial matters and on Zionism. Anti-Semitism had modernized itself, Nathan noted. It no longer based itself on religious arguments, but on purportedly more scientific racial modes of argumentation. Kautsky's work was of value first of all because of the "rich, scientific material" that Kautsky brought to bear in discussing these matters.[10]

Nathan's discussion of Kautsky's views on Zionism was even more laudatory: "As far as I know, Kautsky has never been to Palestine, and he, then, would be one of the few who, free from every religious-mystical agitation, grasped the situation as it is in reality from books."[11] Palestine, Nathan pointed out, was a small strip of land and lacked possibilities for economic development. Neither farmers nor industrialists nor practical politicians who were free from sentimentality could be expected voluntarily to choose Palestine as their field of activity. The Jewish people, however, was predisposed to sentimentality, and sentimentality appeared to have won out over practicality in the decision that Palestine be the focus of those seeking a territory for the Jews. Palestine could potentially become a spiritual center for Jewry, but even this goal could be endangered by the continuation of attempts to turn Palestine into a modern Jewish polity. Nathan endorsed Kautsky's characterization of the Zionist movement as reactionary, noting that Kautsky had predicted that pogroms would follow the Jews to Palestine. As Nathan put it: "[T]he bloody proceedings in Jerusalem and now in Jaffa prove the truth of Kautsky's words."[12]

Nathan was particularly interested in the fate of East European

Jewry. Referring to Kautsky's comments on the Jews of Eastern Europe, Nathan declared, "I thoroughly agree with the Kautskian view."[13] The problems of the Eastern Jews, Nathan continued, would only be solved in the East. Emigration was not the answer. There could be no solution to East European anti-Semitism until the culture of humanity reached a higher plane.

In sum, Nathan, a leading figure in German Jewish circles, writing in the most widely read periodical of German Jewry, explicitly endorsed Kautsky's perspective on all of the major issues discussed in *Rasse und Judentum*. Nathan's view, however, ought to be seen as much more than the response of one Jew, or even one important German Jew, to Kautsky. Most German Jews of the older generation were anti-Zionist and assimilationist. Though Nathan may have had his differences with the CV, Nathan's review probably represented the sentiments of a majority of German Jews of Kautsky's age.[14] Even within the ranks of the CV, however, the liberal-assimilationist ideology was undergoing something of a reinterpretation.

Among some of the Centralverein rank and file, and especially among its young members, the hard-core opposition to Zionism of the older generation seemed passé in light of Zionist practice in Germany. They admired the Zionists' spirit and idealism, and without actually endorsing Jewish nationalism, they advocated limited cooperation [with German Zionists] in cultural, charitable, and self-defense matters.[15]

This new attitude is reflected in several German Jewish responses to Kautsky that appeared in generally liberal publications. The most revealing of these reviews was written by Rabbi Felix Goldmann of Oppeln in 1915. Goldmann, who was born in 1882, and was therefore a full quarter of a century younger than Nathan, played a leading role in the German Jewish student movement closest to the CV, the Kartell Convent of German Academicians of the Jewish Faith. He later became one of the most influential leaders of the CV itself.[16] The periodical in which he published his review, the *Allgemeine Zeitung des Judentums*, was among the oldest of German Jewish papers, having been founded by Rabbi Ludwig Phillippson in 1837. Despite the claim on its masthead to be "a non-partisan organ for all Jewish interests," the *Allgemeine Zeitung* was traditionally more sympathetic to liberal than to orthodox Judaism.[17]

In his review of Kautsky's book Goldmann indicated that he

accepted Kautsky's general argument about races, but he disagreed strongly with Kautsky's discussion of Judaism and Zionism. According-ing to Goldmann, Kautsky considered Jewry as if it were a dead body, without a will of its own—a decisive error.

Whoever wants to give his opinion on Jewish things without investigating and paying attention to the will to live and the spiritual power of the community ought better to keep his hands off the subject. Jewish history, with its heroism, its martyrs and heroes of the spirit, cannot be analyzed and explained by historical materialism, but precisely by idealism, which belongs to the people of the Prophets.[18]

Kautsky, Goldmann insisted, did not understand the essence of Jewry: Jewry's religious meaning and power. He naively expected the mix-ing of Jewry with non-Jewish peoples to result in the disappearance of Jewry, when, in truth, the existence of Jewry was dependent on nothing else but the power of the religious idea.

Kautsky's failure to understand this led him to misunderstand the essence of Zionism as well: "Kautsky does Zionism a decisive injustice when he lets it stand and fall with race theory. For [race theory] in truth determined only the *form* of the [Zionist] move-ment, while [Zionism's] content goes back to altogether different factors."[19] Indeed, a critique of Zionism had to "begin from its position toward religious thought."[20] Zionism "signifies a solution for the question of the Jewish people, not, however, for that of Judaism."[21] Thus Kautsky's book was dangerous, for "the correct-ness of its general part can mislead many" concerning the value of its judgments of Zionism and Jewry.[22] "The opponent of the na-tional Jewish idea . . . ought not to ignore this. For if he uses [Kautsky's] work as a weapon against Zionism, then he may easily live to see a time when it is used as a weapon against himself."[23]

The second edition of *Rasse und Judentum* was reviewed in the *Allgemeine Zeitung des Judentums* by Goldmann's contemporary, Willy Cohn (1888–1942).[24] Cohn's review in the *Allgemeine Zeit-ung* was only seven sentences long,[25] but he published a somewhat longer review early in 1922 in the *Monatsschrift für Geschichte und Wissenschaft des Judentums*, a periodical that has been character-ized as "the leading Jewish scholarly journal in the world" during the era of its publication.[26]

Cohn, who described the increase in literature on race in the

1920s as "a sign of the sickness of our time" in his first review of
Kautsky's book,[27] was, therefore, pleased that Kautsky's book combatted the tendency to think in racial terms: "In this sense we
welcome Karl Kautsky's present work . . . [he] deserves . . . our
thanks, even if we cannot agree with the results of his investiga-
tion."[28] The things Kautsky had to say, however, about the future
of Jewry were less acceptable. Kautsky's claim that Jewry would
completely disappear could not be seriously discussed but could
only be pitted against the belief in the imperishability of Jewry and
in the tasks that it still had to perform. The argument in *Rasse und
Judentum* that Zionism is an unrealizable utopia was "a view which
we are altogether unable to share."[29] Though Kautsky was undoubtedly correct that the Arab question was the most important
one in the Land of Israel, the possibility for a peaceful compromise
with the Arabs, Cohn asserted, still existed. Although Cohn's view
was more critical than Nathan's, he ended his second review by
stressing the positive aspect of Kautsky's work. Kautsky deserved
the thanks of German Jews "for the open and frank way in which
he settled accounts with all of our enemies. . . . The whole book is
a proof of the author's extensive reading and of the extent to which
he is well informed."[30]

   The German Jewish student movement ideologically closest to
the CV, the Kartell Convent of German Academicians of the Jewish
Faith, published a hostile review of *Rasse und Judentum* in its
periodical.[31] While no information is available on F. G. Thur, the
author of the review published in *K. C. Blätter*, the fact that he
wrote for this publication suggests that he was a university student
and may, therefore, have been even younger than Goldmann and
Cohn.

   Thur admitted that Kautsky's discussion of racial issues, while
not innovative, was good and correct. Thur also granted that Kautsky "understands excellently how to make the race theory laughable," by the use of sarcasm, but Thur insisted that Kautsky knew
little about the Jewish question.[32] While Kautsky is "certainly our
friend, he belongs to that well-known sort from whom one is glad
to be defended,"[33] for he believed and hoped that the Jewish question was best answered by complete assimilation. True, many liberal friends of the Jews shared Kautsky's perspective, but this was

merely "a sad example of the fact that even the greatest minds suddenly and radically forget all their former political and scientific axioms . . . as soon as they are dealing 'only' with the Jews."[34]

Kautsky's views on Zionism were also completely incorrect. Thur, too, rejected the Zionist solution to the Jewish question as "certainly false and pernicious."[35] He believed, however, that Kautsky overemphasized the similarities between Zionism and the racial theories, did not devote enough attention to the misery that brought Zionism into being, and, in general, knew little about Zionism.

The differences in attitude among Nathan, Goldmann, Cohn, and Thur may be symbolic of the differences among three generations of German Jewish liberals. While German Jewish liberals born in the mid-nineteenth century (such as Nathan) were usually hostile to Marxism, they were not necessarily hostile to assimilationism or to anti-Zionist arguments. German Jewish liberals of the next generation tended to be more critical of radical assimilationism than were their elders, but still viewed some aspects of Kautsky's position on the Jewish question as similar to their own. But those of student age, while by no means committed to a Zionist program, were generally less inclined to condemn Zionism out of hand.

A three-part article signed "A. L." published as the lead piece in consecutive issues of the widely read weekly of the ZVfD, *Jüdische Rundschau*, beginning in November 1914, contained more extreme charges against Kautsky than any that appeared in liberal periodicals. The author of this article insinuated that Kautsky's motives were sinister:

Even if he had already formulated his thoughts before the outbreak of the war, as he explains in his preface [to *Rasse und Judentum*], the fact that Kautsky is using the moment of the most violent, national, bloody struggles to publish his radical interpretation of the Jewish question remains of import. Does this occur only to console the Jews with the thought that their disappearance in no way signifies a tragic process?[36]

To A. L., the sole and obvious goal of Kautsky's book was to attack Zionism. A. L. makes a number of accusations against Kautsky, including the charge that Kautsky demands Jewish assimilation, but not the assimilation of other nations, and that Kautsky is altogether ignorant of Jewish experience. Unable to substantiate his suspicions that Kautsky was anti-Jewish, A. L. resorted to posing

leading questions. He noted, for example, that there were undoubtedly elements among the Jews which had no desire to assimilate
and asked:

Doesn't it mean the oppression of these elements if one advocates tendencies toward assimilation in opposition to them? . . . Isn't there, obviously,
a real danger that Kautsky's purely abstract expressions of opinion could
ultimately furnish pretexts and motivation for the violent assimilation
attempts of national oppressors?[37]

The fact that Kautsky never advocated forced assimilation was not
mentioned.

Similarly, A. L. noted that Kautsky did not attack the Bund in
*Rasse und Judentum*, but once again raised the possibility that there
might be more here than meets the eye. Perhaps, A. L. suggested,
the failure to tackle the Bund in *Rasse und Judentum* was tactical.
Kautsky, he observed, may have hoped to overpower Zionism first
and only then institute an internal struggle against the Bund in the
socialist world. Nothing Kautsky had written justified this accusation. Moreover, A. L., a Zionist, was certainly no friend of the
Bund. Only by implying that Kautsky was anti-Bundist as well as
anti-Zionist, however, could A. L. justify his charge that Kautsky
was anti-Jewish.

In the second and third parts of this series, A. L. discussed historical materialism and debated Kautsky's explanations of specific
events in ancient Jewish history. A. L., however, saved his fire for
Kautsky's comments on Jewish assimilation. Kautsky had pointed
out that in Italy and Denmark, where the Jews had achieved complete legal emancipation, they had also assimilated: "The examples
of Italy and Denmark show us how correct were those protagonists
of Jewish emancipation who expected from emancipation the complete absorption of Jewry in the peoples among which it lives."[38]
Once again resorting to a strained interpretation of Kautsky's point,
A. L. claimed that those who advocated emancipation only where
it would lead to complete absorption could find support in Kautsky.
Moreover

Whoever . . . does not expect precisely this result from the legal equaliza-
tion of the Jews will also, if he remains true to Kautsky, fight against
Jewish emancipation. . . . [T]he humane oppression which Kautsky inau-
gurates is no less significant than the venemous oppression of a Treitschke.[39]

The attack by A. L. on Kautsky, which deserves the label "venemous" far more than does anything Kautsky ever wrote on the Jewish question, was the only review of *Rasse und Judentum* published in the German Jewish press immediately after the book's appearance. World War I diverted the attention of German Jewry to more pressing matters. Another Zionist critique of *Rasse und Judentum*, however, appeared in Martin Buber's *Der Jude* in March 1922, shortly after the release of the second edition of Kautsky's book.

Buber believed that Jewish liberals undervalued the import of Jewish blood, that is, the extent to which Germans were different from German Jews, and that these liberals therefore were unable to admit the impossibility of Jews becoming truly German. The impossiblity of Jewish assimilation corroborated Zionism, which, for Buber, was grounded in the Jewish right to Palestine. Buber used his journal to advance this Jewish-*völkisch* ideology, clearly expressed by him in a speech in 1928 on the connection of Jews to Palestine: "Only this *Volk* can make of this land what this land is destined to be, and only this land can make of the *Volk* what this *Volk* is destined to be."[40]

The review of *Rasse und Judentum* published by Buber was written in Haifa by Elias Auerbach, a German Zionist who had settled in Palestine around 1909. Auerbach, a doctor, was influenced by the works on race that had appeared in scientific and popular circles in the first few years of the twentieth century and had even written his own studies in this field.[41]

Auerbach, while critical of Kautsky, did not engage in the kind of vitriolic attack on Kautsky's work that had characterized the earlier Zionist review. In fact, Auerbach even described Kautsky's work as "stimulatingly written" and "very much worth reading."[42] Auerbach, however, repeated charges similar to those made by Thur in 1915. According to Auerbach, Kautsky displayed an "ignorance of the true essence of the Zionist movement which is nothing short of astonishing."[43] He also criticized Kautsky for his failure to take into account spiritual factors in assessing Zionism and for his "fundamental ignorance of Palestininan conditions."[44] Auerbach's view of Kautsky's work is best summarized by a phrase from the last sentence of his review: *Rasse und Judentum*, Auerbach wrote, "belongs to a generation which has already begun to go under."[45]

As had Thur's review, Auerbach's assessment underscores a widening gulf between Kautsky and German Jewry. Kautsky's views on the Jewish question did not change during the World War I or Weimar periods. The tenor of opinion within German Jewry did. Not only did younger German Jewish liberals become sympathetic to cooperation with Zionists on specific questions, but a considerable number of German Jews actually became affiliated with the Zionist movement. To German Jews of his own generation, Kautsky's work on the Jewish question was essentially irreproachable. To younger Jewish liberals, and to Zionists of all ages, Kautsky's views were, at best, outmoded.[46]

Significantly, Bernstein's comments during the war on the mission of the Jews and on Zionism were criticized by liberal German Jews. An article attacking Bernstein, for example, was published in *Im deutschen Reich* under the title "Alldeutsch oder International."[47] The author of this article (who signed his work "F. G.") noted, "[I]t is impossible, given the superficiality of the often bizarre train of thought, to seriously" grapple with Bernstein's piece on the tasks of the Jews.[48] According to F. G., and Bernstein to the contrary notwithstanding, Jewry had never advocated the *völkerverbindenden* (solidarity between nations) ideal. Zionism, the author admitted, spoke of a Jewish nationality with national tasks of its own, but religious Jewry, both of the orthodox and of the liberal kind, recognized as the tasks of Jewry only religious tasks and worked for a *Völkerverbindung* only in the sense in which Christianity also strives for this goal. Religious Jewry emphasized wholehearted cooperation with the nation within which the Jews lived.

Bernstein, F. G. asserted, had written a work on the tasks of Jewry with virtually no knowledge of Jewry: "It is altogether certain that we Jews will not go down the road of the Independent Social Democratic Party against our German fatherland in order to please Bernstein. . . . We will, in German matters, go down the quiet and secure road which our conscience prescribes."[49]

An equally critical review of Bernstein's work was written by the editor of the *Allgemeine Zeitung des Judentums*, Ludwig Geiger (1848–1920).[50] Geiger noted that Bernstein grounded his view of the task of Jewry in a supposed *weltbürgerlichen Patriotismus* of the Jews.[51] But, Geiger noted, this very term seemed to contain an inner contradiction. Geiger also referred to Bernstein's pro-Zionist comments as unfortunate.

True, the German Jewish press was not unanimous in its condemnation of Bernstein's views. *Ost und West*, which was particularly interested in fostering both knowledge of East European Jewry and Jewish cultural activities, commented favorably on Bernstein's work in an unsigned article published in 1918.[52] Whereas *Im deutschen Reich* treated Bernstein's ideas with disdain, *Ost und West* referred to Bernstein's book as "one of the most valuable works which the war has brought forth."[53] A brief review by Moritz Güdemann, Chief Rabbi of Vienna, which was published in the *Monatsschrift für Geschichte und Wissenschaft des Judentums*, also praised Bernstein's book.[54] The reviews of Bernstein's work that appeared in *Ost und West* and in the *Monatsschrift*, however, were minority perspectives and ought not to be considered representative of the views of the German Jewish community.

Most German Jews undoubtedly thought of themselves as loyal citizens of the Reich and, as such, had responded enthusiastically to the call to support the war effort. Nevertheless, by 1916, if not earlier, there was an ominous upswing in anti-Semitism.[55] The military defeats suffered by Germany and its allies in the summer of 1916, and the decline in the German standard of living brought on by the war, contributed to the creation of a climate within which anti-Semitic propagandists were able to achieve considerable successes. Jews were frequently accused of avoiding the draft, shirking their duty, and of profiteering.

In their vigorous attempts to refute these charges, the representatives of German Jewry repeatedly stressed the patriotism and loyalty of the German Jewish community[56] and consistently dissociated the community from individual Jews who took strong stands against the war. Time and time again, the German Jewish press stressed that the Jewish community was not responsible for each and every act of, or idea by, persons of Jewish origin. When a particular speech by Oskar Cohn raised a storm of protest, for example, *Im deutschen Reich* pointedly commented that German Jewry had "nothing in common" with Cohn's politics.[57]

The reactions by German Jewry to Bernstein's writings during the war on the tasks of the Jews were motivated by precisely the same sentiments as were the comments on Cohn. Liberal German Jews were distressed by Bernstein's argument that Jews had a distinctive political mission at least in part because they believed that this argument could be used to promote anti-Semitism. Bernstein's World War I-era writings on the Jewish question were criticized by the German Jewish press because these writings were perceived as undermining the defense of the German Jewish community.[58]

Just as a majority of German social democrats continued to accept the traditional (Kautskian) perspective on the Jewish question during the period of war and revolution, so too did a majority of German Jewry continue to think of itself as liberal rather than socialist. It is all but certainly true that the bulk of German Jewry was sympathetic to the German Democratic party in the first few years of the Weimar Republic. Nevertheless, there seems to have been an increase in Jewish support for social democracy between 1914 and 1922. Though precise statistics on the voting patterns of German Jews are unavailable, it is highly likely that a larger percentage of German Jewry voted for either the SPD or the USPD in the elections of 1920 than had voted for the SPD in pre-war Reichstag elections. The pattern of slowly increasing support for the SPD among the German Jewish electorate that had begun to manifest itself in the Wilhelminian era[59] continued in the Weimar years.[60] This pattern eventually culminated in direct, albeit discrete, cooperation between social democracy and German Jewry in the final years of the Weimar era.[61]

My examination of German Jewish reactions to the most prominent socialist works on the Jewish question that appeared during the period between 1914 and 1922, however, demonstrates that increased Jewish support for social democracy was not accompanied by an increase in Jewish support for social democratic perspectives on the Jewish question. To be sure, the fact that leading social democrats regularly condemned anti-Semitism played a significant role in the willingness of Jewish voters to consider the social democratic alternative.[62] The moderation of the rhetoric of the Social Democratic party and the urbanization of German Jewry also contributed to this tendency.[63] But support by individual Jews for the SPD seems to have increased without leading to a diminution in the criticism directed by the publicists of German Jewry against social democratic writings on the Jewish question. German Jewry moved slowly toward social democracy despite social democratic views on assimilation, religion, and Zionism, not because of its agreement with these views.

# Conclusion

Though there have been numerous studies of the attitudes of social democratic writers toward the Jewish question, the bulk of these studies have painted with overly wide brushes. Virtually all of the relevant works have tended to accent the similarities among socialists who have written on the Jewish question and have condemned or applauded the socialist approach accordingly.

It is a major contention of this book that there was no universally accepted socialist or Marxist line on the Jewish question at the end of the nineteenth and beginning of the twentieth centuries. Socialists differed widely among themselves on major components of the Jewish question, just as they did in assessing revisionism, the general strike, the approach that ought to have been taken toward World War I, the Bolshevik Revolution, and many other practical and theoretical issues.

A number of factors, including (but not limited to) differing personalities, family backgrounds, differences in the communities in which they were raised, as well as differing political conditions and differences in their conceptions of socialism, help explain why figures such as Kautsky, Bernstein, Luxemburg, V. Adler, and O. Bauer had quite distinctive approaches to the Jewish question.

Kautsky, who was not of Jewish descent, expressed considerable sympathy for the plight of the Jews throughout his career and seems to have identified himself with persecuted Jews. Kautsky condemned anti-Semitism vigorously and repeatedly and heaped praise on the Bund. He was also a committed assimilationist—a position that was, in his worldview, fully consistent with his admiration for

Jews and for the Bund—and, like much of the Jewish community in German-speaking Europe at the turn of the century, was an anti-Zionist.

Eduard Bernstein, who was raised in a family that was affiliated with the reform Jewish community of Berlin, was also an assimilationist during the first period of his career. During this period, Bernstein disdained orthodox Jews and even rationalized the appearance of political anti-Semitism as a "comprehensible reaction" to the actions of certain individuals of Jewish origin. But the dramatic rise of political anti-Semitism, particularly during and after World War I, eventually led Bernstein to question the viability of assimilationism, to support the labor Zionist movement, to write for Jewish publications, and to allow his name to be used by certain Jewish cultural organizations. Three factors—listed here in chronological order—seem to have played roles in altering and shaping Bernstein's perspective on the issues at hand:

*Bernstein*

1. Bernstein's Jewish family background (which seems to have made him more sensitive to anti-Semitism than was, for example, Friedrich Engels, even during Bernstein's orthodox Marxist phase).
2. Bernstein's revisionism (which may have led him to take "petty bourgeois" movements and the movements of "declining classes" —such as the anti-Semitic movement—more seriously than did certain of his orthodox Marxist contemporaries).
3. The dramatic political and cultural changes that occurred in Europe between the beginning and the end of Bernstein's life (including not only the sharp rise in the power of political anti-Semitism, but also the rise in popularity of Zionism, and the blossoming of a secular culture in the Yiddish language). Unlike Kautsky, who remained committed throughout his life to many of the positions which he first accepted at a young age, Bernstein altered his positions as the world around him changed.

Whereas Bernstein came to respect the need for Yiddish cultural institutions in the post-World War I era, Rosa Luxemburg, who was brought up in a family that had had close links to the maskilim of Zamość, disdained Yiddish. She also differed from Bernstein in her disdainful attitude toward Zionism. Unlike Kautsky, however, Luxemburg was critical not only of the Zionist parties but also of the

*Luxemburg*

Bund. Luxemburg's stance may also be differentiated from that of Kautsky in that Luxemburg tended to ignore rather than condemn Jewish suffering in Eastern Europe. It is highly likely that it was Luxemburg's exposure to maskilish attitudes in her parental home (and not the anti-Semitic attitudes of the non-Jewish population in which she grew to maturity or the anti-Semitic barbs directed toward her throughout her career) that played the primary role in molding the distinctive aspects of her approach to the Jewish question. Luxemburg scorned the values and culture of the Jewish masses of Eastern Europe. In so doing, however, she was, in certain ways, carrying on the tradition in which she was raised.

Anti-semitism seems to have produced a very different reaction in Victor Adler than it did in Luxemburg. Unlike Luxemburg (who either remained silent in the face of anti-Semitism or published anonymous counterattacks on those who had attacked her in anti-Semitic terms), Adler publicly equated anti- and philo-Semitism. Unlike Luxemburg, who merely stopped listing herself as Jewish in official documents, Adler became a formal member of the Protestant community. Luxemburg occasionally made anti-Jewish comments when writing private letters to her closest friends. Adler—by publicly underscoring the Jewish origins of certain of his political opponents—went much further. Luxemburg, in sum, does not appear to have been deeply scarred by the anti-Semitism to which she was subjected. Adler, however, does exhibit scarring of this kind. Anti-Semitism bounced off Luxemburg. It was internalized by the founder of the Austrian Social Democratic Workers' Party.

Though the attitudes toward the Jewish question of the most notable representatives of the SPD's right-wing (Bernstein), center (Kautsky), and left-wing (Luxemburg) line up rather neatly along a continuum that directly parallels the attitude of these thinkers toward other matters of contention, the same cannot be said of the Austrian context. Max Adler, for example, who was among the most insightful theorists of the Austro-Marxist left wing, displayed a sympathy for labor Zionism similar to that of Bernstein. Overarching ideological differences help explain the differing stances taken toward the Jewish question by the social democratic leaders in Central and Eastern Europe in the period between the death of Marx and the beginning of World War II, but examination of the family backgrounds, upbringing, and personalities of these leaders seems to provide even more compelling explanations as to why there was such a broad range of opinion among them.

However broad the range of attitudes toward the Jewish question exhibited by the socialist writers mentioned above, the Jewish communities of Central and Eastern Europe displayed an even broader range of responses to Marxist writings on the Jewish question. There was no such thing as a Jewish response to Marxism, any more than there was a unified Marxist response to the condition of the Jews. In the Russian Empire, in Germany, and in Austria-Hungary, the Jewish population was deeply divided on basic questions. In each of these lands, the responses of Jewish publicists to social democratic ideas on the Jewish question reflected the political map(s) of the Jewish world.

In the Russian Empire, the attitudes of the Marxist theorists toward the Jews became a political football in the first few years of the twentieth century. Because a large portion of the Jewish intelligentsia was sympathetic to socialist ideas, Marxist writings on the Jewish question (and, above all, the ideas of Karl Kautsky and of Otto Bauer) were eagerly read and hotly debated. Each of the four independent Jewish socialist parties of the Russian Empire interpreted the Marxist theorists in a distinctive (and self-serving) fashion. Each attempted to cloak itself in the reputation of the Marxist theorists when so doing would score points with its target audience. Each, moreover, was willing to criticize such theorists as Kautsky and Bauer if it believed such criticism to be necessary.

Jewish publicists in Weimar Germany tended to be far more critical of the attitudes of the leading social democratic writers than these publicists' counterparts in the Czarist Empire had been. Though a significant portion of German Jews voted for the socialist parties, the spokesmen of German Jewry (including, notably, representative figures from the younger generation of German Jews) criticized the ideas of Kautsky and Bernstein in no uncertain terms and gave a cold shoulder to the views of Luxemburg.

Despite the existence of large and important Jewish socialist movements, and despite the fact that a large number of prominent European socialist writers were of Jewish descent, the relationship between European socialists of the pre-World War II era and the

Jews of Europe was far more complex than may at first glance appear to have been the case. ⌈This relationship was neither uniformly warm nor uniformly cold but highly variable and far less amenable to generalization than much of the existing literature on this theme would have us believe.⌋

# Notes

## Introduction

1. The term "the Jewish question" *(die Judenfrage)* evolved over a period of decades. Though it was originally used in German-speaking lands more by anti-Semites than by their opponents, it was commonly accepted in the German-speaking world at the end of the nineteenth century and in the first few decades of the twentieth century not only by anti-Semites, but also by philo-Semites, and not only by non-Jews, but also by Jews holding every conceivable political opinion. By the late nineteenth century, the term itself was a neutral one among German speakers and was not thought of as having either pro- or anti-Jewish connotations. For a discussion of the early development of this term, see Jacob Toury, " 'The Jewish Question': A Semantic Approach," *Leo Baeck Institute Year Book*, XI, 1966, pp. 85–106. Though the connotations of the term have continued to evolve, and are less neutral in the English-speaking world at the end of the twentieth century than in the German-speaking world at the beginning of this century, I use this term for lack of a suitable, pithy alternative. My study of socialist views of the Jewish question concentrates on the attitudes of a handful of leading social democrats, all of whom were active in German-speaking socialist movements and all of whom would have included under the rubric of the Jewish question not only (or even primarily) their attitudes toward Judaism, but their attitudes toward the nature and future of Jewry, anti-Semitism, Zionism, the Jewish socialist and labor movements, and related matters. I, following the lead of my subjects, use the (problematic) term "the Jewish question" as a short-hand way of describing any or all of the above topics.

2. Edmund Silberner, "Was Marx an Anti-Semite?" *Historia Judaica*, XI, 1 (April 1949), p. 50. I have chosen not to discuss Marx's attitude toward the Jewish question in this book, primarily because the subject has been exhaustively and adequately dealt with by a large number of other

scholars in the years since Silberner's piece appeared. See the annotated bilbiography in Julius Carlebach, *Karl Marx and the Radical Critique of Judaism*, The Littman Library of Jewish Civilization (London, Henley, Boston: Routledge & Kegan Paul, 1978), pp. 438–49.

3. Ibid., pp. 51–52.

4. Edmund Silberner, "Anti-Semitism and Philo-Semitism in the Socialist International," *Judaism*, II (1953), p. 122.

5. Hans-Helmuth Knütter, *Die Juden und die deutsche Linke in der Weimarer Republik 1918–1933*, Bonner Schriften zur Politik und Zeitgeschichte, 4 (Düsseldorf: Droste Verlag, 1971), p. 222.

6. P. G. J. Pulzer, *The Rise of Political Anti-Semitism in Germany and Austria*, New Dimensions in History. Essays in Comparative History (New York, London, Sydney: John Wiley & Sons, Inc., 1964), p. 259.

7. Walter Mohrmann, *Antisemitismus. Ideologie und Geschichte im Kaiserreich und in der Weimarer Republik* (Berlin: VEB Deutscher Verlag der Wissenschaften, 1972), p. 63.

8. Shulamit Volkov, "The Immunization of Social Democracy against Anti-Semitism in Imperial Germany," *Juden und jüdische Aspekte in der deutschen Arbeiterbewegung 1848–1918. Internationales Symposium Dezember 1976*, ed. by Walter Grab. Jahrbuch des Instituts für Deutsche Geschichte, Beiheft II (Tel-Aviv: Universität Tel-Aviv, Fakultät für Geisteswissenschaften, Forschungszentrum für Geschichte, Institut für Deutsche Geschichte, 1977), pp. 63–81.

9. Robert S. Wistrich, *Socialism and the Jews: The Dilemmas of Assimilation in Germany and Austria-Hungary*, The Littman Library of Jewish Civilization (Rutherford, Madison, Teaneck, N.J.: Fairleigh Dickinson University Press; London and Toronto: Associated University Presses, 1982), p. 143.

## 1. Karl Kautsky

1. Edmund Silberner, "German Social Democracy and the Jewish Problem Prior to World War I," *Historia Judaica*, XV (1953), p. 41.

2. George L. Mosse, "German Socialists and the Jewish Question in the Weimar Republic," *Leo Baeck Institute Year Book*, XVI (1971), p. 124.

3. See the summary of comments made by Avineri in *Perspectives of German-Jewish History in the 19th and 20th Century* (Jerusalem: Leo Baeck Institute, Jerusalem Academic Press, 1971), p. 88. The Israeli scholar Yehuda Eloni has described the argument that Kautsky made in his famous article on the Kishinev massacre (which is discussed below) as "close to an ideological legitimization of pogroms" (Yehuda Eloni, "The Zionist Movement and the German Social Democratic Party, 1897–1918," *Studies in Zionism*, V, 2 [Autumn 1984], p. 194).

4. Karl Kautsky, *Erinnerungen und Erörterungen*, ed. by Benedikt Kautsky, Quellen und Untersuchungen zur Geschichte der deutschen und

österreichischen Arbeiterbewegung, III (The Hague: Mouton and Co., 1960), p. 105.

5. Ibid., pp. 567, 530.

6. Ibid., p. 546.

7. Ibid., p. 36

8. Ibid., p. 567.

9. Ibid., p. 179.

10. Ibid.

11. Ibid., p. 421.

12. Ibid., p. 422.

13. Ibid.

14. Benedikt Kautsky, ed., *Friedrich Engels' Briefwechsel mit Karl Kautsky* (henceforth: *FEBKK*), Quellen und Untersuchungen zur Geschichte der deutschen und österreichischen Arbeiterbewegung, I (Vienna: Danubia-Verlag, Universitätsbuchhandlung, 1955), pp. 4, 7.

15. Karl Marx to Jenny Longuet (April 11, 1881) in Karl Marx, Friedrich Engels, *Werke* (henceforth: *MEW*), XXXV (Berlin: Dietz Verlag, 1967), p. 178. I follow here the translation in Gary P. Steenson, *Karl Kautsky, 1854–1938: Marxism in the Classical Years* (Pittsburgh: University of Pittsburgh Press, 1978), p. 47.

16. Steenson, op. cit., p. 48.

17. Karl Kautsky, "Karl Kautsky," in *Die Volkswirtschaftslehre der Gegenwart in Selbstdarstellungen*, ed. by Felix Meiner (Leipzig: Verlag von Felix Meiner, 1924), pp. 126–27.

18. The friendship between Kautsky and Engels was strained by Kautsky's divorce from Louise Strasser. Engels thought Kautsky treated Strasser unfairly.

19. Kautsky, "Karl Kautsky," op. cit., p. 126.

20. Robert Wistrich, "Karl Marx, German Socialists and the Jewish Question, 1880–1914," *Soviet Jewish Affairs*, III, 1 (1973), pp. 92–93; Rosemarie Leuschen-Seppel, *Sozialdemokratie und Antisemitismus im Kaiserreich. Die Auseinandersetzungen der Partei mit den konservativen und völkischen Strömungen des antisemitismus 1871–1914*, Reihe: Politik- und Gesellschaftsgeschichte (Bonn: Verlag Neue Gesellschaft GmbH, 1978), pp. 81–86.

21. Paul Massing, *Rehearsal for Destruction: A Study of Political Anti-Semitism in Imperial Germany*, Studies in Prejudice (New York: Harper and Brothers, 1949), p. 158.

22. For a discussion of Engels's views on the Jewish question, see Jack Lester Jacobs, "Kautsky on the Jewish Question" (unpublished Ph.D. dissertation, Columbia University, 1983), pp. 14–52, and the sources cited therein.

23. "Oesterreich-Ungarn," *Der Sozialdemokrat*, 41 (October 5, 1882); cf. Werner Blumenberg, *Karl Kautskys literarisches Werk* (The Hague: Mouton and Co., 1960), no. 237.

24. "Oesterreich-Ungarn," op. cit.

25. "Aus Oesterreich," *Züricher Post*, 212 (September 11, 1883); cf. Blumenberg, op. cit., no. 304.

26. Quoted in Ludwig Brügel, *Geschichte der österreichischen Sozialdemokratie*, III (Vienna: Verlag der Wiener Volksbuchhandlung, 1922), p. 320.

27. Kautsky to Engels (June 23, 1884) in *FEBKK*, op. cit., p. 125.

28. Kautsky to Engels (December 22, 1884), in *FEBKK*, op. cit., p. 159; cf. Kautsky to Engels (November 26, 1888), in *FEBKK*, op. cit., p. 225.

29. C[arolus] Kautsky, "Der Antisemitismus," *Oesterreichischer Arbeiter-Kalender für das Jahr 1885*, p. 100.

30. Ibid., p. 101.

31. Ibid., pp. 102–3.

32. Ibid., p. 104.

33. S., "Das Judenthum," *Die Neue Zeit* (henceforth: *NZ*), VIII (1890), pp. 23–24.

34. Ibid., p. 25.

35. Ibid., p. 27.

36. K. K., Review of *Die Ungarischen Rumänen und die Ungarische Nation* and of *Die Rumänische Frage in Siebenbürgen und Ungarn*, *NZ*, XI, part 1 (1892–93), p. 831.

37. Ibid., p. 832.

38. Kautsky to Emma Adler (April 22, 1895) in Friedrich Adler, ed. *Victor Adler Briefwechsel mit August Bebel und Karl Kautsky sowie Briefe von und an Ignaz Auer, Eduard Bernstein, Adolf Braun, Heinrich Dietz, Friedrich Ebert, Wilhelm Liebknecht, Hermann Müller und Paul Singer* (henceforth: *VABABKK*) (Vienna: Verlag der Wiener Volksbuchhandlung, 1954), p. 175.

39. "Oesterreich-Ungarn," op. cit.

40. Harvey Goldberg, "Jean Jaurès and the Jewish Question: The Evolution of a Position," *Jewish Social Studies*, XX, 2 (April 1958), p. 68.

41. Charles Rappoport [Sharl Rapoport], "Dos lebn fun a revolutsionern emigrant," in *Di yidishe sotsialistishe bavegung biz der grindung fun "bund." forshungen, zikhroynes, materialn*, ed. by E. Tscherikower [Tsherikover], A. Menes, F. Kursky [Kurski], and A. Rosin (Ben-Adir) [Rozin], Historishe shriftn, III, Shriftn fun yidishn visnshaftlekhn institut, XI (Vilna, Paris: Historishe sektsie fun yivo, 1939) (henceforth: *Historishe shriftn*, III) p. 307.

42. Harvey Goldberg, *The Life of Jean Jaurès* (Madison: University of Wisconsin Press, 1968), p. 523.

43. James Joll, *The Second International, 1889–1914* (London and Boston: Routledge & Kegan Paul, 1974), p. 86; Massing, op. cit., p. 274; Silberner, "German Social Democracy and the Jewish Problem Prior to World War I," op. cit., pp. 16–21; Rappoport, loc. cit.

44. [Karl Kautsky], "Jaurès' Taktik und die deutsche Sozialdemokratie,"

*Vorwärts*, 172 (July 26, 1899), p. 3, col. 1; "Un Mot de Kautsky," *La Petite République*, 850 (July 24, 1899), p. 1, col. 5.

45. On Warszawski see J. P. Nettl, *Rosa Luxemburg*, I (London, New York, Toronto: Oxford University Press, 1966), p. 79.

46. The Kishinev massacre—one of the worst pogroms in the history of Russian Jewry—was sparked by the false accusation that Jews had killed a Russian (non-Jewish) boy. Acting with the consent and encouragement of Russian officials, unruly gangs murdered forty-five Jews and seriously wounded eighty-six others (Simon Dubnov, *History of the Jews*, V, trans. by Moishe Spiegel [South Brunswick, New York, and London: Thomas Yoseloff, 1973], pp. 716–19).

47. Warszawski to Kautsky (May 20, 1903), in Kautsky Nachlass, KD XXIII 63, International Institute of Social History (henceforth: IISH).

48. Karl Kautsky, "Das Massaker von Kischeneff und die Judenfrage," *NZ*, XXI, part 2 (1902–03), p. 303.

49. Ibid., p. 308. For an additional comment by Kautsky on the Kishinev pogrom, see Karl Kautsky, "Die Fortsetzung einer unmöglichen Diskussion," *NZ*, XXIII, part 2 (1904–05), p. 719.

50. Blumenberg, op. cit., no. 814. During this period Kautsky also endorsed several resolutions of the ISB condemning anti-Semitism (*International Socialist Review*, II [1901–02], p. 600; "The Kischiniff Massacres," *International Socialist Review*, IV [1903–04], p. 46; Kautsky Nachlass, KG 3, 145, IISH).

51. On July 13, 1914, Kautsky wrote to Adler that he had not yet proofread his work on Jewry (*VABABKK*, op. cit., p. 594).

52. Karl Kautsky, *Rasse und Judentum* (Stuttgart: J. H. W. Dietz, 1914), p. 28, as translated in id. *Are the Jews a Race?* (Westport, Conn.: Greenwood Press, 1972), p. 62.

53. *Are the Jews A Race?*, op. cit., p. 156.

54. Karl Kautsky, *Die Befreiung der Nationen* (Stuttgart: J. H. W. Dietz, 1917), p. 45.

55. Ibid. My thanks to John Kautsky for pointing out this passage to me.

56. On the history of Zionism see Walter Laqueur, *A History of Zionism* (New York: Holt, Rinehart and Winston, 1972).

57. "Das Ergebnis der Reichstagswahl," *Jüdische Rundschau*, 27 (July 3, 1903), pp. 26, ff., cited in Jehuda Eloni, "Die zionistische Bewegung in Deutschland und die SPD 1897–1918," in *Juden und jüdische Aspekte in der deutschen Arbeiterbewegung 1848–1918*, ed. by Walter Grab, op. cit., pp. 90–91.

58. I do not mean to suggest that Kautsky's position on Zionism was a reaction to attacks by Zionists on socialists, but merely to indicate that the mainstream Zionist movement was hostile to socialism. Long before he spoke out against Zionism, Kautsky had allowed anti-Zionist articles to be published in *Die Neue Zeit*. See, for example, S[amuel] Häcker, "Über den Zionismus," *NZ*, XIII, part 2 (1894–95) pp. 759–61; J[akob]

St[ern], Review of *Der Judenstaat*, NZ, XV, part 1 (1896–97), p. 186;
Johann Pollak, "Der politische Zionismus," *NZ*, XVI, part 1 (1897–98),
pp. 596–600.

59. Kautsky, "Das Massaker von Kischeneff und die Judenfrage," p. 308.

60. The article that provoked Chasanowitsch (1880?-1925) to seek out Kautsky
was probably B. Rosin, "Die zionistisch-sozialistische Utopie," *NZ*,
XXVII, part 1 (1908–09), pp. 29–34. B. Rosin was a pseudonym of Boris
Frumkin (Franz Kursky [Frants Kurski], *Gezamlte shriftn* [New York:
Farlag der vecker, 1952], p. 252). Cf. A. L., "Der Poalei-Zionismus; eine
neue Stroemung im russischen Judentum," *NZ*, XXIV, part 1 (1905–06),
pp. 804–13.

61. Kasrial [Leon Chasanowitsch], "Karl kautski un vurm iber der yuden-
frage," *Der yudisher arbeyter. tsentral-organ fun der yudisher sotsialistisher arbeyter-partey poyle-tsien in estreykh*, V, 47 (December 25,
1908), pp. 1–2. Cf. Leon Chasanowitsch [Kasrial] [Khazanovitch], "Vos
kautski veys vegen di yuden frage," *Varhayt*, IV, 1152 (January 13,
1909), p. 4, cols. 4–5.

62. Kautsky, *Are the Jews a Race?*, op. cit., p. 207.

63. Karl Kautsky, *Die materialistische Geschichtsauffassung* (Berlin: Verlag J. H. W. Dietz, 1927), vol. I, p. 690; vol. II, p. 169.

64. Karl Kautsky, "Die Aussichten des Zionismus," *Arbeiter-Zeitung*, 262
(September 22, 1929), p. 4.

65. Ibid.

66. Émile Vandervelde, "Karl Kautsky et le Sionisme," *La Dépêche* (November 2, 1929); *Comité Socialiste pour la Palestine Ouvrière. Bullettin*, 4 (November, 1929), pp. 10–11; *La Vie Socialiste*, VII, série nouvelle 168 (December 14, 1929), pp. 8–9; Camille Huysmans, "Sur le
Sionisme," *Comité Socialiste Pour la Palestine Ouvrière. Bullettin*, 4
(November 1929), pp. 9–10; "A propos de sionisme," *La Vie Socialiste*,
VII, série nouvelle 168 (December 14, 1929), p. 7; Eduard Bernstein,
"Die Aussichten des Zionismus. Eine Antwort an Karl Kautsky," *Vor-
wärts*, 575, 46 Jahrgang, 2. Beilage (December 8, 1929), cf. *Zwei sozial-
istische Antworten auf Karl Kautsky's Artikel "Die Aussichten des
Zionismus*," Bernstein Nachlass, B 10, IISH. For a response to Kautsky's
piece on the prospects of Zionism from the perspective of the Austrian
Poalei-Zion (the Social Democratic Poalei-Zion of Austria, a successor
of the Jewish Socialist Workers' Party Poalei-Zion in Austria), see Karl
Liebstein, "Karl Kautsky zu den Unruhen in Palästina," *Der Jüdische
Arbeiter. Organ der sozialdemokratischen Poale Zion Österreichs*, VI,
11 (November 8, 1929), p. 1.

67. "Je suis tout d'accord avec vous dans les sympathies pour les Sionistes,
particulierement les Socialistes parmi eux." Kautsky to É. Vandervelde
(November 21, 1929), in É. Vandervelde Institute (Brussels) EV/1077/B.

68. Ibid.

69. Karl Kautsky, "Nochmals der Zionismus. Eine Antwort an Eduard Bernstein," *Vorwärts*, XLVI, 586 (December 15, 1929), 2. Beilage, p. 1.

70. Ibid.

71. Ibid.

72. Ibid.

73. Mosse, "German Socialists and the Jewish Question in the Weimar Republic," op. cit., p. 127.

74. Locker to Kautsky, in Kautsky Nachlass, KD XVI, 29, IISH; Jarblum to Kautsky, in Kautsky Nachlass, KD XIII, 375, IISH; Ben-Gurion to Kautsky, in Kautsky Nachlass, KD IV, 128, IISH.

75. Kautsky apparently was open to the possibility of cooperating with a proposed socialist press clearinghouse that was suggested by Chasanowitsch during the Weimar years. Chasanowitsch's idea was that internationally prominent socialist writers would be more willing to write for the socialist press in languages that they could not read if they could be assured that their articles would not appear merely in one or two obscure publications, but in many publications around the world. He therefore proposed that an office be established that would solicit articles from socialists and arrange for their publication abroad. A meeting was held at Kautsky's home that was attended by Bernstein, Stroebel, Breitscheid, and Chasanowitsch, and a secretariat authorized to begin work (made up of Stroebel, Breitscheid, Breitscheid's wife, and Chasanowitsch) was selected at this meeting. Chasanowitsch hoped that if this effort got off the ground, he could obtain exclusive rights to reprint articles in Yiddish for the Labor Zionist press (Leon Chasanowitsch to Zentralkomitee der Poale Zion, n.d., Chazanovitsch File, 104 IV 3, Archives and Museum of the Jewish Labor Movement, Institute of Labour Research in Memory of P. Lavon, [Tel Aviv]). Kautsky's willingness to participate in this effort, however, in no way suggests sympathy with labor Zionist ideas.

76. R[aphael R.] Abramovitch [Rafail Abramovich Rein], "Doyres sotsialistn hobn gelernt sotsializm fun zayne verk," *Forverts* (January 30, 1949), section 2, p. 4, cols. 1–8.

77. Ibid.

78. Henry J. Tobias, *The Jewish Bund in Russia: From its Origins to 1905* (Stanford, Calif.: Stanford University Press, 1972), pp. 88, 93–94.

79. Karl Kautsky [Kautski], "Di bedeytung fun des komunistishen manifest," in *Dos manifest fun di komunistishe partey (mit a forvort fun karl kautski* by Karl Marx and Friedrich Engels (Bund: 1899), pp. 15–24.

80. Karl Kautsky [Kautski], "Der paria unter di proletarier," *Di arbeyter shtimme*, V, 25 (October 1901), p. 5.

81. Ibid.

82. *Vestnik Bunda*, 5 (November 1904), pp. 27–28, quoted in J[acob] S.

Hertz, [I. Sh. Herts], "Di ershte ruslander revolutsie," in *Di geshikhte fun bund*, II, ed. by G. Aronson, S. Dubnow-Erlich [Dubnov-erlikh], J. S. Hertz [I. Sh. Herts], E. Nowogrudski [Novogrudski], Kh. Sh. Kazdan, E. Scherer [Sherer] (New York: Farlag unzer tsayt, 1962), p. 128. His sympathies for the Bund notwithstanding, Kautsky felt obliged to vote against the Bund at this time. The statutes of the Socialist International accorded each delegation two votes at congresses of the International. The Russian delegation, however, was split three ways. There were representatives of the RSDRP, of the PSR, and of the Bund. The RSDRP and the PSR representatives each claimed one of the two Russian votes. The Bund therefore decided to ask for a third Russian vote, and, later, when this proved to be an impossible request given the statutes of the International, it claimed the seat that had also been claimed by the PSR. It was this dispute that was adjudicated by the ISB. Kautsky voted with the majority of the ISB in favor of the PSR representatives, explaining his position by noting that though he was politically closer to the Bund than to the PSR, "I do not have the right to vote according to sympathies or antipathies. I must vote in accord with" the rules of the International. (Hertz, op. cit., pp. 126–28; Vladimir Medem, *The Life and Soul of a Legendary Jewish Socialist*, ed. by Samuel A. Portnoy [New York: KTAV Publishing House, 1979], pp. 324–27).

In a letter dated October 26, 1904, Vladimir Kossovsky, writing on behalf of the foreign committee of the Bund, requested more information from Kautsky about his position regarding the Bund's voting rights. The underground Russian press claimed that the ISB voted against the Bund because the ISB did not want to support the purportedly nationalistic tendencies of the Bund. Kossovsky therefore asked Kautsky whether this was in fact the case, how Kautsky had voted, and also asked him to inform the Bund as to the basis of his vote (Kossowski [Kossovsky] to Kautsky [October 26, 1904], in Kautsky Nachlass KD XIV 274 IISH). The statements by Kautsky published in *Vestnik Bunda* in November 1904 were almost certainly made in response to Kossovsky's letter. For additional details on the charges and countercharges made by the Bund and the RSDRP in the period immediately following the Amsterdam congress, see the letter by Th. Gourvitch [Theodore Dan] to Karl Kautsky dated September 29, 1904 (*Fyodor Ilich Dan pis'ma [1899–1946].* Selected, annotated, and with an outline of Dan's political biography by Boris Sapir. Russian Series on Social History, III [Amsterdam: Stichting Internationaal Instituut voor Sociale Geschiedenis, 1985], p. 111). My attempts to gain access to items 1138 and 1148, listed in B. P. Birman, G. I. Kramol'nikov, and L. Sennikovski, eds., *Sotsial-demokraticheskie listovski 1894–1917 gg bibliograficheskii ukazatel'*, I. (N.p.: Gosydarstvennoe sotsialno-ekonomicheskoye izdatel'stvo, 1931), pp. 222, 224, which contain additional information on Kautsky's position regarding the request of the Bund for a vote at the Amsterdam congress, have been unsuccessful.

83. "Brif tsum 7tn tsuzamenfor fun 'bund,' " *Folkstsaytung*, 159 (September 13–26, 1906). Kautsky was invited to attend this congress by Kursky, writing on behalf of the central committee of the Bund (Kursky to Kautsky [August 29, 1906], in Kautsky Nachlass, KD XIV 354, IISH).

84. "Brif fun k. kautski," *Tsayt*, 21 (May 1914), p. 2. This message from Kautsky was solicited by the foreign committee of the Bund (Kautsky Nachlass, KD II, 140, IISH).

85. B. Rosin, "Die zionistisch-sozialistische Utopie," loc. cit.

86. M. [Nachimson], Review of *Die Judenpogrome in Russland*, NZ, part 2, XXVIII (1909–10), pp. 90–91; M. N[achimson], review of *Die Nationalitätenprobleme der Gegenwart*, NZ, XXVIII, part 2 (1909–1910), pp. 646–47.

87. W[ladimir] Medem [Vladimir Medem], "Ein nationalistischer Vorschlag," NZ, XXVIII, part 2 (1909–10), pp. 748–51; W[ladimir] Medem [Vladimir Medem], "Der moderne Antisemitismus in Russland," NZ, XXIX, part 1 (1910–11), pp. 259–63.

88. L[ippe] Rosenmann, "Ostjudenfrage, Zionismus und Grenzschluss," NZ, XXXIV, part 2 (1915–16), pp. 305–9 (cf. Rosenmann to Kautsky [February 11, 1916], in Kautsky Nachlass, KD XIX 560, IISH).

89. Jak. Pistiner, "Die Juden im Weltkriege," NZ, XXXIV, part 2 (1916), pp. 449–54.

90. W[ladimir] Kossowski [Vladimir Kossovsky], "Die Aussichten der russischen Revolution," NZ, XXVI, part 1 (1907–08), pp. 916–22. According to Kursky, op. cit., p. 305, a young woman active in the Bund named Shenberg also wrote for *Die Neue Zeit*. I have been unable locate this article. Cf. "Der Allgemeine jüdische Arbeiterbund in Litauen, Polen und Russland," NZ, XXII, part 2 (1903–04), pp. 536–40, and the series of articles signed "A. L." ("Der Poalei-Zionismus. Eine neue Strömung im russischen Judentum," NZ, XXIV, part 1 [1905–06], pp. 804–13; "Die prinzipielle Stellung des 'Jüdischen Arbeiterbundes,' " NZ, XXIV, part 2 [1906], pp. 702–5; "Der Jüdische Arbeiterbund," NZ, XXVI, part 1 [1907–08], p. 144; "Der siebente Parteitag des Jüdischen Arbeiterbundes," trans. by A. L. NZ, XXV, part 1 [1906–07], pp. 100–105).

The General Register of *Die Neue Zeit* identifies A. L. as A. Lampert. However, Lampert is almost certainly a pseudonym. Yago-Jung has hypothesized that A. L. was actually A. Litvak (Ilsa Yago-Jung, "Die nationale Frage in der jüdischen Arbeiterbewegung in Russland, Polen und Palästina bis 1929" (unpublished dissertation, Johann Wolfgang Goethe Universität zu Frankfurt am Main, 1976, p. 391). This hypothesis is given further credence by a comparison of the pamphlet signed A. H. entitled *Di sotsialistishe fraktsies in tsienizm* and published by Farlag "di velt" in Warsaw in 1906 with the article by "A. L." on "Der

Poalei-Zionismus" cited above. An authoritative source, Grigori [Gregor] Aronson, "Shimen klevanski," *Doyres bundistn*, ed. by J[acob] S. Hertz [I. Sh. Herts] I [New York: Farlag unzer tsayt, 1956], p. 311) has hazarded the guess that Litvak was involved in putting together the pamphlet.

91. When confronted by a labor Zionist leader who wanted to publish a piece in *Die Neue Zeit*, Kautsky argued that the readers of his journal had little interest in the Jewish question, and that articles by labor Zionists were better suited for the socialist press of Poland and Russia than they were for the Western press (Kasrial [Leon Chasanowitsch], "Karl kautski un vurm iber der yuden-frage," op. cit.). Though Kautsky grudgingly agreed to consider an article written from a Labor Zionist perspective, no such article ever appeared in *Die Neue Zeit*.

92. Maxim Anin [Maks-Aryeh Z. Shats], "Ist die Assimilation der Juden möglich?" *Sozialistische Monatshefte* (Henceforth: *SM*) XII (1908), part 2, pp. 614–19; idem, "Probleme des jüdischen Arbeiterlebens," *SM*, XIII (1909), part 1, pp. 231–35; idem, "Die Judenfrage als Wanderungsproblem," *SM*, XIII (1909), part 2, pp. 849–54; idem, "Das Nationalitätsprinzip in der sozialistischen Internationale," *SM*, XIV (1910), part 2, pp. 885–90; idem, "Das jüdische Proletariat in der Internationale," *SM*, XIV (1910), part 2, pp. 1065–68; idem, "Was will die jüdische Sektion in der sozialistischen Internationale?" *SM*, XV (1911), part 1, pp. 396–401; Leon Chasanowitsch, "Ziele und Mittel des sozialistischen Zionismus," *SM*, XX (1914), part 2, pp. 962–73; Markus Ratner, "Die nationale Frage in den jüdischen sozialistischen Parteien," *SM*, XII (1908), part 3, pp. 1533–41; idem, "Nationalitätsbegriff und nationale Autonomie," *SM*, XIV (1910), part 1, pp. 345–54; idem, "Die nationale Autonomie und das jüdische Proletariat," *SM*, XV (1911), part 3, pp. 1333–42.

93. "Die Dumawahlen," *NZ*, XXXI (1912–13), part 1, pp. 843–44, cf. W. Kossowski [Kossovsky] to Kautsky (January 21, 1913), in Kautsky Nachlass, KD XIV, 275, IISH.

94. Kautsky to Zetterbaum (October 30, 1893), in Kautsky Family Archive, Portfolio 8, Folder 5, IISH.

95. K. Kautsky [Kautski], "Di oyfgabn fun dem yidishn proletariat in england. a bagrisung artikl tsu di 'naye tsayt,' " *Di naye tsayt* (April 1, 1904), p. 5, cols. 1–3. This article was reprinted under the title "Kautsky on the Problems of the Jewish Proletariat in England" in *Justice, the organ of the Social Democracy*, XXI, 1058 (April 23, 1904), p. 4, and under the title "Karl Kautsky über Judentum und jüdisches Proletariat" in *Die Welt*, 50 (December 15, 1905), pp. 4–5. It also appeared in a Russian language organ of the Bund, *Vestnik Bunda*, 3 (June 1904), pp. 20–21.

Kautsky wrote this article for *Di naye tsayt* at the request of Theodore Rothstein, who was already known to Kautsky as a contributor to *Die Neue Zeit*. (Rothstein to Kautsky [March 10, 1904], in Kautsky Nachlass KD XIX, 585, IISH). It was Rothstein who gave the Bund permission to reprint Kautsky's article (Rothstein to Kautsky [April 7, 1904], in Kautsky Nachlass, KD XIX 586, IISH).

96. Karl Kautsky, "Amerikanische und europäische Arbeiter," *Arbeiter-Zeitung*, 265 (September 23, 1928), p. 3. Cf. Kautsky Nachlass KA 149, IISH; B. C. Vladeck to Luise Kautsky (November 28, 1928), in Kautsky Nachlass, KD XXII, 435, IISH; M. Feinstone to Karl Kautsky (May 21, 1928), in Kautsky Nachlass, KD X, 332, IISH.

97. Karl Kautsky [Kautski], "Di oyfgabn fun di yidishe sotsialistn in amerika," *Forverts* (April 23, 1922), section 2, p. 6, cols. 1–8; cf. A. Cahan to Kautsky (January 10, 1922), (March 16, 1922), in Kautsky Nachlass, KD VII, 1 and 2, IISH; Karl Kautsky [Kautski], "Bagrisungen tsum 'forverts,' fun karl kautski," *Forverts* (April 24, 1927), section 4, p. 1, cols. 6–8; cf. letter from Luise Kautsky to Baruch Charney Vladeck (February 10, 1927), Vladeck Papers, Tamiment Library: "My husband had a letter of [sic] Comrade Cahan asking him to write a short article for the jubilee number of 'Forward.' Though Karl is deeply immersed in his big theoretical work on historic materialism, yet he will send something to the 'Forward' one of the next days. He feels that for 'his Jews' he must make an exception."; "Teyere verter tsu unzer yontef fun unzer libn lerer karl kautski," *Forverts* (April 25, 1937), section 2, p. 1, cols. 1–8. The original German language manuscript version of Kautsky's greeting to the *Forverts* on the occasion of the paper's fortieth anniversary has been preserved. See "Zum 40. jährigen Bestehen des 'Jewish Daily Forward,' " in Kautsky Nachlass KA 219, IISH; cf. A. Cahan to Kautsky (March 29, 1937), in Kautsky Nachlass, KD VII, 15, IISH.

98. Kautsky, Karl [Kautski], "A bagrisung tsum 'veker' fun karl kautski," *Der veker* (October 30, 1926), p. 14.

99. Kautsky [Kautski], "Di oyfgabn fun dem yidishn proletariat in england," loc. cit.

100. Kautsky, "Amerikanische und europäische Arbeiter," loc. cit.

101. Kautsky did not believe that the Jewish workers of the Soviet Union also had a unique role. These workers, he wrote in 1923, certainly had a particular interest, both as proletarians and as Jews, in equal rights and in protection for national minorities. "[T]he Jewish proletariat does not have a class interest separate from that of other proletarians," however, and thus does not have a distinct role to play in the Soviet Union (K. Kautsky [Kautski], "Di oyfgabn funm yidishn proletariat in sovet-rusland," *Dos fraye vort*, I, 4 [June 20, 1923], p. 1). This article is unusual in that Kautsky wrote it for a Jewish periodical that (unlike *Di arbeyter shtimme*, *Di naye tsayt*, *Tsayt*, *Forverts*, *Der veker*, and *Tsukunft*) was not explicitly social democratic. *Dos fraye vort* was close to the social revolutionary tradition and was, in general, unable

to attract Bundist and Menshevik contributors. Its editor, Ben-Adir (Avrom Rozin), who had been prominently associated with Vozrozhdeniye, SERP, and the Faraynikte, visited Kautsky and convinced himself that Kautsky's socialism had the same ethical foundation as did his own (Gregor [Grigori] Aronson, *Rusish-yidishe inteligents* [Buenos-Aires: Farlag "yidbukh" bay der "gezelshaft der yidish-veltlekhe shuln in argentina," 1962], p. 222). My thanks to Hillel Kempinski for pointing out this passage to me.

Kautsky may also have had contact with another Jewish periodical that was not explicitly social democratic. An undated note from Kautsky to the left socialist revolutionary and territorialist Shteinberg (in the Shteinberg Collection, File 279, YIVO Institute for Jewish Research, New York [henceforth: YIVO]) indicates that Kautsky had agreed to write an article for a periodical with which Shteinberg was associated. The periodical is unnamed. However, Shteinberg was editor of *Fraye shriftn—farn yidishn sotsialistishn gedank* from 1926 to 1937.

102. John Mill [Yoysef Shloyme Mil], *Pionern un boyer,* II (New York: Farlag der veker, 1949), pp. 135–36.

103. Luise Kautsky expressed Karl's thanks to A. Cahan of the *Forverts* in the following terms: "It is of the greatest value to him that the Forward is one of the rare mouth-pieces from where he is able to influence the brains and the minds of so many thousands of readers. You can easily imagine how sad it is for such an old writer and fighter to see himself bereft at the end of his days of nearly every tribune wherefrom to speak to his public" (Luise Kautsky to A. Cahan [November 26, 1934] in A. Cahan Collection, YIVO).

104. Martov to Kautsky (January 28, 1920), in Nicolaevsky Collection, 17, Box 1, Hoover Institution on War, Revolution and Peace, Stanford University, California.

105. Ibid.

106. Ibid.

107. Cahan to Kautsky (December 12, 1931), in Kautsky Nachlass, KD VII, 7, IISH.

108. Ibid.

109. Ibid.

110. Karl Kautsky [Kautski], "Fun a rumfuler fargangenhayt tsu a herlekher tsukunft," *Naye folkstsaytung* (November 10, 1937), p. 10. Cf. the letters from the central committee of the Bund to Kautsky, dated October 12, October 22, and December 29, 1937 (Kautsky Nachlass, KD VI, 740, 741, 742, IISH).

111. Kautsky, "Der Antisemitismus," op. cit., p. 100. Emphasis added.

112. S., "Das Judenthum," op. cit., pp. 25, 27.

113. "Brif tsum 7tn tsuzamenfor fun 'bund,' " op. cit.

114. Ibid.
115. Karl Kautsky, "Die Nationalitätenfrage in Russland," *Leipziger Volkszeitung*, 4 Beilage z. Nr. 98 (April 29, 1905).
116. Ibid.
117. I have been unable to determine whether or not Kautsky also supported the program of the Bund's sister party in Austria-Hungary, the ŽPSD. He certainly knew of the existence of such a party (R. Hilferding to Kautsky [May 27, 1905], in Kautsky Nachlass, KD XII, 590, IISH) but never wrote about it.
118. Kautsky, *Are the Jews a Race?*, op. cit., p. 243.
119. Shlomo Avineri, "Marx and Jewish Emancipation," *Journal of the History of Ideas*, 25(3) (1964), pp. 445–50.
120. Karl Kautsky, "Karl Kautsky," in *Die Volkswirtschaftslehre der Gegenwart in Selbstdarstellungen*, ed. by Felix Meiner (Leipzig: Verlag von Felix Meiner, 1924), p. 117; Kautsky, *Erinnerungen und Erörterungen*, op. cit., p. 557, 547. Kautsky's Czech roots are discussed in Frant. Soukup, "Karlu Kautskému," *Právo lidu* XXIII, 241 (October 12, 1924), pp. 11–12; idem "Karlu Kautskému," in Karl Kautsky, *Historické dílo Karle Marxe* (Prague, 1933); Jaroslav Vozka, *Karel Kautský. Učitel československého proletariátu. 1854–1934* (Prague: Ústřední Dělnické Knihkupectví a Nakladatelství, 1934); Zdeněk Šolle, "Vzpomínka Karla Kauského na Břevnovský sjezd Českoslovanské Sociální Demokracie," *Československý Časopis Historický*, XIII, 2 (1965), pp. 269–79. My thanks to Michaela Harnick, Alena Ptak-Danchak, and Peter Kussi for aid in translating these sources.
121. Kautsky, *Erinnerungen und Erörterungen*, op. cit., p. 161.
122. Kautsky, "Karl Kautsky," op. cit., p. 118.
123. Kautsky, *Erinnerungen und Erörterungen*, op. cit., p. 206.
124. Ibid., p. 207.
125. "Die nationale Frage," *Der Volksstaat*, VII, 26 (March 5, 1875), p. 1; VII, 28 (March 10, 1875), p. 1; VII, 29 (March 12, 1875), p. 1.
126. Kautsky, *Erinnerungen und Erörterungen*, op. cit., p. 209.
127. Kautsky to Adler (November 12, 1896) in *VABABKK*, op. cit. , p. 221.
128. Kautsky believed that the articles in *Revolution and Counter-Revolution in Germany* had been written by Marx. They had actually been written by Engels under Marx's name. The attitudes of Marx and Engels toward the Slavs is discussed in Hermann Wendel, "Marxism and the Southern Slav Question," *The Slavonic Review*, II (December 1923), pp. 289–307; Roman Rosdolsky, "Friedrich Engels und das Problem der 'geschichtslosen' Völker (Die Nationalitätenfrage in der Revolution 1848–1849 im Lichte der 'Neuen Rheinischen Zeitung.')," *Archiv für Sozialgeschicht*, IV (1964), pp. 87–282; H. Malcolm Macdonald, "Karl Marx, Friedrich Engels, and the South Slavic Problem in 1848–49," *University of Toronto Quarterly*, VIII (July 1939), pp. 452–60;

William George Vettes, "The German Social Democrats and the Eastern Question 1848–1900," *The American Slavic and East European Review*, XVII, 1 (February 1958), pp. 86–100.

129. Kautsky, "Vorrede des Uebersetzers," *Revolution und Kontre-Revolution in Deutschland* by Karl Marx (Stuttgart: Dietz, 1896), p. XXI.

130. Ibid., p. XXIX, cf. Kautsky to Hugo Heller (April 23, 1896), in *VABABKK*, op. cit., p. 206.

131. Kautsky, "Vorrede des Uebersetzers," op. cit., p. XXX.

132. Adler to Kautsky (July 21, 1897) in *VABABKK*, op. cit., p. 233.

133. Kautsky to Adler (August 5, 1897) in *VABABKK*, op. cit., p. 236.

134. Karl Kautsky, "Der Kampf der Nationalitäten und das Staatsrecht in Oesterreich," *NZ*, part 1, XVI (1897–98), pp. 516–24, 557–64.

135. Arthur G. Kogan, "The Social Democrats and the Conflict of Nationalities in the Habsburg Monarchy," *The Journal of Modern History*, XXI, 3 (September 1949), pp. 206–7; Edmund Silberner, "Austrian Social Democracy and the Jewish Problem," *Historia Judaica*, XIII, part 2 (October 1951), p. 124.

136. Kogan, op. cit., p. 210.

137. Kautsky to Modráček (October 22, 1899) in Zdeněk Šolle, "Die Sozialdemokratie in der Habsburger Monarchie und die tschechische Frage," *Archiv für Sozialgeschichte*, VI/VII (1966–67), p. 383. Modráček, editor of the Czech socialist review *Akademie*, had written a letter to Kautsky in which he had criticized the national program of the Austrian party (Kautsky Nachlass, KD XVII 570, IISH). Kautsky's comments to Modráček on the Brünn Resolution were made in response to Modráček's criticisms and were published for the first time in 1900 ("K narodnostní otázce," *Revue socialistická—Akademie*, IV [1900], pp. 33–35; Šolle, op. cit., pp. 369–70).

138. "Socialism and Internationalism," *The Social-Democrat*, IX (1905), p. 541.

139. K. Kautsky, "Das Böhmische Staatsrecht und die Sozialdemokratie," *NZ*, XVII, part 1 (1899), p. 295, 301.

140. "Die Krise in der tschechischen Sozialdemokratie," *Oesterreichischer Metallarbeiter*, XX, 15 (April 14, 1910), p. 1. The Czech socialists had also attempted to use Kautsky's authority in 1896. At that time Kautsky had written an article in which he had discussed the movement for the creation of a Polish state in sympathetic terms ("Finis Poloniae?" *NZ*, XIV, part 2 [1895–96], pp. 484–91; 513–25). The Czech socialists altered a portion of Kautsky's article and reprinted it in their party organ under the title "Czech Sovereignty and Social Democracy." The Czechs completely distorted Kautsky's intent by replacing the words *Poland*, and *Polish* with the words *Bohemia* and *Czech* at various points in Kautsky's article (K. K, "Samostatnost ceská a so-

ciální demokracie," *Sociální Demokrat*, VI, 18, 19 [August 7, August 21, 1896]). This incident is discussed by Šolle, op. cit., pp. 358–59.

141. Kautsky to Beer (January 5, 1909), in "Die Krise in der tschechischen Sozialdemokratie," op. cit.

142. Ibid.

143. K. Kautsky, "Eine Frage," *Der Kampf*, IV, 11 (August 1, 1911), p. 485.

144. K. Kautsky, "Separatismus, Nationalismus und Sozialismus," *NZ*, XXX, part 1 (1911–12), p. 523.

145. Among the most influential critiques of Kautsky's ideas are those of Karl Korsch, "Die materialistische Geschichtsauffassung: Eine Auseinandersetzung mit Karl Kautsky," *Archiv für die Geschichte des Sozialismus und der Arbeiterbewegung*, IV, 2 (1929), pp. 179–279, and Erich Matthias, "Kautsky und der Kautskyanismus," Marxismus-studien, II (1957), pp. 151–97. The bibliographies in Gary P. Steenson, *Karl Kautsky, 1854–1938: Marxism in the Classical Years* (Pittsburgh: University of Pittsburgh Press, 1978), pp. 291–301, and in Reinhold Hünlich, *Karl Kautsky und der Marxismus der II. Internationale*, Schriftenreihe für Sozialgeschichte und Arbeiterbewegung, XXII (Marburg: Verlag Arbeiterbewegung und Gesellschaftswissenschaft GmbH, 1981), pp. 331–36, list most of the major works on Kautsky. Works not listed by Steenson or Hünlich include Dick Geary, *Karl Kautsky* (New York: St. Martin's Press, 1987); Ingrid Gilcher-Holtey, *Das Mandat der Intellektuellen. Karl Kautsky und die Sozialdemokratie* (Berlin: Siedler Verlag, 1986), and Massimo Salvadori, *Karl Kautsky and the Socialist Revolution 1880–1938*, translated by Jon Rothschild (London: NLB, 1979).

146. In addition to German and Czech ancestors, Kautsky also had ancestors of Italian and Polish origin and ancestors who had lived in Hungary (Kautsky, "Karl Kautsky," op. cit., p. 117).

147. There is virtually no published biographical information available on Kautsky's first wife, Louise Strasser. Kautsky's second wife, Luise Ronsperger, formally left the Jewish community in the spring of 1890, shortly before her marriage to Kautsky (Kautsky Family Archive, 1952, IISH. My thanks to Leo J. van Rossum for providing me with this citation). "In Vienna, a Jew could not marry a non-Jew without prior conversion of the Jewish or the non-Jewish partner. Thus intermarriage was a much more radical step than elsewhere in Central or Western Europe or in America. . . . For a mixed couple to marry, one of the partners had to convert either to the religion of the other or to the neutral category, *konfessionslos*, 'without religious affiliation.' This legal impediment minimized the numbers of Jews and gentiles who married each other." (Marsha L. Rozenblit, *The Jews of Vienna, 1867–1914: Assimilation and Identity*. SUNY Series in Modern Jewish History [Albany: State University of New York Press, 1983], p. 128).

Nevertheless, though certainly not religiously observant, Luise Ronsperger considered herself to be a Jew throughout her life. She did not maintain particularly close ties with the Ronsperger family after she married Kautsky, but all of her closest friends were of Jewish origin. In the late 1930s, Luise was very involved with other Jewish refugees living, as she did, in the Netherlands (Ilse Kautsky Calabi to Jack Jacobs [August 31, 1981]). She was deported to Auschwitz in August 1944 and died there in December of that year ("Tod einer Emigrantin —wie die Witwe Karl Kautskys starb," in *Sie flohen vor dem Hakenkreuz*, ed. by Walter Zadek [Reinbek bei Hamburg: Rowohlt Taschenbuch Verlag GmbH, 1981], pp. 117–18).

148. John Kautsky to Jack Jacobs (December 1, 1981). In this same letter John Kautsky discusses the extent to which Karl's sons identified themselves as Jewish and noted that "obviously they detested anti-Semitism and hated and feared the Nazis and they 'identified' with German Jewry, in the sense of complete sympathy, in the Nazi period. But I'm not 100% sure that they would have 'identified' themselves as Jewish—or as non-Jewish, for that matter. They were totally divorced from Jewish religion and largely from Jewish culture (e.g. they had no knowledge of Jewish customs or holidays). . . . Jewishness was simply not an issue in the Kautsky family."

149. Erich Matthias and Susanne Miller, ed. *Das Kriegstagebuch des Reichstagsabgeordneten Eduard David 1914 bis 1918*, Quellen zur Geschichte des Parlamentarismus und der politischen Parteien, erste Reihe: Von der konstitutionellen Monarchie zur parlamentarischen Republik, IV (Düsseldorf: Droste Verlag, 1966), p. 136.

150. Werner Mosse, ed. *Deutsches Judentum in Krieg und Revolution 1916–1923*, Schriftenreihe Wissenschaftlicher Abhandlungen des Leo Baeck Instituts, XXV (Tübingen: J. C. B. Mohr [Paul Siebeck], 1971), p. 30, 217; Karl Paumgartten, *Judentum und Sozialdemokratie* (Graz: Heimatverlag Leopold Stocker, n.d.), p. 30; Donald Niewyk, *Socialist, Anti-Semite, and Jew: German Social Democracy Confronts the Problem of Anti-Semitism, 1918–1933* (Baton Rouge: Louisiana State University Press, 1971), p. 84.

151. Kautsky, *Erinnerungen und Erörterungen*, op. cit., pp. 36–37.

152. Ibid., p. 36.

153. Karl Kautsky, *The Dictatorship of the Proletariat* (Ann Arbor: University of Michigan Press, 1971), p. 90.

154. K. Kautsky, "Zwischen Baden und Luxemburg," *NZ*, XXVIII, part 2 (1909–10), p. 667.

## 2. Eduard Bernstein

1. Zalman Shazar [Shneyer Zalman Rubashev], "Eduard bernshteyn," *Der tog-morgen zhurnal*, July 17, 1966, p. 3. On Gans see H. G. Reissner,

"Rebellious Dilemma: The Case Histories of Eduard Gans and Some of his Partisans," *Leo Baeck Institute Year Book*, II (1957), pp. 179–93.

2. Eduard Bernstein, *Von 1850 bis 1872. Kindheit und Jugendjahre* (Berlin: Erich Reiss Verlag, 1926), p. 4.

3. Eduard Bernstein, "Wie Ich als Jude in der Diaspora aufwuchs," *Der Jude*, II, 3 (June 1917), p. 187. Though undoubtedly written in German, this article was especially written for and first published in Yiddish by a labor Zionist periodical. Cf. "Vi ikh bin oyfgevaksn in goles als yid," *Der yidisher kempfer* (December 1, 1916), pp. 4, 6; (December 22, 1916), p. 4; (December 29, 1916), pp. 4, 5.

4. Bernstein, "Wie Ich als Jude in der Diaspora aufwuchs," op. cit., p. 189.

5. Ibid., pp. 187–89.

6. Bernstein, *Von 1850 bis 1872*, op. cit., p. 5; Eduard Bernstein, *Sozialdemokratische Lehrjahre* (Berlin: Der Bücherkreis GmbH, 1928), p. 12.

7. Aron Bernstein (1812–1884), born in Danzig, studied Talmud for a number of years before moving to Berlin, where he became a student of the humanities and of the natural sciences. He published numerous books on Jewish and non-Jewish themes, including the popular novels *Vögele der Magid* and *Mendel Gibbor*. His influence and prestige in the world at large, however, were based primarily on his position as editor in chief of Berlin's most popular liberal paper, the *Volkszeitung*. Aron's close ties to the reform community are symbolized by the fact that a poem by him was part of the service conducted by the reform congregation of Berlin (S. Wininger, *Große jüdische National-Biographie* [Cernăuți: Buchdruckerei "Arta," n.d.], pp. 350–51). Bernstein once asserted that Aron had "no noteworthy influence" on his intellectual development, both because Jakob's family lived quite far from Aron's (and thus saw relatively little of Aron), and because Eduard felt greatly reserved in his uncle's presence. "As a boy, if I visited him or he visited us, I avoided, in an almost fearful manner, attracting his attention. I never ventured to direct a substantive question to him, but only admired him from afar" (Eduard Bernstein, "Entwicklungsgang eines Sozialisten," in *Die Volkswirtschaftslehre der Gegenwart in Selbstdarstellungen*, ed. by Felix Meiner [Leipzig: Verlag von Felix Meiner, 1924], pp. 2–3). Aron, however, influenced Eduard despite these facts. When Eduard first entered the socialist movement, Aron was so widely known that Eduard first attained notice as the nephew of the great liberal editor (see, for example, Morris Winchevsky [Moris Vintshevski], *Gezamlte verk*, ed. by Kalman Marmor, X [New York: Farlag "frayhayt," 1927], p. 274; Bernstein, *Sozialdemokratische Lehrjahre*, op. cit., p. 7). Moreover, on at least one occasion, Eduard himself allegedly claimed that Aron had "exercised a tremendous influence in his life" ("Eduard Bernstein: On the Occasion of His Seventy-Fifth Birthday," *Jewish Telegraphic Agency. Daily News Bulletin*, VI, 8 [January 9, 1925], p. 3).

8. Ismar Schorsch, *Jewish Reactions to German Anti-Semitism, 1870–1914*.

Columbia University Studies in Jewish History, Culture, and Institutions, III (New York and London: Columbia University Press; Philadelphia: Jewish Publication Society of America, 1972), p. 6.

9. Bernstein, "Entwicklungsgang eines Sozialisten," op. cit., p. 2.

10. Bernstein, "Wie Ich als Jude in der Diaspora aufwuchs," op. cit., p. 191; Robert S. Wistrich, Revolutionary Jews from Marx to Trotsky (London: Harrap, 1976), p. 60.

11. Bernstein, "Entwicklungsgang eines Sozialisten," op. cit., p. 3.

12. Bernstein, "Wie Ich als Jude in der diaspora aufwuchs," op. cit., p. 187.

13. Ibid., p. 188.

14. Bernstein, Von 1850 bis 1872, op. cit., p. 41.

15. Bernstein, "Wie Ich als Jude in der Diaspora aufwuchs," op. cit., p. 191.

16. Bernstein, Von 1850 bis 1872, op. cit., pp. 41–42.

17. Shazar, loc. cit. In 1850 Jews were granted the right to vote, own land, and enter the professions by the King of Prussia. Nineteen years later, legal restrictions applying only to Jews were lifted throughout the North German Confederation. Finally, in 1871, all Jews living in the German Empire were granted full legal emancipation (Donald L. Niewyk, "German Social Democracy and the Problem of Anti-Semitism, 1906–1914," [unpublished M.A. thesis, Tulane University, 1964], pp. 5–6).

18. Eleonore Sterling, "Jewish Reactions to Jew-Hatred in the First Half of the Nineteenth Century," Leo Baeck Institute Year Book, III (1958), pp. 107–9.

19. Bernstein, "Wie Ich als Jude in der Diaspora aufwuchs," op. cit., p. 190.

20. Ibid., p. 194.

21. Bernstein, "Entwicklungsgang eines Sozialisten," op. cit., p. 10.

22. Ibid., p. 11. Bernstein apparently did attempt to discuss the question of anti-Semitism with Dühring on one occasion, only to find that Dühring denied having any prejudice against the Jews (Bernstein, Sozialdemokratische Lehrjahre, op. cit., p. 53). Wistrich mistakenly claims, "Bernstein only broke with Dühring in 1879, when the latter began systematically to attack the 'Jewish' press and the 'Judaized' Social Democracy" (Wistrich, Revolutionary Jews From Marx to Trotsky, op. cit., p. 62). In fact, Bernstein broke from Dühring before he arrived in Switzerland in October 1878 (Kautsky, Erinnerungen und Erörterungen, op. cit., p. 436).

23. Bernstein, "Entwicklungsgang eines Sozialisten," op. cit., p. 9. Cf. Eduard Bernstein, Die Geschichte der Berliner Arbeiter-Bewegung. Ein Kapitel zur Geschichte der deutschen Sozialdemokratie, I (Berlin: Buchhandlung Vorwärts, 1907), pp. 350–53.

24. Moses Aronson to Bernstein (August 12, 1928), unpublished letter in Bernstein Nachlass, D20, IISH. Aronson, born in Mohilev in 1854, received traditional rabbinical training. After having been influenced by Enlightenment ideas, however, he left the Russian Empire for Berlin,

where he became a student of medicine. He became acquainted with the other Russian Jewish students living in Berlin at that time, adopted the radical ideology popular among these students, and rapidly became a leading member of the Jewish Section. Aronson first met Bernstein in December 1874 and became sufficiently friendly with him to be introduced to Bernstein's family. Along with Gurevitch and Lieberman, Aronson was a defendant in the Nihilist trial of 1879. He served a brief prison term, emigrated to Switzerland (where he lived in the same villa as Bernstein and Kautsky), and later married Bernstein's sister, Martha. See ibid.; Kalman Marmor, ed., *Arn libermans briv* (New York: Yidisher visnshaftlekher institut—yivo, 1951), p. 192; Marius (Moses Aronson), "Erinnerungen aus meinem Leben," *Sonntagsblatt der N.Y. Volkszeitung* (August 16, 1908), Erste Beilage, p. 13; (August 23, 1908), Erste Beilage, p. 16; idem, "Erinnerungen und Gedanken zur Halbjahrhundert Feier der 'N.Y. Volkszeitung,' " *Sonntagsblatt der N.Y. Volkszeitung*, (January 29, 1928), section III, p. 8c; Herts Burgin, *Di geshikhte fun der yidisher arbeter bavegung in amerika, rusland un england* (New York: Fareynigte yidishe geverkshaftn, 1915), p. 25; G. Gurevitch, "Der protses fun a. lieberman, g. gurevitch un m. aronson in berlin," *Royter pinkes. tsu der geshikhte fun der yidisher arbeter-bavegung un sotsialistishe shtremungen bay yidn*, II (Warsaw: Farlag kultur-lige, 1924), pp. 107–11; idem, "Zikhroynes 1873–1880," in *Historishe shriftn*, III, op. cit., pp. 224, 237.

25. Bernstein, *Sozialdemokratische Lehrjahre*, op. cit., pp. 98–102.

26. Joel Efron, born into a well-to-do Russian Jewish family in Vilna, began to study in the University of Berlin in 1874. He was a member of the Jewish Section but was only in Berlin until 1876. At that time, he returned to the Russian Empire, where he was soon arrested for revolutionary activities. Efron later escaped abroad, lived, at various times, in Germany, Switzerland, and France, and eventually established a medical practice in the last of these three countries. See E. Tscherikower [Tsherikover], "Bamerkungen un derklerungen tsu di zikhroynes fun grigori gurevitch," *Historishe shriftn*, III, op. cit., p. 248; Ephim H. Jeshurin, "Vilner frayhayts kemfer," in Ephim H. Jeshurin, ed., *Vilna. a zamlbukh gevidmet der shtot vilna* (New York: Vilner brentsh 367 arbeter ring, 1935), p. 722; Marmor, op. cit., p. 56. Efron was introduced to Bernstein by Bernstein's cousin Hermann Lisso (Bernstein, *Sozialdemokratische Lehrjahre*, op. cit., p. 99), who, it appears, was a professional photographer and took a number of photographs of the members of the Jewish Section (Gurevitch, "Zikhroynes," op. cit., p. 238).

27. On "Grischa" (Grigori Gurevitch), see Bernstein, *Sozialdemokratische Lehrjahre*, op. cit., pp. 99–100.

28. Aron Sundelvitch (1852–1923) was born in Vilna into a large, poor family. He first came into contact with the revolutionary movement while in the Vilna Rabbinical Seminary, where he organized a small

revolutionary study group. When a police search in July 1875 uncovered some of the literature being used by this circle, Sundelvitch fled to Germany. He became active in arranging the transport of illegal literature from Western Europe to Russia and also engaged in organizing efforts among the German workers. In 1878 Sundelvitch became one of the most important activists in the newly organized Russian revolutionary organization Zemlia i Volia (Earth and Freedom), and, a year later, he became active in the terrorist group Narodnaia Volia (People's Will). He was captured by the Russian police, sentenced to lifelong exile in the eastern part of the empire, and remained in exile for a quarter of a century. Sundelvitch spent the period from 1907 to 1923 in England (D. Shub, "Arn sundelvitch," in Jeshurin, ed., *Vilna*, op. cit., pp. 96–126; Boris Sapir, "Jewish Socialists around 'Vpered,' " *International Review of Social History*, X [1965], p. 372).

29. Vladimir (Benyomin) Jochelson, born in 1855, was a native of Vilna. His family was religious and relatively well-off. While in the Vilna Rabbinical Seminary, he became a member of the revolutionary circle organized by Sundelvitch. When the circle was broken by the Czarist police, Jochelson fled to Berlin. He returned to Russia in 1876, where he acted as a courier for illegal literature and printing materials. In 1885, Jochelson was sentenced to ten years in Siberia. He used the period of his sentence to study ethnology and anthropology and later had a distinguished career in these fields. Jochelson came to the United States in 1922 and died in New York in the 1930s. See E. Tscherikower (Tsherikover), "Yidn-revolutsionern in rusland in di zekhtsiker un zibtsiker yorn," *Historishe shriftn*, III, pp. 156–57; Louis Greenberg, *The Jews in Russia. The Struggle for Emancipation*, I (New York: Schocken Books, 1976), p. 153.

30. Dr. Dimitri Alexandrovitch Klemenz (1848–1914) was a non-Jewish Russian revolutionary who arrived in Berlin toward the end of 1874 and who was close to the members of the Jewish Section. Klemenz was arrested in Germany in the summer of 1879. See Marmor, op. cit., pp. 77, 124; E. Tscherikower, (Tsherikover), "Bamerkungen un derklerungen tsu di zikhroynes fun grigori gurevitch," op. cit., p. 248; Abraham Ascher, *Pavel Axelrod and the Development of Menshevism* (Cambridge, Mass.: Harvard University Press, 1972), p. 27.

31. Leizer Zuckerman (1852–1887), born in Mohilev and active in the revolutionary movement in that city in the early 1870s, left the Russian Empire for Berlin in 1873, where he wrote poetry while working first in a soap factory and later in print shops. He was arrested in Russia in 1880 and was sentenced to exile in the east, where he committed suicide in 1887. See Leo Deich (Daytsh), "Leyzer tsukerman—der belibster yid in der revolutsie," *Tsukunft*, XXI (1916), pp. 240–45; G. Gurevitch, "Tsu der biografie fun l. tsukerman," *Royter pinkes*, II, op.

cit., pp. 112–18; N. Mayzil, "Leyzer tsukerman," *Royter pinkes*, op. cit., I (1921), pp. 92–112.

32. On Lieberman and his work, see Ber Borochov [Borokhov], "Arn liberman—der foter funem yidishn sotsializm un di ershte hebreish-sotsialistishe tsaytshrift 'haemes,' " *Shprakh-forshung un literatur-geshikhte* (Tel-Aviv: I. l. perets farlag, 1966), pp. 271–80; Leo Deich [Daytsh], "Der ershter yidish-sotsialistisher propagandist," *Tsukunft*, XXI (1916), pp. 677–81; S. L. Citron [Sh. L. Tsitron], *Dray literarishe doyres*, II (Vilna: Farlag sh. shreberk, 1921), pp. 3–49; E. Tscherikower [Tsherikover], "Der onhoyb fun der yidisher sotsialistisher bavegung," *Historishe shriftn*, I. Yidisher visnshaftlekher institut, historishe sektsie (Warsaw: Kooperativer farlag "kultur-lige," 1929), pp. 469–532; Boris Sapir, "Lieberman et le socialisme russe," *International Review for Social History*, III (1938), pp. 25–88; B. Weinryb, *Be-reshit ha-sotsyalizm ha yehudi* (Jerusalem: Rubin Mass, 1940); Zivion (Dr. B. Hoffman) [Tsivyon (Dr. b. hofman)], *Far fuftsik yor. geklibene shriftn* (New York: E. laub farlag ko., 1948), pp. 103–17; Kalman Marmor, ed., *Arn libermans briv* (New York: Yidisher visnshaftlekher institut—yivo, bibliotek fun yivo, 1951); William J. Fishman, *Jewish Radicals. From Czarist Stetl to London Ghetto* (New York: Pantheon, 1974), pp. 97–134; Jonathan Frankel, *Prophecy and Politics. Socialism, Nationalism and the Russian Jews, 1862–1917* (Cambridge: Cambridge University Press, 1981), pp. 28–47. Aronson's charge that Bernstein fails to mention either Leizer Zuckerman or Aron Lieberman is unfounded. Bernstein explicitly notes that Gurevitch was actively involved in the socialist commune Obschtschina, "which was created in the second half of the seventies of the last century by Russian socialists studying in Berlin under the leadership of the students Zuckermann and Liebermann" (Bernstein, *Sozialdemokratische Lehrjahre*, op. cit., p. 100). Bernstein also mentions that Gurevitch introduced him to some of the members of this commune (ibid.). Though it is likely that Bernstein was introduced to Lieberman, he apparently did not know him well. In his description of the Nihilist trial in *Die Geschichte der Berliner Arbeiter-Bewegung*, II, op. cit., p. 34, Bernstein mistakenly gives Lieberman's first name as Rudolf.

33. Aronson to Bernstein (August 12, 1928), op. cit.

34. The Jewish Section, also known as the Berlin Section, was an informally organized group made up largely of young Russian Jewish radicals active in smuggling illegal literature into the Russian Empire and in smuggling letters, reports, and comrades out of the Empire. See Sapir, "Jewish Socialists around 'Vpered,' " p. 369. Also see Lieberman to Smirnov (January 29, 1877) in Marmor, op. cit., p. 120; Marmor, op. cit., p. 35; Sapir, Lieberman et le socialisme russe," op. cit., pp. 51–52.

35. Gurevitch, "Zikroynes," op. cit., p. 234.

36. Kautsky, *Erinnerungen und Erörterungen*, op. cit., p. 440.
37. "Following the passing of Bismarck's anti-socialist laws," Wistrich claims, "Bernstein felt obliged to emigrate to Switzerland" (Wistrich, *Revolutionary Jews from Marx to Trotsky*, op. cit., p. 62). Bernstein left Germany for Lugano on October 12, 1878. The antisocialist law was passed on October 19. Though the law was already being debated when Bernstein left Germany, he emigrated not because of this legislation, but because he received a job offer from Höchberg.
38. F. Kursky [Kurski], "Di zhenever 'grupe sotsialistn-yidn' un ir oyfruf," *Historishe shriftn*, III, op. cit., p. 558; E. Tsch(erikower) [Tsherikover], "Nokh vegn der zhenever 'grupe sotsialistn-yidn,' " *Historishe shriftn*, III, op. cit., p. 565.
39. Bernstein, *Sozialdemokratische Lehrjahre*, op. cit., pp. 100–101.
40. In the 1880s Bernstein married Regina Zadek and Romm married Regina's sister July (Julka).
41. Eduard Bernstein, *Aus den Jahren meines Exils. Erinnerungen eines Sozialisten* (Berlin: Erich Reiss Verlag, 1918), p. 122. On Axelrod, see Abraham Ascher, op. cit.; Leo Deich [Daytsh], "Pavel akselrod," *Tsukunft*, XVIII (1913), pp. 897–905. The best source on Deich is his own book *Yidn in der rusisher revolutsie. zikhroynes vegn yidn-revolutsionern*, trans. by E. Korman (Berlin: Yidisher literarishe farlag, 1924).
42. Quoted in D. Shub, "Arn sundelevitch," op. cit., p. 103.
43. Quoted in Greenberg, op. cit., p. 148. Also note: Lieberman to Smirnov (November 23, 1876) in Marmor, op. cit., p. 82; Erich Goldhagen, "The Ethnic Consciousness of Early Russian Jewish Socialists," *Judaism*, XXIII, 4 (Fall 1974), pp. 479–96.
44. Bernstein, *Sozialdemokratische Lehrjahre*, op. cit., pp. 99–100, 133.
45. Ibid., p. 98.
46. In *Die Geschichte der Berliner Arbeiterbewegung*, II, op. cit., p. 34, Bernstein describes Aronson, Gurevitch, and Lieberman as "Russian Social Democrats." He also, however, describes the contents of a letter used in the Nihilist trial in which the grouping of his friends is explicitly described as a Russian-Jewish section of the International (ibid.).
47. On the attitude of Bernstein's parents, see Bernstein, *Von 1850 bis 1872*, op. cit., p. 41.
48. Bernstein, "Wie Ich als Jude in der Diaspora aufwuchs," op. cit., p. 194. Cf. E. Bernstein, "Vospominaniia o Mikhaile Dragomanove i Sergee Podolinskom," *Letopis' Revoliutsii*, I (Berlin, St. Petersburg, Moscow: 1923), p. 63, as quoted in Vladimir Nikolaevich Pavloff, "Revolutionary Populism in Imperial Russia and the National Question in the 1870s and 1880s," in *Socialism and Nationalism*, ed. by Eric Cahm and Vladimir Claude Fisera, I (Nottingham: Spokesman, 1978), p. 70: "Any consideration of the Jews as a separate nationality appeared to me either impossible or as the worst form of reaction."

49. Wistrich, *Socialism and the Jews: The Dilemmas of Assimilation in Germany and Austria-Hungary*, op. cit., pp. 94–101.

50. Dragomanow (1841–1895), who had been removed from a teaching position at the University of Kiev because of his political views, lived in Switzerland between 1876 and 1884 and was generally acknowledged to be the leader of the Ukrainian radicals. See Tscherikower [Tsherikover], "Bamerkungen un derklerungen tsu di zikhroynes fun grigori gurevitch," op. cit., pp. 247–48.

51. Dragomanow was opposed to the Russification of the Ukraine and was worried that the Jews of the Ukraine would become agents of Russification. He therefore sympathized with efforts to disseminate socialist literature in Yiddish because he believed that these efforts might lead to strengthening of progressive Jewish culture and thus weaken the forces of Russification among the Jews. Dragomanow preferred the existence of a (relatively weak) Jewish nation living amidst the Ukrainians and committed to the use of its own language to the possiblity of a Russo-Jewish alliance, which would, he feared, undermine Ukrainian culture (Kursky, "Di zhenever 'grupe sotsialistn-yidn' un ir oyfruf," op. cit., pp. 559–60). The question of just how much of a role Dragomanow played in writing the proclamation of 1880 favoring Yiddish socialist literature is addressed by J. S. H(ertz) [I. Sh. Herts], "M. dragomanow un der oyfruf fun der 'grupe sotsialistn-yidn' (tsu zayt 53)," in *Di geshikhte fun bund*, op. cit., I (1960), pp. 359–60.

52. Tsch(erikower), "Nokh vegn der zhenever 'grupe sotsialisten-yidn,' " op. cit., p. 567.

53. *Der Sozialdemokrat*, 21 (May 22, 1881), p. 4, col. 1.

54. Ibid.

55. Several decades later Bernstein offered to write an article on Dragomanow for the *Forverts* (Bernstein to A. Cahan [September 17, 1922], in A. Cahan Collection, YIVO). Dragomanow, Bernstein noted, was "an advocate of specific national rights for the Jews in Russia and Poland," but did not advocate "Zionistic ideas" (ibid.). Cahan rejected the idea that Bernstein write such an article for the *Forverts* (A. Cahan to Bernstein [November 2, 1922], in Bernstein Nachlass, IISH, D89), but Bernstein proceeded to publish a piece on this theme in Russian (Bernstein, "Vospominaniia o Mikhaile Dragomanove i Sergee Podolinskom," op. cit., pp. 58–65).

56. Gurevitch, for example, was deeply shaken by the pogroms and began to explore the feasibility of Jewish immigration from Eastern Europe to Palestine. See Leo Deich (Daytsh), "Der ershter revolutsioner—'tsienist,' " *Tsukunft*, XXI (1916), pp. 777–81. At least in part because of the influence on him of his close friend Gurevitch, Axelrod also reconsidered his approach to the Jewish question and came to believe that the Jewish socialists ought not to "have forsaken the Jewish masses" (Pavel

Borisovich Axelrod, "Socialist Jews Confront the Pogroms," in *The Golden Tradition*, ed. by Lucy S. Dawidowicz [Boston: Beacon Press, 1967], p. 410). Cf. Abraham Ascher, "Pavel Axelrod: A Conflict Between Jewish Loyalty and Revolutionary Dedication," *Russian Review*, XXIV (1965), pp. 249–65.

57. On the Jewish socialist movement in England in the 1880s and 1890s, see Burgin, op. cit., pp. 42–67, 228–91; E. T[s]cherikower [Tsherikover], "London un ir pionerishe role in der bavegung," *Geshikhte fun der yidisher arbeter-bavegung in di fareynikte shtatn*, ed. by E. T[s]cherikower [Tsherikover], II (New York: Yidisher visnshaftlekher institut—yivo, 1945), pp. 97–137; Lloyd P. Gartner, *The Jewish Immigrant in England, 1870–1914* (London: Ruskin House, George Allen and Unwin Ltd., 1960), pp. 106–41; Fishman, *Jewish Radicals: From Czarist Stetl to London Ghetto*, op cit.

58. Fishman, op. cit., p. 165, notes that estimates as to the size of the crowd varied markedly.

59. Ibid., p. 183.

60. As the revisionist controversy gained momentum, Eleanor wrote to Kautsky, "Ede is so dear a friend that it is horrible to see things as they are just now" (Eleanor Marx to Kautsky [March 15, 1898], in Kautsky Nachlass, IISH, KD XVI 489; cf. Edmund Silberner, "Eleanor Marx. Ein Beitrag zu ihrer Biographie und zum Problem der jüdischen Identität," *Jahrbuch des Instituts für Deutsche Geschichte*, VI [1977], p. 275).

61. Eduard Bernstein, "Eleanor Marx," NZ, XVI, part 2 (1897–98), p. 122. According to Chaim Zhitlovsky, Bernstein once described Eleanor's attitude as "nearly Zionistic." See Solomon F. Bloom, "Kh. zhitlovski un karl marks vegn anti-semitizm," *Afn shvel*, 3 (19) (April-May 1944), p. 11. No other evidence on the attitudes or activities of Eleanor Marx supports this description. Though it is not clear precisely when Bernstein made this comment, he may have been projecting his own post-World War I "nearly Zionistic" attitude onto his late friend Eleanor. One other primary source corroborates Bernstein's description of Eleanor's tendency to identify herself as a Jew at public meetings. At an evening of memoirs organized by the YIVO division in London on January 9, 1939, a certain Perkov is said to have declared, "One time Eleanor Marx Aveling was supposed to speak in the Hall Leeds Institute, but she was not allowed to do so, so she spoke in the open, and, in so doing, shouted out 'I am a Jewess!' " (T[s]cherikower, "London un ir pionerishe role in der bavegung," op. cit., p. 135).

62. Eduard Bernstein, "Einige Bemerkungen über die jüdische Einwanderung in England," in *Jüdische Statistik*, ed. by Verein für Jüdische Statistik (Berlin: Jüdischer Verlag, 1903), p. 336. For documentation of a speech by Bernstein delivered in London to an audience containing Jewish socialists, see "Londener internatsionaler sotsial-demokratisher klub," *Di arbayter tsaytung*, 17 (April 22, 1892), p. 3.

63. Stepniak (Sergius Kravtschinsky) was the author of the popular books *Underground Russia* and *The Career of a Nihilist*. A prominent Narodnik, he had, in 1878, executed the chief of the Czarist police, Mezentsev. He had been a guest at Engels's home on a number of occasions and had been very friendly with Bernstein, but had had a falling out with the Germans. See Tscherikower, "Bamerkungen un derklerungen tsu di zikhroynes fun grigori gurevitch," op. cit., pp. 249–50; Eduard Bernstein, *My Years of Exile. Reminiscences of a Socialist*, trans. by Bernard Miall (London: Leonard Parsons, 1921), pp. 214–15; James W. Hulse, *Revolutionists in London* (Oxford: Clarendon Press, 1970), pp. 29–52.

64. "Stepniak's levayeh," *Der arbayter fraynd*, XI, 13 (January 13, 1895), p. 51.

65. Kursky, *Gezamlte shriftn*, op. cit., p. 314. According to Kursky there were three hundred workers in the procession at Stepniak's funeral (ibid.).

66. Eduard Bernstein, *My Years of Exile: Reminiscences of a Socialist*, op. cit., pp. 215–16.

67. Arno Herzig, "The Role of Antisemitism in the Early Years of the German Workers' Movement," *Leo Baeck Institute Year Book*, XXVI (1981), pp. 248–55.

68. Tölcke (1817–1893) became president of the ADAV in 1865. Despite the bitter polemics in which he engaged during the early 1870s, it was Tölcke who eventually led the Lassalleans to unite with the SDAP[D]. See F. Osterroth, ed., *Biographisches Lexicon des Sozialismus*, I (Hannover: Verlag J. H. W. Dietz Nachf. GmbH, 1960), p. 311.

69. *Neuer Sozialdemokrat* (January 22, 1873), quoted in Herzig, op. cit., p. 250.

70. Wilhelm Hasselmann, born in 1844, served as editor of several socialist periodicals, including the *Neuer Sozialdemokrat* and was a member of the Reichstag from 1874 to 1876 and from 1878 to 1880. In 1880 he was expelled from the party because of anarchistic tendencies (Osterroth, op. cit., p. 115).

71. Bernstein, *Sozialdemokratische Lehrjahre*, op. cit., p. 26.

72. Ed[uard] Bernstein, "Zur Abwehr," *Volkstaat* (February 19, 1873).

73. Bernstein, "Wie Ich als Jude in der Diaspora aufwuchs," op. cit., p. 194.

74. Bernstein to Engels (July 23, 1881), in Helmut Hirsch, ed., *Eduard Bernsteins Briefwechsel mit Friedrich Engels*, Quellen und Untersuchungen zur Geschichte der deutschen und österreichischen Arbeiterbewegung, Neue Folge, I (Assen: Van Gorcum & Comp. N.V., 1970) (henceforth: *EBBFE*), pp. 27–28. For another indication of the degree to which Bernstein took the anti-Semitic movement seriously, see Bernstein, *Die Geschichte der Berliner Arbeiterbewegung*, II, op. cit., pp. 58 ff.

75. Bernstein to Engels (July 7, 1882), in *EBBFE*, op. cit., p. 112. Cf. Bern-

stein to Engels (September 9, 1881), in *EBBFE*, op. cit., p. 34; Bernstein to Engels (September 1, 1882), in *EBBFE*, op. cit., p. 123; Bernstein to Engels (November 17, 1882), in *EBBFE*, op. cit., p. 163.

76. Bernstein to Engels (July 7, 1882), in *EBBFE*, op. cit., p. 112.
77. Bernstein to Engels (November 10, 1883), in *EBBFE*, op. cit., p. 228. Also note Bernstein's letter to Engels of April 15, 1884, *EBBFE*, op. cit., p. 260, in which Bernstein wrote that Singer's chances for election were doubtful, "Since he is a Jew [and] we must reckon with the petty-bougeoisie in the fourth electoral district."
78. Bernstein to Engels (April 7, 1884), in *EBBFE*, op. cit., p. 257.
79. Bernstein to Engels (August 18, 1884), in *EBBFE*, op. cit., p. 293.
80. Ibid.
81. Bernstein to Engels (September 24, 1884), in *EBBFE*, op. cit., p. 299. Pierre Angel, *Eduard Bernstein et l'évolution du socialisme allemand*, Germanica, II (Paris: Marcel Didier, 1961), pp. 417–18, refers to a letter from Bernstein to Motteler written in 1881 and stored in the IISH in which Bernstein objected to Hirsch's underestimation of anti-Semitism. I have been unable to locate this letter.
82. Eduard Bernstein, "Das Schlagwort und der Antisemitismus," *NZ*, XI, part 2 (1892–93), p. 234.
83. Ibid., p. 233.
84. Ibid.
85. Ibid., p. 234.
86. Wistrich, "Socialism and the Jewish Question in Germany and Austria (1880–1914)" (Ph.D. dissertation, University College, London, 1974), p. 195.
87. Bernstein, "Wie Ich als Jude in der Diaspora aufwuchs," op. cit., pp. 187, 193, 195.
88. On the revisionist controversy, and on Bernstein's views during that controversy, see Peter Gay, *The Dilemma of Democratic Socialism* (New York: Collier Books, 1962); Angel, loc. cit.; Thomas Meyer, *Bernsteins konstruktiver Sozialismus. Eduard Bernsteins Beitrag zur Theorie des Sozialismus*, Internationale Bibliothek, CIV (Berlin, Bonn-Bad Godesburg: Verlag J. H. W. Dietz Nachf. GmbH, 1977); Horst Heimann and Thomas Meyer, eds., *Bernstein und der demokratische Sozialismus. Bericht über den wissenschaftlichen Kongreß "Die historische Leistung und aktuelle Bedeutung Eduard Bernsteins,"* Internationale Bibliothek, CXIV (Berlin, Bonn: Verlag J. H. W. Dietz Nachf. GmbH, 1978).
89. Bernstein, "Das Schlagwort und der Antisemitismus," op. cit., p. 234.
90. Ibid.
91. Eduard Bernstein, review of *Der Antisemitismus und die Juden im Lichte der modernen Wissenschaft*, NZ, XII, part 2 (1893–94), p. 406. During this same period, Bernstein also commented on anti-Semitism in his article "Die deutsche Ausgabe einer Hauptschrift des Giordano

Bruno," *NZ*, XII, part 1 (1893–94), pp. 653–54. Cf. Bernstein to Engels (February 22, 1894), in *EBBFE*, op. cit., p. 404.

92. Ed[uard] Bernstein, "Das realistische und das ideologische Moment im Sozialismus," *NZ*, XVI, part 2 (1897–98), p. 232. In this article Bernstein cites a work by the Jewish social revolutionary Chaim Zhitlovsky (ibid., p. 225). By 1900, Bernstein was directly in contact with Zhitlovsky. See Bernstein to Schitlowsky (March 20, July 1, July 20, October 9, 1900), in Zhitlovsky Collection, File 177, YIVO.

93. The passage in question in full reads: "My parting question was, 'What do you think of the anti-Jewish attacks of some Socialists?' The reply was short and decisive: 'Apart from any agitation in this country, where my opinion might be resented, I have stated, a year ago in the *Neue Zeit*, that *although in no way connected with any Jewish movement as such*, I think it is my duty to be a "philo-Semite" in all cases where I meet anti-Semitism. As a Social Democrat I fight for all political reforms Jews can reasonably demand.' " See "Evolutionary Socialism. Interview with Herr Eduard Bernstein," *The Jewish Chronicle* (November 24, 1899), p. 21; emphasis in the original.

94. See the comments by Helmut Hirsch in Heimann and Meyer, eds., *Bernstein und der Demokratische Sozialismus*, op. cit., p. 467.

95. Edmund Silberner, "German Social Democracy and the Jewish Problem Prior to World War I," op. cit., pp. 46–47; Donald L. Niewyk, "German Social Democracy and the Problem of Anti-Semitism, 1906–1914" (M.A. thesis, Tulane University, 1964, pp. 33–34); Robert S. Wistrich, "German Social Democracy and the Problem of Jewish Nationalism 1897–1917," *Leo Baeck Institute Year Book*, XXI (1976), pp. 125–30; Jehuda Eloni, "Die zionistische Bewegung in Deutschland und die SPD 1897–1918," in *Juden und jüdische Aspekte in der deutschen Arbeiterbewegung 1848–1918*, op. cit., p. 102. For accounts of the life and work during the pre-World War I years of Josef Bloch, the longtime editor of the *Socialistische Monatshefte*, see Roger Fletcher, "Revisionism and Empire: Joseph Bloch, the *Socialistische Monatshefte* and German tionalism, 1907–14," *European Studies Review*, X (1980), pp. 459–85 and the sources cited therein.

96. A. Nossig to Bernstein (March 25, 1902, February 11, 1903, October 17, 1903, January 12, 1904), in Bernstein Nachlass, D 505, IISH; T. Zlocisti to Bernstein (June 6, 1902), in Bernstein Nachlass, D 857, IISH; A.J. Kastelianski to Bernstein (October 23, 1902), in Bernstein Nachlass, D 341, IISH.

97. Chaim Weizmann to Vera Khatzman (August 29, 1902) in Leonard Stein, ed. *The Letters and Papers of Chaim Weizmann*, series A, volume I (London: Oxford University Press, 1968), p. 389. Cf. Weizmann to Kasteliansky (December 4, 1902), in Meyer W. Weisgal, ed., *The Letters and Papers of Chaim Weizmann*, series A, volume II (London: Oxford

University Press, 1971), p. 63. The journal to which Weizmann was referring, which was to have been called *Der Jude*, never appeared (Weisgal, ed., op. cit., p. 293).

98. Julius Moses, ed., *Die Lösung der Judenfrage. Eine Rundfrage* (Berlin: C. Wigand, 1907), p. 50.

99. On Fornberg, see Zalmen Reyzen, *Leksikon fun der yudisher literatur un prese* (Warsaw: Farlags-gezelshaft "tsentral," 1914), cols. 463–65.

100. "Eduard bernshteyn iber di yudenfrage in [sic] iber di yudishe arbey-ter-frage," *Der yudisher arbeyter*, IV, 31 (August 2, 1907), p. 2. *Der yudisher arbeyter*, which was published at that time in Cracow, was the central organ of the Jewish Socialist Workers' Party Poalei-Zion in Austria.

101. "Eduard bernshteyn iber di yudenfrage in [sic] iber di yudishe arbey-ter-frage," loc. cit.

102. Ibid.

103. Later in this same interview, Bernstein also discussed his attitude toward the various Jewish political parties of the Russian Empire, and, according to Fornberg, demonstrated quite a bit of knowledge about them. He reportedly said that the Bund had at an earlier point played a significant role, but that it had also made colossal blunders. Bernstein also criticized the position of the Bund in "Fragen der Taktik in Russland," *Sozialistische Monatshefte* (1906), i, pp. 213–17.

104. Ed[uard] Bernstein, "Der Schulstreit in Palästina," *NZ*, XXXII, part 1 (1913–14), p. 752. Responses to Bernstein's critical comments on Zion-ism were published in the *Jüdische Rundschau* and in the Viennese organ of the Poalei-Zion, *Neuer Weg*. E. Hamburger pointedly com-mented that Zionism was not merely seeking entrance into the social-ist world, but had long since found entrance into this world (E. Ham-burger, "Eduard Bernstein über den Zionismus," *Jüdische Rundschau*, XIX, 13 [March 27, 1914], p. 132). The unsigned article in *Neuer Weg* insisted that Bernstein would never have written his article had he been better acquainted with conditions in Palestine: "He does not know the productive Jewry of the new *yishuv*" ("Ed. Bernstein und der Sprachenkampf," *Neuer Weg*, I, 3–4 [March-April 1914], p. 3).

105. Among those with whom Bernstein corresponded during this period (albeit not about the Jewish question) was Martin Buber, Bernstein to Buber (May 13, June 2, June 4, June 29, July 3, 1905; July 13, 1909; January 13, February 26, April 24, 1910), Bernstein File, Martin Buber Archive, Jewish National and University Library, Jerusalem. Bernstein also continued to speak out against anti-Semitism, as he had done even before the revisionist controversy. See, for example, *Sixième Congrès Socialiste International tenu à Amsterdam du 14 au 20 août 1904. Compte-rendu analytique* (Brussels: Le Secrétariat Socialiste In-ternational, 1904), p. 94, which indicates that the Socialist Interna-tional endorsed: "Une motion signée par Bebel, Bernstein, Anseele,

etc., proteste contre la persécution antisémite en Russie." Cf. *Verhandlungen des Reichstags. XIII Legislaturperiode. I Session. Band 289. Stenographische Berichte. Von der 131 Sitzung am 3 April bis zur 150 Sitzung am 26 April 1913* (Berlin: Verlag der norddeutschen Buchdruckerei und Verlagsanstalt, 1913), pp. 4736, 4800–4801, for the transcript of a speech by Bernstein condemning Rumanian anti-Semitism, and Paul Nathan to Bernstein (May 2, 1913), Bernstein Nachlass, D 490, IISH, for Nathan's reaction to Bernstein's speech.

106. Ed[uard] Bernstein, "Vom Patriotismus der Juden," *Die Friedens-Warte,* XVIII (1916), p. 248.

107. Eduard Bernstein [Bernshteyn], "Di yidn als fermitler tsvishn di felker," *Der yidisher kempfer* (September 27, 1916), p. 4; (October 6, 1916), p. 4; (October 11, 1916), p. 6. It was, apparently, the Labor Zionist Berl Locker who approached Bernstein on behalf of *Der yidisher kempfer.* See Berl Locker, *Me-kitov ad yerushalayim* (Jerusalem: Ha-sifriyah ha-tsiyonit, 1970), p. 170. Bernstein also wrote several other works at the request of this periodical: "Vi ikh bin oyfgevaksen in goles als yid" (December 1, 8, 15, 22, 29, 1916); "Vos di sotsialistn hobn nit gedarft ignorirn" (May 18, 1917). The editors of *Der yidisher kempfer* considered it a great coup to have attracted a contributor of Bernstein's stature: "Eduard bernshteyn mitarbayter fun'm 'yidishn kempfer,' " *Der yidisher kempfer* (August 18, 1916), p. 2; "Eduard bernshteyn far'n 'yidishn kempfer,' " *Der yidisher kempfer* (September 15, 1916), p. 1; "Eduard bernshteyn vegn yidishkayt," *Der yidisher kempfer* (September 27, 1916), p. 4.

108. Bernstein to Chasanowitsch (April 18, November 12, November 17, 1913; May 31, 1914), A 277/8/8, Leon Chasanowitsch Papers, Central Zionist Archives, Jerusalem; Locker, op. cit., p. 169; Bernstein to Locker (March 16, 1916), Abraham Schwadron Collection, Jewish National and University Library, Jerusalem. Zerubawel asserted that Chasanowitsch interviewed Bernstein (in 1908 or 1909) in Zerubawel [Zerubavel], "Leon khazanovitsh," in *Yidisher arbeter pinkes (tsu der geshikhte fun der poyle-tsien bavegung),* ed. by Zerubawel, I (Warsaw: Kooperativer farlag "naye kultur," 1927), p. 581. I have, however, been unable to confirm Zerubawel's assertion. Chasanowitsch did publish interviews with Karl Kautsky and Emmanuel Wurm at that time —Kasrial [Leon Chasanowitsch], "Karl kautski un vurm iber der yuden-frage," op. cit.

109. Bernstein, *Von den Aufgaben der Juden im Weltkriege* (Berlin: Erich Reiss Verlag, 1917), p. 8. For additional information on this work, see Silberner, "German Social Democracy and the Jewish Problem Prior to World War I," op. cit., pp. 28, 29, and 32.

110. Chasanowitsch to Bernstein, (January 8, 1918), in Bernstein Nachlass, D 317, IISH; Chasanowitsch to Leo Hermann (January 23, 1918), in Records of the Central Zionist Office, (Zionistisches Zentralbureau),

Berlin, Z 3/1055, Central Zionist Archives. Chasanowitsch had originally suggested that Bernstein write on the moral significance of the Jewish people for humanity: Chasanowitsch to Leo Hermann (December 14, 1917), in Records of the Central Zionist Office (Zionistisches Zentralbureau), Berlin, Z 3/1055, Central Zionist Archives; Chasanowitsch to Bernstein (January 8, 1918), in Bernstein Nachlass, D 317, IISH. Neither Bernstein's article nor the volume for which it was written were ever published. Robert Wistrich has hypothesized that Bernstein wrote this article "around 1916/17," in Wistrich, "Eduard Bernstein and the Jewish Problem," *Jahrbuch des Instituts für deutsche Geschichte*, VIII (1979), p. 253. It seems more likely that Bernstein wrote his piece in 1918 after receiving Chasanowitsch's invitation. The existence of Bernstein's article was apparently first noted by Mosse in "German Socialists and the Jewish Question in the Weimar Republic," op. cit., p. 129. For further information on the anthology in which Bernstein's piece was supposed to have been printed, see Simon Dubnow [Shimen Dubnov], *Dos bukh fun mayn lebn. zikhroynes un rayoynes. materialn far der geshikhte fun mayn tsayt*, II, trans. by I. Rapaport (Buenos Aires: Alveltlekher yidisher kultur-kongres, 1962), p. 267.

111. Ed. Bernstein, "Die demokratische Staatsidee und die jüdisch-nationale Bewegung," K 13/26, Central Zionist Archives. The manuscript of this article is in the Bernstein Nachlass, A 114, IISH.

112. Ed. Bernstein, "Zum Aufsatz über die Demokratie und die nationale Minderheiten," p. 1. K 13/26, Central Zionist Archives. This addition to Bernstein's original article was apparently written at Chasanowitsch's request in order to clarify the ways in which the theoretical passages in Bernstein's original essay could be applied to the specific case of the Jews. Cf. Bernstein to Leo Hermann (May 21, 1918), in Records of the Central Zionist Office, (Zionistisches Zentralbureau), Berlin, Z 3/1055, Central Zionist Archives.

113. Bernstein, "Zum Aufsatz über die Demokratie und die nationale Minderheiten," loc. cit.

114. Ibid., p. 2.

115. Roger Fletcher, "Revisionism and Nationalism: Eduard Bernstein's Views on the National Question, 1900–1914," *Canadian Review of Studies in Nationalism*, XI, I (Spring 1984), p. 104. Cf. Hans Mommsen, *Arbeiterbewegung und Nationale Frage. Ausgewählte Aufsätze*, Kritische Studien zur Geschichtswissenschaft, XXXIV (Göttingen: Vandenhoeck & Ruprecht, 1979), pp. 109–24.

116. Eduard Bernstein, "Wie Fichte und Lassalle national waren," *Archiv für die Geschichte des Sozialismus und der Arbeiterbewegung*, V (1915), p. 161.

117. The Poalei-Zion was relatively small in Germany. Though no membership figures are available, it is known that the Poalei-Zion received

940 of the 14,442 valid ballots cast in the elections to the assembly of representatives of the Berlin Jewish Community in 1920 (*Jüdische Rundschau*, XXV, 43, p. 346). Reinhold Cohn (son of the German social democrat Oskar Cohn) has asserted that the German Poalei-Zion was "originally made up almost exclusively of non-German [East European] Jews living in Germany," in Reinhold Cohn to Ernst Hamburger (November 1, 1971), Ernst Hamburger collection, AR 7034, Box 11, folder 6, Leo Baeck Institute Archives. For additional information on the Poalei-Zion in Germany, see Felix A. Theilhaber, "Die sozialistisch-zionistische Arbeiterpartei Poalei-Zion," in *Das deutsche Judentum. Seine Parteien und Organizationen. Eine Sammelschrift* (Berlin, Munich: Verlag der neuen jüdischen Monatshefte, 1919), pp. 38–43.

118. Shazar, loc. cit. The events at the Amsterdam conference are discussed in "Die Amsterdamer Sozialistenkonferenz für die zionistischen Forderungen," *Jüdische Rundschau*, XXIV, 31 (May 2, 1919), p. 237; "Die Sozialistenkonferenz in Amsterdam zur Judenfrage," *Jüdische Rundschau*, XXIV, 32 (May 6, 1919), p. 247; "Die Verhandlungen über die Judenfrage auf der Amsterdamer Konferenz," *Jüdische Rundschau*, XXIV, 37 (May 23, 1919), pp. 282–83.

119. "Die Amsterdamer Sozialistenkonferenz und die jüdischen Forderungen (Eine Kundgebung der Berliner Gruppe der Poale Zion)," *Jüdische Rundschau*, XXIV, 33 (May 9, 1919), p. 255.

120. "Eduard Bernstein," *Mitteilungs-Blätter der Liga für das Arbeitende Palästina in Oesterreich*, 6/7 (November-December 1932), p. 12. Bernstein's name appears on a membership list of the Deutsches Komitee pro Palästina dated February 28, 1930 (Bernstein Nachlass, K2, IISH).

121. Eduard Bernstein, "Die Reichstagswahlen und die Juden," *Der Neue Weg*, 1 (December 1924), pp. 2–6. *Der Neue Weg* was published by the Jewish Social Democratic Workers' Organization Poalei-Zion in Germany. The program of this organization is reproduced in *Programm und Dokumente des allweltlichen Jüdischen Sozialistischen Arbeiter-Verbandes Poale-Zion*. Poale-zionistische Bibliothek, Heft I (Berlin: Sekretariat der Poale-Zion-Gruppen in Deutschland, n.d.).

122. Edouard Bernstein, "Les nationalistes arabes et le mandat palestinien," *Comité Socialiste pour la Palestine Ouvrière*. *Bulletin*, 5 (May 1930), p. 12. For yet another example of a piece by Bernstein dealing with Zionism in a sympathetic manner, see his review of Vandervelde's *Schaffendes Palästina* (manuscript, Bernstein Nachlass, A126, IISH), which he sent to Palestine (Lilli Popper to Bernstein [January 1, 1931], in Bernstein Nachlass, D548, IISH). For additional information on Lilli Popper, neé Zadek, who emigrated to Palestine, see the introduction by Robert Weltsch to *Leo Baeck Institute Year Book*, XV (1970), pp. XIII-XIV and Lil[l]i Zadek [Tsadek], *Devarim meshelah ve-alehah* (Tel Aviv: Davar, 1970). It may be significant that Bernstein was willing

to use his influence in order to help Lilli Zadek obtain permission to enter Palestine (Bernstein to Captain Warburton [March 10, 1920], in Bernstein File, Abraham Schwadron Collection, Jewish National and University Library). Zadek published an article on her memories of the Bernstein family in *Davar* (1930), p. 4, on the occasion of Eduard's eightieth birthday.

123. Receipts for contributions made to the Keren Kajemeth signed by Bernstein and dated November 12, 1928, and September 11, 1930, are preserved in the Bernstein Nachlass, H9, IISH.

124. On February 18, 1924, for example, Bernstein addressed a meeting organized by the Berlin committee "Für das arbeitende Erez-Israel." In his remarks to this meeting Bernstein stressed several times that he was not a Zionist, that he disagreed with many of the theses of the Zionists, but that he advocated aid to to the Jewish workers of Palestin, whose idealism and hard work he clearly respected. See "Öffentliche Volksversammlung in Berlin für das arbeitende Erez-Israe(l)," typescript (43) 69, III, file 23, Archives and Museum of the Jewish Labour Movement, The Institute of Labour Research in Memory of P. Lavon, Tel Aviv. Cf. "Eine Kundgebung für das arbeitende Palästina," *Jüdische Rundschau*, XXIX, 15 (February 22, 1924), p. 99. Eduard Bernstein, "Für das arbeitende Palästina," *Der Neue Weg*, 3/4 (February-March 1925), pp. 72–73; *Ershter kongres farn arbetndn erets-yisroel* (Tel Aviv: Velt-lige farn arbetndn erets-yisroel, 1931), pp. 12–15. Bernstein signed a letter of invitation to a conference for socialists arranged by the Poalei-Zion and convened in Brussels on August 9, 1928. See M[arc] Jarblum, *The Socialist International and Zionism*, trans. by Maximilian Hurwitz (New York: Poale Zion-Zeire Zion of America, 1933), p. 18 and a similar letter of invitation to a conference for labor Palestine held in Berlin in December 1928 (*Comité Socialiste Pour la Palestine Ouvrière. Bulletin*, 2 [April 1929], p. 11).

125. When the International Socialist Committee for the Organized Jewish Workers in Palestine adopted a resolution protesting against the British White Paper on Palestine, Bernstein submitted the resolution to the *Vorwärts* and requested that it be published (Richard Bernstein to Eduard Bernstein [January 22, 1931], in Bernstein Nachlass, D 806, IISH).

126. "Massen-Kundgebung für das arbeitende Erez-Jisroel in Leipzig. Ein Bekenntnis von Edward Bernstein," *Jüdische Presszentrale Zürich*, VII, 285 (March 20, 1924), p. 8. Cf. *Jewish Telegraphic Agency. Daily News Bulletin* (March 20, 1924). During this period, Bernstein delivered talks on behalf of the "Komitee für das arbeitende Erez-Israel" not only in Berlin and Leipzig, but also in Magdeburg and other locations (Siegfried Jacoby, "Eduard Bernstein als Mitarbeiter im "Komitee für das arbeitende Erez Israel," *Jüdische Presszentrale Zürich*, VII, 307 [August 28, 1924], p. 5).

127. See, for example, "Wahlversammlung der Poale Zion," *Jüdische Rund-schau*, XXX, 7 (January 23, 1925), p. 63; "Eduard Bernstein, Veteran Socialist Leader, on His Jewishness," *Jewish Telegraphic Agency. Daily News Bulletin*, VI, 21 (January 24, 1925), p. 6; *Alveltlikher yidisher sotsialistisher arbeter-farband poyle-tsien farbands-bureau. yedies*, 10 (March 25, 1925).

128. Bernstein, "Wie Ich als Jude in der Diaspora aufwuchs," op. cit., p. 187; Wistrich, *Revolutionary Jews from Marx to Trotsky*, op. cit., p. 74.

129. Eduard Bernstein [Bernshteyn], "Di yidishe heym in erets yisroel. an untershtitser fun dem pro-palestine komitet un dokh nit kayn tsionist," *Tsukunft*, XXXIV (March 1929), p. 157. Having made these caveats, Bernstein indicated that he believed that under the conditions of the day, including anti-Semitism, a "large scale Jewish agrarian home is very necessary" (ibid.). Bernstein wrote this piece at the request of the editor of *Tsukunft*, A. Liessin, who requested an article on the Pro-Palestine Committee and who claimed, "It is necessary to enlighten the minds of the last remnants of anti-nationalists who are still imprisoned in their outlived dogmas" (A. Liessin to Bernstein [December 12, 1928], in Bernstein Nachlass, 415, IISH). In another piece published in 1929, Bernstein noted that "if one means by Zionism a movement for the transformation of Palestine into a nationalistically constituted Jewish state, I am not a Zionist" (Eduard Bernstein, "Die Aussichten des Zionismus. Eine Antwort an Karl Kautsky," *Vorwärts*, XLVI, 575 [December 8, 1929], 2. Beilage). Zionism in this sense, Bernstein suggests, deserves to be condemned. But, Bernstein, continues, it is altogether different to condemn the striving for a Jewish homeland in Palestine secured under public law. This Bernstein was clearly unwilling to do, for he believed such a homeland to be desirable (ibid.).

130. "Konferenz der Poale-Zion in Deutschland," *Der jüdische Arbeiter. Organ der sozialdemokratischen Poale Zion Österreichs*, VII, 2 (January 17, 1930), p. 4. Of course Bernstein's declaration of membership in the Poalei-Zion should not be taken to mean that he agreed with the policies of the mainstream Zionist movement: "Ich bedaure sehr," Bernstein wrote to his niece and nephew (who lived in Palestine) "daß es so viele Zionisten giebt, die durch unverständige Artikel über die Ziele des Zionismus die Lage der Juden in Palästina womöglich noch verschlechtern. Wer nicht Maß zu halten versteht, ist der größte Feind des jüdischen Volkes" (Bernstein to Lilli and Ernst Popper [January 18, 1930], Handschriftenabteilung, 16216, Stadt- und Landesbibliothek, Dortmund).

131. Kursky, *Gezamlte shriftn*, op. cit., p. 313. Kursky was a prominent and committed Bundist and, as such, an opponent of Zionism. Thus Kursky may not have wanted to believe that Bernstein, whom he admired and respected, would adhere to an ideology that the Bundists con-

sidered to be fundamentally flawed (A. Liessin, *Tsukunft* [October 1933], p. 578).

132. Isaiah Eisenshtat (known in the socialist movement as Vitali Yudin) attended the celebration of Bernstein's eightieth birthday, which was held in Berlin in January 1930, as a representative of the Bund (Kursky, op. cit., p. 308). Works written by Bernstein for the American Jewish socialist press include: "Di yidn un di daytshe sotsial-demokratie," *Tsukunft*, XXVI (March 1921), pp. 145–52; "Di natsionale shtremungen tsvishn der yidish-akademisher yugnt in daytshland," *Tsukunft*, XXVI (September 1921), pp. 520–25; "Di ershte kampf far ekzistents vos di arbayter-prese hot durkhgemakht in europ," *Forverts* (April 23, 1922), section 4, p. 5; "Di entshteyung fun dem internatsionalen gedank," *Der veker* (August 11, 1923), pp. 5–7; "Vi azoy vet der sotsializm farvirklikht vern?" *Der veker* (November 10, 1923), pp. 6–8; "Di mizrekh-yidn in daytshland. di yidishe vanderer, di antisemiten un di sotsialisten," *Tsukunft*, XXVIII (November 1923), pp. 664–69; "Di yidishe heym in erets yisroel," op. cit. Bernstein was particularly eager to write for the Yiddish-language socialist press after he stepped down from the Reichstag and subsequently lost what had been a major source of income (Bernstein to Abraham Cahan [November 9, 1928], Abraham Cahan Collection, YIVO). Cf. M. Aronson to Abraham Cahan (May 3, 1928), Abraham Cahan Collection, YIVO, in which Aronson urges Cahan to allow Bernstein to become a regular contributor to the *Forverts*, and stresses the urgency of the matter by noting, "His fate, I think, depends on you."

133. The *Jüdisch-liberale Zeitung* solicited a brief piece, dealing with how leading public personalities from various political perspectives responded to anti-Semites, from Bernstein as a representative of the Vereinigte Sozialdemokratische Partei Deutschlands (VSPD)—the United Social Democratic Party of Germany, which was formed in 1922 through a merger of the SPD with virtually all of the membership of the Unabhängige Sozialdemokratische Partei Deutschlands (USPD). See Schriftleitung der *Jüdisch-liberale Zeitung* to Bernstein (April 29, 1924), in Bernstein Nachlass, D318, IISH. Bernstein's article was published under the title "Die politischen Parteien zur Judenfrage," *Jüdisch-liberale Zeitung*, IV, 12 (May 2, 1924), pp. 2–3.

134. As he did throughout this period, Bernstein spoke of the spread of anti-Semitism and urged his listeners not to allow themselves to be intimidated ("Tagung der jüdischen Studenten," *Jüdische Rundschau*, XXX, 14 [February 17, 1925], p. 132). According to Simon Dubnow, who, along with Bernstein and with the chairman of the orthodox Jewish community of Berlin, also addressed this conference of Jewish students, Bernstein noted that "one must match the national tendency with the commands of the great French revolution." See Simon Dub-

now [Shimen Dubnov], *Dos bukh fun mayn lebn*, op. cit., III, trans. by I. Birnboym (1963), p. 39.

135. "Eduard Bernstein über Lassalle," *Jüdische Rundschau*, XXX, 35 (May 5, 1925), p. 323. For additional information on the Scholem Alechemklub, see *Israelitisches Familienblatt*, XXVII, 1 (January 2, 1925), p. 4.

136. See the letter from the Zentral-Verwaltung des Verbandes der Gesellschaften zur Förderung des Handwerks und der Landwirtschaft unter den Juden "Ort" to Leo Chasanowitsch (August 14, 1925), 104 IV, file 5, Chazanovitsch collection, Archives and Museum of the Jewish Labour Movement, The Institute of Labour Research in Memory of P. Lavon; " 'Ort'-Aktion in Deutschland zur Förderung des Handwerks und der landwirtschaft unter den Juden," *Jüdische Presszentrale Zürich*, IV, 382 (February 5, 1926), p. 4.

137. Bernstein's membership cards in the Hilfsverein for the years 1927, 1929, and 1930 are extant (Bernstein Nachlass, H2, IISH). Cf. Katarina von Kardorff to Bernstein (May 23, 1930), in Bernstein Nachlass, D 339, IISH.

138. Eduard Bernstein [Bernshteyn], "Glik tsum yidishn 'forverts,' " *Forverts* (April 23, 1922), Section 2, p. 1.

139. Ibid.

140. "Das Kuratorium des Instituts," *Mitteilungen der Auslandszentrale des Jiddischen Wissenschaftlichen Instituts*, Berlin, (May 1, 1930), p. 2. The IISH possesses the first page of a manuscript by Bernstein on the YIVO dating from 1929 (Bernstein Nachlass, L8, IISH).

141. Bernstein to Franz Kursky (November 27, 1928), in Kursky, op. cit., pp. 321–22. Bernstein had several sources of information on the Jewish secular schools. An article entitled "Die jüdische weltliche Schule in Polen" by Sch. Rudel appeared in the first issue of *Der Neue Weg, Monatsschrift der jüdischen sozialdemokratischen Arbeiter-Organisation Poale Zion in Deutschland* (December 1924), pp. 18–20. Since this issue contained an article by Bernstein ("Die Reichstagswahlen und die Juden," loc. cit.), it can be safely assumed that Bernstein was aware of Rudel's article. More important, Bernstein met with Shloyme Mendelson, general secretary of the TSYSHO and discussed the work of the schools with him. See Mendelson to Bernstein (April 6, 1929), in Bernstein Nachlass D 381, IISH. Cf. Shloyme Mendelson, *Shloyme mendelson. zayn lebn un shafn* (New York: Farlag "unzer tsayt," 1949), p. 251.

142. Bernstein to Kursky (November 27, 1928), in Kursky, op. cit., pp. 321–22.

143. In 1930, for example, when the leaders of the SPD were being urged by some to take more energetic measures against the Nazis, Otto Landsberg quipped "I have already survived three anti-Semitic waves, and I

will also endure the fourth," as quoted in Niewyk, *Socialist, Anti-Semite and Jew: German Social Democracy Confronts the Problem of Anti-Semitism, 1918–1933*, op. cit., p. 199.

144. Bernstein, "Die Reichstagswahlen und die Juden," op. cit., p. 3.
145. "Eduard Bernstein über Lassalle," op. cit.
146. Ibid.
147. Bernstein, "Für das arbeitende Palästina," op. cit., p. 72.
148. Max Reinheimer, "Eduard Bernstein als Jude," *Israelitisches Familienblatt*, XXXII, 1 (January 2, 1930). Though the rise of anti-Semitism seems to have been the most important factor in explaining the change in Bernstein's position, other factors may also have contributed to this change. An unsigned obituary for Bernstein issued by the Jewish Telegraphic Agency suggests that Bernstein's conversations with Benno Chajes (who was married to Käte "Kitty" Schattner, Regina's daughter, and who was a nephew of the man who was chief rabbi of Vienna during the years of the Austrian First Republic, Hirsch [Zevi] Perez Chajes), may have led Bernstein to clarify his own views toward Jewry and the Jewish question, but provides no evidence to support this contention. See "Eduard Bernstein, der grosse Theoretiker des Sozialismus, gestorben," *Juedische Telegraphen-Agentur (J. T. A.)*, XI, 289 (December 20, 1932), p. 1. My thanks to Florian Tennstedt for sending me a copy of this article. Berl Locker once asserted that Bernstein's wife, Regina, was descended from the Romm family—a Jewish family widely known and respected in Vilna and elsewhere in Eastern Europe—and indicated that Regina's origins and background fostered Bernstein's change in consciousness (Locker, *Me-kitov ad yerushalayim*, op. cit., p. 170). But Locker's claim may have been based on a misunderstanding. Though Regina was related to the Romms, the relationship was more distant than Locker's account would suggest. July "Julka" Zadek, Regina's sister, married Maxim Davidowitsch Romm, and emigrated with him to the U.S. in 1890 (Florian Tennstedt, "Arbeiterbewegung und Familiengeschichte bei Eduard Bernstein und Ignaz Zadek. Hilfswissenschaftliche Mitteilungen zu persönlichen Aspekten von Revisionismus und Sozialreform bei deutschen Sozialdemokraten," *IWK Internationale wissenschaftliche Korrespondenz zur Geschichte der deutschen Arbeiterbewegung*, XVIII, 4 [December 1982], p. 475, 480). Robert Wistrich, while stressing the impact that the "resurgence of nationalist anti-Semitism in the early years of the Weimar Republic" and the "xenophobic campaign against die [sic] *Ostjuden* in Germany" had on Bernstein's approach to Zionism (Wistrich, "Eduard Bernstein and the Jewish Problem," op. cit., p. 255), has also hypothesized that Bernstein's "attitude to Zionism and the Jewish problem was the product of an ethical, rather than an ideological stance. Bernstein was influenced by his liberal, Jewish heritage to adopt a cosmopolitan position on certain political questions" (Robert

S. Wistrich, "Back to Bernstein? A Neo-Revisionist Renaissance," *Encounter*, L, 6 [June 1978], p. 77). This formulation strikes me as problematic. While it is highly likely that Bernstein's Jewish family background sensitized him to anti-Semitism, and while it may well be that the values of the reform Jewish congregation of Berlin were ultimately echoed, however faintly, in Bernstein's revisionism, it is decidely unlikely that Bernstein's "liberal, Jewish heritage" per se led him during the Weimar years to express sympathy for labor Zionism (or for East European Jews or for the secular Jewish institutions operating in the Yiddish-language sphere). The hostility of German Jewry toward Zionism weakened somewhat during the 1920s and 1930s. Nevertheless, most German Jews of the Weimar era who shared Bernstein's "liberal, Jewish heritage" were not sympathetic to Zionism, had negative views about East European Jews, and were not supportive of efforts to foster Yiddish culture.

149. Paul Kampffmeyer, "Eduard Bernstein. Zu seinem 80. Geburtstage," *C.V. Zeitung*, IX, 1 (January 3, 1930), p. 6.

150. Ibid.

151. Karl Kautsky, "Die Aussichten des Zionismus," *Arbeiter-Zeitung*, 262 (September 22, 1929), p. 4; Bernstein, "Die Aussichten des Zionismus. Eine Antwort an Karl Kautsky," loc. cit.; Karl Kautsky, "Nochmals der Zionismus," *Vorwärts*, LXVI, 587 (December 15, 1929), 2. Beilage.

152. Karl Kautsky, "Zum 80. Geburtstag Eduard Bernstein," *Der Kampf*, XXIII, 1 (January 1930), p. 15. My thanks to the late Alexander Erlich for pointing out this passage to me. A typescript of this article by Kautsky is in the Kautsky Nachlass, IISH.

153. Bernstein to Kautsky (September 13, 1929), in Kautsky Nachlass, KD, V, 556, IISH.

154. Eva Reichmann-Jungmann, "Trotz allem Jude . . . Zu Eduard Bernsteins Tod," *C.V. Zeitung*, XI, 52 (December 23, 1932), p. 529.

155. Among the obituaries published in the Jewish press were "Eduard Bernstein," *Jüdische Rundschau*, XXXVII, 101 (December 20, 1932), p. 493, and "Eduard Bernstein," *Israelitisches Familienblatt*, XXXIV, 51 (December 22, 1932). For a more critical view, see Hans Rosby, "Zum Tode Eduard Bernstein," *Jüdisch-liberale Zeitung*, XII, 19 (January 1, 1933). The social democrats who spoke at Bernstein's funeral allegedly did not so much as mention that Bernstein was of Jewish origin. See Simon Dubnow [Shimen Dubnov], *Dos bukh fun mayn lebn*, III, op. cit., pp. 113–14. Hermann Badt, who was to have spoken in the name of the United Zionist-Socialist Party, the League for Labor Palestine and the Pro-Palestine Committee, did not in fact address those assembled because the earlier speakers had used up too much time. See "Eduard Bernstein, der grosse Theoretiker des Sozialismus, gestorben," *Der jüdische Arbeiter*, X, 1 (January 4, 1933), p. 4.

## 3. A Familial Resemblance

1. Nettl, *Rosa Luxemburg* I, op. cit., 51–52. Cf. Elżbieta Ettinger, ed., *Comrade and Lover. Rosa Luxemburg's Letters to Leo Jogiches* (Cambridge, Mass., and London: MIT Press, 1979), p. 1: "The Luxemburgs had no connections with the Jewish community of Zamość. . . . Each parent leaned toward a different way of shedding Jewishness"; Stephen Eric Bronner, *A Revolutionary For Our Times: Rosa Luxemburg* (London: Pluto Press, 1981), p. 13: "Her family exemplified the cosmopolitan attitudes of 'enlightened' Jewry; they had no ties to the strong and cultured Jewish community of the town." It ought to be noted, however, that Nettl suspected that Luxemburg's family history had been adjusted by earlier biographers on whom he was heavily dependent: "There is at least a suspicion of some 'adjustment' of Rosa's background. Frölich and Oelssner, both orthodox Marxists, would consider it progressive for anyone to 'overcome' an orthodox religious background. It was probably not quite as 'comfortable' or as assimilated as they make out" (Nettl, op. cit., I, p. 52).

2. The information on Zamość given below is derived primarily from Jacob Shatzky [Yankev Shatski], book review of *Dr. shloyme etingers ksovim*, in *Pinkes. a fertlyoriker zshurnal far yidisher literaturgeshikhte, shprakhforshung, folklor, un bibliografie*, I (1927–28), pp. 281–82; idem, "Perets-shtudies," *Yivo bleter*, XXVIII (1946), pp. 40–46; idem, "Haskole in zamoshtsh," *Yivo bleter*, XXXVI (1952), pp. 24–62; and Nahum Socolow [Nakhum Sokolov], *Perzenlekhkeyten*, trans. by Moises Senderey [Moyshe Shenderey]. Dos poylishe yidntum, XXXVIII (Buenos Aires: Tsentral-farband fun poylishe yidn in argentine, 1948), pp. 22–24.

3. Biographical research on Rosa Luxemburg's father is complicated by the fact that he used several different names. He was, for example, known both as Eliasch (Eliasz) and as Eduard (or Edward), may have used both Luksenburg and Luksemburg as his family name, and may, moreover, also have been known as Abraham (Nettl, op. cit., I, pp. 52, 95). An "Edward Luksemburg" is mentioned in passing as a one-time student of the rabbinical school of Warsaw in Jakob R. "Synagogi postępowe w Warszawie. (Z moich wspomnień)," *Izraelita* (1906), p. 74, a translation of which was published in Jacob Shatzky [Yankev Shatski], *Geshikhte fun yidn in varshe*, II (New York: Yidisher visnshaftlekher institut, historishe sektsye, 1948), pp. 275–77. A comprehensive list of those who had attended the rabbinical school includes an "Eliasz Luxemburg" (but not an "Edward Luksemburg"), *Z dziejów gminy starozakonnych w Warszawie w XIX stuleciu*, I, 1907, p. 130. The claim that the Luksemburg referred to in *Izraelita* was Rosa Luxemburg's father was first made by Abraham Bick [Avrom Bik], *In baginen* (New York: 1952), p. 6. In a memorial book for the Jewish population of

Zamość published by former Jewish residents of that town, I. Tsudiker notes that Rosa Luxemburg's father had studied in the rabbinical school but adds that Eliasz was "far from the rabbinate" and also describes Eliasz as an "assimilated Jew who did not have any special connection with Judaism [yidishkayt]." See I. Tsudiker, "Di odlerin vos iz aroysgefloygn fun zamoshtsh," in *Pinkes zamoshtsh*, ed. by Mordekhai V. Bernshtayn (Buenos Aires: Tsentral komitet far pinkes zamoshtsh, 1957), p. 537. The lack of consistency in use of first name may be explained by the fact that Rosa's father conducted business in several languages— including Yiddish, German, and Polish—and may have preferred to be known to various customers by names that would sound familiar and comfortable to them in their native tongue. He may have been named Abraham at birth, been known as Eduard to his German-speaking acquaintances, and known as Eliasz among most of his Polish-speaking friends.

4. For further information on the rabbinical school, see Aron Sawicki, "Szkoła rabinów w warszawie (1826–1863)," *Miesięcznik Żydowski*, 3 (1933), pp. 244–74; Jacob Shatzky [Yankev Shatski], *Yidishe bildungspolitik in poiln fun 1806 biz 1866* (New York: Yidisher visnshaftlekher institut, historishe sektsye, 1943), pp. 37 ff., 122 ff.; idem, *Geshikhte fun yidn in varshe*, II, op. cit., passim.

5. As quoted in Raphael Mahler, *Hasidism and the Jewish Enlightenment: Their Confrontation in Galicia and Poland in the First Half of the Nineteenth Century*, trans. from the Yiddish by Eugene Orenstein; trans. from the Hebrew by Aaron Klein and Jenny Machlowitz Klein (Philadelphia, New York, Jerusalem: Jewish Publication Society of America, 1985), p. 220.

6. Ibid., pp. 220–21.

7. Ezra Mendelsohn, "A Note on Jewish Assimilation in the Polish Lands," in *Jewish Assimilation in Modern Times*, ed. by Bela Vago (Boulder, Col.: Westview Press, 1981), p. 144.

8. Jacob Shatzky [Yankev Shatski], "Der bilbl oyf zamoshtsher yidn in 1870 in likht fun peretses zikhroynes," *Yivo bleter*, XXXVI (1952), p. 331. In this piece, Shatzky indicates that Eduard Luksenburg also used the name Abraham. An Abraham Luksenburg is listed among the financial contributors to a work entitled *Hazrot ha-Shir* (Warsaw: 1840) written by Feivel Schiffer, who was raised in the district of Zamość. Cf. Shatzky, "Haskole in zamoshtsh," op. cit., pp. 46–47, in which the author identifies Rosa's father as a financial contributor to maskilish literature, but in which he refers to Abraham Luksenburg and Eduard Luksenburg as if they were two different, related individuals.

9. Shatzky, *Geshikhte fun yidn in varshe*, op. cit., II, 276.

10. Shatzky, "Der bilbl oyf zamoshtsher yidn in 1870 in likht fun peretses zikhroynes," op. cit., p. 330.

11. The Luksenburgs's use of non-Jewish languages has often been taken as

evidence of their extreme assimilation. But the Jews of Zamość prided themselves on the extent to which knowledge of German and Polish was common among them. In an ode to Zamość published by the maskil Dovid Shifman in 1878 (which was several years after the Luksenburgs had left Zamość), Shifman boasted that "there was not a single person" among the Jewish proprietors of Zamość "who could not read and write Polish," as quoted in Nachman Meisel [Nakhman Mayzil], *I. l. perets. zayn lebn un shafn, ophandlungen un materialn* (New York: Ikuf farlag, 1945), p. 17. On knowledge of German by Zamość Jewry, see Shatzky, "Haskole in zamoshtsh," op. cit., p. 28.

12. Meisel, op. cit., p. 16. Shatzky once noted that at the end of the eighteenth and beginning of the nineteenth centuries precisely the opposite had been the case: "The struggles in Zamość between *khasidim* [adherents of a Jewish religious movement that tended to be sympathetic toward mysticism] and *misnagdim* [opponents of the *khasidim* within Jewish Orthodoxy], *maskilim* and their opponents were, comparatively speaking, much sharper and keener than in other Jewish cities of that size." (Shatzky, "Perets-shtudies," op. cit., p. 41). Cf. Sh. Niger, *I. l. perets, zayn lebn, zayn firndike persenlekhkeyt, zayne hebreishe un yidishe shriftn, zayn virkung* (Buenos Aires: Argentiner opteyl fun alveltlekhn yidishn kultur-kongres, 1952), p. 43; Yehuda Arye Klausner, "Studies on the Life and Work of Yishaq Leyb Peretz, with special reference to an Unknown Manuscript" (unpublished Ph.D. dissertation, University of London, 1958), p. 31.

13. J. Altberg, "Gmina Izraelska w Zamościu," *Jutrzenka*, I, 20 (November 15, 1861), p. 162. A Yiddish translation of this article appears in Bernshtayn, ed., *Pinkes zamoshtsh*, op. cit., pp. 366–72.

14. Nettl asserts, "The Jewish community of Zamość at any rate did not approve of families like the Luxemburgs; it is significant that none of the children ever played any part in Jewish movements or affairs" and cites Shatzky's "Der bilbl oyf zamoshtsher yidn in 1870 in likht fun peretses zikhroynes" in support of these contentions (Nettl, op. cit., I, p. 52). Shatzky's article, however, says nothing whatsoever about Rosa's siblings, nor does it indicate that the Luxemburgs were not approved of by their *landslayt*.

15. Shatzky, "Der bilbl oyf zamoshtsher yidn in 1870 in likht fun peretses zikhroynes," op. cit., pp. 330–31. Cf. footnote 17, infra, for details of this incident.

16. Luise Kautsky, *Rosa Luxemburg. Ein Gedenkbuch* (Berlin: E. Laubsche Verlagsbuchhandlung G.m.b.H., 1929), p. 23.

17. Ibid.; article on Bernhard Löwenstein in *Encyclopedia Judaica*, XI, p. 451. According to Silberner, Bernhard Löwenstein began to serve as a preacher in Lemberg in 1863 (not 1862) and remained in that post until his death in 1889. See Edmund Silberner, "Rosa Luxemburg, ihre Partei und die Judenfrage," *Jahrbuch des Instituts für deutsche Geschichte,*

VII (1978), p. 300. Ettinger asserts that Bernhard Löwenstein and Lina Luksenburg "maintained no contact" during their adult years and hypothesizes that their failure to maintain contact may have been "an indication that Lina's family disapproved of her marriage outside the Orthodox faith" (Elżbieta Ettinger, *Rosa Luxemburg. A Life* [Boston: Beacon Press, 1986], p. 5). Whether or not Lina's parents approved of her marriage, her brother would have been unlikely to object to it on the grounds that Eliasz was insufficiently orthodox, since Bernhard was himself an active advocate of religious reform. Evidence provided by Shatzky, moreover, suggests that the Luksenburgs may well have been in contact with Bernhard Löwenstein as late as 1870. At that time, eight Jews in Zamość were accused of theft and were in danger of being executed. The rest of the Jewish community of Zamość decided to attempt to come to the aid of those arrested by appealing to world-renowned Jewish leaders and, in order to establish contact with such leaders, decided to request the help of Bernhard Löwenstein. How, Shatzky rhetorically asks, would Zamość Jewry have known of the existence of Löwenstein (who was himself far from being world re-nowned)? And Shatzky replies: It was in all likelihood Eliasz Luksenburg, Bernhard's brother-in-law, who suggested contacting Bernhard and who arranged the trip to Lemberg to meet with Löwenstein (Shatzky, "Der bilbl oyf zamoshtsher yidn in 1870 in likht fun peretses zikroynes," op. cit., pp. 330–31).

18. A. B. [J. S. Hertz], "Tsurikgeshmust," *Unzer tsayt* (July-August 1959), p. 32. In a conversation with me on March 23, 1982, Hertz noted that the letters from Lina Luksenburg to Rosa Luxemburg were at one time in the possession of the Bund archives and that they were probably given by Rosa Luxemburg to John Mill and by Mill to the archives. Portions of the collection of the Bund archives were, however, de-stroyed during World War II. I have been unable to locate any letters by Lina Luksenburg in the extant portions of the Bund archives' collec-tion.

19. Anna Luksenburg to Rosa Luxemburg (undated, after September 30, 1897), as quoted in Elżbieta Ettinger, "Rosa Luxemburg: Letters from Warsaw," *Formations*, IV, 3 (Winter 1988), p. 32.

20. Ettinger, *Rosa Luxemburg. A Life*, op. cit., p. 5.

21. Ibid., p. 6.

22. Klausner, "Studies," op. cit., p. 130.

23. Klausner, "Studies," op. cit., p. 128. It is likely that Peretz knew the Luksenburgs. Peretz allegedly made a favorable reference to Rosa Lux-emburg in a conversation following a speech delivered in Lodz in 1908 or 1909 (without, however, indicating at that time whether or not he had been personally acquainted with Luxemburg's family). See Yitshok Gordin, "Roza luksemburg—odler fun revolutsie," *Morgn frayhayt* (December 31, 1967), p. 11. Shatzky has claimed that a section of

Peretz's memoirs referring to a certain "A . . . L . . . ," who is described as living on the edge of Zamość, and as having a hunchback as his only daughter, was in fact a veiled allusion to Rosa Luxemburg and to her father. See Shatzky, "Der bilbl oyf zamoshtsher yidn in 1870 in likht fun peretses zikhroynes," op. cit., p. 331; see also I. L. Peretz [Perets], *In mayn vinkele. mayne zikhroynes*, 2d ed. *Di verk fun itskhok leybush perets*, XIII, ed. by Dovid Pinski (New York: Farlag "yidish," 1920, p. 77. Shatzky's claim has been contested by Helmut Hirsch, who pointed out that Rosa was not a hunchback, that Peretz's description of the location at which "A . . . L . . ." lived did not correspond to the location at which the Luksenburg family is known to have resided, and that Rosa's father had two daughters, not one. See Helmut Hirsch, *Rosa Luxemburg in Selbstzeugnissen und Bilddokumenten* (Reinbek bei Hamburg: Rowholt, 1969), p. 131.

24. Ettinger, *Rosa Luxemburg. A Life*, op. cit., p. 8.

25. The specific catalyst for the family's move may well have been the cholera epidemic of 1873, which led many families to leave Zamość (Klausner, "Studies," op. cit., p. 130). Economic factors probably also played a role. Changing economic conditions led large numbers of Jews to move to Warsaw in the latter half of the nineteenth century. There were 41,062 Jews in Warsaw in 1856, and 219,141 in 1897 (Mendelsohn, "A Note on Jewish Assimilation in the Polish Lands," op. cit., p. 147). By drawing attention to factors specific to the cultural climate of Zamość that may have contributed to the Luksenburgs's decision to move, I do not intend to deny that other factors probably played a major role in that decision.

26. Anna Luksenburg to Rosa Luxemburg (undated, after September 30, 1897), as quoted in Ettinger, "Rosa Luxemburg: Letters from Warsaw," op. cit., p. 32.

27. Ettinger, *Rosa Luxemburg. A Life*, op. cit., p. 68. Ettinger, "Rosa Luxemburg: Letters from Warsaw," op. cit., pp. 35, 36, 39, 40, 41.

28. The information presented above raises the intriguing question of why Luxemburg has traditionally been presented as descended from an all but completely assimilated family. One answer, suggested by Nettl (see note 1, supra), is that certain of Luxemburg's early biographers misstated Luxemburg's family background in order to make it more politically palatable to themselves. A second, complementary answer (first suggested by Ettinger) is that Luxemburg obfuscated her own background. Ettinger has asserted, for example, that Luxemburg "started to weave a legend about her own life and family, a legend which has become part of her official biographies. . . . [H]er origins oppressed her, . . . in order to liberate herself from Polish Jewry she created these legends," as quoted in Muriel Cohen, "Presenting Her Past," *The Boston Globe Magazine* (May 31, 1987), p. 46. The creation of this legend seems to have been aided by Rosa's siblings, who were interviewed by

several of Luxemburg's biographers. In a letter written by Rosa's brother Josef Luxenburg in the summer of 1922 to Luise Kautsky (who had been a close friend of Rosa, and who later wrote a widely known biographical sketch of Rosa's life), Josef mentions that he had received a request for an interview about Rosa's childhood and family home from a woman who intended to write an article about these matters for a German Jewish newspaper and who indicated that Luise had suggested contacting Josef. The reporter, Josef notes, was particularly interested in Rosa's Jewish consciousness. "Speaking openly," Josef continues, "I do not know if it is right for a person who is wholly unknown to me to write so personally about Rosa without further ado, and I would appreciate hearing your opinion in this matter. I answered the woman provisionally that I am prepared to [be interviewed] after I return from my vacation, but emphasized at the same time that there was no Jewish consciousness to be discovered in the development of Rosa's view of the world." In Josef Luxenburg to Luise Kautsky (July 29, 1922), Kautsky Family Archive, Portfolio 14, Map 1, International Institute of Social History, Amsterdam. This passage suggests that Josef may well have been engaging in a deliberate cover-up. It also suggests that Luise Kautsky may have been privy to more information than she revealed to her readers in her own biography of Luxemburg.

29. Luxemburg almost certainly would have insisted that her position on the Jewish question was rooted first and foremost in Marxist principles. Luxemburg's perspective was, however, overdetermined. "Clinically, 'overdetermination' means that every symptom and symbol has many layers of meaning from the present and the psychodynamic past. Functionally, for the psychohistorian, it means that when a person strongly and passionately takes a position, there are invariably private (rational and irrational) reasons as well as the reasons of public discourse for the intensity of the commitment." (Peter Loewenberg, *Decoding the Past. The Psychohistorical Approach* [Berkeley, Los Angeles, London: University of California Press], pp. 183–84).

30. See, for example, Luxemburg to Jogiches (June 24, 1898) in Feliks Tych, ed. *Róża Luksemburg Listy do Leona Jogichesa-Tyszki*, I (Warsaw: Książka i Wiedza, 1968), p. 213.

31. Mill, *Pionern un boyer*, op. cit., I, pp. 179–80.

32. Quoted in A. B., "Tsurikgeshmust," op. cit., p. 32. Cf. Ettinger, *Rosa Luxemburg. A Life*, op. cit., p. 219.

33. A.B., "Tsurikgeshmust," op. cit., p. 31. The other non-Jew to whom Luxemburg refers is Feliks Dzierżyński. On Dzierżyński's knowledge of Yiddish, see Karl Radek, *Portraits and Pamphlets* (London: Wishart Books Ltd., 1935), p. 100.

34. In 1886 Jogiches organized the first Jewish workers' circle in Vilna. When, in 1887, the handful of revolutionaries in Vilna divided tasks among themselves in order to facilitate their work, Jogiches was put in

charge of agitating among non-Jewish workers and of fostering contacts with soldiers and officers. He was also made manager of an illegal library of revolutionary materials. Jogiches was, moreover, the leader of a strike by thirty typesetters that occurred in Vilna in 1888. On Jogiches's role in Vilna, see Avrom Gordon [Avrom Rezshtsik], *In friling fun vilner yidisher arbeter bavegung* (Vilna, 1926), pp. 13–14; Z[almen] Reyzen, "L. jogiches-tishka un der baginen fun der yidisher arbeter-bavegung," *Yivo bleter*, I (1931), pp. 432–48; T. M. Kopelzon, "Yidishe arbeter bavegung in vilna sof akhtsiker un onhoyb nayntsiker yorn," trans. from Russian into Yiddish by Ephim Jeshurin; *Vilna*, ed. by Ephim H. Jeshurin (New York: Vilner brentsh 367 arbeter ring, 1935), pp. 58, 61; Pati [Kremer], "Zikhroynes vegn arkadin," in *Arkadi. zamlbukh tsum ondenk fun grinder fun "bund" arkadi kremer (1865–1935)* (New York: Farlag "unzer tsayt," 1942), pp. 44–45.

35. Mill, op. cit., I, p. 98. Mill reports that the Jewish socialists had wanted to send the transcript to Plekhanov, but were not directly in contact with him. The transcript was, therefore, sent to Jogiches, with a request that he forward the material. Because of a longstanding feud with Plekhanov, however, Jogiches refused to honor this request and published the transcripts himself (ibid., p. 99). Charles Rappaport [Sharl Rapoport], "Dos lebn fun a revolutsionern emigrant. zikhroynes," in *Historishe shriftn*, III, op. cit., p. 299, claims that the transcript was sent to him, but that it somehow fell into Jogiches's hands. Both the claim that Luxemburg wrote the introduction to this transcript (Nettl, op. cit., I, p. 68) and the claim that Jogiches was the author of the introduction ("Fir redes fun yidishe arbeter oyf der mai-fayerung 1892 in vilna," in *Historishe shriftn*, III, op. cit., p. 610) have been forcefully refuted. The introduction was actually written by Boris Krichevsky. See I. Hart [J. S. Hertz], "Nisht ganvenen un nisht felshn," *Unzer tsayt* (September 1961), p. 24; Moshe Mishkinski, Letter to the editor, *Soviet Studies*, XIX, 3 (January 1968), p. 454.

36. Mill, op. cit., I, p. 180.

37. Kursky, *Gezamlte shriftn*, op. cit., p. 171.

38. Mill reported that he was too busy to fill Luxemburg's request, and that the article was written by someone else, but that he no longer remembered who it was that had written the piece in question. Mill was probably referring to the article on the Bund by L. Bernstein that appeared in *Przegląd Socjaldemokratyczny* in 1902. See Arkadi Kremer to L. Bernstein (September 1902) in *Arkadi, zamlbukh tsum ondenk fun grinder fun "bund" arkadi kremer (1865–1935)*, op. cit., p. 342.

39. "Noch einmal der Pariser Socialisten-Congress und die jüdischen 'Genossen,' " *Die Welt*, IV, 46 (November 16, 1900), pp. 11–12.

40. Mill, op. cit., I, p. 216.

41. Ibid., p. 225.

42. Ibid.
43. Ibid., I, p. 248. The SDKP, founded in 1892–93, became the SDKPiL when the Lithuanian Social Democrats merged with the Polish Social Democratic group.
44. As quoted in J. L. Talmon, *The Myth of the Nation and the Vision of Revolution. The Origins of Ideological Polarisation in the Twentieth Century* (London: Secker & Warburg; Berkeley and Los Angeles: University of California Press, 1980), p. 218.
45. Efrim Kupfer, "Tsu der frage fun kamf fun SDKPL far der klasn-aynhayt fun di poylishe un yidishe arbeter," *Bleter far geshikhte*, VII, 2–3 (April-August 1954), pp. 175–76.
46. Ibid., pp. 176–77.
47. At that time, the SKDPiL and the Bund generally felt closer to each other than to the PPS. The SKDPiL and the Bund were both hostile to the notion that socialists ought to demand the recreation of an independent Polish state (which was the defining characteristic of the program of the PPS). Moreover, both the Bund and the SKDPiL thought of themselves as Marxist parties and of the PPS as a non-Marxist grouping. In addition, some leaders of the SKDPiL were eager to work with the Bund because they believed that it could be used as a vehicle for the assimilation of Jewish workers (Jerzy Holzer, "Relations between Polish and Jewish left wing groups in interwar Poland," in *The Jews in Poland*, edited by Chimen Abramsky, Maciej Jachimczyk, and Antony Polonsky [Oxford: Basil Blackwell, 1986], p. 141). Wistrich suggests that Bundist leaders may also have been less distrustful of the SDKPiL leadership than of the PPS because so many of the key figures in the SKDPiL leadership were themselves of Jewish origin (Wistrich, *Revolutionary Jews*, op. cit., p. 82). The points made above notwithstanding, relations between the SKDPiL and the Bund were by no means always cordial. For further details on the relationship between these parties see M. K. Dziewanoski, *The Communist Party of Poland. An Outline of History*, 2d ed. (Cambridge, Mass., and London: Harvard University Press, 1976), pp. 37–38; Tobias, op. cit., pp. 290 ff; Georg W. Strobel, *Die Partei Rosa Luxemburgs, Lenin and die SPD. Der polnische "europäische" Internationalismus in der russischen Sozialdemokratie* (Weisbaden: Franz Steiner Verlag GmbH, 1974), pp. 242–47; John Bunzl, *Klassenkampf in der Diaspora. Zur Geschichte der jüdischen Arbeiterbewegung*, Schriftenreihe des Ludwig-Boltzmann-Instituts für Geschichte der Arbeiterbewegung, 5 (Vienna: Europa Verlag, 1975), pp. 93–95.
48. Luxemburg to Jogiches (June 17, 1905), as quoted in Ettinger, *Rosa Luxemburg. A Life*, op. cit., p. 126. At the time of the second congress of the RSDRP in 1903, Luxemburg had had a different stance—or at least had suggested a different formulation of her stance for public consumption. In a letter of instruction to Adolph Warszawski (Warski), Luxemburg had declared that the SKDPiL delegates to the RSDRP

congress should pronounce unification of the Bund with the RSDRP "correct but at present impracticable." See H. Shukman, "The Relations between the Jewish Bund and the RSDRP, 1897–1903" (unpublished D. Phil. thesis, Oxford University, 1961), p. 285.

49. This incident is mentioned in the memoirs of a number of leading Bundists. See B[eynish] Michalewicz [Mikhalevitsh] [Joseph Isbitzki], *Zikhroynes fun a yudishn sotsialist,* III (Warsaw: Farlag "di velt," 1923), pp. 148–50; Vladimir Medem, *Fun mayn leben,* II ([New York]: Vladimir medem komite, 1923), pp. 182–83; Zivion (Dr. B. Hoffman) Tsivyon (Dr. b. hofman)], *Far fuftsik yor. geklibene shriftn* (New York: E. laub farlag ko., 1948), pp. 119–20; R[aphael] R. Abramovitch [Rafail Abramovich Rein], *In tsvey revolutsies. di geshikhte fun a dor,* I (New York: Farlag "arbeter-ring," 1944), p. 306.

50. Luxemburg to Clara Zetkin (June 4, 1907), Rosa Luxemburg, *Gesammelte Briefe,* II (Berlin: Dietz Verlag, 1982), p. 294.

51. Rosa Luxemburg, "The National Question and Autonomy," in *The National Question. Selected Writings by Rosa Luxemburg,* ed. by Horace B. Davis (New York and London: Monthly Review Press, 1976), pp. 266–67.

52. B. Nelin [Boris Markovitsh Frumkin], "Der internatsionaler sotsialistisher kongres in shtutgart," *Folkstsaytung,* 429 (August 26, 1907), p. 1.

53. F.B. "Notitsn," *Eyn tog* (1907), p. 3. In her articles on autonomy (Luxemburg, "The National Question and Autonomy," op. cit., p. 149), Luxemburg mentions the SERP and refers to "its ultimate goal, territorial (!) autonomy for the Jews." Her punctuation succinctly sums up her view of SERP's platform.

54. Rosa Luxemburg, "Fragment über Krieg, nationale Frage und Revolution," in *Gesammelte Werke,* IV, 2d ed. (Berlin: Dietz Verlag, 1979), pp. 367–68.

55. Studies of Luxemburg's views on the national question include: Joseph A. Petrus, "The Theory and Practice of Internationalism: Rosa Luxemburg's Solution to the National Question," *East European Quarterly,* IV, 4 (January 1971), pp. 442–56; Arieh Yaari, "Rosa Luxemburg ou le nihilisme national," *Les nouveaux cahiers* (Hiver 1974–75), pp. 27–31; Jürgen Hentze, *Nationalismus und Internationalismus bei Rosa Luxemburg,* Beiträge zur Politikwissenschaft, IV (Bern: Herbert Lang; Frankfurt/M.: Peter Lang, 1975); Michael Löwy, "Marxists and the National Question," *New Left Review,* 96 (March-April 1976), pp. 85–89; the introduction by Horace B. Davis to *The National Question. Selected Writings by Rosa Luxemburg,* op. cit., pp. 9–23; A. Walicki, "Rosa Luxemburg and the Question of Nationalism in Polish Marxism (1893–1914)," *The Slavonic and East European Review,* LXI (October 1983), pp. 565–82; and Anna K. Shelton, "Rosa Luxemburg and the National Question," *East European Quarterly,* XXI (September 1987), pp. 297–303.

56. Rosa Luxemburg, "Die nationalen Kämpfe in der Türkei und die Sozial-demokratie," in *Gesammelte Werke*, op. cit., I, 1, p. 63.
57. Ibid., p. 65.
58. See Rosa Luxemburg, "The Polish Question at the International Congress in London," in *The National Question: Selected Writings by Rosa Luxemburg*, op. cit., pp. 49–59; and the articles in *Gesammelte Werke*, op. cit., I, 1, pp. 14 ff.
59. Rosa Luxemburg, *The Industrial Development of Poland*, trans. by Tessa DeCarlo (New York: Campaigner Publications, University Editions, 1977).
60. Luxemburg, "The National Question and Autonomy," op. cit., pp. 112, 152.
61. Ibid., p. 125.
62. As quoted in Ettinger, ed., *Comrade and Lover*, op. cit., p. 16.
63. Luxemburg to Jogiches (June 9, 1898), *Listy*, I, 197, as quoted in Ettinger, *Rosa Luxemburg. A Life*, op. cit., p. 78.
64. Rosa Luxemburg to Jogiches (January 28, 1902), adapted from the translation in Ettinger, ed., *Comrade and Lover*, op. cit., p. 122. Ettinger's translation of the word *zydłaków* as "kikes" strikes me as somewhat too strong.
65. Luxemburg to Konstantin Zetkin (May 12, 1907), in Rosa Luxemburg, *Gesammelte Briefe*, op. cit., II, p. 289.
66. My thanks to W. G. Zimmermann of the Stadtarchiv Zürich for sending me a photocopy of this form. A photograph of this form has been published in Verena Stadler-Labhart, *Rosa Luxemburg an der Universität Zürich 1889–1897*, Schriften zur Zürcher Universitäts- und Gelehrtengeschichte, II (Zurich: Verlag Hans Rohr, 1978), illustration 3. The form in question was filled out by a city official rather than by Luxemburg, but was presumably based on answers given by Luxemburg to questions posed by this official. Jewish students from Russia who moved to Zurich were not pressured by the government officials responsible for *Einwohnerkontrolle* to have themselves listed as Jewish, and were free to describe themselves as *konfessionslos* if they so desired (Jacques E. Picard to Jack Jacobs [November 24, 1988], citing Daniela Neumann, *Studentinnen aus dem Russischen Reich in der Schweiz [1867–1914]*, Die Schweiz und der Osten Europas, I [Zurich: Verlag Hans Rohr, 1987]). Luxemburg's decision to have herself listed as Jewish did not oblige her to pay dues to an official organization of the Jewish community (Werner G. Zimmermann to Jack Jacobs [December 28, 1988]). Significantly, a large number of Luxemburg's contemporaries who were not Swiss citizens, who were of Jewish origin, and who were living in Zurich, did in fact choose to have themselves listed as konfessionslos in the same period during which Luxemburg chose to have herself listed as Jewish. See *Die Ergebnisse der eidgenössischen Volkszählung vom 1. Dezember 1900 in der Stadt Zürich*. 1. Heft (Zürich: Kommissionsverlag

Ed. Rascher's Erben [Meyer & Zeller's Nachfolger], 1905), table XXVI. Though Luxemburg's decision to have herself listed as *jued.* rather than *konfessionslos* was significant, her designation as *jued.* rather than *israelitisch* or *mosaisch* on this form has no particular significance. These terms were used synonymously by the relevant city officials (Werner G. Zimmermann to Jack Jacobs [December 28, 1988]). Luxemburg did not describe herself as Jewish at the end of her life (Hirsch, *Rosa Luxemburg*, op. cit., 18). Cf. Hauptstaatsarchiv Düsseldorf, Rep. 17, Bd. I (=208), Bl. 92; Hauptstaatsarchiv Düsseldorf, Rep. 17, Bd. II (=209), Bl. 1. My thanks to Helmut Hirsch for sending me copies of these two documents.

67. "Friedenkertum und Sozialdemokratie," *Vorwärts*, 226 (September 27, 1910), pp. 1–2; "Dwa Obozy," *Młot*, 9 (October 1, 1910), pp. 9–10; "Po Pogromie," *Młot*, 10 (October 8, 1910), pp. 1–2; "Odwrót na calej linji," *Młot*, 11 (October 15, 1910), pp. 9–10; "Ostatnia Próba," *Młot*, 13 (October 29, 1910), pp. 3–5; "Dyskusja," *Młot*, 14 (November 5, 1910), pp. 5–7; "Ein literarisches Bravo," *Vorwärts*, 274 (November 23, 1910), p. 2; "Pozegnanie z p. Niemojewskim," *Młot*, 18 (December 3, 1910), pp. 8–9; "Befremdende Kampfmethoden," *Vorwärts*, 292 (December 14, 1910), p. 3. The single best discussion of these articles is that of G. Haupt and P. Korzec, "Les socialistes et la campagne antisémite en Pologne en 1910: un épisode inédit," *Revue du Nord*, LVII, 225 (April-June 1975), pp. 185–94.

68. Robert Wistrich's use of the concept of Jewish self-hatred in his work *Revolutionary Jews from Marx to Trotsky* has been criticized by a number of reviewers: Lionel Kochan, "Moved to Revolution," *TLS* (August 20, 1976), p. 1029; Hyman Maccoby, "On the Left," *Commentary*, LXIII (April 1977), p. 80; Ferdinand Mount, "Revolutionaries. Their Mind, Body, and Soul," *Encounter*, XLIX (December 1977), p. 64; William H. Friedland, Review of *Revolutionary Jews*, *American Journal of Sociology*, LXXXIII (1978), p. 1552. It ought to be noted, however, that, whatever his position may have been on this point when writing *Revolutionary Jews*, Wistrich subsequently denied that Luxemburg suffered a classic case of self-hatred: "Though Rosa Luxemburg, like Marx avoided all reference to her Jewish origin, she does not appear to have suffered from the obvious symptoms of self-hatred which many revolutionaries from a similar background exhibited. There are for example almost none of the sarcastic remarks about Jews in her correspondence that one can readily find in Marx, Lassalle, or Victor Adler." See Robert Wistrich, "The Jewish Origins of Rosa Luxemburg," *Olam*, 3 (Winter-Spring 1977), p. 5.

69. Ettinger, *Rosa Luxemburg. A Life*, op. cit., p. xiii.

70. Ibid., p. 218.

71. Certain components of Luxemburg's position on the Jewish question also bear a somewhat fainter resemblance to the positions held by most

German Jews in Luxemburg's day. But these latter similarities did not lead Luxemburg and German Jewry to sympathize with one another. In fact, Luxemburg studiously avoided commenting on German anti-Semitism and also avoided contact with the German Jewish community or with its members. In an unpublished memoir (a copy of which is held by the Leo Baeck Institute in New York) Bernhard Kahn, a leading member of the Hilfsverein der Deutschen Juden, once asserted that his wife, Dora, "was from her student time also a friend of Rosa Luxemburg" (Kahn, p. 66). This relationship, however, was apparently strictly personal, not political. Luxemburg's origins to the contrary notwithstanding, she did not think of herself as a Jew and did not feel any affinity with or sympathy for the German Jewish community per se.

Luxemburg's lack of sympathy for German Jewry was matched by an equally studied lack of sympathy for Luxemburg on the part of German Jewry. The class backgrounds, religious sensibilities, and political inclinations of German Jewish leaders contributed to a consistent predilection by German Jewry to avoid Luxemburg in a manner directly paralleling her avoidance of it. The propensity of German Jewish publicists to avoid mention of Luxemburg was almost certainly reinforced by knowledge of the intense animosity against Luxemburg in certain sectors of the non-Jewish population. German Jewish leaders apparently believed—quite legitimately—that any indication of interest in Luxemburg by German Jews could be used by anti-Semites against the German Jewish community. Given the intensity of the emotions that Luxemburg raised, German Jewish leaders seem to have concluded, it made even more sense for them to ignore Luxemburg than it did for them to combat her. The organs of German Jewry did not review her works, discuss her activities, debate her ideas, or even condemn her murder. In fact, to the best of my knowledge, Luxemburg was never even mentioned in any of the German Jewish periodicals of her day. But it was not Rosa Luxemburg's position on the Jewish question that led German Jewry to keep as much distance as it could from Luxemburg, but rather her position on the monarchy and on the road to socialism. In fact, German Jewry kept an equally studied distance from all of the revolutionaries of East European Jewish origin who were active on German soil—i.e., Jogiches, Parvus, Leviné, and Radek.

#### 4. Austrian Social Democrats and the Jews

1. See, for example, Victor Adler to Engelbert Pernerstorfer (May 30, 1872), Adler-Archiv, Mappe 138, Verein für Geschichte der Arbeiterbewegung (Vienna), in which Adler complains about Max von Gruber's attitude toward Jews.

2. Adler-Archiv, Mappe 6/V, Verein für Geschichte der Arbeiterbewegung. The document in question dates from the mid-1860s and was published

decades later by Pernerstorfer (Storfer [E. Pernerstorfer], "Viktor Adlers erstes Flugblatt," *Der Arbeiter-Zeitung. Scherzblatt zum 60. Geburtstag ihres Chefs*, 2 (June 24, 1912), p. 1. A photograph of this document is reproduced in Julius Braunthal, *Victor und Friedrich Adler. Zwei Generationen Arbeiterbewegung*, (Vienna: Wiener Volksbuchhandlung, 1965), between pages 48 and 49. Cf. Max Ermers, *Victor Adler. Aufstieg und Grösse einer sozialistischen Partei* (Vienna and Leipzig: Verlag Dr. Hans Epstein, 1932), p. 20; Friedrich Adler to Adolf Schaerf (January 4, 1957), Adler-Archiv, Mappe 6/V, Verein für Geschichte der Arbeiterbewegung; Wistrich, *Revolutionary Jews*, op. cit., p. 99. In an undated memoir, Pernerstorfer claimed that during his student years "there was on the whole no anti-Semitism in the population of Vienna" ("Kinderjahre," typescript, Pernerstorfer Nachlaß, Verein für Geschichte der Arbeiterbewegung).

3. Theodor Billroth, *Über das Lehren und Lernen der medicinischen Wissenschaften an den Universitäten der Deutschen Nation nebst allgemeinen Bemerkungen über Universitäten. Eine culturhistorische Studie* (Vienna: Carl Gerold's Sohn, 1876), as quoted in Dennis B. Klein, *Jewish Origins of the Psychoanalytic Movement* (Chicago and London: University of Chicago Press, 1985), p. 50. I follow Klein throughout the following discussion on Billroth.

4. Billroth, as quoted in Klein, *Jewish Origins of the Psychoanalytic Movement*, op. cit., pp. 50–51.

5. Billroth, as quoted in Klein, *Jewish Origins of the Psychoanalytic Movement*, op. cit., p. 51. For information on the context within which Billroth made these remarks, see Erna Lesky, *The Vienna Medical School of the 19th Century* (Baltimore and London: Johns Hopkins University Press, 1976), pp. 261–62.

6. Klein, *Jewish Origins of the Psychoanalytic Movement*, op. cit. pp. 51–52.

7. William J. McGrath, *Dionysian Art and Populist Politics in Austria* (New Haven and London: Yale University Press, 1974), p. 33–34.

8. Ibid:, p. 39.

9. Friedrich Adler to Julius Braunthal (April 27, 1948), Adler-Archiv, Mappe 99, Verein für Geschichte der Arbeiterbewegung.

10. My account of Adler's lecture is derived from Braunthal, *Victor und Friedrich Adler*, op. cit., p. 19.

11. Klein, *Jewish Origins of the Psychoanalytic Movement*, op. cit., p. 52.

12. As evidence of Adler's continued affiliation with the *Leseverein*, see the library card dated February 12, 1877, in the Adler-Archiv, Mappe 6, Verein für Geschichte der Arbeiterbewegung.

13. In a letter written at the age of nineteen, for example, Adler describes the young woman who was at that time the object of his affections and comments, "Imagine! I, a poor, stuttering, ugly Jew, clumsy, awkward,

and she, beautiful, brilliant, educated—how do I dare?" (Victor Adler to Engelbert Pernerstorfer [September 19, 1871], Adler-Archiv, Mappe 138, Verein für Geschichte der Arbeiterbewegung). Cf. Victor Adler to Engelbert Pernerstorfer (November 23, 1874), Adler-Archiv, Mappe 138, Verein für Geschichte der Arbeiterbewegung. The notion that Pernerstorfer's attitude toward Jews may have had an impact on Adler was suggested by Ermers, *Victor Adler*, op. cit., p. 230.

14. In a will dated November 7, 1913, Victor Adler indicates that he became a Protestant only in order to make his children's separation from Judaism "more thorough and easier" and in order to save them from the difficulties that were at that time encountered by Austrians who were not affiliated with any religious community (Adler-Archiv, Mappe 1, Verein für Geschichte der Arbeiterbewegung).

    Though by the end of the nineteenth century "Vienna's Jewish conversion rate far outranked that of any other city in the Dual Monarchy or elsewhere in Europe" (Rozenblit, *The Jews of Vienna, 1867–1914: Assimilation and Identity*, op. cit., p. 132), the number of individual Viennese males who converted from Judaism in any given year in the late 1870s or early 1880s was still small. A total of 61 males, for example, converted in 1880. In Adler's circle, however, his conversion was far from unique. Adler's brother-in-law, Heinrich Braun, for example, also converted at some point (Wistrich, *Revolutionary Jews*, op. cit., p. 101).

15. See the *ksuba* (marriage certificate) in Adler-Archiv, Mappe 31, Verein für Geschichte der Arbeiterbewegung.

16. Emma Adler, "Biographie Victor Adler," typescript, p. 13, Adler-Archiv, Mappe 29, Verein für Geschichte der Arbeiterbewegung. Emma, who was of Jewish origin, did not undergo baptism.

17. Emma Adler, "Biographie Victor Adler," typescript, pp. 13–14, Adler-Archiv, Mappe 29, Verein für Geschichte der Arbeiterbewegung.

18. Rudolf G. Ardelt, *Friedrich Adler. Probleme einer Persönlichkeitsentwicklung um die Jahrhundertwende* (Vienna: Österreichischer Bundesverlag, 1984), p. 29. Whereas Braunthal seems to emphasize that this pithy characterization was meant to be droll, Ardelt asserts that this characterization was nevertheless an accurate one (Ardelt, *Friedrich Adler*, op. cit., p. 243).

19. On Schönerer, see Oscar Karbach, "The Founder of Modern Political Antisemitism: Georg von Schoenerer," *Jewish Social Studies*, VII, 1 (January 1945), pp. 3–30.

20. Pulzer, *The Rise of Political Anti-Semitism in Germany and Austria*, op. cit., pp. 150 ff.

21. In a letter to Schönerer dated April 22, 1883, Pernerstorfer noted that "the form of anti-Semitism which seems today to be, or at least to be becoming, Party dogma among us, appears completely unacceptable to me. The struggle, it seems to me, is leveled far more against the Jews

than against *Judaism*" (Pernerstorfer Nachlaß, Mappe 1, Verein für Geschichte der Arbeiterbewegung). My thanks to Wolfgang Maderthaner for providing me with a transcript of this letter. Pernerstorfer's case provides evidence in support of the argument made by Scheichl concerning the difference between the private prejudices of certain Austrian social democrats on the one hand and their public attitudes on the other (Sigurd Paul Scheichl, "The Contexts and Nuances of Anti-Jewish Language: Were All the 'Antisemites' Antisemites?" *Jews, Antisemitism and Culture in Vienna*, edited by Ivar Oxaal, Michael Pollak, and Gerhard Botz [London and New York: Routledge & Kegan Paul, 1987], pp. 92–94).

22. Pulzer, *The Rise of Political Anti-Semitism in Germany and Austria*, op. cit., pp. 152–53.
23. McGrath, *Dionysian Art and Populist Politics in Austria*, op. cit., p. 196.
24. The single best discussion of opposition to Zionism by Viennese Jews is that of Robert S. Wistrich, *The Jews of Vienna in the Age of Franz Joseph* (Oxford: Littman Library, Oxford University Press, 1989), pp. 458–93.
25. Hertz, "Di ershte ruslander revolutsie 1903–1907," op. cit., p. 120.
26. According to a labor Zionist who discussed the Jewish question with Adler in 1912, Adler "on the whole did not like" the Bund. See Moyshe Nakhman Silberroth [Zilberot], "A unterhaltung mit viktor adler," *Der yudisher arbeyter*, IX, 39 (September 25, 1912), p. 3.
27. Barkai mistakenly indicates that the bill in question was proposed in 1901 (A. Barkai, "The Austrian Social Democrats and the Jews," *Wiener Library Bulletin*, XXIV, 1, n.s. 18 [1970], p. 35).
28. The hostility of the social democratic leadership to Zionism was reciprocated. For examples of the bitter reaction of Austrian Zionists to the social democratic leadership, see "Arbeiterzeitungsjuden," *Jüdische Zeitung. National-jüdisches Organ*, IV, 22 (June 3, 1910), p. 1; "Sozialdemokratie und jüdische Nationalität," *Jüdische Zeitung. National-jüdisches Organ*, IV, 34 (August 26, 1910), pp. 1–2; "Rote Assimilanten als Judenfeinde," *Jüdische Zeitung. National-jüdisches Organ*, V, 18 (May 4, 1911), p. 2.
29. Sh. B. "Di fartretung fun der ts.s.a.p. oyfn shtutgarter kongres," *Unzer veg*, 1 (August 19, September 1, 1907), cols. 15–16. *Unzer veg* was an organ of the SS. Cf., for marginally different versions of Adler's remarks, V. Latski-Bertoldi, *Erdgayst. geklibene shriftn*, I (Paris, Berlin, Warsaw, Vilna: Aroysgegeben funm yobl-komitet, n.d.), pp. 252–53; Nelin "Der internatsionaler sotsialistisher kongres in shtutgart," op. cit.; and Adolf Gaisbauer, *Davidstern und Doppeladler. Zionismus und Jüdischer Nationalismus in Österreich 1882–1918*, Veröffentlichungen der Kommission für neuere Geschichte, LXXVIII (Vienna, Cologne, Graz: Böh-

lau Verlag, 1988), p. 374, citing *Jüdische Zeitung* (September 20, 1907), p. 5. On the identification of Nelin as Frumkin, see Kursky, *Gezamlte shriftn*, op. cit., p. 252. For the reaction to Adler's remarks by the Jewish Socialist Workers' Party Poalei-Zion in Austria (which did not, unlike the ESDRP-PZ, its sister party in Russia, consider itself to be an orthodox Marxist organization), see "Dr. adler iber di estreykhishe poyle tsien," *Der yudisher arbeyter*, IV, 37 (September 13, 1907), pp. 2–3. Adler's comments did not persuade a majority of those with voting rights in the ISB, which voted narrowly in favor of giving a consultative status to the SS. The bid for admission made by the SS was vigorously opposed by the RSDRP and by the Bund. Though Adler's comments concerning the motion to admit the SS were strongly worded, they were no harsher than were those of the Bundist delegates to the congress of the International.

30. For information on Galician Jewish politics at the time of the formation of the ŻPSD, see Leila P. Everett, "The Rise of Jewish National Politics in Galicia, 1905–1907," *Nationbuilding and the Politics of Nationalism. Essays on Austrian Galicia*, ed. by Andrei S. Markovits and Frank E. Sysyn. Harvard Ukrainian Research Institute Monograph Series (Cambridge, Mass.: Harvard Ukrainian Research Institute, Harvard University Press, 1982), pp. 149–77.

31. Pernerstorfer to Victor Adler (July 24, 1904), Adler-Archiv, Mappe 141, Verein für Geschichte der Arbeiterbewegung.

32. Rosa Luxemburg, *Gesammelte Briefe*, I (Berlin: Dietz Verlag, 1982), p. 667.

33. Yoysef Kisman, "Di yidishe sotsial-demokratishe bavegung in galitsie un bukovine," *Di geshikhte fun bund*, op. cit., III (1966), p. 360.

34. Emil Häcker to Victor Adler (April 17, 1905), Adler-Archiv, Mappe 176, Verein für Geschichte der Arbeiterbewegung.

35. "Die Gesamtexekutive und die jüdischen Separatisten in Galizien," *Arbeiter-Zeitung* (May 17, 1905), p. 7. This article has been attributed to Victor Adler (Henryk Piasecki, *Sekcja Żydowska PPSD i Żydowska Partia Socjalno-Demokratyczna 1892–1919/20* [Wrocław, Warsaw, Cracow, Gdańsk, Lodz: Zakład Narodowy im. Ossolińskich wydawnictwo Polskiej Akademii Nauk, 1982], p. 353).

36. *Protokoll über die Verhandlungen des Gesamtparteitages der Sozialdemokratischen Arbeiterpartei in Oesterreich. Abgehalten zu Wien vom 30. Oktober bis zum 2. November 1905* (Vienna: Verlag der Wiener Volksbuchhandlung, 1905), p. 16. Though the resolution of the Executive Committee was supported by all those who ultimately voted in that Committee, the Czech socialist leaders present when this resolution was discussed purportedly supported recognition of the Jewish group during the debate (Raimund Löw, *Der Zerfall der "Kleinen Internationale." Nationalitäten-konflikte in der Arbeiterbewegung des al-*

*ten Oesterreich [1889–1914]*, Ludwig Boltzmann Institut für Geschichte der Arbeiterbewegung, Materialien zur Arbeiterbewegung, 34 [Vienna: Europa Verlag, 1984], p. 64).

37. *Protokoll über die Verhandlungen des Gesamtparteitages der Sozialdemokratischen Arbeiterpartei in Oesterreich. Abgehalten zu Wien vom 30. Oktober bis zum 2. November 1905*, op. cit., p. 87.

38. "An die Sozialdemokraten in Oesterreich!" Broadsheet, File MG-7-29–32, Bund Archives of the Jewish Labor Movement (New York).

39. "Der estreykhisher parteytog," *Der sotsial-demokrat. organ fun der yudisher sotsial-demokratisher partey in galitsien*, I, 6 (November 10, 1905), p. 2.

40. *Protokoll über die Verhandlungen des Gesamtparteitages der Sozialdemokratischen Arbeiterpartei in Oesterreich. Abgehalten zu Wien vom 30. Oktober bis zum 2. November 1905*, op. cit., p. 70.

41. Ibid., p. 90. Cf. "Der estreykhisher sotsial-demokratisher parteytog," *Der yudisher arbeyter*, II, 20 (December 1, 1905), p. 7. Henryk Grossmann, a leader of the ŻPSD, wrote to Adler in order to emphasize his dismay at the failure of the All-Austrian party to admit the ŻPSD; see Grossmann to Adler (October 23, 1905), Adler-Archiv, Mappe 176, Verein für Geschichte der Arbeiterbewegung. It is not known whether Adler replied to Grossmann's letter. The Ukrainian Social Democrats of Galicia were supportive of the ŻPSD and critical of the position taken by the Gesamtpartei Executive. See Mychajlo Lozynskyj, "Die jüdische Frage in Galizien und die österreichische Sozialdemokratie," *Ukrainische Rundschau*, IV, 5 (May 1906), pp. 168–74; IV, 6 (June 1906), pp. 208–14.

42. Silberroth reports he encountered Victor and Emma Adler accidently, on September 15, 1912, in Switzerland, while he was en route to visit the Yiddish writer Sholem Aleichem, and that he ended up riding in the same railway car as did the Adlers for an hour and a half. Though he was loath to disturb the Adlers while they were on their vacation, he decided to take the opportunity in order to discuss a business matter with Emma Adler, publisher of the *Arbeiterinnen-Zeitung*, to which Silberroth had recently submitted an article (which was later published under the title "Landarbeitsheime für genesende Lungenkranke," *Arbeiterinnen-Zeitung. Sozialdemokratisches Organ für Frauen und Mädchen*, XXI, 22 [October 29, 1912], pp. 4–5). He therefore introduced himself, explained that he had contributed the piece, and later began the discussion with Victor Adler reported below (Silberroth, "A unterhaltung mit viktor adler," op. cit.). In Silberroth's piece, Adler indicates, in passing, that he knew how to read Yiddish ("I am the only one in Vienna who reads Jargon. When Zionists come to see me, I read to them aloud in Yiddish, which they do not know.").

43. Yoysef Kisman, "Yidishe sotsialistishe fareynikung in galitsie. (a kapitl bundishe geshikhte—mit 50 yor tsurik," *Unzer tsayt* (November 1961),

p. 26. Recent works dealing with the ŻPSD include Piasecki, *Sekcja Żydowska PPSD i Żydowska Partia Socjalno-Demokratyczna 1892–1919/20*, op. cit., and Shabtai Unger, "The Jewish Workers' Movement in Galicia on the Eve of World War I: The Failure to Unify," [In Hebrew] *Gal-Ed*, X (1987), pp. 121–46.

44. McCagg's statement that "the Galician section of the SDPÖ" (by which he appears to mean the PPSD) "set up a new Jewish section," in 1911, "which then by subtle mergers absorbed the independent one" (the ŻPSD) (William O. McCagg Jr., *A History of Habsburg Jews, 1670–1918* [Bloomington and Indianapolis: Indiana University Press, 1989], p. 185) is inaccurate. The Jewish section of the PPSD was organized in 1906, as the result of a decision reached at the tenth party conference of the PPSD. This Jewish section was renamed Jewish Social Democracy in Galicia in 1907 and continued to function under this name until it merged with the ŻPSD in 1911 (Kisman, "Di yidishe sotsial-demokratishe bavegung in galitsie un bukovine," op. cit., pp. 428 ff). I disagree with the assertion that the Jewish Social Democracy in Galicia "absorbed" the ŻPSD, as McCagg suggests or, for that matter, with the suggestion made by Wistrich, "By 1911 the Jewish Social Democrats of Galicia had capitulated to the Polish party, by accepting fusion with the 'Jewish section' of Daszynski's party" (Robert S. Wistrich, "Austrian Social Democracy and the Problem of Galician Jewry 1890–1914," *Leo Baeck Institute Year Book*, XXVI [1981], p. 114). The ŻPSD was much larger than was the Jewish section and succeeded in imposing its perspective on the new, unified organization. It was the PPSD that had capitulated, not the ŻPSD. The concessions made by the ŻPSD leadership in 1911 were temporary and minor.

45. Ibid., p. 27. Opposition within the ŻPSD to the agreement reached with the PPSD revolved around a compromise to which the ŻPSD leadership had agreed—that is, that the demand for national cultural autonomy for Galician Jewry (which had been a key part of the platform of the ŻPSD since 1906) would remain an "open question" within the new, unified Jewish group, to be resolved at a later date.

46. "Der fareynigungs-kongres fun der yudisher sotsialdemokratisher partey," *Der sotsial-demokrat*, VII, 42 (October 20, 1911); I. [Yakov] Bros, "Tsu der geshikhte fun der i.s.d.p. in galitsie," *Royter pinkes. tsu der geshikhte fun der yidisher arbeter-bavegung un sotsialistishe shtremungen bay yidn*, op. cit., p. 47; Kisman, "Yidishe sotsialistishe fareynikung in galitsie," op. cit., p. 27.

47. Kisman, "Yidishe sotsialistishe fareynikung in galitsie," op. cit., p. 28.

48. Silberroth "A unterhaltung mit viktor adler," op. cit.

49. In 1911, during the election campaign for the Reichsrat, Leopold Fuchs came upon a handbill "written in Hebrew letters" that he was unable to read. When he and a friend of his brought the handbill to Adler, Adler teasingly said, "What kind of Jews are you?, Shame on you" and

claimed that he knew how to translate Hebrew (Leopold Fuchs to Brandl [January 31, 1930], Adler-Archiv, Mappe 25, Verein für Geschichte der Arbeiterbewegung). The document that Fuchs remembers Adler having translated at that time, however, was in all probability written in Yiddish, not Hebrew.

50. L. [S. R. Landau?], " 'Patentierte' Arbeiterführer," *Der jüdische Arbeiter. Organ für die Interessen der jüdischen Arbeiterschaft,* I, 2 (September 1, 1898), p. 1. For a second example of comparable criticism of Adler, see "Zum Parteitag der österreichischen Sozialdemokratie," *Der jüdische Arbeiter; Organ für die Interressen der jüdischen Arbeiter und Handangestellten,* I, 2 (November 1903), p. 4.

51. On Locker, see Zalmen Reyzen, *Leksikon fun der yidisher literatur, prese un filologie,* II, 3d ed. (Vilna: Farlag fun b. kletskin, 1930), c. 82–84.

52. B[erl] L[ocker], "Viktor adler (tsu zayn zekhtsinsten [sic] geburtstog)," *Der yudisher arbeyter. tsentral-organ fun der yudisher sotsialistisher arbeyter-partey poyle-tsien in estreykh,* IX, 26 (June 28, 1912).

53. Ibid.

54. Ibid.

55. Ibid.

56. Ibid.

57. Ibid.

58. For additional information on the attempts by the SS, the SERP, and the ESDRP-PZ to have the International recognize a Jewish section, see Maxim Anin [Maks-Aryeh Z. Shats], "Das Nationalitätsprinzip in der sozialistischen Internationale," *SM,* XIV, 2. Band (1910), pp. 885–90; W. Medem, "Ein nationalistischer Vorschlag," *NZ,* XXVIII, 2. Band (1909–10), pp. 748–51; Maxim Anin, "Das jüdische Proletariat in der Internationale," *SM,* XIV, 2. Band (1910), pp. 1065–68; Maxim Anin, "Was will die jüdische Sektion in der sozialistischen Internationale?" *SM,* XV, 1. Band (1911), pp. 396–401; V[ladimir] K[ossovsky] [Nokhum Mendl Levinson], "Di fartretung in'm internatsional," *Fragen fun leben zamelbukh* (Vilna: 1911), pp. 25–39; the manuscript by Kossovsky, "Ist in der Organisation der Internationale das nationale Prinzip zulässig?" MG1–161, Bund Archives of the Jewish Labor Movement; and Ezra Mendelsohn, "The Jewish Socialist Movement and the Second International, 1889–1914: The Struggle for Recognition," *Jewish Social Studies,* XXVI (1964), pp. 142–45.

59. L[ocker], "Viktor adler (tsu zayn zekhtsinsten [sic] geburtstog)," op. cit.

60. Ibid.

61. Ibid.

62. R. Nss, "Ein führender Sozialdemokrat über den Nationalitätsgedanken," *Die Welt,* IX, 37 (September 15, 1905), p. 10.

63. "Engelbert pernerstorfer," *Der sotsial-demokrat*, VI, 17 (April 30, 1910), p. 5.

64. Engelbert Pernerstorfer, "Zur Judenfrage," *Der Jude*, I, (1916–17), pp. 313, 311. Cf. Engelbert Pernerstorfer, "Allerlei Kriegsliteratur," *Süddeutsche Monatshefte*, XIII (May 1916), p. 271. When, in late 1917, the Labor Zionist movement hoped to publish an anthology on the Jewish question, Leon Chasanowitsch proposed that Pernerstorfer be invited to write for this book. See Leon Chasanowitsch to Leo Hermann (December 14, 1917), Records of the Central Zionist Office, (Zionistisches Zentralbureau), Berlin, Z 3/1055, Central Zionist Archive (Jerusalem). For an appreciation of Pernerstorfer from the perspective of the Labor Zionist movement, see E. L., "Engelbert Pernerstorfer und die Judenfrage," *Der jüdische Arbeiter*, V, 1 (February 1, 1928), pp. 2–3.

65. [Victor Adler], "Der Antisemitismus," *Gleichheit*, I, 20 (May 7, 1887).

66. For an example of a piece forthrightly condemning anti-Semitism and apparently written by a non-Jewish Austrian socialist, see E[ngelbert] P[ernerstorfer], "Das neue Ghetto," *Arbeiter-Zeitung*, XI, 7 (January 8, 1898), pp. 5–6: "the great traditions of the German people will not disappear, and the time will come again in which Lessing's plain and simple words will be remembered: 'I am no friend of general judgements against whole peoples.' For the time being, we must fight hot and bitter battles, in order first of all to force merely the theoretical recognition of the correctness of this sentence once again." This article is identified as having been written by Pernerstorfer in the index to the *Arbeiter-Zeitung* stored in the Verein für Geschichte der Arbeiterbewegung.

67. For additional details concerning this incident, see Silberner, "Anti-Semitism and Philo-Semitism in the Socialist International," op. cit., pp. 117–20, and Mendelsohn, "The Jewish Socialist Movement and the Second International, 1889–1914: The Struggle for Recognition," op. cit., pp. 133–34.

68. "Zum Brüsseler Kongreß," *Arbeiter-Zeitung* (August 28, 1891), reproduced in *Victor Adlers Aufsätze, Reden und Briefe*, VII (Vienna: Verlag der Wiener Volksbuchhandlung, 1929), pp. 65–66.

69. Ab[raham] Cahan, *Bleter fun mayn leben*, III (New York: "Forverts" asosieyshon, 1926), pp. 162–63.

70. Ibid., p. 163.

71. Ibid., p. 160.

72. Ibid., p. 313.

73. Ibid.

74. *Verhandlungen des sechsten österreichischen Sozialdemokratischen Parteitages abgehalten zu Wien vom 6. bis einschließlich 12. Juni 1897 im Saale des Hotel Wimberger* (Wien: Erste Wiener Volksbuchhandlung [Ignaz Brand], 1897), p. 87.

75. Ibid., p. 103. Cf. *Victor Adlers, Aufsätze, Reden und Briefe*, VIII: Victor

Adler der Parteimann. Reden und Aufsätze, gesammelt und in vier Heften zusammengestellt von Dr. Gustav Pollatschek, mit einer Einleitung von Dr. Otto Bauer. 3: Österreichische Politik (Vienna: Verlag der Wiener Volksbuchhandlung, 1929), p. 387. For discussion of responses to Brod's remarks made by other delegates to the party congress, see Wistrich, Socialism and the Jews, op. cit., pp. 264–69.

76. Verhandlungen des sechsten österreichischen Sozialdemokratischen Parteitages, op. cit., p. 103.

77. Adler's emphasis on the Jewish background of members of the Viennese bourgeoisie distorted the actual class divisions within the Jewish community of Vienna and within Austro-Hungarian Jewry as a whole. The occupational structure of Jews in late Habsburg Austria, and even in late Habsburg Vienna, was far more complex than Adler's comments suggest (Ivar Oxaal and Walter R. Weitzmann, "The Jews of Pre-1914 Vienna: An Exploration of Basic Sociological Dimensions," Leo Baeck Institute Year Book, XXX (1985), pp. 420 ff.

78. Benno Karpeles to Victor Adler (May 16, 1907), Adler-Archiv, Mappe 123, Verein für Geschichte der Arbeiterbewegung. Cf. Benno Karpeles to Victor Adler (July 29, 1897), Adler-Archiv, Mappe 123, Verein für Geschichte der Arbeiterbewegung. Though Karpeles was angered by Adler's comment in 1897, by 1907 he thought that Adler had, after all, been right. For additional information on Karpeles, see Friedrich Adler, ed., VABABKK, op. cit., pp. 204–6; Jean Maitron and Georges Haupt, eds., Dictionnaire biographique du mouvement ouvrier international, I, Autriche (Paris: Les éditions ouvrières, 1971), p. 159. The incident involving Karpeles referred to above provides evidence in support of Ermers's contention (in a portion of his biography of Adler in which he is referring specifically to Adler's attitude toward Jews) that Adler "repelled many capable minds" who desired to work in the party and "drove them into other camps or into emigrating to Germany" (Ermers, Victor Adler, op. cit., p. 231).

79. Hendrik de Man, Gegen den Strom. Memoiren eines europäischen Sozialisten (Stuttgart: Deutsche Verlags-Anstalt, 1953), pp. 91–92. Whatever Renner's position in 1907 may have been, Renner seems to have been concerned about the charges made by anti-Semites regarding the percentage and visibility of socialist leaders of Jewish origin during the First Republic (Friedrich Austerlitz to Karl Renner [October 31, 1929], Das Alte Partei Archiv, Mappe 85, Verein für Geschichte der Arbeiterbewegung).

80. Ermers, Victor Adler, op. cit., p. 230.

81. For evidence of contact between Bundists and Adler, see W. [Vladimir] Kossovsky to Victor Adler (October 26, 1904), Adler-Archiv, Mappe 175, Verein für Geschichte der Arbeiterbewegung; Foreign Committee of the Bund to Victor Adler (May 5, 1905), Adler-Archiv, Mappe 176, Verein für Geschichte der Arbeiterbewegung; Pinsk Organization of the

Bund to Victor Adler (June 19, 1905), Adler-Archiv, Mappe 176, Verein für Geschichte der Arbeiterbewegung.

82. "Die Wiener Sozialdemokratie und der Beilis-prozess," *Neuer Weg*. I, 1 (January 1914), p. 5. Morton indicates that Adler signed a petition to the Czar on Beilis's behalf. See Frederic Morton, *Thunder at Twilight*. *Vienna 1913/1914* (New York: Charles Scribner's Sons, 1989), p. 117. I have been unable to corroborate this information.

83. Ber Borochov, *Ketavim*, III (Tel Aviv: Sifriath Poalim and Hakibbutz hameuchad, 1955), p. 265, as translated in Barkai, "The Austrian Social Democrats and the Jews," op. cit., p. 38. Adler's reaction to the Beilis trial may be contrasted with that of Trotsky. Though Trotsky's involvement in Russian political affairs would help explain why he would have a far more intense interest in the trial than would Adler, it does not explain why he would publicly condemn the trial when Adler would not. Trotsky, like Adler, was a social democrat, he lived in Vienna throughout the period of the Beilis affair, he was of Jewish origin, he was quite assimilated, he was not involved in Jewish life, and he was unsympathetic to either Zionism or other movements demanding national rights for Jews. But, unlike Adler, Trotsky was deeply moved by the Beilis case. He wrote an article on the case for *Die Neue Zeit* in which he noted that "reading the reports of the case calls forth above all a feeling of insurmountable physical nausea" (N. Trotzky, "Die Beilis-Affäre," *NZ*, XXXII, part 1 [1913–14], p. 318).

84. C. Huysmans, "Sur le sionisme. Réponse à Kautsky," *Comité socialiste pour la palestine ouvrière. Bulletin*, 4 (1929), p. 10.

85. Jacob Toury, "Defense Activities of the Österreichisch-Israelitische Union before 1914," *Living with Anti-Semitism: Modern Jewish Responses*, ed. by Jehuda Reinharz, Tauber Institute for the Study of European Jewry Series, VI (Hanover and London: Brandeis University Press, University Press of New England, 1987), p. 182.

86. Engelbert Pernerstorfer, "Der Typus Danneberg," *Volkstribüne*, XXIV, 17 (April 28, 1915), p. 5.

87. Ibid.

88. Viktor Adler, "Das Märchen von den 'Formeln' und das Typus," *Volkstribüne*, XXIV, 18 (May 5, 1915), p. 5.

89. Victor Adler, *Aufsätze, Reden und Briefe*, op. cit., XI: Victor Adler der Parteimann. Reden und Aufsätze von Victor Adler gesammelt und zusammengestellt von Dr. Gustav Pollatschek; 6: Parteigeschichte und Parteipolitik. Nachträge und Ergänzungen, p. 106.

90. Ibid., p. 108.

91. Ibid., pp. 108, 110.

92. "The Jewish Background of Victor and Friedrich Adler. Selected Biographical Notes," *Leo Baeck Institute Year Book*, X (1965), p. 266.

93. Braunthal, *Victor und Friedrich Adler*, op. cit., p. 143.

94. For a brief sketch of the life of Kathia Adler, born Katharina Jacovlena

Germanischskaja in Lida in 1879, see "Abschied von Kathia Adler,"
*Volksrecht* (May 7, 1969). When Kathia insisted that she and Fritz be
married in a Jewish ceremony, Victor advised his son to go along with
her desires. "A Jewish heart, after all," Victor writes, "is also a heart,
and this is more important than our own cultural or aesthetic require-
ments" ("The Jewish Background of Victor and Friedrich Adler: Selected Biographical Notes," op. cit., p. 273).

95. As cited in Ardelt, op. cit., p. 116.

96. Bauer's name appears in both the 1920 and the 1924 lists of those
eligible to vote in elections of the Viennese Jewish community (which
could only be the case if he had paid his membership dues to that
community). See Steueramt Israelitische Kultusgemeinde Wien, Jewish
Historical General Archive, Ohaleh Josef Depository, (Jerusalem), as
cited in Loewenberg, *Decoding the Past. The Psychohistorical Approach*, op. cit., p. 163.

97. Ernst Fischer, *An Opposing Man*, trans. by Peter and Betty Ross (London: Allen Lane, 1974), p. 134.

98. "Protokoll der Sitzung des Zionistischen Parteirates vom 13. Februar
1927," typescript, pp. 10–11, Records of the Palestine Foundation Fund
(Keren Hayesod), Head Office, Jerusalem, KH 4 277 I, in Central Zionist
Archives. My thanks to Harriet Freidenreich for informing me of the
existence of this document and of other relevant materials.

99. Josiah C. Wedgwood to Dr. Gelber (February 2, 1927), Records of the
Zionist Organization/The Jewish Agency for Palestine—Central Office,
London, Z4 3563/1, in Central Zionist Archives (Jerusalem). Cf. a copy
of a letter to Walter Preuss dated February 19, 1930, in the Berl Locker
papers, A 263/27, Central Zionist Archives: "In der Delegations-Ange-
legenheit habe ich in Wien mit Braunthal, Pollack und [sic] Otto Bauer,
in Zuerich mit Adler und in Berlin mit Naphtali, Alfringhaus und
Furtwaengler gesprochen. Um zuerst vom Erfreulichen zu reden: Die
Stimmung, fuer die palastinensische Arbeiterbewegung ist selbst in Oesterreich weit guenstiger, als ich es je erwartet habe. Otto Bauer hat
sich mit mir fast 3 Stunden Ueber Palaestina und den Mittleren Osten
unterhalten. Er kennt die Dinge viel tiefer, wie man allgemein annimt
und er waere sogar bereit gewesen, nach Palaestine zu kommen, aber
er kann nicht, da er im Herbst Neuwahlen in Oesterreich erwartet
werden. Braunthal dagegen hat fuer die Angelegenheit lebhaftes Inter-
esee. Friedrich Adler hat natuerlich abgelehnt."

100. Otto Bauer, *Die Nationalitätenfrage und die Sozialdemokratie*, Marx-
Studien. Blätter zur Theorie und Politik des wissenschaftlichen Sozialismus, II (Vienna: Verlag der Wiener Volksbuchhandlung, 1907),
p. 368.

101. Ibid., p. 370.

102. Ibid., p. 376.

103. Ibid., p. 378.
104. Ibid., p. 379.
105. Ibid. As Bauer put it "Wo eine Ganze Nation—wie nach Marxens Ansicht die Tschechen, nach unserer Ansicht zum Beispiel die Juden —einzelne Volkssplitter,—wie viele tschechische Minderheiten im deutschen, viele deutsche Minderheiten im tschechischen Gebiete— durch die ökonomische Entwicklung zum Untergang verurteilt sind, dort ist es kleinbürgerlich, reaktionär, utopistisch, sich dieser unvermeidlichen Entwicklung zu widersetzen." "Where . . . the Jews . . . are condemned to downfall through economic development, it is petty bourgeois, reactionary, utopian to resist this inevitable development" (Otto Bauer, Schlusswort zur Minoritätenfrage," Der Kampf IV, 5 [February 1911], p. 206, as cited in Spira, op. cit., p. 59).
106. L. Waynshtayn, "Di natsional-kulturele oytonomie un di yuden," Der sotsial-demokrat, V, 4 (January 22, 1909), supplement, pp. 2–3; V, 5 (January 29, 1909), supplement, pp. 2–3; V, 6 (February 5, 1909), supplement, pp. 2–3. For a response to Bauer published in Bukovina, see Max Rosenfeld, Nationale Autonomie der Juden in Oesterreich. Sonderabdruck aus dem vom Jued.-Nat. Akad. Vereine "Emunah," Czernowitz, herausgegebenen Sammelwerke "Heimkehr" (Erschienen in Verlag Louis Lamm, Berlin), (Czernowitz: Buchdruckerei "Gutenberg," 1912).
107. Waynshtayn, op. cit. (January 22, 1909), p. 2.
108. Waynshtayn, op. cit. (January 22, 1909), p. 3.
109. Waynshtayn, op. cit. (January 29, 1909), p. 3.
110. Waynshtayn, op. cit. (February 5, 1909), p. 3.
111. Otto Bauer, "Galizische Parteitage," Der Kampf, V, 4. Heft (January 1, 1912), p. 159. An article submitted to Der Kampf during this period that apparently dealt with the national question from a Bundist perspective was rejected by Bauer (letter from Bauer [July 10, 1911], MG 10–18, Bund Archives of the Jewish Labor Movement).
112. Bauer, "Galizische Parteitage," op. cit., p. 159.
113. Ibid.
114. Ibid., p. 160. Several months after having published this rebuke of the ŻPSD, Bauer published a more theoretical article in which he sketched out the conditions under which assimilation is likely to occur and the conditions that tend to hinder assimilation (Otto Bauer, "Die Bedingungen der nationalen Assimilation," Der Kampf, V [1912], pp. 246–63). A retort to this article from the standpoint of the Austrian Poalei-Zion was published in Martin Buber's Der Jude during World War I (Berl Locker, "Die allgemeinen Gesetze der Assimilation und die Ostjuden," Der Jude, I [1916–17], pp. 504–29).
115. Andrzej Niemojewski, editor of Myśl Niepodległa, a Polish review, viciously attacked Rosa Luxemburg and other members of the SDKPiL

using anti-Semitic arguments (Nettl, *Rosa Luxemburg* I, op. cit., p. 86) and had also attempted to justify his generally anti-Semitic stance by referring to the works of Marx, Kautsky, Lassalle, Mehring, and other well-known socialists (Haupt and Korzec, "Les socialistes et la campagne antisémite en Pologne en 1910: un épisode inédit," op. cit., p. 188) including Bauer. In response, the SDKPiL solicited replies to Niemojewski from major figures in the socialist world, including Bebel and Jaurès. In a letter to Jogiches in which Luxemburg proposed this tactic, she suggests that the Polish social democrat Julian Marchlewski could write to Bauer in order to solicit a piece from him. See Luxemburg to Jogiches (October 7, 1910), in Tych, ed., *Róża Luksemburg Listy do Leona Jogichesa-Tyszki*, III, (1971), op. cit., pp. 177–78; Rosa Luxemburg, *Gesammelte Briefe*, III, op. cit., pp. 238–39.

116. See the letter by Bauer dated October 21, 1910, and probably written to Marchlewski, in Centralne Archiwum, KC PZPR, Warsaw, in which Bauer indicates that he had considered writing a piece for *Der Kampf* contra-Häcker even before he had received the request from the SDKPiL to disavow Niemojewski, because he feared that nationalistic or anti-Semitic tendencies among the Poles of Galicia and Bukowina would strengthen the separatist tendencies among Ruthenians and Jews. Having considered the matter, however, Bauer notes, he had initially decided not to write such a piece, because he did not want to become involved in a polemic with the Polish socialists in Galicia while he was also involved in a conflict with the Czech socialists. The letter from the SDKPiL, Bauer continues, led him to change his mind. He therefore indicates in response to the request of the SDKPiL that he send a letter disavowing Niemojewski to *Młot* that he will write a gloss on Niemojewski in which he will also include "a few polemical words against Häcker," that he will publish this piece in *Der Kampf*, and that this piece could then be republished in *Młot*. Bauer indicates that he believes this procedure suits his purposes more than does a letter by him published in *Młot* because *Der Kampf* had a considerable number of readers, and considerable authority, in Galicia. In this manner, Bauer concludes, his attack on Niemojewski would gain in power in the Austro-Hungarian context while not losing power in the Russian-ruled portion of Poland (in which the SDKPiL operated). The piece by Bauer was first published under the title "Sozialismus und Antisemitismus," *Der Kampf*, IV, 2. Heft (November 1, 1910), pp. 94–95, and was promptly reprinted by the SDKPiL, "Otto Bauer o antisemityzmie i miedzynarodowosci," *Młot*, 16 (November 19, 1910), p. 8. Cf. the letter by Bauer dated November 1, 1910, and also probably written to Marchlewski, Centralne Archiwum, KC PZPR.

117. Otto Bauer, "Sozialismus und Antisemitismus," op. cit., p. 94.

118. Ibid.

119. Ibid.

120. "Sozialismus und Antisemitismus," *Jüdische Zeitung. National jü-disches Organ*, IV, 45 (November 11, 1910), p. 5.
121. Ibid., p. 6.
122. Bauer warded off the charge that Austrian social democracy was "Ju-daized," for example, by claiming that the function of anti-Semitism had changed. Whereas anti-Semitism had at an earlier point in time been the slogan of the lower middle class in its struggle against the upper levels of the bourgeoisie, Bauer asserted in 1924, it now served the interests precisely of these latter bourgeois elements. In this con-text, "the Jewish capitalist gladly pays the printing costs of anti-Semitic electoral leaflets in order to weaken Social Democracy." See Otto Bauer, "Der Kampf um die Macht," in *Otto Bauer. Eine Auswahl aus seinem Lebenswerk*, ed. by Julius Braunthal (Vienna: Verlag der Wiener Volksbuchhandlung, 1961), p. 278. Cf. Otto Bauer, *Die Öster-reichische Revolution* (Vienna: Verlag der Wiener Volksbuchhand-lung, 1965), p. 226, for a similar comment. It ought to be noted that Bauer vigorously attacked anti-Semitism after the fall of the First Republic. See, for example, the manuscript by Otto Bauer, "Juden-hetze als Herrschaftsmittel," Bauer Teilnachlass, Item 30, IISH.
123. Christoph Hinteregger, *Der Judenschwindel* (Vienna: Verlag der Wie-ner Volksbuchhandlung, 1923), pp. 23, 56. For an example of a similar claim made in the socialist daily press, see "Die Juden beim Seipel," *Arbeiter-Zeitung* (December 3, 1925), p. 4. Other propagandistic works published under socialist auspices that were aimed against the anti-Semitic parties include *Kauft nicht bei Juden*, Die Drei Pfeile, 3 (Vi-enna: Sozialdemokratischer Verlag, G.m.b.H., n.d.); and *Wir Haken-kreuzler*, Vienna.
124. *Wenn Judenblut vom Messer spritzt* (Vienna: Verlag der Wiener Volks-buchhandlung, n.d.), pp. 5, 13.
125. *Der Jud ist Schuld* (Vienna: Verlag der Wiener Volksbuchhandlung, n.d.), p. 11.
126. "Juden von Hitlers Gnaden," *Das kleine Blatt*, VIII, 3 (January 4, 1934), p. 2.
127. Robert Danneberg, *Die Schiebergeschäfte der Regierungsparteien; der Antisemitismus im Lichte der Tatsachen* (Vienna: Verlag der Wiener Volksbuchhandlung, 1926), p. 11.
128. For a defense of the Austrian social democratic use of this tactic, see J. W. Bruegel, "The Antisemitism of the Austrian Socialists, a Reas-sessment," *Wiener Library Bulletin*, vol. 25, 3/4, n.s. 24/25 (1972), p. 42: "there are indeed various ways of fighting [anti-Semitism]. It can be done by impassioned condemnations or by ridicule, thus laying bare the lie and the inconsistencies at its root. Intellectuals will prefer the first method, but a political party appealing to millions of people will be better served by the other approach. This is what the Austrian social democrats did, and what all parties do in similar circum-

stances." Cf. Barkai's rebuttal to Bruegel, *Wiener Library Bulletin*, vol. 25, 3/4, n.s. 24/25 (1972), p. 45.

129. Among the bitterest condemnations by Jewish socialists of Austrian social democrats were those made when Austrian social democracy supported the policy of expelling refugees who had fled to Vienna from the Eastern parts of Austria-Hungary during World War I (many of whom were Jewish) from the First Republic. See, for example, "Die Judenhatz bei Austerlitz," *Freie Tribüne*, I, 29 (August 2, 1919), p. 3; "Di oysvayzungen. mir protestiren!" *Der veker. organ fun der yudisher sotsialistisher (bundisher) organizatsie in vien*, I, 8 (September 24, 1919), p. 3; "Ferfolgung fun di fremde," *Der veker. organ fun der yudisher sotsialistisher (bundisher) organizatsie in vien*, I, 12 (November 21, 1919), p. 1; "Judenausweisungen," *Freie Tribüne*, II, 18 (May 1, 1920), pp. 2–3; "Wir klagen an!" *Freie Tribüne*, III, 7 (February 24, 1921), p. 1.

130. "Der jüdische Dreh eines arischen Advokaten," *Arbeiter-Zeitung*, XXXV, 158 (June 11, 1923), p. 2.

131. "Das neue Wappen der Hakenkreuzler," *Arbeiter-Zeitung* (October 11, 1925). For additional examples of this kind, see Dieter A. Binder, "Der 'reiche Jude': Zur sozialdemokratischen Kapitalismuskritik und zu deren antisemitischen Feindbildern in der Ersten Republik," *Geschichte und Gegenwart*, IV, 1 (March 1985), pp. 43–55.

132. Otto Bauer, "Die Bedingungen der nationalen Assimilation," op. cit., pp. 246–63.

133. Victor Adler to Friedrich Adler (April 19, 1902), Adler-Archiv, Mappe 71, Verein für Geschichte der Arbeiterbewegung, as quoted in Ardelt, op. cit., p. 116.

134. Ardelt, op. cit., p. 275.

135. Friedrich Adler to Victor Adler (April 21, 1902), Adler-Archiv, Mappe 76, Verein für Geschichte der Arbeiterbewegung, as quoted in Ardelt, op. cit., p. 116.

136. Friedrich Adler to Sara Rappeport (December 30, 1918), Adler-Archiv, Mappe 57, Verein für Geschichte der Arbeiterbewegung.

137. Friedrich Adler, "Einige Reminiszenzen," *Volksrecht*, LII, 121 (May 24, 1949), as translated in "The Jewish Background of Victor and Friedrich Adler," op. cit., p. 275. The typescript of Adler's article is in the Adler-Archiv, Mappe 235, Verein für Geschichte der Arbeiterbewegung. The article that provoked Adler into writing the statement quoted above was, "Die Judenfrage und ihre Lösungsmöglichkeiten. Eine Unterredung mit Adler, ehemaligem Generalsekretär der II. Internationale," *Die Tat* (February 2, 1948). Cf. Friedrich Adler to Julius Braunthal (April 27, 1948), Adler-Archiv, Mappe 99, Verein für Geschichte der Arbeiterbewegung, in which Adler describes the portion of Bauer's book *Die Nationalitätenfrage und die Sozialdemokratie* entitled "National Autonomy of the Jews?" as "extraordinarily inter-

esting," and in which he characterizes the presentation of the problem of assimilation in that portion of Bauer's work as "extraordinarily good."

138. Though all but certainly well aware of Adler's lack of sympathy for the Zionist movement, Berl Locker and Shloyme Kaplansky nevertheless invited Adler to attend a world conference of the Poale-Zion in 1920 (Locker and Kaplansky to Friedrich Adler [July 24, 1920], Adler-Archiv, Mappe 200, Verein für Geschichte der Arbeiterbewegung).

139. "Kampf der Poale Zion auf dem Kongreß der Sozialistischen Internationale," Das Jüdische Volksblatt, I, 12 (August 10, 1928), p. 1. For correspondence between Friedrich Adler in his capacity as secretary of the LSI and the leadership of both the mainstream Zionist organization and the labor Zionist movement, see Labour and Socialist International Archive, 338/13; 355/13–16, 21–22; 356/53–58; IISH. Additional details concerning Adler's attitude toward the Poalei-Zion may be gleaned from Johannes Glasneck, "Die internationale Sozialdemokratie und die zionistische Palästina-Kolonisation in den Jahren 1929/30." Wissenschaftliche Zeitschrift der Martin-Luther Universität Halle-Wittenberg, Gesellschafts- und Sprachwissenschaftliche Reihe, XXVI, 4 (1977), pp. 39–50.

140. Jacques Hannak, "Das Judentum am Scheidewege," Der Kampf, XII (1919), p. 651.

141. Jacques Hannak, "Die Krise des Zionismus," Der Kampf, XX (1927), pp. 455–56.

142. Friedrich Adler to Abraham Cahan (June 16, 1920), Adler-Archiv, Mappe 199, Verein für Geschichte der Arbeiterbewegung. Cahan responded very positively to Adler's note. See Abraham Cahan to Friedrich Adler (1920), Adler-Archiv, Mappe 199, Verein für Geschichte der Arbeiterbewegung. Friedrich Adler continued to have a good relationship with the Forverts after the fall of the First Republic, as evidenced by the greeting that he sent to that paper when it celebrated the fortieth anniversary of its founding. See H. Lang, "Der fertsikster geburtstog fun forverts," Forverts (April 25, 1937), Section 1, p. 17.

143. Labour and Socialist International Archive, 356/25, IISH.

144. F. Adler, "Tsum fertsik-yorikn yoyvl fun 'bund,' " Naye folkstsaytung (November 19, 1937), p. 10.

145. "Der parteytog fun der estreykhisher sotsialdemokratie," Poyle-tsien-istishe yedies, 13 (1923), p. 9.

146. "Gen. Dr. Max Adlers Stellung zum Zionismus," Jüdische Arbeiter-Jugend. Organ des Verbands der jüdisch-sozialistischen Arbeiter-Jugend Österreichs, II, 2 (March 1928), p. 9.

147. Jarblum, The Socialist International and Zionism, op. cit., p. 19.

148. "Dans les Ligues pour la Palestine Ouvrière," Comité socialiste pour la palestine ouvrière. Bulletin, 5 (May 1930), p. 27.

149. Max Adler, "Sozialismus und Zionismus," Der Jüdische Arbeiter, VII, 5 (March 27, 1931), p. 1, col. 1.
150. Max Adler, Das Verhältnis der nationalen zur sozialistischen Idee. Bemerkungen zum Poale-Zionismus (Vienna: Verlag Zukunft ["Der Jüdische Arbeiter"], [1933]).
151. Comité socialiste pour la palestine ouvrière. Bulletin, 5 (May 1930), p. 27. After the fall of the First Republic, Braunthal visited Palestine and was enormously impressed by the accomplishments of the Labor Zionists with whom he met there (Julius Braunthal, In Search of the Millenium [London: V. Gollancz, 1945], pp. 306–14). See also Brigitte Robach, "Julius Braunthal als politischer Publizist. Ein Leben im dienste des Sozialismus" (unpublished dissertation, Universität Wien, 1983), pp. 540–68. My thanks to Dr. Robach for allowing me to see the relevant portions of this work.
152. Braunthal, In Search of the Millenium, op. cit., p. 298.
153. See, for example, Mendel Singer, "Judenfrage und Zionismus," Der Kampf, XX (1927), pp. 574–80; Hugo Steiner, "Der Kampf der jüdischen Arbeiter," Der Kampf, XXIII (1930), pp. 136–40; Hugo Steiner, "Palästina und die Judenfrage," Arbeiter-Zeitung (September 2, 1929), pp. 1–2; Émile Vandervelde, "Das arbeitende Palästina," Der Kampf, XXIII (1930), pp. 31–34. The Arbeiter-Zeitung declined to print a rejoinder to Steiner's "Palästina" article submitted by Josef Kissmann [Yoysef Kisman]. See letter to Kissmann from the Arbeiter-Zeitung, (September 20, 1929), Kissmann file, Bund Archives of the Jewish Labor Movement, New York. It did, however, soon thereafter publish Karl Kautsky's "Die Aussichten des Zionismus," Arbeiter-Zeitung, op. cit.
154. Shlomo Shafir, "Julius Braunthal and his Postwar Mediation Efforts between German and Israeli Socialists," Jewish Social Studies, XLVII (1985), p. 269.
155. Barkai, "The Austrian Social Democrats and the Jews," Wiener Library Bulletin, XXIV, 2, n.s. 19, p. 21.
156. Richard Berczeller, "Robert Danneberg," in Norbert Leser and Richard Berczeller, Als Zaungäste der Politik. Österreichische Zeitgeschichte in Konfrontationen (Vienna, Munich: Jugend und Volk, 1977), p. 185. N.b. Leon Kane, Robert Danneberg, Ein pragmatischer Idealist (Vienna, Munich, Zurich: Europaverlag, 1980), p. 166. Danneberg was incarcerated in Dachau beginning with May 1938 and was in Buchenwald beginning with the end of September 1938 (Kane, op. cit., p. 184). He died in Auschwitz in mid-December 1942 (Leser and Berczeller, op. cit., p. 182).
157. Walter B. Simon, "The Jewish Vote in Austria," Leo Baeck Institute Year Book, XVI (1971), p. 110.
158. Classic examples of antisocialist propaganda stressing the Jewish origin of some Austrian social democratic leaders include "Österreich unter Juda's Stern," Auf gut deutsch. Wochenschrift für Ordnung u.

*Recht,* II, 13/14 (1920); Karl Paumgartten, *Judentum und Sozialde-mokratie* (Graz: Heimatverlag Leopold Stocker, n.d.), and the post-First Republic work by Aurelia Gerlach, *Der Einfluss der Juden in der österreichischen Sozialdemokratie* (Vienna: W. Braumüller, 1939).

159. Among the relevant differences between the Austrian and the German social democratic parties was that the Austrian movement is widely believed to have had a far higher percentage of individuals of Jewish origin in highly visible positions in the 1920s and early 1930s than did its German counterpart.

160. Niewyk, *Socialist, Anti-Semite, and Jew: German Social Democracy Confronts the Problem of Anti-Semitism, 1918–1933,* op. cit., pp. 105–6, 190 ff. For additional information on the relationship between the CV and the SPD in the final years of the Weimar Republic, see Arnold Paucker, *Der jüdische Abwehrkampf gegen Antisemitismus und Nationalsozialismus in den letzten Jahren der Weimarer Republik.* Hamburger Beiträge zur Zeitgeschichte, IV (Hamburg: Leibniz-Verlag, 1968), especially pp. 111–28. English-language summaries of Paucker's research include Arnold Paucker, "Jewish Defence Against Nazism in the Weimar Republic," *Wiener Library Bulletin,* XXVI, 1/2, n.s. 26/7 (1972), pp. 27–30 and idem, "The Jewish Defense against Antisemitism in Germany, 1893–1933," in *Living With Antisemitism. Modern Jewish Responses,* ed. by Jehuda Reinharz (Hanover and London: Brandeis University Press, University Press of New England, 1987), pp. 123–32. Cf. Mosse, "German Socialists and the Jewish Question in the Weimar Republic," op. cit., pp. 123–51 and Knütter, op. cit.

161. N. Gelber to the "Keren Hajessod-Direktorium, Jerusalem" (March 17, 1927), Records of the Palestine Foundation Fund (Keren Hayesod), Head Office, Jerusalem, KH 4 277 I, in Central Zionist Archives.

162. On Jewish voting patterns in the First Republic, see Simon, "The Jewish Vote in Austria," op. cit., pp. 97–121. For an impressionistic explanation of "the affinity of the Jewish electorate to the Socialist movement in the First Republic," see Robert Schwarz, "Antisemitism and Socialism in Austria, 1918–1962," *The Jews of Austria,* ed. by Josef Fraenkel (London: Vallentine Mitchell, 1967), p. 445.

163. E. Tramer, "Der republikanische Schutzbund" (unpublished dissertation, Erlangen, 1969), pp. 84 ff., as cited in John Bunzl, "Arbeiterbewegung und Antisemitismus in Österreich vor und nach dem Ersten Weltkrieg," *Zeitgeschichte,* IV, 5 (February 1977), p. 167.

164. Simon, "The Jewish Vote in Austria," op. cit., p. 121. Robert Wistrich has expressed an opinion on this point differing from my own: "The antisemitism of the socialists was inevitably tempered, not so much by their 'Jewish' leadership as by the importance of the Jewish concentration in Vienna, their main stronghold" (Robert S. Wistrich, "[A]n Austrian variation on socialist antisemitism," *Patterns of Prejudice,* VIII, 4 [July-August 1974], p. 6).

## 5. Each Took in Accord with His Needs

1. Among the works dealing with the early history of the Bund are Aronson, Dubnow-Erlich, Hertz, Nowogrudski, Kazdan, and Scherer, eds., *Di geshikhte fun bund*, vols. I-III, op. cit.; Frankel, op. cit., pp. 171–257; Ezra Mendelsohn, *Class Struggle in the Pale: The Formative Years of the Jewish Workers' Movement in Tsarist Russia* (Cambridge: Cambridge University Press, 1970); Aaron L. Patkin, *The Origins of the Jewish Workers Movement in Tsarist Russia* (Melbourne: F. W. Cheshire, 1947); Yoav Peled, *Class and Ethnicity in the Pale: The Political Economy of Jewish Workers' Nationalism in Late Imperial Russia* (New York: St. Martin's Press, 1989); Harold Shukman, "The Relations between the Jewish Bund and the RSDRP, 1897–1903" (unpublished D.Phil thesis, Oxford University, 1961); Tobias, op. cit.

2. On the SS, see Gregor Aronson, "Ideological Trends among Russian Jews," in *Russian Jewry, 1860–1917*, ed. by Jacob Frumkin, Gregor Aronson, Alexis Goldenweiser, trans. by Mirra Ginsburg (New York: Thomas Yoseleff, 1966), p. 164; Michael Astour [Mikhel Astur], *Geshikhte fun der frayland-lige un funem teritorialistishn gedank*, I (Buenos Aires: Frayland-lige, 1967), pp. 10–17; Herts Burgin, *Di geshikhte fun der yidisher arbeyter bavegung in amerika, rusland un england* (New York: Fareynigte yidishe geverkshaften, 1915), pp. 523–24; Abraham G. Duker, "Introduction. The Theories of Ber Borochov and Their Place in the History of the Jewish Labor Movement," in Ber Borochov, *Nationalism and the Class Struggle: A Marxian Approach to the Jewish Problem* (New York: Poale Zion-Zeire Zion of America, and Young Poale Zion Alliance of America, 1937), pp. 29–30; Frankel, op. cit., pp. 324–28; Zvi Y. Gitelman, *Jewish Nationality and Soviet Politics: The Jewish Sections of the CPSU, 1917–1930* (Princeton, N.J.: Princeton University Press, 1972), pp. 72–73; Oscar I. Janowsky, *The Jews and Minority Rights (1898–1919). Studies in History, Economics and Public Law*, 384 (New York: Columbia University Press; London: P. S. King & Son, 1933), pp. 134–36; and the excerpts from "Unzere oyfgabn," *Der nayer veg*, 1 (April 28, 1906), reprinted in *Der yidisher gedank in der nayer tsayt*, ed. by Abraham Menes, I (New York: Alveltlekher yidisher kultur-kongres, 1957), pp. 175–78.

3. Aronson, "Ideological Trends," op. cit., p. 164.

4. On Vozrozhdeniye and SERP, see Aronson, "Ideological Trends," op. cit., p. 163; Astour, op. cit., pp. 17–19; Ben-Adir [Avrom Rozin], "Tsum oyfkum fun der 'yidisher sotsialistisher arbeter partay' (y s)," *Sotsialistisher teritorializm. zikhroynes un materialn tsu der geshikhte fun di partayen s"s, y"s, un "fareynikte*," I ([Paris], Arkhiv komisie fun di partayen s"s, y"s, un fareynikte [1934]), pp. 9–56; N. A. Buchbinder [Bukhbinder], *Di geshikhte fun der yidisher arbeter-bavegung in rusland loyt nit-gedrukte arkhiv-materialn*, trans. into Yiddish by Dovid

Roykhel (Vilna: Farlag "tomor," 1931), pp. 398–402; Burgin, op. cit.,
pp. 525–29; Duker, op. cit., pp. 31–32; Frankel, op. cit., pp. 279–83;
Gitelman, loc. cit., Janowsky, op. cit., pp. 68–71, 126–30; M. Zilberfarb,
"Di grupe 'vozrozhdenie.' (vi zi iz antshtanen un zikh antviklt),"
*Royter pinkes. tsu der geshikhte fun der yidisher arbeter-bavegung un
sotsialistishe shtremungen bay yidn*, I (Warsaw: Farlag kultur-lige,
1921), pp. 113–30; and "Di yidishe sotsialistishe arbeter-partey 'serp,' "
*S.E.R.P.*, I (1907), trans. and reprinted in Menes, op. cit., pp. 172–75.

5. Vozrozhdeniye felt a strong need to maintain ties with a non-Jewish
   general socialist movement and recognized that the RSDRP would not
   be interested in being associated with it. There were Marxists within
   Vozrozhdeniye. These Marxists, however, were among the strongest
   supporters within Vozrozhdeniye of fostering contact with the PSR.
   The contacts between Vozrozhdeniye and the PSR notwithstanding,
   Vozrozhdeniye rejected the label pinned on it by the Bund and others
   that it was ideologically committed to a Jewish form of "S.R.ism" (Ben-
   Adir, op. cit., pp. 39–40).

6. The individuals identified with Vozrozhdeniye who attended the founding
   meeting of the SS were Benie Fridland, Yoysef Bregman, and Shimen
   Dobin. See M. Gutman, "Tsu der forgeshikhte fun 's.s.,' " *Royter pinkes.
   tsu der geshikhte fun der yidisher arbeter-bavegung un sotsialistishe
   shtremungen bay yidn*, I, op. cit., p. 172.

7. The sympathy of certain leaders of the SERP for the PSR was reciprocated, as evidenced, for example, by the support given by Rubanovich
   in the name of the central committee of the PSR to the SERP in August
   1907 when the SERP applied for admission into the Socialist International. See A. Litovski, "Di zitsungen fun der ruslandisher sektsie. (a
   brif fun shtutgart)," *Di shtime. zamelbukh* (Vilna, 1907), col. 30. *Di
   shtime* was issued by the SERP. The sympathy of SERP leaders like
   Ratner for the PSR ought not to be taken as indicative of the attitude of
   the rank-and-file. Many of the local branches of the SERP thought of
   themselves as Marxist in orientation and as Chernov has reported "did
   not want to have anything at all in common with the [P.]S.R." See
   Victor Chernov [Viktor Tshernov], *Yidishe tuer in der partay sotsialistn
   revolutsionern. biografishe eseyen*, trans. by Viktor Shulman (New
   York: Gregori gershuni brentsh 247, Arbeter ring, 1948), p. 308. Cf.
   Frankel, op. cit., p. 283. This attitude on the part of the local organizations notwithstanding, some members of the national leadership, and
   particularly those who had been active in Vozrozhdeniye, appear to
   have retained an affinity for PSR ideology. The SERP entered a formal
   alliance with the PSR in 1907.

8. Aronson, "Ideological Trends," op. cit., p. 163.

9. In 1910, that is, several years after the formation of the SERP, in a piece
   apparently written by Vladimir Kossovsky, the Bundist theorist reportedly conceded that conditions in Russia made it desirable for the Jewish

community to have control over somewhat broader functions (Burgin, op. cit., p. 529).

10. The history and ideology of the ESDRP-PZ are discussed in Aronson, "Ideological Trends," op. cit., pp. 164–65; Burgin, op. cit., pp. 517–23; Duker, op. cit., pp. 33 ff.; Frankel, op. cit., pp. 345–51; Janowsky, op. cit., pp. 130–34; "Oystsugn fun dem program-proiekt fun der yidisher sotsial-demokratisher arbeterpartey poyle-tsien," *Der yidisher arbeter,* II, pp. 387–94, reprinted in Menes, op. cit., pp. 146–50; Zerubavel, "Der grindungs-period fun der i.s.d.a.p. poyle-tsien in rusland," *Royter pinkes,* I, op. cit., pp. 131–51.

11. Janowsky, op. cit., p. 34. On the history of Zionism in Russia, see Louis Greenberg, *The Jews in Russia: The Struggle for Emancipation,* II (New York: Schocken Books, 1976), pp. 160–202; Walter Laqueur, *A History of Zionism* (New York: Rinehart and Winston, 1972), passim.

12. See the text of the Helsingfors Program in Menes, op. cit., p. 179.

13. Aronson, "Ideological Trends," op. cit., pp. 160–61; Janowsky, op. cit., pp. 114–18. The platform of the Folkspartay is reproduced in Menes, op. cit., pp. 180–82.

14. Kursky, *Gezmalte shriftn,* op. cit., p. 105.

15. Mill, *Pionern un boyer,* op. cit., II, p. 53.

16. Ibid. Celina Dowgierd was a wealthy Polish socialist who aided the Bund both by smuggling socialist literature into the Russian Empire and by contributing financially to Bundist causes. Mill, *Pionern un boyer,* op. cit., I, p. 139.

17. Kautsky, "Der Kampf der Nationalitäten und das Staatsrecht in Oesterreich," op. cit., p. 517.

18. Ibid., p. 518.

19. Ibid., p. 558.

20. Mill, *Pionern un boyer,* op. cit., II, p. 54.

21. The ideas of the Austro-Marxists are discussed in Kogan, op. cit., pp. 204–17.

22. Koppel S. Pinson, "Arkady Kremer, Vladimir Medem, and the Ideology of the Jewish 'Bund,' " *Jewish Social Studies,* VII (1945), p. 250. Mishinsky is also among those who claim that the Bund's national program was based on the ideas of the Austro-Marxists. Moshe Mishkinsky, "The Jewish Labor Movement and European Socialism," *Cahiers d'Histoire Mondiale,* XI (1968–69), p. 291.

23. In making this claim, I do not mean to deny the manifest impact of the Austro-Marxists on the Bund, but merely to affirm Kautsky's influence. Of course, neither Kautsky's influence nor that of the Austro-Marxists fully explains why the Bund became more interested in the national question. The underlying reasons for this change in attitude are still debated in the literature. One reason often cited in older literature on this theme is the influx of new members who were less assimilated and

more nationally conscious than the pioneers. The need to respond to Zionist rivals has also been mentioned. Frankel emphasizes the political rather than the sociological origins of this change. Peled, however, has recently (and compellingly) argued that the experience of Russian Jewish workers "in the labour market of an emergent Russian capitalism caused them to become more cognisant of their ethnic, as well as their class identity, and to develop . . . 'ethno-class' consciousness" (Peled, op. cit., p. 3). Cf. Kh. Sh. Kazdan, "Der 'bund'—biz dem finftn tsuzamenfor," Di geshikhte fun bund, op. cit., I, pp. 154, 184–85; Pinson, op. cit., p. 250; Tobias, op. cit., p. 108; Frankel, op. cit., p. 176.

24. Tom Bottomore and Patrick Goode, eds., Austro-Marxism (Oxford: Clarendon Press, 1978), p. 9.

25. Hans Mommsen, Die Sozialdemokratie und die Nationalitätenfrage im habsburgischen Vielvölkerstaat (Vienna: Europa-Verlag, 1963), p. 314; Šolle, "Die Sozialdemokratie in der Habsburger Monarchie und die tschechishe Frage," op. cit., p. 383.

26. Vladimir Medem, who had published a pathbreaking series of articles under the title "Social Democracy and the National Question" in Vestnik Bunda in 1904, notes in his memoirs that he "derived great satisfaction" when he first became aware of Otto Bauer's Die Nationalitätenfrage und die Sozialdemokratie, which was published in 1907. Bauer's book, as Medem read it, did not merely have a title that was virtually identical with the title of Medem's earlier piece, but also enunciated the same principles. "Of course," Medem admits, "his exposition was different: it was deeper, better, and clearer than mine. Indeed, his is an uncommonly brilliant mind (without question the finest mind in today's socialist movement), but on the essential matter we had found a common ground." See Medem, The Life and Soul of a Legendary Jewish Socialist, op. cit., pp. 315–16. For the Yiddish original, see Medem, Fun mayn leben, op. cit., II, p. 56. A far more critical assessment of Bauer that appeared in the Bundist anthology, Simoni [sic?], "Otto bauer vegen di yuden," Tsayt-fragen, I (1909), pp. 31–41, seems to have been written by Shimen Dobin (1869–1944), who used the pseudonym Shimoni during this period. Dobin, however, was new to the Bund at that point in time and may well have been unrepresentative of the Bundist perspective. On the identification of Shimoni as Dobin, see Buchbinder, op. cit., p. 389. Shimen Dobin, who had worked closely with Ber Borochov in 1900–01 (ibid.), and who had also participated in the Vozrozhdeniye conference in 1903 (ibid., p. 398), had so-called Palestinian sympathies at the time of the founding of the SS (M. Gutman, "Tsu der forgeshikhte fun 's.s.,' " Royter pinkes, I, p. 172), but nevertheless became a member of the first central committee of the the the SS (ibid., p. 173). Like other members of Vozrozhdeniye, however, Dobin soon found that he disagreed with the orientation of the SS and resigned from that

party ("Vozrozhdeniye," Encyclopaedia Judaica, XVI, col. 230). In 1906–07, Dobin edited Folksshtime, the organ of the SERP (article on Dobin in Encyclopaedia Judaica, VI, col. 142).

27. Karl Kautsky, "Der kampf fun di natsionen in estraych," Der yidisher arbeyter, 8 (December 1899), pp. 8–12. Mill used Kautsky's article as early as issue 6 of Der yidisher arbeyter (March 1899)—the first issue to be edited by Mill. Frankel, op. cit., p. 218.

28. Tobias, op. cit., pp. 106–7.

29. Kazdan, "Der 'bund'—biz dem finftn tsuzamenfor," p. 180.

30. Karl Kautsky, "Der 'paria' unter di proletarier," Di arbeyter shtimme, 25 (October 1901), p. 5.

31. Kazdan, "Der 'bund'—biz dem finftn tsuzamenfor," op. cit., p. 260; K. Kautsky, Pariia sredi proletariev (London: Zagranichnago komiteta "bunda," n.d.).

32. Vladimir Lenin, "Does the Jewish Proletariat Need an 'Independent Political Party?' " in Lenin on the Jewish Question, ed. by Hyman Lumer (New York: International Publishers, 1974), p. 23.

33. Kazdan, "Der 'bund'—biz dem finftn tsuzamenfor," op. cit., p. 260.

34. Karl Kautsky, Die soziale Revolution, 2d ed. (Berlin: Buchhandlung Vörwarts, 1907), pp. 34–35.

35. Kautsky, "Das Massaker von Kischeneff und die Judenfrage," op. cit., pp. 304–5.

36. Ibid., p. 306.

37. Karl Kautsky, "Kishinevskaia reznia i evreiski vopros'," Iskra, 42 (June 15, 1903), pp. 1–2. Blumenberg, Karl Kautskys literarisches Werk, op. cit., no. 814.

38. "Di diskusie vegn der natsionaler frage afn tsuzamenfor fun 'bund,' yuni 1903, tsurikh. (fun di protokoln fun tsuzamenfor)," Unzer tsayt (Warsaw), I, 4 (December 1927), p. 85. On Frumkin, see Zalmen Reyzen, Leksikon fun der yidisher literatur (Vilna: Farlag fun b. kletskin, 1926–29), VII, col. 462.

39. Tobias, op. cit., p. 205. Frumkin's hostility to Kautsky's view was, however, apparently widely known in Bundist circles. See, for example, A. Liessin's footnote to the article by Vladimir Kossovsky written on the occasion of Kautsky's sixty-fifth birthday (V. Kossovsky [Kosovski], "Tsum 65tn geburtstog fun karl kautski," Tsukunft, XXV [January 1920], p. 43).

40. G. Aronson, "Di nationale un organizatsionele frage," Di geshikhte fun bund, II, op. cit., p. 516. On Mark Liber [Mikhail Isaakovich Goldman], see article by Gregory [Gregori] Aronson in Doyres bundistn, ed. by J. S. Hertz [Herts], I, op. cit., pp. 196–225.

41. Vladimir Lenin, "The Position of the Bund in the Party," in Lenin on the Jewish Question, p. 47.

42. Ibid., pp. 47, 49.

43. Ibid., p. 47. Cf. Karl Kautsky, "Die Krisis in Österreich," *NZ*, XXII, part 1 (1903–04), pp. 39–46, 72–79.

44. Lenin, "The Position of the Bund in the Party," p. 48.

45. L. Bassin, "Natsiya li evrei?" *Vestnik Bunda*, 1–2 (January-February 1904), pp. 12–14; (Vladimir Kossovsky), "Nationalitet un asimilatsie," *Der yidisher arbeter*, 15 (June 1904), pp 25–37; 16 (August 1904), pp. 15–26. Cf. *Vestnik Bunda*, 1–2 (January-February 1904), pp. 2–9; 3 (June 1904), pp. 1–6. On Kossovsky's authorship of this article, see Medem, *Fun mayn lebn*, op. cit., II, p. 54.

46. Bassin, op cit., p. 13.

47. Ibid. My thanks to George Nemetsky, who translated this and all following quotes from Bassin's article for me.

48. Ibid., p. 14.

49. On Kossovsky, pseudonym of Nokhum Mendl Levinson (1867–1941), see Hertz's article in Hertz, ed. *Doyres bundistn*, I, op. cit., pp. 11–67 and my article on him in Robert A. Gorman, ed., *Biographical Dictionary of Neo-Marxism* (Westport, Conn.: Greenwood Press, 1985), pp. 242–44.

50. Kossovsky, "Nationalitet un asimilatsie," op. cit., issue 15, p. 25. The phrase "one of the most prominent of Marxist theoreticians" was used by Lenin in "The Position of the Bund in the Party," op. cit., p. 47.

51. Kossovsky, op. cit., p. 27.

52. Ibid., p. 32.

53. Ibid., issue 16, p. 22.

54. Ibid., issue 16, p. 24.

55. Kautsky, "Di oyfgabn fun dem yidishn proletariat in england. a bagrisung artikl tsu di 'naye tsayt,' " loc. cit.; Karl Kautsky, "Pis'mo Kautskago," *Vestnik Bunda*, 3 (June 1904), pp. 20–21.

56. Lenin and the Bund continued to use Kautsky's works to buttress their respective views on the Jewish question for many years after the exchange of articles discussed here. A number of works by Lenin written between spring 1913 and winter 1914 cite Kautsky's works in an approving manner. Kautsky, Lenin repeatedly claimed, did not recognize the need for national autonomy for the Jews, thought of the Jews of Eastern Europe (Galicia and Russia) as a caste, rather than as a nation, and of the Jews "in the civilized world" as already assimilated. See Vladimir Lenin, "Draft Program of the Fourth Congress of Social-Democrats of the Latvian Area," *Lenin on the Jewish Question*, p. 71; "Theses on the National Question," ibid., p. 79; "The National Problem of the R.S.D.L.P. (Excerpt)," ibid., p. 97; "Critical Remarks on the National Question," ibid., p. 137. In making these points, Lenin apparently relied on Russian translations of Kautsky's works. He repeatedly referred, for example, to what is purportedly a quote for *Nationalität und Internationalität*.

According to Lenin, who seems to have been using the Russian version
of this work, Kautsky had written, "The Jews in Galicia and Russia are
more of a caste than a nation, and attempts to constitute Jewry as a
nation are attempts at perserving a caste." The German original, however, reads somewhat differently: "Will man die Rolle kennzeichnen,
die das Judenthum im Mittelalter spielte und heute noch in Osteuropa
spielt, so geschiet dies weit besser als durch die Bezeichnung Nation
durch die Bezeichnung Kaste. Nicht unter den Nationen des modernen
Europa, mit denen wir es hier zu tun haben, sondern unter den Kasten
Indiens finden wir Erscheinungen, die dem Judentum entsprechen, wie
es sich nach der Zerstörung Jerusalems und dem Aufkommen des Chris-
tentums gestaltet hat. Die Versuche, das Judentum als Nation aufrecht
zu halten, sind tatsächlich nur Versuche, seine Existenz als besondere
Kaste fortzufristen, Solches Streben wäre unerklärlich in einem modernen Staate. Es kann nur gedeihen unter der infamen Wirtschaft der
moskowitischen Bureaukratie oder des rumänischen Bojarentums."
Lenin's version of this quote is inaccurate in several respects. First,
Kautsky did not specifically refer to Galicia, an area that included
territory under the control of Austria-Hungary. Galicia was a trouble-
some point in Kautsky's theory and was never dealt with at length in
any work by Kautsky on the Jewish question. Second, and more important, Kautsky's wording (but not Lenin's) implies that the attempts to
maintain the Jews as a nation can succeed in the Russian Empire,
precisely because of the backwardness of the Russian economy (Karl
Kautsky, "Nationalität und Internationalität," *Erganzungshefte zur
Neuen Zeit*, 1 [January 18, 1908], p. 7).

Lenin, as is well known, broke sharply with Kautsky at the beginning of World War I over matters that had nothing whatever to do with
the Jewish question. Some scholars have claimed, however, that Lenin's rejection of Kautsky during and after 1914 included a repudiation
of Kautsky's position on the Jewish question. See, for example, Norman
Levine, "Lenin on Jewish Nationalism," *Wiener Library Bulletin*, XXXIII,
n.s. 51–52 (1980), p. 46. There is, however, no evidence of such a
repudiation in Lenin's writings. Moreover, Lenin's actions in the years
after the revolution, which have occasionally been cited as a de facto
repudiation of Kautsky, actually demonstrate nothing of the kind.
Kautsky's hope that assimilation would occur has frequently been con-
fused with advocacy of forced assimilation, which Kautsky most certainly never endorsed. On Lenin and the Jewish question, cf. Hyman
Lumer, ed., *Lenin on the Jewish Question*, pp. 1–19; Paul Novick,
"Lumer vs. Lenin on the Jewish Question," *Jewish Currents* (July-
August 1977), pp. 22–28; Harold Shukman, "Lenin's Nationalities Pol-
icy and the Jewish Question," *Bulletin on Soviet and East European
Affairs*, 5 (May 1970), pp. 43–50. As it had in an earlier period, the
Bund responded to Lenin's use of Kautsky in 1913–14 by soliciting and

publishing a letter from Kautsky endorsing the work of the Bund ("Brif
fun k. kautski," loc. cit.

57. On Avrom Rozin, see Reyzen, op. cit., I, pp. 310–16; Shumel Niger and
Yankev Shatski, eds., *Leksikon fun der nayer yidisher literatur*, I (New
York: Alveltlekher yidisher kultur kongres, 1956), pp. 336–39.

58. Ben-Adir [Avrom Rozin], "Teritorialistishe shtremungen in sotsialistishn tsionizm," in Menes, op. cit., pp. 167–68.

59. Ben Ader [Ben-Adir] [Avrom Rozin], *Evreiskii vopros' v osveshchenii K.
Kautskago i S. N. Iuzhakova* (St. Petersburg: Viktor Kugel, 1906), p. 1.

60. Ibid., p. 4.

61. Ibid., p. 11.

62. Kautsky, "Das Massaker von Kischeneff," op. cit., pp. 303–4.

63. Ben Ader, *Evreiskii vopros'*, op. cit., p. 12.

64. Ibid.

65. Ibid., p. 40.

66. Rozin's assessment of Kautsky altered markedly over the years. In the
1920s Rozin moved to Berlin and began publishing a journal entitled
*Dos fraye vort*. Grigori Aronson, who was intimately involved in the
publication of this journal, reports that "in Ben-Adir's eyes Kautsky's
authority was especially high at that time, and he strongly wanted to
obtain for . . . *Dos fraye vort* an article from the famous Marxist."
Rozin visited Kautsky in connection with this article and felt "even
closer" to the Marxist after the visit than he had previously. It is clear
from the context of Aronson's comments that Rozin's reassessment was
sparked by Kautsky's anti-Bolshevik stance—a stance with which Rozin was in wholehearted agreement. The result of Rozin's visit, however, was an article by Kautsky not on general socialist theory, but on
the tasks of the Jewish workers in the Soviet Union. Rozin felt comfortable enough with Kautsky's views as expressed in this article to publish
it (Kautski, "Di oyfgabn funm yidishn proletariat in sovet-rusland,"
op. cit., pp. 1–7). Kautsky's views on the tasks of the Jewish proletariat
had not changed. Rozin had. See Aronson, *Rusish-yidishe inteligents*,
op. cit., p. 222.
    Markus Ratner (1871–1917), another leading member of the SERP,
sharply criticized Kautsky's views in a somewhat later article addressed
toward a West European audience. After quoting the passage from
"Nationalität und Internationalität" in which Kautsky indicated that
the role of East European Jewry could be better characterized by the
term caste than by the term nation, Ratner comments: "Viel ist über
das Wesen und die Eigentümlichkeiten der jüdischen Nationalität ge-
stritten worden, aber niemand kam bisher auf den ungeheuerlichen
Gedanken das nach Millionen zählende jüdische Volk mit einer in-
dischen Kaste zu vergleichen. . . . Das heißt wirklich Mißbrauch mit
Analogieen treiben" (Ratner, "Die nationale Autonomie und das jüdische Proletariat," op. cit., p. 1341).

67. On Lestchinsky, see Paul Glikson, "Jacob Lestchinsky: A Bibliographical Survey," *Jewish Journal of Sociology*, IX, 1 (June 1967), pp. 48–57.
68. Jacob Lestchinsky, *Marks i Kautskii o evreiskom vopros'*, 2 (Moscow: Pereval', 1907). My thanks to Jonathan Boyarin for allowing me access to his unpublished commentary on and translation of excerpts from this booklet. All further quotes from Lestchinsky's works are cited as in Boyarin's unpaginated translation.
69. Lestchinsky, op. cit.
70. Ibid.
71. Ibid.
72. Kautsky, "Brif tsum 7tn tsuzamenfor fun "bund," *Folkstsaytung*, 159 (September 13–26, 1906).
73. Lestchinsky, op. cit. Moyshe Shalit (1885–1941), who was active in Vozrozhdeniye, SERP, and later in the Poalei-Zion (Berl Kahn, Israel Knox [Noks], Elihu Shulman, eds., *Leksikon fun der nayer yidisher literatur* VII [New York: Alveltlekher yidisher kultur kongres, 1981], p. 523), reviewed Lestchinsky's essay in *Folksshtime*, a journal of the SERP, 9 (June 27, 1907), col. 46. Shalit claimed that Lestchinsky's work suffered from an overdose of historical materialism—a typical social revolutionary critique of a social democratic perspective—and that it was not clear what Lestchinsky hoped to prove. In general, however, Shalit agreed with Lestchinsky's criticisms of Kautsky. According to Shalit, Lestchinsky "exposes successfully and with conviction the great errors" that lie at the base of Marx's and Kautsky's views on the Jewish question. The Russian and Yiddish translations of Kautsky's works were reviewed by Shalit in his bibliography of literature on the Jewish and national questions (M. Shalit, "Bibliografie," *Folksshtime*, 4 [Febraury 23, 1907], cols. 94–100). Shalit, who is known to have written for the Zionist organ *Dos yidishe folk*, is, moreover, almost certainly the author of the work signed M. Sh. and published in that periodical under the title "Karl kautski un di natsionale frage" (18 [September 12, 1906], pp. 10–12; 19 [September 19, 1906], pp. 8–10). M. Sh. discusses "Die moderne Nationalität," *NZ*, V (1887), pp. 392–405, 442–51), "Der Kampf der Nationalitäten," op. cit., "Die Krisis in Oesterreich," op. cit., and "Die Nationalitätenfrage in Russland," op. cit., and comes to the conclusion that there had been a great change in Kautsky's perspective. In Kautsky's early work on the national question, M. Sh. claims, Kautsky had prophesied that the small nations would assimilate into the large ones and that a worldwide language would replace existing languages. In his later works, Kautsky is said to have recognized the deep roots of the modern national idea and to have acknowledged that economic development was leading even small nations to develop national literatures. M. Sh. applauds Kautsky's new approach as in accord with the "best part of contemporary society" (*Dos yidishe folk*, 19, p. 10).
74. On Shats, see Reyzen, op. cit., I (1926), cols. 117–19; Kahn, Knox, and

Shulman, eds., *Leksikon fun der nayer yidisher literatur*, op. cit., VIII, pp. 544–46.

75. M. Anin [Maks-Aryeh Z. Shats], "Di natsionale frage—oder natsionale fragn?" *Unzer veg*, 8–9 (November 1–14, 1907), cols. 18–24.

76. Ibid., col. 18.

77. Ibid., col. 21.

78. Ibid.

79. Ibid., col. 7.

80. Ibid., col. 9.

81. Ibid., col. 14.

82. On Ratner, see Reyzen, *Leksikon fun der yudisher literatur un prese*, op. cit., cols. 587–88; *Tsum ondenk fun m. b. ratner. zamlbukh*, ed. by the Ratner fond ([Kiev]: Kiever farlag: [1919]); Kahn, Knox, and Shulman, eds., *Leksikon fun der nayer yidisher literatur*, op. cit., VIII, pp. 367–68, and *Encyclopaedia Judaica*, XIII, pp. 1572–73.

83. Ratner, "Die nationale Frage in den jüdischen sozialistischen Parteien," op. cit., pp. 1535–36.

84. Ibid., p. 1536. In a later work, Ratner refers to the chapter in Bauer's book dealing with the question of Jewish national autonomy as "doubtless the weakest part of this book which is otherwise worth reading" (Ratner, "Die nationale Autonomie und das jüdische Proletariat," op. cit., pp. 1333–42). Chaim Zhitlovsky, who was also closely affiliated with the SERP, wrote a sharp critique of Bauer, in which he labeled Bauer an anti-Semite (Chaim Zhitlovsky [Khayim Zhitlovski], *Gezamlte shriftn*, XIII, Der sotsializm un di natsionale frage [Warsaw: Ch. Brzoza (Kh. Bzhoza), 1935], p. 227).

85. On Borochov and his ideas, see Frankel, op. cit., pp. 329–63; Moyshe Menachowski [Menakhovski], *Ber borokhov—zayn lebn un zayn shafn* (Buenos Aires: Farlag "unzer vort," 1959); Zerubawel [Zerubavel] [Yakov Vitkin], *Ber borokhov. zayn leben un shafen*, I (Warsaw: Arbeterheim [Arbeter-heym], 1926); and the introductory essays (listed here in chronological order) in D. B. Borochov [Borokhov], *Poyle tsien shriftn*, I (New York: Poyle tsien farlag, 1920); B. Borochov [Borokhov], *Geklibene shriftn*, II, ed. by B. Lo[c]ker (New York: Borokhov-brentsh 14, yidish-natsionaler arbeter-farband, 1928); Borochov, *Nationalism and the Class Struggle*, op. cit.; and Ber Borochov, *Class Struggle and the Jewish Nation. Selected Essays in Marxist Zionism*, ed. by Mitchell Cohen (New Brunswick, London: 1984). I have not had direct access to the works of Matityahu Mintz, including *Ber borokhov: ha-máagal harishon (1900–1906)* (Tel Aviv: Tel Aviv University and the Kibbutz Meuhad Publishing House, 1976).

86. Ber Borochov [Borokhov], "Unzer platform," in D. B. Borochov [Borokhov], *Poyle tsien shriftn*, op. cit., pp. 173, 178. Ber Borochov [Borokhov], "Di rol fun der arbeterklas in der realizirung funm teritorializm," in B. Borochov [Borokhov], *Geklibene shriftn*, p. 32.

87. Gitelman, op. cit., p. 48.
88. Ber Borochov [Borokhov], "Di klasn-interesn un di natsionale frage," in D. B. Borochov [Borokhov], *Poyle tsien shriftn*, op. cit., p. 73.
89. D. Pasmanik, *Di natsionale frage farn mishpet fun di sotsialdemokratn*, (Odessa: Farlag "kedimeh," 1906). Dubnow used the Russian-language version of this booklet, also published by Farlag "kedimeh" in 1906.
90. Simon Dubnow [Shimen Dubnov], *Briv vegn altn un nayem yidntum*, translated by Moisés [Moyshe] and Saúl [Shaul] Ferdman (Mexico City: Shloyme mendelson fond bay der gezelshaft far kultur un hilf, 1959), p. 89. On Dubnow, see Sofia Dubnow-Erlich [Dubnov-erlikh], *Dos lebn un shafn fun shimen dubnov*, trans. by Moisés Ferdman (Mexico City: Shloyme mendelson fond bay der gezelshaft far kultur un hilf, 1952). The introduction to *Briv vegn altn un nayem yidentum*, op. cit., written by Kh. Sh. Kazdan, and the introduction by K. S. Pinson to the English translation of Dubnow's Letters on Old and New Jewry (*Nationalism and History* [Philadelphia: Jewish Publication Society of America, 1958]) are helpful in clarifying various aspects of Dubnow's thought. Robert M. Seltzer, "Simon Dubnow: A Critical Biography of his Early Years" (unpublished Ph.D. dissertation, Columbia University, 1970), provides much useful information on Dubnow's life and milieu.
91. Dubnow, *Briv vegn altn un nayem yidentum*, p. 90.

## 6. Cooperation without Agreement

1. In April 1917 both Kautsky and Bernstein left the SPD and became founding members of USPD. Throughout this chapter the terms "socialist" and "social democratic" (without capitals) will be used to describe individuals affiliated with either one of these two parties. The terms "Socialist" and "Social Democratic," however, will be used to refer only to the SPD.
2. On German Jewish voting patterns, see J. Toury, *Die politischen Orientierungen der Juden in Deutschland. Von Jena bis Weimar* (Tubingen: J. C. B. Mohr, 1966), especially p. 275.
3. Donald L. Niewyk, *The Jews in Weimar Germany* (Baton Rouge: Louisiana State University Press, 1980), pp. 28–29.
4. Stephen N. Poppel, *Zionism in Germany, 1897–1933* (Philadelphia: Jewish Publication Society of America, 1977), tables 2 and 3.
5. Poppel, op. cit., table 3.
6. Of course, the fact that *Rasse und Judentum* was a book and not an article also helps explain the attention it received.
7. Poppel, op. cit., p. 34. On the Centralverein, see the annotated bibliography appended to Arnold Paucker's "Die Abwehr des Antisemitismus in den Jahren 1893–1933," in *Antisemitismus. Von der Judenfeindschaft zum Holocaust*, ed. by Herbert A. Strauss and Norbert Kampe. Schriftenreihe der Bundeszentrale für politische Bildung, CCXIII (Frankfurt-

am-Main and New York: Campus Verlag, 1985), pp. 164–71; Schorsch, *Jewish Reactions to German Anti-Semitism, 1870–1914*, op. cit., pp. 103–48; Jehuda Reinharz, *Fatherland or Promised Land. The Dilemma of the German Jew, 1893–1914* (Ann Arbor: University of Michigan Press, 1975), pp. 37–89; Marjorie Lamberti, *Jewish Activism in Imperial Germany: The Struggle for Civil Equality*. Yale Historical Publications, Miscellany, 119 (New Haven and London: Yale UniversityPress, 1978).

8. Schorsch, op. cit., p. 120. Niewyk's assertion (Niewyk, op. cit., p. 28) that the *Israelitisches Familienblatt* was "by far the largest newspaper for German Jews" is correct only if *Im deutschen Reich*, which had a larger circulation, is thought of as a journal rather than as a newspaper.

9. On Nathan, see Ernst Feder, *Politik und Humanität. Paul Nathan. Ein Lebensbild* (Berlin: Deutsche Verlagsgesellschaft für Politik und Geschichte m.b.H., 1929); idem, "Paul Nathan and His Work for East European and Palestinian Jewry," *Historia Judaica*, XIV, part 1 (April 1952), pp. 3–26; idem, "Paul Nathan, the Man and His Work," *Leo Baeck Institute Year Book*, III (1958), pp. 60–80. Nathan corresponded with Kautsky in 1905 and in 1914: Nathan to Kautsky (September 8, 1905, January 17, 1914, January 21, 1914), in Kautsky Nachlass, KD XVIII 93–5, IISH. Eduard Bernstein was a personal friend of Nathan's and had defended Nathan in the pages of *Die Neue Zeit* in 1914. See Robert Wistrich, "Eduard Bernstein and the Jewish Problem," *Jarbuch des Instituts für deutsche Geschichte*, VIII (1979), p. 252. Cf. Ed. Bernstein, "Der Schulstreit in Palastina," *NZ*, XXXIII (1913–14), pp. 744–52. Nathan became disillusioned with the liberal Democratic party in November 1921 and at some point thereafter became a member of the SPD.

10. Paul Nathan, "Rasse und Judentum," *Im deutschen Reich*, XXVII, 7/8 (July-August 1921), p. 203.

11. Ibid., p. 205.

12. Ibid.

13. Ibid., p. 206.

14. Schorsch has pointed out that there is no firm evidence that Nathan was a formal member of the CV and that Nathan may have had some ideological differences with that organization (Schorsch, op. cit., p. 242). These differences notwithstanding, the decision of the editors of *Im deutschen Reich* to publish Nathan's review of what was clearly perceived of as an extremely important book indicates that these editors considered Nathan's views as consistent with the tone of their journal. Cf. Reinharz, op. cit., where Nathan is described as "an important member of the executive board of the C.V.," and in which Reinharz cites sources supporting this description (Reinharz, op. cit., p. 54, 255–56).

15. Niewyk, op. cit., p. 160.

16. On Felix Goldmann, see S. Wininger, *Grosse Jüdische National-Biographie*, VII (Cernăuţi: Arta, n.d.), pp. 18–19.
17. On the *Allgemeine Zeitung*, see Margaret T. Edelheim-Muehsam, "The Jewish Press in Germany," *Leo Baeck Institute Year Book*, I (1956), pp. 166–67.
18. Felix Goldmann, "Rasse und Judentum," *Allgemeine Zeitung des Judentums*, LXXIX, 22 (May 28, 1915), p. 254.
19. Ibid.
20. Ibid.
21. Ibid.
22. Ibid.
23. Ibid.
24. On Willy Cohn, see *Kurschners deutscher Gelehrten-Kalender 1931* (Berlin: Walter de Grunter and Co., 1931).
25. Willy Cohn, review of *Rasse und Judentum*, *Allgemeine Zeitung des Judentums*, LXXXV, 17 (August 19, 1921), p. 202.
26. Schorsch, op. cit., p. 173. Edelheim-Muehsam, op. cit., p. 164.
27. Cohn, op. cit.
28. Willy Cohn, review of *Rasse und Judentum*. *Monatsschrift für Geschichte und Wissenschaft des Judentums*, LXVI, 1/3 (January-March 1922), p. 75.
29. Cohn in *Allgemeine Zeitung des Judentums*, op. cit.
30. Cohn in *Monatschrift für Geschichte und Wissenschaft des Judentums*, op. cit., p. 76.
31. Edelheim-Muehsam, op. cit., p. 168, maintains that the Kartell Convent "fought for the ideology of the Centralverein." Poppel, op. cit., p. 23, describes the Kartell Convent as "basically committed to assimilationism." Cf. Adolph Asch, *Geschichte des K.C.* (London: Published privately by the author, 1964).
32. F. G. Thur, review of *Rasse und Judentum*, *K.C. Blatter*, 6 (July-August 1915), p. 434.
33. Ibid., p. 435.
34. Ibid.
35. Ibid.
36. A. L., "Der Angiff Kautskys auf den Zionismus," *Jüdische Rundschau*, 48 (November 27, 1914), p. 435.
37. Ibid., p. 436.
38. Kautsky, as cited by A. L., op. cit., 1 (January 1, 1915), p. 2.
39. A. L., op. cit.
40. *Bayerische Israelitische Gemeindezeitung*, IV (1928), pp. 136–38, as quoted by Niewyk, op. cit., p. 132.
41. On Auerbach, see Siegmund Kaznelson, ed., *Juden im deutschen Kulturbereich* (Berlin: Jüdischer Verlag, 1962), p. 996; Laqueur, *A History of Zionism*, op. cit., pp. 213, 386.
42. Elias Auerbach, "Rassenkunde," *Der Jude*, VI, 6 (March 1922), p. 385.

43. Ibid.
44. Ibid.
45. Ibid. *Rasse und Judentum* was also reviewed in a German Jewish publication that was not ideologically oriented—see Max Grunwald, "Rasse, Volk, Nation," *Jahrbuch für jüdische Volkskunde* (1924–25), pp. 307–10, 335–36—and by the Zionist Felix A. Theilhaber (1884–1956) *Archiv für Rassen- und Gesellschafts- Biologie*, XII, 1 (1916–17), pp. 91-92. Theilhaber's works on Jewish demographics were cited by Kautsky in his chapter on the physical characteristics of the Jews in *Rasse und Judentum*.
46. In 1929 the *Jüdische Rundschau* replied to Kautsky's "Die Aussichten des Zionismus" by asserting, "That which Kautsky writes about Palestine work demonstrates that he does not know the character of this work at all. . . . One can be an important Marxist and nevertheless know very little about a real undertaking and its actual conditions" ("Palästina und der Sozialismus," *Jüdische Rundschau*, XXIV, 78/79 [October 4, 1929], p. 522).
47. F. G. "Alldeutsch oder International," *Im deutschen Reich*, XXIII, 12 (December 1917), pp. 499–505.
48. Ibid., p. 499.
49. Ibid., p. 506.
50. Ludwig Geiger, "Literarische Übersicht," *Allgemeine Zeitung des Judentums*, LXXXII, 27 (July 5, 1918), p. 320. On Geiger, see *Jüdisches Lexikon*, II (Berlin: Jüdischer Verlag, 1928), p. 944.
51. Geiger, "Literarische Übersicht," op. cit.
52. "Sein oder nichtsein?" *Ost und West. Illustrierte Monatsschrift für das gesamte Judentum*, XVIII, 1/2 (January-February 1918), pp. 1–16. On *Ost und West*, see Edelheim-Muehsam, op. cit., p. 168 and Steven E. Aschheim, *Brothers and Strangers: The East European Jew in German and German Jewish Consciousness, 1800–1923* (Madison, Wis.: University of Wisconsin Press, 1982), p. 117.
53. "Sein oder nichtsein?" p. 3.
54. M. Güdemann, review of E. Bernstein, "Von den Aufgaben der Juden im Weltkriege," *Monatsschrift für Geschichte und Wissenschaft des Judentums*, LXII, Neue Folge, 26 (1918), pp. 64–65.
55. Werner Jochmann, "Die Ausbreitung des Antisemitismus," in *Deutsches Judentum in Krieg und Revolution 1916–1923*, ed. by Werner E. Mosse. Schriftenreihe Wissenschaftlicher Abhandlungen des Leo Baeck Instituts, XXV (Tübingen: J. C. B. Mohr, [Paul Siebeck], 1971), pp. 409–510.
56. David Joshua Engel, "Organized Jewish Responses to German Antisemitism during the First World War" (Ph.D. dissertation, University of California, Los Angeles, 1979).
57. "Zur Reichstagsrede des Herrn Abg. Dr. Cohn," *Im deutschen Reich*, XXIII, 7/8 (July-August 1917), p. 315.
58. The fear that Bernstein's views would fan anti-Semitism was altogether

justified. Jochmann notes, "Die Antisemiten haben die Aüsserungen Bernsteins später tendenziös entstellt und agitatorisch ausgenutzt" (Jochmann, op. cit., p. 446).

59. Jacob Toury, *Die politischen Orientierungen der Juden in Deutschland. Von Jena bis Weimar*, Schriftenreihe Wissenschaftlicher Abhandlungen des Leo Baeck Instituts, XV (Tübingen: J. C. B. Mohr, 1966), p. 275.

60. Ernst Hamburger and Peter Pulzer, "Jews as Voters in the Weimar Republic," *Leo Baeck Institute Year Book*, XXX (1985), pp. 48–49.

61. Paucker, *Der jüdische Abwehrkampf*, pp. 89, 96–97; Donald L. Niewyk, *Socialist, Anti-Semite, and Jew: German Social Democracy Confronts the Problem of Anti-Semitism, 1918–1933* (Baton Rouge: Louisiana State University Press, 1971), pp. 190–91.

62. Leaders of both the SPD and the USPD repeatedly condemned anti-Semitism during and after World War I. These condemnations were regularly noted by Jewish periodicals. See, for example, *Im deutschen Reich*, XXII, 9/10 (September-October 1916), p. 204: "Sozialdemokratie und Antisemitische Beschuldigungen," *Im deutschen Reich*, XXIV, 11 (November 1918), p. 441; *Allgemeine Zeitung des Judentums*, LXXXIII, 12 (March 21, 1919), pp. 111–12; *Allgemeine Zeitung des Judentums*, LXXXIII, 13 (March 28, 1919), p. 125; "Sozialdemokratische Führer gegen die antisemitische Hetzpropaganda," *Allgemeine Zeitung des Judentums*, LXXXIII, 27 (July 4, 1919), pp. 291–92; "Reichswehrminister Noske gegen die antisemitische Hetze," *Mitteilungen der Jüdischen Presszentrale Zürich*, 49 (August 15, 1919), p.7; "Die unabhängige Sozialdemokratie gegen den Antisemitismus," *Im deutschen Reich*, XXVI, 2 (February 1920), p. 90.

63. Hamburger and Pulzer, "Jews as Voters in the Weimar Republic," op. cit., p. 34.

# Bibliography

## I. Unpublished Sources

### ARCHIVAL MATERIAL

Archives and Museum of the Jewish Labour Movement, Institute of Labour
  Research in Memory of P. Lavon, Tel Aviv:
  Chazanovitsch, Leon
  Committee for Working Eretz-Israel in Germany
Bund Archives of the Jewish Labor Movement, New York:
  Foreign Committee of the Bund
  Jewish Social Democratic Party of Galicia
  Kautsky, Benedikt
  Kautsky, Karl
  Kissmann, Josef
Central Zionist Archives, Jerusalem:
  Central Zionist Office (Zionistisches Centralbureau), Berlin
  Chasanowitsch, Leon
  Locker, Berl
  Palestine Foundation Fund (Keren Hayesod) Head Office, Jerusalem
  The Zionist Organization/The Jewish Agency for Palestine—Central Of-
  fice, London
Centralne Archiwum KC PZPR, Warsaw
Hauptstaatsarchiv, Düsseldorf:
  Gerichte
Hoover Institution on War, Revolution and Peace, Stanford, California:
  Nicolaevsky, Boris
International Institute of Social History, Amsterdam:
  Bauer, Otto
  Bernstein, Eduard
  Hertz, Paul
  Kautsky, Karl
  Kautsky Family

Labour and Socialist International
Motteler, Julius
Jewish National and University Library, Jerusalem:
Buber, Martin
Schwadron, Abraham
Leo Baeck Institute, New York
Hamburger, Ernst
Kahler, Erich
Kahn, Bernhard
Tamiment Library, New York:
Debs, Eugene Victor
Lee, Algernon
Vladeck, Baruch Charney
Stadtarchiv, Zürich:
Registerkarten
Stadt- und Landesbibliothek, Dortmund:
Handschriftenabteilung
É. Vandervelde Institute, Brussels:
Vandervelde, É.
Verein für Geschichte der Arbeiterbewegung, Vienna:
Adler, Friedrich and Victor
Archive of the Austrian Social Democratic Workers' Party
Kautsky, Benedikt
Pernerstorfer, Engelbert
YIVO Institute for Jewish Research, New York:
Cahan, Ab.
Lestchinsky, Jacob
Liessin, Abraham
Osherowicz, Mendel
Shteinberg, I. N.
Zhitlovsky, Chaim
Zivilstandesamt, Basel-Stadt, Basel:
Ehe-Register

### ESSAYS AND DISSERTATIONS

Elliot, C. J. "Freedom and Revolution: Rosa Luxemburg and the Marxist Legacy." Ph.D. dissertation, Harvard, 1963.

Engel, David Joshua. "Organized Jewish Responses to German Antisemitism During the First World War." Ph.D. dissertation, University of California, Los Angeles, 1979.

Geary, R.J. "Karl Kautsky and the Development of Marxism." Ph.D. dissertation, Emmanuel College, Cambridge, 1970.

Gilles, Hermann. "Die Sozialdemokratie und ihr Verhältnis zum Antisemitismus unter historisch-politikwissenschaftlichem Gesichtspunkt." Hausarbeit, Cologne, 1979.

Kautsky, John H. "The Political Thought of Karl Kautsky." Ph.D. dissertation, Harvard, 1951.

Klausner, Yehuda Arye. "Studies on the Life and Work of Yishaq Leyb Peretz with Special Reference to an Unknown Manuscript." Ph.D. dissertation, University of London, 1958.

Koch, Henriette. "Die SPD und ihre Stellung zu den Juden in der Weimarer Republik." Zwischenprüfungsarbeit, Aachen, 1979.

Marks, Harry J. "Movements of Reform and Revolution in Germany from 1890 to 1903." Ph.D. dissertation, Harvard, 1937.

Niewyk, Donald L. "German Social Democracy and the Problem of Anti-Semitism, 1906–1914." M.A. thesis, Tulane University, 1964.

Petrus, Joseph Anthony. "Marxism, Marxists on the National Question." Ph.D. dissertation, University of Texas at Austin, 1965.

Reichard, Richard W. "Karl Kautsky and the German Social Democratic Party, 1863–1914." Ph.D. dissertation, Harvard, 1950.

Riemer, Yehuda. "Peretz Naphtali. A Social Democrat in the Zionist Movement and in Eretz-Israel" (in Hebrew). Ph.D. dissertation, Tel-Aviv University, 1983.

Robach, Brigitte. "Julius Braunthal als politischer Publizist. Ein Leben im Dienste des Sozialismus." Universität Wien, 1983.

Seltzer, Robert M. "Simon Dubnow: A Critical Biography of his Early Years." Ph.D. dissertation, Columbia, 1970.

Shukman, H. "The Relations between the Jewish Bund and the RSDRP, 1897–1903." D.Phil. thesis, Oxford, 1961.

Stone, B. "Nationalist and Internationalist Currents in Polish Socialism: The PPS and SDKPiL, 1893–1921." Ph.D. dissertation, University of Chicago, 1965.

Wistrich, Robert S. "Socialism and the Jewish Question in Germany and Austria (1880–1914)." Ph.D. dissertation, University College, London, 1974.

Yago-Jung, Ilsa. "Die nationale Frage in der jüdischen Arbeiterbewegung in Russland, Polen und Palästina bis 1929." Ph.D. dissertation, Johann Wolfgang Goethe Universität zu Frankfurt am Main, 1976.

## II. Published Sources

### CORRESPONDENCE

Adler, Friedrich, ed. *Victor Adler Briefwechsel mit August Bebel und Karl Kautsky sowie Briefe von und an Ignaz Auer, Eduard Bernstein, Adolf Braun, Heinrich Dietz, Friedrich Ebert, Wilhelm Liebknecht, Hermann Müller und Paul Singer.* Vienna: Verlag der Wiener Volksbuchhandlung, 1954.

Bernstein, Eduard, ed. *Die Briefe von Friedrich Engels an Eduard Bernstein mit Briefen von Karl Kautsky an ebendenselben*. Berlin: J. H. W. Dietz, 1925.

Billroth, Theodor. *Briefe von Theodor Billroth*. 6th ed. Hannover and Leipzig: Hahnsche Buchhandlung, 1902.

Birman, B. P., G. I. Kramol'nikov, and L. Sennikovski, eds. *Sotsialdemokraticheskie listovki 1894–1917 gg. bibliograficheskii ukazatel'*. I. N.p.: Gosydarstvennoe Sotsialno-Ekonomicheskoye Izdatel'stvo, 1939.

Blumenberg, Werner, ed. *August Bebels Briefwechsel mit Friedrich Engels*. Quellen und Untersuchungen zur Geschichte der deutschen und österreichischen Arbeiterbewegung, VI. The Hague: Mouton and Co., 1965.

Bronner, Stephen Eric, ed. *The Letters of Rosa Luxemburg*. Boulder, Col.: Westview Press, 1978.

Eckert, George, ed. *Wilhelm Liebknecht Briefwechsel mit Karl Marx und Friedrich Engels*. Quellen und Untersuchungen zur Geschichte der deutschen und österreichischen Arbeiterbewegung, V. The Hague: Mouton and Co., 1963.

Engels, Friedrich. *Paul et Laura Lafargue. Correspondance*. Edited by Émile Bottigelli. 3 vols. Paris: Editions Sociales, 1956–1959.

Ettinger, Elżbieta, "Rosa Luxemburg: Letters from Her Father." *Formations* IV, 2 (Fall 1987), pp. 8–16.

———. "Rosa Luxemburg: Letters from Warsaw." *Formations* IV, 3 (Winter 1988), pp. 23–41.

———. ed. *Comrade and Lover, Rosa Luxemburg's Letters to Leo Jogiches*. Cambridge, Mass.: M.I.T. Press, 1979.

Hirsch, Helmut, ed. *Eduard Bernsteins Briefwechsel mit Friedrich Engels*. Quellen und Untersuchungen zur Geschichte der deutschen und österreichischen Arbeiterbewegung, Neue Folge, I. Assen: Van Gorcum & Co. N.V., 1970.

Kautsky, Benedikt, ed. *Friedrich Engels' Briefwechsel mit Karl Kautsky*. Quellen und Untersuchungen zur Geschichte der deutschen und österreichischen Arbeiterbewegung, I. Vienna: Danubia-Verlag, Universitätsbuchhandlung, 1955.

Kautsky, Luise, ed. *Rosa Luxemburg. Briefe an Karl und Luise Kautsky (1896–1918)*. Berlin: E. Laub'sche Verlagsbuchhandlung, G.m.b.H., 1923.

Luxemburg, Rosa. *Briefe an Leon Jogiches*. Frankfurt am Main: Europäische Verlagsanstalt, 1971.

———. *Briefe aus dem Gefängnis*. Berlin: Dietz Verlag, 1974.

———. *Gesammelte Briefe*. 5 vols. Institut für Marxismus-Leninismus beim ZK der SED. Berlin: Dietz Verlag, 1982–1984.

Marmor, Kalman, ed. *Arn libermans briv*. New York: Yidisher visnshaftlekher institut—yivo, bibliotek fun yivo, 1951.

Marx, Karl, and Friedrich Engels. *Briefwechsel*. IV. Berlin: Dietz Verlag, 1950.

———. *Selected Correspondence*. Moscow: Foreign Languages Publishing House, n.d.

Meier, Olga, ed. *The Daughters of Karl Marx. Family Correspondence 1866–1898*. Translated by Faith Evans. New York: Harcourt Brace Jovanovich, 1982.

Procacci, Giuliano, ed. "Antonio Labriola e la revisione del marxismo attraverso l'epostolario con Bernstein e con Kautsky 1895–1904." *Instituto Giangiacomo Feltrinelli Annali* III (1960), pp. 264–341.

Sapir, Boris, ed. *Fyodor Ilich Dan pis'ma (1899–1946)*. Selected, annotated and with an outline of Dan's political biography by Boris Sapir. Russian Series on Social History, III. Amsterdam: Stichting Internationaal Instituut voor Sociale Geschiedenis, 1985.

Tych, Feliks, ed. *Róża Luksemburg Listy do Leona Jogichesa-Tyszki*. 3 vols. Warsaw: Książka i Wiedza, 1968–1971.

Weizmann, Chaim. *The Letters and Papers of Chaim Weizmann*. Series A, Volume II. Edited by Meyer W. Weisgal. London: Oxford University Press, 1971.

PRIMARY SOURCES

Abramovitch, Raphael [Rafail Abramovich Rein]. "Doyres sotsialistn hobn gelernt sotsializm fun zayne verk." *Forverts* (January 30, 1949), section 2, p. 4.

———. *In tsvey revolutsies. di geshikhte fun a dor*. 2 vols. New York: Farlag "arbeter-ring," 1944.

———. "Zionismus, Judenfrage und Sozialismus." *Der Kampf* XXII (1929), pp. 509–19.

Adler, Friedrich. "Einige Reminiszenzen." *Volksrecht* LII, 121 (May 24, 1949).

———. "Tsum fertsik-yorikn yoyvl fun 'bund.' " *Naye folkstsaytung* (November 19, 1937), p. 10.

Adler, Max. "Sozialismus und Zionismus." *Der Jüdische Arbeiter. Organ der sozialdemokratischen Poale Zion Österreichs* VII, 5 (March 27, 1931), p. 1.

———. *Das Verhältnis der nationalen zur sozialistischen Idee. Bemerkungen zum Poale-Zionismus*. Vienna: Verlag Zukunft ("Der Jüdische Arbeiter"), 1933.

Adler, Victor. "Der Antisemitismus." *Gleichheit* I, 20 (May 7, 1887), p. 2.

———. *Aufsätze, Reden und Briefe*. 11 vols. Vienna: Verlag der Wiener Volksbuchhandlung, 1922–1929.

———. "Das Märchen von den 'Formeln' und das Typus." *Volkstribüne* XXIV, 18 (May 5, 1915), p. 5.

"Der Allgemeine Jüdische Arbeiterbund in Litauen, Polen und Russland." *Die Neue Zeit* XXII, part 2 (1903–04), pp. 536–40.

"Der allweltliche Kongreß für das arbeitende Palästina." *Der jüdische Arbeiter* VII, 17 (September 1, 1930), p. 2.

"Die Amsterdamer Sozialistenkonferenz für die zionistischen Forderungen."
*Jüdische Rundschau* XXIV, 31 (May 2, 1919), p. 237.

"Die Amsterdamer Sozialistenkonferenz und die jüdischen Forderungen
(Eine Kundgebung der Berliner Gruppe der Poale Zion)." *Jüdische Rundschau* XXIV, 33 (May 9, 1919), p. 255.

Anin, Maxim [Maks-Aryeh Z. Shats]. "Ist die Assimilation der Juden möglich?" *Sozialistische Monatshefte* XII, part 2 (1908), pp. 614–19.

————. "Die Judenfrage als Wanderungsproblem." *Sozialistische Monatshefte* XIII, part 2 (1909), pp. 849–54.

————. "Das jüdische Proletariat in der Internationale." *Sozialistische Monatshefte* XIV, part 2 (1910), pp. 1065–68.

————. "Das Nationalitätsprinzip in der sozialistischen Internationale."
*Sozialistische Monatshefte* XIV, part 2 (1910), pp. 885–90.

————. "Di natsionale frage—oder natsionale fragn?" *Unzer veg* 8–9 (November 1–14, 1907), c. 18–24.

————. "Probleme des jüdischen Arbeiterlebens." *Sozialistische Monatshefte* XIII, part 1 (1909), pp. 231–35.

————. "Was will die jüdische Sektion in der sozialistischen Internationale?" *Sozialistische Monatshefte* XV, part 1 (1911), pp. 396–401.

"Arbeiterzeitungsjuden." *Jüdische Zeitung. National-jüdisches Organ* IV, 22 (June 3, 1910), p. 1.

*Arkadi. zamlbukh tsum ondenk fun grinder fun "bund" arkadi kremer (1865–1935)*. New York: Farlag unzer tsayt, 1942.

Aronson, Gregor [Grigori]. *Rusish-yidishe inteligents*. Buenos Aires: Farlag "yidbukh" bay der "gezelshaft der yidish-veltlekhe shuln in argentina," 1962.

Auerbach, Elias. "Rassenkunde." *Der Jude* VI, 6 (March 1922), pp. 382–87.

Austerlitz, Friedrich. "Die Wahlen in Wien." *Die Neue Zeit* XXIX, part 2 (1910–1911), pp. 507–12.

Axelrod, Pavel Borisovich. "Socialist Jews Confront the Pogroms." In *The Golden Tradition*. Edited by Lucy S. Dawidowicz. Boston: Beacon Press, 1967, pp. 405–10.

B., Sh. "Di fartretung fun der ts.s.a.p. oyfn shtutgarter kongres." *Unzer veg* 1 (August 19 [September 1], 1907), pp. 5–16.

Bahr, Hermann, ed. *Der Antisemitismus. Ein internationales Interview.* Berlin: S. Fischer, 1894.

Bassin, L. "Natsiya li evrei?" *Vestnik Bunda* 1–2 (January-February 1904), pp. 12–14.

Bauer, Otto. "Die Bedingungen der nationalen Assimilation." *Der Kampf* V, 4. Heft (March 1912), pp. 246–63.

————. "Galizische Parteitage." *Der Kampf* V, 4. Heft (January 1, 1912), pp. 154–62.

————. *Die Nationalitätenfrage und die Sozialdemokratie.* Marx-Studien. Blätter zur Theorie und Politik des wissenschaftlichen Sozialismus, II. Vienna: Verlag der Wiener Volksbuchhandlung, 1907.

————. *Die Österreichische Revolution.* Vienna: Verlag der Wiener Volksbuchhandlung, 1965.

————. "Schlusswort zur Minoritätenfrage." *Der Kampf* IV, 5. Heft (February 1, 1911), pp. 201–9.

————. "Sozialismus und Antisemitismus." *Der Kampf* IV, 2. Heft (November 1910), pp. 94–95.

Bebel, August. *Sozialdemokratie und Antisemitismus.* 2d ed. Berlin: Buchhandlung Vorwärts, 1906.

Beer, Max. "Ein Beitrag zur Geschichte des Klassenkampfes im hebräischen Alterthum." *Die Neue Zeit* XI, part 1 (1892–93), pp. 444–48.

————. *Fifty Years of International Socialism.* London: George Allen and Unwin Ltd., 1935.

————. "Der Talmud." *Die Neue Zeit* XII, part 2 (1894) pp. 379–84, 408–16.

————. "Der Talmud." *Die Neue Zeit* XII, part 2, (1894), p. 603.

————. Review of *Die Judenfrage eine ethische Frage*, by Leopold Caro. *Die Neue Zeit* XI, part 2 (1893), pp. 118–19.

————. Review of *Die Staatsverfassung der Juden*, by Eduard Schall. *Die Neue Zeit* XIV, part 2 (1896), pp. 569–70.

————. "Die russischen und polnischen Juden in London." *Die Neue Zeit* XII, part 2 (1894), pp. 730–34.

Belfort-Bax, E. "Der sozialismus einer gewöhnlichen Menschenkindes gegenüber dem Sozialismus des Herrn Bernstein." *Die Neue Zeit* XVI, part 1 (1897–98), pp. 824–29.

Ben Ader [Ben-Adir] [Avrom Rozin]. *Evreiskii vopros' v osveshchenii k. kautskago i S. N. Iuzhakova.* St. Petersburg: Viktor Kugel, 1906.

Berger, H. Review of *Zum jüdisch-arabischen Problem*, by M. Beilinson. *Der Kampf* XXIII (1930), pp. 444–45.

Bernstein, Eduard. *Aus den Jahren meines Exils. Erinnerungen eines Sozialisten.* Berlin: Erich Reiss Verlag, 1918.

————. "Die Aussichten des Zionismus. Eine Antwort an Karl Kautsky." *Vorwärts* 2. Beilage z. no. 575 (December 8, 1929).

————. "Die deutsche Ausgabe einer Hauptschrift des Giordano Bruno." *Die Neue Zeit* XII, part 1 (1893–94), pp. 652–59.

————. "Einige Bemerkungen über die jüdische Einwanderung in England." In *Jüdische Statistik.* Berlin: Jüdischer Verlag, 1903.

————. "Eleanor Marx." *Die Neue Zeit* XVI, part 2 (1898), pp. 118–23.

————. "Die entsteung fun dem internatsionaln gedank." *Der veker* (August 11, 1923), pp. 5–7.

————. "Entwicklungsgang eines Sozialisten." In *Die Volkswirtschaftslehre der Gegenwart in Selbstdarstellungen.* Edited by Felix Meiner. Leipzig: Verlag von Felix Meiner, 1924, pp. 1–58.

————. "Di ershte kampf far ekzistents vos di arbayter-prese hot durkhgemakht in europ." *Forverts* (April 23, 1922), Section 4, p. 5.

————. "Fragen der Taktik in Russland." *Sozialistische Monatshefte* I (1906), pp. 208–17.

————. "Für das arbeitende Palästina." *Der Neue Weg* 3–4 (February-March 1925), pp. 72–73.

————. *Geschichte der Berliner Arbeiter-Bewegung. Ein Kapitel zur Geschichte der deutschen Sozialdemokratie.* 3 vols. Berlin: Buchhandlung Vorwärts, 1907–1910.

————. "Glik tsum yidishn 'forverts.' " *Forverts* (April 23, 1922), section 2, p. 1.

————. "Die Internationale der Arbeiterklasse und der europäische Krieg." *Archiv für Sozialwissenschaft und Sozialpolitik* XL, 2 (January 1915), pp. 267–322.

————. "Der Kampf der Sozialdemokratie und die Revolution der Gesellschaft." *Die Neue Zeit* XVI, part 1 (1897–98), pp. 484–97.

————. "Di mizrekh-yidn in daytshland. di yidishe vanderer, di antisemiten un di sotsialisten." *Tsukunft* XXVIII (November 1923), pp. 664–69.

————. *My Years of Exile. Reminiscences of a Socialist.* Translated by Bernhard Miall. London: Leonard Parsons, 1921.

————. "Les nationalistes arabes et le mandat palestinien." *Comité socialiste pour la Palestine ouvrière. Bulletin* 5 (May 1930), p. 12.

————. "Di natsionale shtremungen tsvishn der yidish-akademisher yugnt in daytshland." *Tsukunft* XXVI (September 1921), pp. 520–25.

————. "Das realistische und das ideologische Moment im Sozialismus." *Die Neue Zeit* XVI, part 2 (1897–98), pp. 225–32.

————. "Die Reichstagswahlen und die Juden." *Der Neue Weg* 1 (December 1924), pp. 2–6.

————. Review of *Der Antisemitismus und die Juden im Lichte der modernen Wissenschaft,* by C. Lombroso. *Die Neue Zeit* XII, part 2 (1893–94), pp. 405–7.

————. Review of *Die Sozialdemokratie und das jüdische Proletariat,* by David Balakan. *Dokumente des Sozialismus* V (1905), p. 357.

————. Review of *Das Stiefkind der Sozialdemokratie,* by Matthias Acher. *Dokumente des Sozialismus* V (1905), pp. 298–99.

————. Review of *Studien zur Wirtschaftsstellung der Juden,* by Felix Pinkus. *Dokumente des Sozialismus* V (1905), pp. 343–44.

————. Review of *Das Wesen des Judentums,* by J. Fromer. *Dokumente des Sozialismus* V (1905), pp. 145–47.

————. "Das Schlagwort und der Antisemitismus." *Die Neue Zeit* XI, part 2 (1893), pp. 228–37.

————. "Der Schulstreit in Palästina." *Die Neue Zeit* XXXII, part 1 (1913–14), pp. 744–52.

————. *Sozialdemokratische Lehrjahre.* Berlin: Der Bücherkreis GmbH, 1928.

————. "Überschätzte Friedensmächte." *Die Friedens-Warte* XVII, 4 (1915), pp. 127–33.

————. "Vi azoy vet der sotsializm farvirklikht vern?" *Der veker* (November 10, 1923).

———. "Vi ikh bin oyfgevaksn in goles als yid." *Der yidisher kempfer* (December 1, 8, 15, 22, and 29, 1916).

———. "Vom Mittlerberuf der Juden." *Neue Jüdische Monatshefte* 14 (April 25, 1917), pp. 397–401.

———. "Vom Patriotismus der Juden." *Die Friedens-Warte* XVIII (1916), pp. 243–48.

———. *Von 1850 bis 1872. Kindheit und Jugendjahre.* Berlin: Erich Reiss Verlag, 1926.

———. *Von den Aufgaben der Juden im Weltkriege.* Berlin: Erich Reiss Verlag, 1917.

———. "Vos di sotsialisten hobn nit gedarft ignorirn." *Der yidisher kempfer* (May 18, 1917).

———. "Vospominaniia o Mikhaile Dragomanove i Sergee Podolinskom." In *Letopis' Revoliutsii* I. Berlin, St. Petersburg, Moscow: 1923, pp. 58–65.

———. "Wie Fichte und Lassalle national waren." *Archiv für die Geschichte des Sozialismus und der Arbeiterbewegung* V (1915), pp. 143–62.

———. "Wie Ich als Jude in der Diaspora aufwuchs." *Der Jude* II (1917–18), pp. 186–95.

———. "Di yidishe heym in erets yisroel. an untershtitser fun dem pro-palestine komitet un dokh nit kayn tsionist." *Tsukunft* XXXIV (1929), pp. 157–58.

———. "Di yidn als fermitler tsvishn di felker." *Der yidisher kempfer* (September 27, 1916), p. 4; (October 6, 1916), p. 4; (October 11, 1916), p. 6.

———. "Di yidn un di daytshe sotsial-demokratie." *Tsukunft* XXVI (March 1921), pp. 145–52.

———. "Zur Abwehr." *Volksstaat* (February 19, 1873).

Billroth, Theodor. *The Medical Sciences in the German Universities. A Study in the History of Civilization.* Introduction by William H. Welch. New York: Macmillan Company, 1924.

———. *Prof. Dr. Th. Billroth's Antwort auf die Adresse des Lesevereines der deutschen Studenten Wien's.* Vienna: Carl Gerold's Sohn, 1875.

———. *Über das Lehren und Lernen der medicinischen Wissenschaften an den Universitäten der Deutschen Nation nebst allgemeinen Bemerkungen über Universitäten. Eine culturhistorische Studie.* Vienna: Carl Gerold's Sohn, 1876.

Blum, Klara. Review of *Die Soziologie der Juden*, by Arthur Ruppin. *Der Kampf* XXIV (1931), p. 462.

Borochov, Ber. *Class Struggle and the Jewish Nation. Selected Essays in Marxist Zionism.* Edited and with an introduction by Mitchell Cohen. New Brunswick, London: Transaction Books, 1984.

———. [Borokhov]. *Geklibene Shriftn.* II. Edited by B. Lo[c]ker. New York: Borokhov brentsh 14, yidish-natsionaler arbeter-farband, 1928.

————. [D. B. Borokhov]. *Poyle tsien shriftn*. I. New York: Poyle tsien farlag, 1920.

Braunthal, Julius. *In Search of the Millenium*. London: V. Gollancz, 1945.

Braunthal, Julius, ed. *Otto Bauer. Eine Auswahl aus seinem Lebenswerk*. Vienna: Verlag der Wiener Volksbuchhandlung, 1961.

Brügel, Fritz. Review of *Burschenschaft und Judenfrage*, by Oskar Franz Scheuer. *Der Kampf* XX (1927), pp. 293–94.

C[ahan], A[braham]. "Eleanora marks-aveling." *Tsukunft* VI (February 1897) pp. 1–3.

————. *Bleter fun mayn lebn* II and III. New York: Forverts asosiashon, 1926.

Chasanowitsch, Leon [Kasrial] [Khazanovitch]. "Karl kautski un vurm iber der yuden-frage." *Der yudisher arbeyter. tsentral-organ fun der yudisher sotsialistisher arbeyter-partey poyle-tsien in estreykh* V, 47 (December 25, 1908), pp. 1–2.

————. "Vos kautski veys vegen di yuden frage." *Varhayt* IV, 1152 (January 13, 1909), p. 4, cols. 4–5.

————. "Ziele und Mittel des sozialistischen Zionismus." *Sozialistische Monatshefte* XX, part 2 (1914), pp. 962–73.

Cohn, Willy. Review of *Rasse und Judentum. Allgemeine Zeitung des Judentums* LXXXV, 17 (August 19, 1921), p. 202.

————. Review of *Rasse und Judentum. Monatsschrift für Geschichte und Wissenschaft des Judentums* LXVI, 1/3 (January-March 1922), pp. 75–76.

Cunow, [Heinrich]. Review of *Grundzüge zur Judenfrage*, by O. V. Boenick. *Die Neue Zeit* XIII, part 1 (1894–95), pp. 823–24.

Daszynski, Ignaz. "Die Lage in Oesterreich." *Die Neue Zeit* XVI, part 1 (1897–98), pp. 718–23.

Deich, Leo [Daytsh]. "Arn sundelevitch." *Tsukunft* XIX (1914), pp. 831–39.

————. "Der ershter revolutsioner-'tsienist.'" *Tsukunft* XXI (1916), pp. 771–81.

————. "Der ershter yidish-sotsialistisher propagandist." *Tsukunft* XXI (1916), pp. 677–81.

————. "Der ershter yidisher revolutsioner in rusland." *Tsukunft* XVIII (1913), pp. 438–50.

————. "Leyzer tsukerman—der belibster yid in der revolutsie." *Tsukunft* XXI (1916), pp. 240–45.

————. "Pavel akselrod." *Tsukunft* XVIII (1913), pp. 897–905.

————. *Yidn in der rusisher revolutsie. zikhroynes vegn yidn-revolutsionern*. Translated by E. Korman. Berlin: Yidisher literarisher farlag, 1923.

————. "Di yidn in der rusisher revolutsionerer bavegung." *Tsukunft* XVIII (1913), pp. 248–57.

"Di diskusie vegn der natsionaler frage oyfn tsuzamenfor fun 'bund,' yuni 1903, tsurikh." *Unzer tsayt* I, 4 (December 1927).

"Dr. adler iber di estraykhishe poyle tsien." *Der yudisher arbeyter* IV, 37 (September 13, 1907), pp. 2–3.

Dubnow, Simon [Shimen Dubnov]. *Briv vegn altn un nayem yidentum.* Translated by Moiśes [Moyshe] and Saúl [Shaul] Ferdman. Introduction by Kh. Sh. Kazdan. Mexico City: Shloyme mendelson fond bay der gezelshaft far kultur un hilf, 1959.

———. *Dos bukh fun mayn lebn. zikhroynes un rayoynes. materialn far der geshikhte fun mayn tsayt.* 3 vols. Volumes I and III translated by I. Birnboym. Volume II translated by I. Rapaport. Buenos-Aires, New York: Alveltlekher yidisher kultur-kongres, 1962–63.

Eckstein, G. "Entgegnung auf die Zuschrift d. zionistischen Vereinigung." *Die Neue Zeit* XXIX, part 1 (1910–11), p. 158.

"Ed. Bernstein und der Sprachenkampf." *Neuer Weg* I, 3–4 (March-April 1914), p. 3.

"Eduard Bernstein." *Israelitisches Familienblatt* XXXIV, 51 (December 22, 1932).

"Eduard Bernstein." *Der jüdische Arbeiter* VII, 2 (January 17, 1930), pp. 1–2.

"Eduard Bernstein." *Jüdische Rundschau* XXXVII, 101 (December 20, 1932), p. 493.

"Eduard Bernstein." *Mitteilungs-Blätter der Liga für das arbeitende Palästina in Oesterreich* 6–7, (November-December 1932), p. 12.

"Eduard Bernstein, der grosse Theoretiker des Sozialismus, gestorben." *Der jüdische Arbeiter* X, 1 (January 4, 1933), p. 4.

"Eduard Bernstein, der grosse Theoretiker des Sozialismus, gestorben." *Jüdische Telegraphen-Agentur (J. T. A.)* XI, 289 (December 20, 1932), pp. 1–2.

"Eduard Bernstein: On the Occasion of his Seventy-Fifth Birthday." *Jewish Telegraphic Agency. Daily News Bulletin* VI, 8 (January 9, 1925), p. 3.

"Eduard Bernstein, Veteran Socialist Leader, On his Jewishness." *Jewish Telegraphic Agency. Daily News Bulletin* VI, 21 (January 24, 1925), p. 6.

"Eduard bernshteyn far'n 'yidishn kempfer.'" *Der yidisher kempfer* (September 15, 1916), p. 1.

"Eduard bernshteyn iber di yudenfrage in [sic] iber di yudishe arbeyterfrage." *Der yudisher arbeyter* IV, 31 (August 2, 1907), p. 2.

"Eduard bernshteyn mitarbayter fun'm 'yidishn kempfer.'" *Der yidisher kempfer* (August 18, 1916), p. 2.

"Eduard bernshteyn vegn yidishkayt." *Der yidisher kempfer* (September 27, 1916), p. 4.

"Eine Kundgebung für das arbeitende Palästina." *Jüdische Rundschau* XXIX, 15 (February 22, 1924), p. 99.

Emanuel, B. "Über den Zionismus." *Die Neue Zeit* XIII (1895), pp. 599–603.

"Engelbert pernerstorfer." *Der sotsial-demokrat. organ fun der yudisher sotsial-demokratisher partey in galitsien* VI, 17 (April 30, 1910), pp. 5–6.

Engels, Friedrich. "Die Bauernfrage in Frankreich und Deutschland." *Die Neue Zeit* XIII (1894–95), pp. 292–306.

———. *Condition of the Working-Class in England in 1844*. London: George Allen and Unwin Ltd., 1892.

———. "Herrn Eugen Dührings Umwälzung der Wissenschaft." In *Werke*, XX, by Karl Marx and Friedrich Engels. Berlin: Dietz Verlag, 1962.

———. "Kann Europa abrüsten?" In *Werke*, XXII, by Karl Marx and Friedrich Engels. Berlin: Dietz Verlag, 1970.

———. "Preussischer Schnaps im deutschen Reichstag." In *Werke*, XIX, by Karl Marx and Friedrich Engels. Berlin: Dietz Verlag, 1962.

———. *Profile. Eine Auslese aus seinen Werken und Briefen*. Edited by Helmut Hirsch. Wupertal-Barmen: Peter Hammer Verlag, GmbH, 1970.

———. "Über den Antisemitismus." In *Werke*, XXII, by Karl Marx and Friedrich Engels. Berlin: Dietz Verlag, 1970.

*Ershter kongres farn arbetndn erets-yisroel. berlin IX-27—X-1 1930*. Tel Aviv, Warsaw: Velt-lige farn arbetndn erets-yisroel, 1931.

"Der estreykhisher parteytog." *Der sotsial-demokrat. organ fun der yudisher sotsial-demokratisher partey in galitsien* I, 6 (November 10, 1905), pp. 2–3.

"Der estreykhisher sotsial-demokratisher parteytog." *Der yudisher arbeyter* II, 20 (December 1, 1905), pp. 6–7.

"Evolutionary Socialism. Interview with Herr Eduard Bernstein." *The Jewish Chronicle* (November 24, 1899), p. 21.

"Der fareynigungs-kongres fun der yudisher sotsialdemokratisher partey." *Der sotsial-demokrat. organ fun der yudisher sotsial-demokratisher partey in galitsien* VII, 42 (October 20, 1911).

"Ferfolgung fun di fremde." *Der veker. organ fun der yudisher sotsialistisher (bundisher) organizatsie in vien* I, 12 (November 21, 1919), p. 1.

Fischer, Ernst. *An Opposing Man*. Translated by Peter and Betty Ross. London: Allen Lane, 1974.

G., F. "Alldeutsch oder International." *Im deutschen Reich* XXIII, 12 (December 1917), pp. 499–505.

"Gedanken eines Juden." *Die Neue Zeit* III (1885), p. 284.

Geiger, Ludwig. "Literarische Übersicht." *Allgemeine Zeitung des Judentums* LXXXII, 27 (July 5, 1918), pp. 320–22.

"Gen. Dr. Max Adlers Stellung zum Zionismus." *Jüdische Arbeiter-Jugend. Organ des Verbands der jüdisch-sozialistischen Arbeiter-Jugend Österreichs* II, 2 (March 1928), pp. 9–10.

Gerlach, Aurelia. *Der Einfluss der Juden in der österreichischen Sozialdemokratie*. Vienna: W. Braumüller, 1939.

Goldmann, Felix. "Rasse und Judentum." *Allgemeine Zeitung des Judentums* LXXIX, 22 (May 28, 1915), pp. 253–54.

Gordon, Avrom [Avrom Rezshtsik]. *In friling fun vilner yidisher arbeter bavegung.* Vilna, 1926.

Grunwald, Max. "Rasse, Volk, Nation." *Jahrbuch für jüdische Volkskunde* (1924–25), pp. 307–43.

Güdemann, M. Review of *Von den Aufgaben der Juden im Weltkriege. Monatsschrift für Geschichte und Wissenschaft des Judentums,* Neue Folge, LXII, 26 (1918), pp. 64–65.

Gurevitch, G. "Der protses fun a. liberman, g. gurevitch un m. aronson in berlin." In *Royter pinkes. tsu der geshikhte fun der yidisher arbeter-bavegung un sotsialistische shtremungen bay yidn.* II. Warsaw: Farlag kultur-lige, 1924, pp. 107–11.

———. "Tsu der biografie fun l. tsukerman." In *Royter pinkes. tsu der geshikhte fun der yidisher arbeter-bavegung un sotsialistische shtremungen bay yidn.* II. Warsaw: Farlag kultur-lige, 1924, pp. 12–118.

———. "Zikhroynes 1873–1880." In *Di yidishe sotsialistishe bavegung biz der grindung fun "bund." forshungen, zikhroynes, materialn.* Edited by E. Tscherikower [Tsherikover], A. Menes, F. Kursky [Kurski], and A. Rosin (Ben-Adir) [Rozin]. *Historishe shriftn,* III. Shriftn fun yidishn visnshaftlekhn institut, XI. Vilna, Paris: Historishe sektsie fun yivo, 1939, pp. 224–44.

H., A. *Di sotsialistishe fraktsies in tsienizm.* Warsaw: Farlag "di welt," 1906.

Häcker, S. "Der Sozialismus in Polen." *Die Neue Zeit* XIV, part 2 (1896), pp. 324–32.

———. "Über den Zionismus." *Die Neue Zeit* XIII, part 2 (1895), pp. 759–61.

Hamburger, E. "Eduard Bernstein über den Zionismus." *Jüdische Rundschau* XIX, 13 (March 27, 1914), pp. 131–32

Hannak, Jacques. "Judenfrage." *Der Kampf* XIII (1920), pp. 117–20.

———. "Das Judentum am Scheidewege." *Der Kampf* XII (1919), pp. 649–53.

———. "Die Krise des Zionismus." *Der Kampf* XX (1927), pp. 454–58.

———. Review of *Sozialismus im Zionismus,* by Max Brod. *Der Kampf* XIII (1920), pp. 245–46.

Hinteregger, Christoph. *Der Judenschwindel.* Vienna: Verlag der Wiener Volksbuchhandlung, 1923.

Huysmans, Camille. "Sur le sionisme. Réponse à Kautsky." *Comité socialiste pour la palestine ouvrière. Bulletin* 4 (1929), p. 10.

Ignatjeff, I. [Alexander Israel Helphand]. "Russisch-jüdische Arbeiter über die Judenfrage." *Die Neue Zeit* XI, part 1 (1892–93), pp. 175–79.

Ivanovitsh, S. "Karl kautski. (tsu zayn 70 yorign yubileum.)" *Der veker* (October 18, 1924), pp. 6–8.

Jacoby, Siegfried. "Eduard Bernstein als Mitarbeiter im 'Komitee für das arbeitende Erez Israel.' " *Jüdische Presszentrale Zürich* VII, 307 (August 28, 1924), pp. 5–6.

J., O. (Jenssen.) Review of *Rasse und Judentum. Der Bibliothekar und Ratgeber für Hausbüchereien* XIII (1921), p. 1936.

Jenssen, O. "Anti-Semitismus, Zionismus, Sozialismus." *Leipziger Volkszeitung* 3. Beilage z. no. 76 (April 2, 1921).

*Der Jud ist Schuld*. Vienna: Verlag der Wiener Volksbuchhandlung, n.d.

"Die Juden beim Seipel." *Arbeiter-Zeitung* (December 3, 1925), p. 4.

"Juden von Hitlers Gnaden." *Das Kleine Blatt* VIII, 3 (January 4, 1934), p. 2.

"Judenausweisungen." *Freie Tribüne* II, 18 (May 1, 1920), pp. 2–3.

"Die Judenfrage und ihre Lösungsmöglichkeiten. Eine Unterredung mit Adler, ehemaligem Generalsekretär der II. Internationale." *Die Tat* (February 2, 1948).

"Die Judenhatz bei Austerlitz." *Freie Tribüne* I, 29 (August 2, 1919), p. 3.

"Der jüdische Dreh eines arischen Advokaten." *Arbeiter-Zeitung* XXXV, 158 (June 11, 1923), p. 2.

"Die jüdischen Kolonien in Palästina." *Die Neue Zeit* I (1883), p. 199.

"Kampf der Poale Zion auf dem Kongreß der Sozialistischen Internationale." *Das Jüdische Volksblatt* I, 12 (August 10, 1928), p. 1.

*Kauft nicht bei Juden*. Die Drei Pfeile, 3. Vienna: Sozialdemokratischer Verlag, G.m.b.H., n.d.

Kautsky, Karl. "Amerikanische und europäische Arbeiter." *Arbeiter-Zeitung* 265 (September 23, 1928), p. 3.

———. "Der Antisemitismus." *Oesterreichischer Arbeiter-Kalender für das Jahr 1885*, pp. 98–104.

———. *Are the Jews a Race?* Westport, Conn.: Greenwood Press, 1972.

———. "Aus Oesterreich." *Züricher Post* 212 (September 11, 1883), p. 1.

———. "Die Aussichten des Zionismus." *Arbeiter-Zeitung* 262 (September 22, 1929), p. 4.

———. "L'Avenir du sionisme." *La Vie socialiste* VII, 168 (December 14, 1929), pp. 5–6.

———. "A bagrisung tsum 'veker' fun karl kautski." *Der veker* (October 30, 1926), p. 14.

———. "Bagrisungen tsum 'forverts' fun karl kautski." *Forverts* (April 24, 1927), Section 4, p. 1, c. 6–8.

———. "Di bedeytung fun des komunistishen manifest." In *Dos manifest fun di komunistishe partey*, by Karl Marx and Friedrich Engels. N.p.: Bund, 1899, pp. 15–24.

———. *Die Befreiung der Nationen*. Stuttgart: J. H. W. Dietz, 1917.

———. "Das böhmische Staatsrecht und die Sozialdemokratie." *Die Neue Zeit* XVII, part 1 (1898–99), pp. 292–301.

———. "Brif fun k. kautski." *Tsayt* 21 (May 1914), p. 2.

———. "Brif tsum 7tn tsuzamenfor fun 'bund.' " *Folkstsaytung* 159 (September 13–26, 1906).

————. "Die Differenzen unter den russischen Sozialisten." *Die Neue Zeit* XXIII, part 2 (1904–05), pp. 68–79.

————. *The Dictatorship of the Proletariat.* Ann Arbor: University of Michigan Press, 1971.

————. *Die Diktatur des Proletariats.* Vienna: Verlag der Wiener Volksbuchhandlung, 1918.

————. "Die Dumawahlen." *Die Neue Zeit* XXXI, part 1 (1912–13), pp. 843–44.

————. "Ein Bildchen aus Oesterreich." *Züricher Post* 88 (April 17, 1883), p. 1, c. 1–3.

————. "Ein Brief." *Der Kampf* I (1907–08), pp. 9–11.

————. "Eine Erinnerung an Masaryk." *Prager Presse* XVII, 260 (September 21, 1937), p. 2.

————. "Eine Frage." *Der Kampf* IV (1911), pp. 482–85.

————. "Einige Ursachen und Wirkungen des deutschen Nationalsozialismus." *Der Kampf* XXVI (1933), pp. 235–45.

————. *Erinnerungen und Erörterungen.* Edited by Benedikt Kautsky. Quellen und Untersuchungen zur Geschichte der deutschen und österreichischen Arbeiterbewegung, III. The Hague: Mouton and Co., 1960.

————. "Finis Poloniae?" *Die Neue Zeit* XIV, part 2 (1896), pp. 484–91, 513–25.

————. "Die Fortsetzung einer unmöglichen Diskussion." *Die Neue Zeit* XXIII, part 2 (1904–05), pp. 681–92; 717–27.

————. "Fun a rumfuler fargangenhayt tsu a herlekher tsukunft." *Naye folkstsaytung* (November 19, 1937), p. 10.

————. "Jaures' Taktik und die Sozialdemokratie." *Vorwärts* 172 (July 26, 1899), p. 3, c. 1.

————. "Das Judenthum." *Die Neue Zeit* VIII (1890), pp. 23–30.

————. *Der kamf fun di natsionalitetn un dos statsrecht in estraych.* Vilna: Ferlag "kamf," 1906.

————. "Der kamf fun di natsionen in estraykh." *Der yidisher arbeyter* 8 (December 1899), 8–12.

————. "Der Kampf der Nationalitäten und das Staatsrecht in Oesterreich." *Die Neue Zeit* XVI, part 1 (1897–98), pp. 516–24, 557–64.

————. "Karl Kautsky." In *Die Volkswirtschaftslehre der Gegenwart in Selbstdarstellungen.* Edited by Felix Meiner. Leipzig: Verlag von Felix Meiner, 1924, pp. 117–53.

————. "Karl Kautsky über Judentum und jüdisches Proletariat." *Die Welt* 50 (December 15, 1905), pp. 4–5.

————. "Kautsky on the Problems of the Jewish Proletariat in England." *Justice. The Organ of the Social Democracy* XXI, 1058 (April 23, 1904), p. 4.

————. "Kishinevskaia reznia i evreiskii vopros'." *Iskra* 42 (June 15, 1903), pp. 1–2.

————. "Die Krisis in Österreich." *Die Neue Zeit* XXII, part 1 (1903–04), pp. 39–46, 72–79.

————. "Das Massaker von Kischeneff und die Judenfrage." *Die Neue Zeit* XXI, part 2 (1902–03), pp. 303–9.

————. *Die materialistische Geschichtsauffassung.* 2 vols. Berlin: J. H. W. Dietz, 1927.

————. "Die moderne Nationalität." *Die Neue Zeit* V (1887), pp. 392–405, 442–51.

————. "Nachschrift der Redaktion." *Die Neue Zeit* XXIII, part 2 (1904–05), pp. 739–40.

————. "Die 'nationale' Bewegung in Böhmen." *Der Sozialdemokrat* 30 (July 21, 1881), p. 2, c. 1–2.

————. "Die nationale Frage." *Der Volksstaat* VII, 26 (March 5, 1875), p. 1; VII, 28 (March 10, 1875), p. 1.

————. "Nationalität und Internationalität." *Erganzungshefte zur Neuen Zeit* 1 (January 18, 1908).

————. "Die Nationalitätenfrage in Russland." *Leipziger Volkszeitung* 4. Beilage z. no. 98 (April 29, 1905).

————. "Nochmals der Kampf der Nationalitäten in Oesterreich." *Die Neue Zeit* XVI, part 1 (1897–98), pp. 723–26.

————. "Nochmals der Zionismus." *Vorwärts* 2. Beilage z. no. 587 (December 15, 1929), p. 1.

————. "Oesterreich-Ungarn." *Der Sozialdemokrat* 41 (October 5, 1882).

————. "Di oyfgabn fun dem yidishn proletariat in england. a bagrisung artikl tsu di 'naye tsayt.' " *Di naye tsayt* (April 1, 1904), p. 5, c. 1–3.

————. "Di oyfgabn fun di yidishe sotsialistn in amerika." *Forverts* (April 23, 1922), Section 2, p.6, c. 1–8.

————. "Di oyfgabn funm yidishn proletariat in sovet-rusland." *Dos fraye vort* 4 (June 20, 1923), pp. 1–7.

————. "Der 'paria' unter di proletarier." *Di arbeyter shtimme* 25 (October 1901), p. 5.

————. "A Pariah among Proletarians." *Justice. The Organ of the Social Democracy* XIX, 945 (February 22, 1902), p. 2.

————. *Pariia sredi proletariev.* London: Zagranichnago komiteta "bunda."

————. "Die Parteiorganisation in Österreich." *Die Neue Zeit* XXX, part 1 (1911–12), pp. 675–79.

————. "Particularismus und Sozialdemokratie." *Die Neue Zeit* XVII, part 1 (1898–99), pp. 292–301.

————. "Di perspektiven fun'm tsionizm." *Der veker* (November 2, 1929), pp. 8–10.

————. "Pis'mo Kautskago." *Vestnik Bunda* 3 (June 1904), pp. 20–21.

————. "Das prager Programm von 1878." In Šolle, Zdeněk, "Vzpomínka Karla Kautského na břevnovský sjezd československé sociální demokracie." *Československý časopis historický* XIII, 2 (1965), pp. 275–79.

———. "Rasse und Judentum." *Erganzungshefte zur Neuen Zeit* 20 (October 30, 1914). Second edition: Stuttgart: J. H. W. Dietz, 1921.

———. Review of *Judenthum und Sozialdemokratie*, by Alexander Berg. *Die Neue Zeit* X, part 1 (1891–92), p. 757.

———. Reviews of *Die Ungarischen Rumänen und die Ungarische Nation* and of *Die Rumänische Frage in Siebenbürgen und Ungarn*. *Die Neue Zeit* XI, part 1 (1892–93), pp. 830–32.

———. "Die Revision des Programms der Sozialdemokratie in Oesterreich." *Die Neue Zeit* XX, part 1 (1901–02), pp. 68–82.

———. "Separatismus, Nationalismus und Sozialismus." *Die Neue Zeit* XXX, part 1 (1911–12), pp. 520–32.

———. "Separatizmus, natsionalizmus un sotsializmus." *Tsukunft* 3 (1912), pp. 238–42; 4 (1912), pp. 278–84.

———. "Socialism and Internationalism." *The Social Democrat* IX (1905), pp. 540–43.

———. *Die soziale Revolution*. Berlin: Buchhandlung Vorwärts, 1902.

———. *Sozialisten und Krieg*. Prague: Orbis-Verlag A.-G., 1937.

———. "Tayere verter tsu unzer yontef fun unzer libn lerer karl kautski." *Forverts* (April 25, 1937), Section 2, p. 1, c. 1–8.

———. "Die Theilung Böhmens." *Züricher Post* 190 (August 16, 1883), p.1, c. 1–3.

———. "Un mot de Kautsky." *La Petite République Socialiste* 850 (July 24, 1899), 1st page, c. 5.

———. *Vegn der natsionaler frage in rusland*. Vilna: Di velt, 1906.

———. "Viktor Adler. Erinnerungsblätter zu seinem 60. Geburtstag." *Die Neue Zeit* XXX, part 2 (1912), pp. 417–27.

———. "Vorrede des Uebersetzers." In *Revolution und Kontre-Revolution in Deutschland*, by Karl Marx. Stuttgart: Dietz, 1896, pp. VII-XXX.

———. "Zum 80. Geburtstag Eduard Bernsteins." *Der Kampf* XXIII (1930), pp. 7–16.

———. "Zum Nationalitätenkampf in Oesterreich." *Der Sozialdemokrat* 52 (December 24, 1885).

Kaznelson, Siegmund. "Volk und Nation." *Jüdische Rundschau* XXVI, 77 (September 27, 1921), p. 569.

Kisman, Yoysef. "Yidishe sotsialistishe fareynikung in galitsie. (a kapitl bundishe geshikhte—mit 50 yor tsurik.)" *Unzer tsayt* (November 1961), pp. 24–28.

Kon, Felix. "Die Juden in Polen." *Die Neue Zeit* XXXIV, part 1 (1915–16), pp. 169–78.

"Konferenz der Poale-Zion in Deutschland." *Der jüdische Arbeiter. Organ der sozialdemokratischen Poale Zion Österreichs.* VII, 2 (January 17, 1930), p. 4.

Kopelzon, T. M. "Yidishe arbeter bavegung in vilna sof akhtsiker un onhoyb nayntsiker yorn." Translated by Ephim Jeshurin. In *Vilna. a zamlbukh gevidmet der shtot vilna.* Edited by Ephim H. Jeshurin. New York: Vilner brentsh 367 arbeter ring, 1935, pp. 57–74.

Kossovsky, Vladimir [Kosovski] [Nokhum Mendl Levinson]. "Di fartretung in'm internatsional." In *Fragen fun leben zamelbukh,* Vilna: 1911, pp. 25–39.

———. "Die Aussichten der russischen Revolution." *Die Neue Zeit* XXVI, part 1 (1907–08), pp. 916–22.

———. "Natsionalitet un asimilatsie." *Der yidisher arbeter* 15 (June 1904), pp. 25–37; 16 (August 1904), pp. 15–26.

———. "Tsum 65tn geburtstog fun karl kautski." *Tsukunft* XXV (1920), pp. 41–44.

"Die Krise in der tschechischen Sozialdemokratie." *Oesterreichischer Metallarbeiter* XX, 15 (April 14, 1910), pp. 1–2.

"Das Kuratorium des Instituts." *Mitteilungen der Auslandszentrale des Jiddischen Wissenschaftlichen Instituts* 1 (May 1930), pp. 2–3.

Kursky, Franz [Frants Kurski]. *Gezamlte shriftn.* New York: Farlag der veker, 1952.

L., A. "Der Angriff Kautskys auf den Zionismus." *Jüdische Rundschau* XIX, 48 (November 27, 1914), pp. 435–37; XIX, 51 (December 18, 1914), pp. 459–60; XX, 1 (January 1, 1915), pp. 1–2.

———. "Der Jüdische Arbeiterbund." *Die Neue Zeit* XXVI, part 1 (1907–08), p. 144.

———. "Der Poalei-Zionismus. Eine neue Strömung im russischen Judentum." *Die Neue Zeit* XXIV, part 1 (1905–06), pp. 804–16.

———. "Die prinzipielle Stellung des 'Jüdischen Arbeiterbundes.'" *Die Neue Zeit* XXIV, part 2 (1906), pp. 702–5.

L., E. "Engelbert Pernerstorfer und die Judenfrage." *Der jüdische Arbeiter* V, 1 (February 1, 1928), pp. 2–3.

Lafargue, P. "Die Beschneidung, ihre soziale und religiöse Bedeutung." *Die Neue Zeit* VI (1888), pp. 496–505.

Lang, H. "Der fertsikster geburtstog fun forverts." *Forverts* (April 25, 1937), Section 1, p. 17.

Latski-bertoldi, V[olf]. *Erdgayst. geklibene shriftn.* I. Paris, Berlin, Warsaw, Vilna: Aroysgegeben funm yobl-komitet, n.d.

Leder, Z. [W. Feinstein]. "Zur Judenfrage in Russland." *Die Neue Zeit* XXX, part 1 (1911–12), pp. 704–13.

Lenin, Vladimir [Vladimir Ilich Ulianov]. *Lenin on the Jewish Question.* Edited by Hyman Lumer. New York: International Publishers, 1974.

Lestchinsky, Jacob. *Marks i Kautskii o evreiskom vopros'.* Vol. 2. Moscow: Pereval', 1907.

Levy, Amy. "Ruben Sachs. Ein Charakterbild aus der jüdischen Gesellschaft Londons." *Die Neue Zeit* X, part 1 (1891–92), pp. 27–32, 58–64, 90–96, 125–28, 153–60, 188–92, 220–24, 252–56, 285–88, 313–20, 345–52, 376–84.

Liebknecht, Wilhelm. "Nachträgliches zur 'Affaire.'" *Die Fackel* I, 18 (September 1899), pp. 1–10.

Liebstein, Karl. "Karl Kautsky zu den Unruhen in Palästina." *Der Jüdische Arbeiter. Organ der sozialdemokratischen Poale Zion Oesterreichs* VI, 11 (November 8, 1929), p. 1.

Litovski, A. "Di zitsungen fun der ruslandisher sektsie. (a brif fun shtutgart)." In *Di shtime. zamelbukh*. Vilna: 1907, cols. 22–34.

Locker, Berl. "Die allgemeinen Gesetze der Assimilation und die Ostjuden." *Der Jude* I (1916–17), pp. 504–29.

———. "Karl Kautsky und der Zionismus." *Der Neue Weg* 1 (December 1924), pp. 6–13.

———. *Me-kitov ad yerushalayim*. Jerusalem: Ha-sifriyah ha-tsiyonit, 1970.

———. "Viktor adler (tsu zayn zekhtsinsten [sic] geburtstog)." *Der yudisher arbeyter. tsentral-organ fun der yudisher sotsialistisher arbeyterpartey poyle-tsien in estreykh* IX, 26 (June 28, 1912).

———. "Wirkungen des Kapitalismus im ostjüdischen Leben." *Der Neue Weg* 2 (January 1925), pp. 38–47.

Lozynskyj, Mychajlo. "Die jüdische Frage in Galizien und die österreichische Sozialdemokratie." *Ukrainische Rundschau* IV, 5 (May 1906), pp. 168–74; IV, 6 (June 1906), pp. 208–14.

Luxemburg, Rosa. "Diskussion." In *Marxisten gegen Antisemitismus*, edited by Iring Fetscher. Hamburg: Hoffmann und Campe Verlag, 1974, pp. 141–50.

———. *Gesammlte Werke*. 5 vols. Berlin: Dietz Verlag, 1970–75.

———. *The Industrial Development of Poland*. Translated by Tessa DeCarlo. New York: Campaigner Publications, University Editions, 1977.

———. *Internationalismus und Klassenkampf*. Edited by Jürgen Hentze. Neuwied: Luchterhand, 1971.

———. "Nach dem pogrom." In *Marxisten gegen Antisemitismus*. Edited by Iring Fetscher. Hamburg: Hoffmann und Campe, 1974, pp. 127–35.

———. *The National Question*. Edited by Horace B. Davis. New York: Monthly Review Press, 1976.

———. "Ostatnia Próba." *Młot.Tygodnik społeczny, polityczny i literacki* 13 (October 29, 1910), pp. 3–5.

———. Review of *Polska Partja Socjalistyczna o żydowskim ruchu robotniczym. Przegląd Socjaldemokratyczny* II, 4 (April 1903), pp. 159–62.

———. "Rückzug auf der ganzen Linie." In *Marxisten gegen Antisemitismus*. Edited by Iring Fetscher. Hamburg: Hoffmann und Campe Verlag, 1974, pp. 136–40.

———. *Le socialisme en France (1898–1912)*. Edited by Daniel Guérin. Paris: Editions Pierre Belfond, 1971.

M. Review of *Die Judenpogrome in Rußland. Die Neue Zeit* XXVIII, part 2 (1909–10), pp. 90–91.

Man, Hendrik de. *Gegen den Strom. Memoiren eines europäischen Sozialisten*. Stuttgart: Deutsche Verlags-Anstalt, 1953.

Marius [Moses Aronson]. "Erinnerungen aus meinem Leben." *Sonntags-*

*blatt der N.Y. Volkszeitung* (August 16, 1908), Erste Beilage, p. 13; (August 23, 1908), Erste Beilage, p. 16.

――――. "Erinnerungen und Gedanken zur Halbjahrhundert Feier der 'N.Y. Volkszeitung.' " *Sonntagsblatt der N.Y. Volkszeitung* (January 29, 1928), Section III, p. 8c.

"Massen-Kundgebung für das arbeitende Erez-Jisroel in Leipzig." *Jüdische Presszentrale Zürich* VII, 285 (March 20, 1924), p. 8.

Marx, Karl and Friedrich Engels. "Manifest der komunistischer partey." Introduced and freely translated by Ab. Cahan. *Tsukunft* VI (1897).

――――. *Werke.* Vols. XIX-XXXIX. Berlin: Dietz Verlag, 1962-70.

Matthias, Erich and Susanne Miller, eds. *Die Kriegstagebuch des Reichstagsabgeordneten Eduard David 1914 bis 1918.* Quellen zur Geschichte der Parlamentarismus und der politischen Parteien, Erste Reihe: Von der konstitutionellen Monarchie zur parlamentarischen Republik, IV. Düsseldorf: Droste Verlag, 1966.

Medem, Vladimir. *Fun mayn lebn.* Vol. II. New York: Vladimir medem komite, 1923.

――――. *The Life and Soul of a Legendary Jewish Socialist.* Edited and translated by Samuel A. Portnoy. New York: KTAV Publishing House, 1979.

――――. "Der moderne Antisemitismus in Rußland." *Die Neue Zeit* XXIX, part 1 (1910-11), pp. 259-63.

――――. "Ein nationalistischer Vorschlag." *Die Neue Zeit* XXVIII, part 2 (1909-10), pp. 748-51.

Mehring, F. "Anti- und philosemitisches." *Die Neue Zeit* IX, part 2 (1891), pp. 585-88.

――――. "Berliner Geschichten." *Die Neue Zeit* X, part 2 (1892), pp. 225-29.

――――. "Canossa in Berlin." *Die Neue Zeit* X, part 2 (1892), pp. 321-24.

――――. "Drillinge." *Die Neue Zeit* XII, part 2 (1894), pp. 577-82.

――――. "Im Wechsel der Zeiten." *Die Neue Zeit* XI, part 2 (1893), pp. 1-4.

――――. "Kapitalistische Agonie." *Die Neue Zeit* X, part 2 (1892), pp. 545-48.

――――. "Mönch und Rabbi." *Die Neue Zeit* XI, part 1 (1892-93), pp. 841-44.

――――. "Sauve qui peut!" *Die Neue Zeit* XI, part 2 (1893), pp. 161-64.

――――. "Sic vos, non vobis." *Die Neue Zeit* XI, part 1 (1892-93), pp. 361-64.

――――. "Treffliche Minirer." *Die Neue Zeit* XI, part 1 (1892-93), pp. 393-96.

――――. "Zu viel und zu wenig." *Die Neue Zeit* XIII, part 1 (1894-95), pp. 737-41.

Mendelson, Shloyme. *Shloyme mendelson. zayn lebn un shafn.* New York: Farlag "unzer tsayt," 1949.

Michalewicz, B[eynish]. [Mikhalevitsh] [Joseph Isbitzki]. "Karl kautski, tsu zayn 65tn geburtstog." *Lebns-fragn* 230 (October 24, 1919).

———. *Zikhroynes fun a yudishn sotsialist.* 3 vols. Warsaw: Farlag lebens-fragen (Vols. 1 and 2); Farlag di velt (Vol. 3), 1921–1923.

Mill, John. [Yoysef Shloyme Mil]. *Pionern un boyer.* 2 vols. New York: Farlag der veker, 1946–49.

Moses, Julius, ed. *Die Lösung der Judenfrage. Eine Rundfrage.* Berlin: C. Wigand, 1907.

MZM. [Max Zetterbaum]. Review of *Organisaczca Zydow w Polsce. Die Neue Zeit* XIX, part 1 (1900–1901), p. 411.

N., M. "Eduard Bernstein über Lassalle." *Jüdische Rundschau* XXX, 35 (May 5, 1925), p. 323.

N[achimson]. M. Review of *Die Nationalitätenprobleme der Gegenwart,* by Maxim Anin. *Die Neue Zeit* XXVIII, part 2 (1909–10), pp. 646–47.

Nathan, Paul. "Rasse und Judentum." *Im deutschen Reich* XXVII, 7–8 (July-August 1921), pp. 202–7.

Nelin, B. [Boris Markovitsh Frumkin]. "Der internatsionaler sotsialistisher kongres in shtutgart." *Folkstsaytung* 429 (August 26, 1907), p. 1.

"Das neue Wappen der Hakenkreuzler." *Arbeiter-Zeitung* 279 (October 11, 1925).

Nss, R. "Ein führender Sozialdemokrat über den Nationalitätsgedanken." *Die Welt* IX, 37 (September 15, 1905), pp. 9–10.

"Österreich unter Juda's Stern." *Auf gut deutsch. Wochenschrift für Ordnung u. Recht* II, 13–14 (1920).

"Otto Bauer o antisemityzmie i międzynarodowości." *Młot. Tygodnik społeczny, polityczny i literacki* 16 (November 19, 1910), p. 8.

"'Ort'-Aktion in Deutschland zur Förderung des Handwerks und der Landwirtschaft unter den Juden." *Jüdische Presszentrale Zürich* IX, 382 (February 5, 1926), p. 4.

"Di oysvayzungen. mir protestiren!" *Der veker. organ fun der yudisher sotsialistisher (bundisher) organizatsie in vien* I, 8 (September 24, 1919), pp. 2–4.

"Palästina und der Sozialismus." *Jüdische Rundschau* XXIV, 78/79 (October 4, 1929), p. 522.

"Der partaytog fun der estraykhisher sotsialdemokratie." *Poyle-tsienistishe yedies* 13 (1923), p. 9.

"'Patentierte' Arbeiterführer." *Der jüdische Arbeiter. Organ für die Interessen der jüdischen Arbeiterschaft* I, 2 (September 1, 1898), pp. 1–4.

Pati [Kremer]. "Zikhroynes vegn arkadin." In *Arkadi. zamlbukh tsum ondenk fun grinder fun "bund" arkadi kremer.* New York: Farlag unzer tsayt, 1942.

Paumgartten, Karl. *Judentum und Sozialdemokratie.* Graz: Heimatverlag Leopold Stocker, n.d.

Pernerstorfer, Engelbert. "Allerlei Kriegsliteratur." *Süddeutsche Monatshefte* XIII (May 1916), pp. 261–72.

———. "Das neue Ghetto." *Arbeiter-Zeitung* XI, 7 (January 8, 1898), pp. 5–6.

———. "Der Typus Danneberg." *Volkstribüne* XXIV, 17 (April 28, 1915), p. 5.

———. "Viktor Adlers erstes Flugblatt." *Der Arbeiter-Zeitung. Scherzblatt zum 60. Geburtstag ihres Chefs* 2 (June 24, 1912), p. 1.

———. "Zur Judenfrage." *Der Jude* I (1916–17), pp. 308–15.

Pistiner, Jak. "Die Juden im Weltkriege." *Die Neue Zeit* XXXIV, part 2 (1915–16), pp. 449–54.

"Die politischen Parteien zur Judenfrage." *Jüdisch-liberale Zeitung* IV, 12 (May 2, 1924), pp. 2–3.

Pollack, Johann. "Der politische Zionismus." *Die Neue Zeit* XVI, part 1 (1897–98), pp. 596–600.

*Programm und Dokumente des allweltlichen Jüdischen Sozialistischen Arbeiter-Verbandes Poale-Zion.* Poale-zionistische Bibliothek, Heft I. Berlin: Sekretariat der Poale-Zion-Gruppen in Deutschland, n.d.

*Protokoll über die Verhandlungen des Gesamtparteitages der Sozialdemokratischen Arbeiterpartei in Oesterreich. Abgehalten zu Wien vom 30. Oktober bis zum 2. November 1905.* Wien: Verlag der Wiener Volksbuchhandlung, 1905.

R. [Max Beer]. Review of *Das Talmudjudentum*, by W. Rubens. *Die Neue Zeit* XII, part 1 (1893–94), pp. 724–25.

Rappaport, Charles [Sharl, Rapoport]. "Dos lebn fun a revolutsionern emigrant. zikhroynes." In *Di yidishe sotsialistishe bavegung biz der grindung fun "bund." forshungen, zikhroynes, materialn.* Edited by E. Tscherikower [Tsherikover], A. Menes, F. Kursky [Kurski], and A. Rosin (Ben-Adir) [Rozin]. *Historishe shriftn*, III. Shriftn fun yidishn visnshaftlekhn institut, XI. Vilna, Paris: Historishe sektsie fun yivo, 1939, pp. 283–312.

———. Review of *Die Organization des jüdischen Proletariats in Rußland*, by Sara Rabinovitsch. *Die Neue Zeit* XXII, part 2 (1903–04), pp. 541–43.

Ratner, Markus. "Die nationale Autonomie und das jüdische Proletariat." *Sozialistische Monatshefte* XV, 3. Band (1911), pp. 1333–42.

———. "Die nationale Frage in den jüdischen sozialistischen Parteien." *Sozialistische Monatshefte* XII, part 3 (1908), pp. 1533–41.

———. "Nationalitätsbegriff und nationale Autonomie." *Sozialistische Monatshefte* XIV, part 1 (1910), pp. 345–54.

Ravesteijn, W. van. "Kapitalismus und Judentum." *Die Neue Zeit* XXX, part 2 (1911–12), pp. 708–16.

Redaktion des "Jüdischen Arbeiters." "Probleme der jüdisch-proletarischen Bewegung." *Die Neue Zeit* XIX, part 1 (1900–1901), pp. 605–7.

Reinheimer, Max. "Eduard Bernstein als Jude." *Israelitisches Familienblatt* XXXII, 1 (January 2, 1930).

Rezawa (Stanislaus Mendelsohn). "Die Judenausweisungen in Rußland und die polnische Frage." *Die Neue Zeit* XII, part 2 (1894), pp. 324–33.

Rosby, Hans. "Zum Tode Eduard Bernstein." *Jüdisch-liberale Zeitung* XII, 19 (January 1, 1933).

Rosenfeld, Max. *Nationale Autonomie der Juden in Oesterreich. Sonderab-*

*druck aus dem vom Jued.-Nat. Akad. Vereine "Emunah," Czernowitz, herausgegebenen Sammelwerke "Heimkehr" (Erschienen in Verlag Louis Lamm, Berlin).* Czernowitz: Buchdruckerei "Gutenberg," 1912.

Rosenmann, L[ippe]. "Ostjudenfrage, Zionismus und Grenzschluß." *Die Neue Zeit* XXXIV, part 2 (1915–16), pp. 305–9.

Rosin, B. [Boris Frumkin]. "Die zionistisch-sozialistische Utopie." *Die Neue Zeit* XXVII (1908–09), pp. 29–34.

"Rote Assimilanten als Judenfeinde." *Jüdische Zeitung. National-jüdisches Organ* V, 18 (May 4, 1911), p. 2.

S., M. "Der wildgewordene Kleinbürger und Bauer und die Wahlen." *Die Neue Zeit* XI, part 2 (1893), pp. 389–92.

Salomon. "Kautski vegen di foderungen fun 'poyle-tsien.'" *Di arbayter tsaytung* 2 (November 22, 1918), pp. 2–3.

Scheidemann, Philipp. "Wandlungen des Antisemitismus." *Die Neue Zeit* XXIV, part 2 (1905–06), pp. 632–36.

Schippel, Max. "Die Konservativen und der Antisemitismus." *Die Neue Zeit* XI, part 2 (1893), pp. 298–302.

"Sein oder Nichtsein?" *Ost und West. Illustrierte Monatsschrift für das gesamte Judentum* XVIII, 1/2 (January-February 1918), pp. 3–16.

Shalit, M[oyshe] "Karl kautski un di natsionale frage." *Dos yidishe folk* 18 (September 12, 1906), pp. 10–12; 19 (September 19, 1906), pp. 8–10.

———. "Bibliografie." *Folksshtime* 4 (February 23, 1907), pp. 94–99.

———. "Bibliografie." *Folksshtime* 9 (June 27, 1907), cols. 45–48.

Shazar, Zalman [Shneyer Zalman Rubashev]. "Eduard bernshteyn." *Der tog-morgen zhurnal* (July 10, 17, 31, 1966).

———. *Morning Stars.* Philadelphia: Jewish Publication Society of America, 1967.

Shub, D. "Arn sundelevitch." In *Vilna. a zamlbukh gevidmet der shtot vilna.* Edited by Ephim H. Jeshurin. New York: Vilner brentsh 367 arbeter ring, 1935, pp. 96–126.

"Der siebente Parteitag des Jüdischen Arbeiterbundes." Translated by A. L. *Die Neue Zeit* XXV, part 1 (1906–07), pp. 100–105.

Silberroth, Moyshe Nakhman. "Landarbeitsheime für genesende Lungenkranke." *Arbeiterinnen-Zeitung. Sozialdemokratisches Organ für Frauen und Mädchen* XXI, 22 (October 29, 1912), pp. 4–5.

———. "A unterhaltung mit viktor adler." *Der yudisher arbeyter* IX, 39 (September 25, 1912), pp. 3–4.

Simoni. "Otto bauer vegen di yuden." *Tsayt-fragen* I (1909), pp. 31–41.

Singer, Mendel. "Judenfrage und Zionismus." *Der Kampf* XX (1927), pp. 574–80.

———. "Zum Problem der Assimilation der Juden." *Der Kampf* XXI (1928), pp. 295–302.

*Sixième Congrès Socialiste International tenu à Amsterdam du 14 au 20 août 1904. Compte-rendu analytique.* Brussels: Secrétariat Socialiste International, 1904.

Sorow, E. "Die jüdische Sozialdemokratie in Rußland." *Die Neue Zeit* XX, part 1 (1901–02), pp. 812–19.

Soukup, Frant. "Karlu Kautskému." *Právo lidu* XXIII, 241 (October 1924), pp. 11–12.

———. "Karlu Kautskému." In *Historické dílo Karle Marxe*, by Karl Kautsky. Prague: 1933.

"Sozialdemokratie und jüdische Nationalität." *Jüdische Zeitung. National-jüdisches Organ* IV, 34 (August 26, 1910), pp. 1–2.

"Sozialismus und Antisemitismus." *Jüdische Zeitung. National-jüdisches Organ* IV, 45 (November 11, 1910), pp. 5–6.

"Die Sozialistenkonferenz in Amsterdam zur Judenfrage." *Jüdische Rundschau* XXIV, 32 (May 6, 1919), p. 247.

Sp. Review of *Le Juif errant d'aujourd'hui*, by L. Hersch. *Die Neue Zeit* XXXII, part 1 (1913–14), p. 381.

Stampfer, Fr[iedrich]. "Föderalismus und Sozialdemokratie in Oesterreich." *Die Neue Zeit* XVII, part 1 (1898–99), pp. 502–4.

———. "Für das böhmische Staatsrecht." *Die Neue Zeit* XVII, part 1 (1898–99), pp. 275–78.

Steiner, Hugo. "Der Kampf der jüdischen Arbeiter." *Der Kampf* XXIII (1930), pp. 136–40.

"Stepniak's levaye." *Der arbayter fraynd* XI, 13 (January 3, 1895), pp. 51–52.

Stern, Jacob. Review of *Das Recht der unfreien und der freien Arbeiter nach jüdisch-talmudischem Rechte*, by D. Farbstein. *Die Neue Zeit* XV, part 1 (1896–97), pp. 282–83.

———. Review of *Der Judenstaat*, by Theodor Herzl. *Die Neue Zeit* XV, part 1 (1896–97), p. 186.

———. Review of *Die jüdischen Speisegesetze*, by A. Wiener. *Die Neue Zeit* XIII, part 2 (1895), pp. 180–81.

———. "Der Talmud." *Die Neue Zeit* XII, part 2 (1894), pp. 536–39.

Sturmthal, Adolf. Review of *Das Völkerbundmandat für Palästina*, by Georg Schwarzenberger. *Der Kampf* XXIII (1930), pp. 93–94.

"Tagung der deutschen Poale Zion." *Israelitisches Familienblatt* XXII, 2 (January 9, 1930).

"Tagung der jüdischen Studenten." *Jüdische Rundschau* XXX, 14 (February 17, 1925), p. 132.

Theilhaber, Felix A. Review of *Rasse und Judentum*. *Archiv für Rassen- und Gesellschaftsbiologie* XII, 1 (1916–17), pp. 91–92.

Thur, F. G. Review of *Rasse und Judentum*. *K.C. Blätter* 6 (July-August, 1915), pp. 434–35.

Trebitsch, Oskar. Review of *Die Krise des Pazifismus, des Antisemitismus, der Ironie*, by Rudolf Jeremias. *Der Kampf* XXV (1932), pp. 235–36.

Trotsky, N. [Lev Davidovich Bronstein] "Die Beilis-Affäre." *Die Neue Zeit* XXXII (1913–14), pp. 310–20.

Vandervelde, Émile. "Das arbeitende Palästina." *Der Kampf* XXIII (1930), pp. 31–34.

———. "Karl Kautsky et le Sionisme." *Vie Socialiste* VII, 168 (December 14, 1929), pp. 8–9.

"Die Verbreitung der Juden in Deutschland." *Die Neue Zeit* XI, part 1 (1892–93), pp. 57–59.

*Verhandlungen des Parteitages der deutschen Sozialdemokratie Oesterreichs abgehalten zu Linz vom 29. Mai bis einschließlich 1. Juni 1898.* Wien: Erste Wiener Volksbuchhandlung (Ignaz Brand), 1898.

*Verhandlungen des Reichstags. XIII Legislaturperiode. I Session. Band 289. Stenographische Berichte. Von der 131 Sitzung am 3 April bis zur 150 Sitzung am 26 April 1913.* Berlin: Verlag der norddeutschen Buchdruckerei und Verlagsanstalt, 1913.

*Verhandlungen des sechsten österreichischen Sozialdemokratischen Parteitages abgehalten zu Wien vom 6. bis einschließlich 12. Juni 1897 im Saale des Hotel Wimberger.* Wien: Erste Wiener Volksbuchhandlung (Ignaz Brand), 1897.

"Die Verhandlungen über die Judenfrage auf der Amsterdamer Konferenz." *Jüdische Rundschau* XXIV, 37 (May 23, 1919), pp. 282–83.

"Die Vermehrung der Juden in Deutschland." *Die Neue Zeit* XI, part 2 (1893), p. 796.

Verus. "Der Kampf der Nationalitäten in Österreich." *Die Neue Zeit* XVI, part 1 (1897–98), pp. 665–66.

Vozka, Jaroslav. *Karel Kautský. Učitel československého proletariátu. 1854–1934.* Prague: Ústřední Dělnické Knihkupectví a Nakladatelství, 1934.

"Wahlversammlung der Poale Zion." *Jüdische Rundschau* XXX, 7 (January 23, 1925), p. 63.

Waynshtayn, L. "Di natsional-kulturele oytonomie un di yuden." *Der sotsial-demokrat. organ fun der yudisher sotsial-demokratisher partey in galitsien* V, 4 (January 22, 1909), supplement, pp. 2–3; V, 5 (January 29, 1909), supplement, pp. 2–3; V, 6 (February 5, 1909), supplement, pp. 2–3.

Wendel, Hermann. "Die Juden in der Provinz Posen." *Die Neue Zeit* XXIX, part 1 (1910–11), pp. 434–40.

*Wenn Judenblut vom Messer spritzt.* Vienna: Verlag der Wiener Volksbuchhandlung, n.d.

"Die Wiener Sozialdemokratie und der Beilis-prozess." *Neuer Weg* I, 1 (January 1914), pp. 5–6.

Winchevsky, Morris [Moris Vintshevski]. *Gezamlte verk.* VIII–X. Edited by Kalman Marmor. New York: Farlag "frayhayt," 1927.

*Wir Hakenkreuzler.* Vienna, 1927.

"Wir klagen an!" *Freie Tribüne* III, 7 (February 24, 1921), p. 1.

Yanovsky, Sh. [Yanovski]. *Ershte yorn fun yidishn frayhaytlekhn sotsializm.* New York: Fraye arbeter shtime, 1948.

Zadek, Lil[l]i [Tsadek]. *Devarim meshelah ve-alehah*. Tel Aviv: Davar, 1970.

Zetterbaum, Max. "Klassengegensätze bei den Juden." *Die Neue Zeit* XI, part 2 (1893), pp. 4–12, 36–43.

———. "Probleme der jüdisch-proletarischen Bewegung." *Die Neue Zeit* XIX, part 1 (1900–1901), pp. 324–30, 367–73.

Zhitlovsky, Chaim [Khayim Zhitlovski]. *Gezamlte shriftn*, XIII, Der sotsializm un di natsionale frage. Warsaw: Ch. [Kh.] Brzoza, 1935.

"Zionistische Vereinigung für Deutschland. (Zuschrift v. Zionistischen Vereinigung für Deutschland.)" *Die Neue Zeit* XXIX, part 1 (1910–11), pp. 157–58.

Zollschan, J. "Tatsächliche Berichtigung." *Jüdische Rundschau* XXVI, 84/85 (October 21, 1921), p. 608.

"Zum Parteitag der österreichischen Sozialdemokratie." *Der jüdische Arbeiter; Organ für die Interressen der jüdischen Arbeiter und Handangestellten* I, 2 (November 1903), pp. 4–5.

### SECONDARY SOURCES

Abramovitch, Raphael R. [Rafail Abramovich Rein] "The Jewish Socialist Movement in Russia and Poland (1897–1919)." In *The Jewish People, Past and Present*. II. New York: Jewish Encyclopedic Handbooks. Central Yiddish Cultural Organization (CYCO), 1948, pp. 369–98.

Altshuler, M. "The Attitude of the Communist Party of Russia to Jewish National Survival, 1918–1930." *YIVO Annual of Jewish Social Science* XIV (1969), pp. 68–69.

Angel, Pierre. *Eduard Bernstein et l'évolution du socialisme allemand*. Germanica, II. Paris: Marcel Didier, 1961.

Angress, Werner T. " 'Between Baden and Luxemburg.' Jewish Socialists on the Eve of the First World War." *Leo Baeck Institute Year Book* XXII (1977), pp. 3–34.

Arato, Andrew. "The Second International: a Reexamination." *Telos* 18 (Winter 1973–74), pp. 2–52.

Ardelt, Rudolf G. *Friedrich Adler. Probleme einer Persönlichkeitsentwicklung um die Jahrhundertwende*. Vienna: Österreichischer Bundesverlag, 1984.

Arendt, Hanna. "Rosa Luxemburg. 1871–1919." In *Men in Dark Times*. New York: Harcourt, Brace, and World, 1968, pp. 33–56.

Aronson, Gregor. "Ideological Trends among Russian Jews." In *Russian Jewry. 1860–1917*. Edited by Jacob Frumkin, Gregor Aronson, and Alexis Goldenweiser. Translated by Mirra Ginsburg. New York, London: Thomas Yoseleff, 1966, pp. 144–71.

———. "Di natsionale un organizatsionele frage." In *Di geshikhte fun bund*. I. Edited by G. Aronson, S. Dubnow-Erlich [Dubnov-erlikh], J. S.

Hertz [I. Sh. Herts], E. Nowogrudski [Novogrudski], Kh. Sh. Kazdan, and E. Scherer [Sherer]. New York: Farlag unzer tsayt, 1960, pp. 483–536.

———. "Shimen klevanski." In *Doyres bundistn.* I. Edited by J[acob] S. Hertz [I. Sh. Herts]. New York: Farlag unzer tsayt, 1956, pp. 307–16.

Asch, Adolph. *Geschichte des K.C.* London: Published by author, 1964.

Ascher, Abraham. "Axelrod and Kautsky." *Slavic Review* 26 (1967), pp. 94–112.

———. "Pavel Axelrod: A Conflict between Jewish Loyalty and Revolutionary Dedication." *Russian Review* XXIV, 3 (July 1965), pp. 249–65.

———. *Pavel Axelrod and the Development of Menshevism.* Cambridge, Mass.: Harvard University Press, 1972.

Aschheim, Steven E. *Brothers and Strangers. The East European Jew in German and German Jewish Consciousness, 1800–1923.* Madison, Wis.: University of Wisconsin Press, 1982.

Astour, Michael [Mikhel Astur]. *Geshikhte fun der frayland-lige un funem territorialistishn gedank.* I. Buenos Aires: Frayland lige, 1967.

Avineri, Shlomo. "Marx and Jewish Emancipation." *Journal of the History of Ideas* XXV (1964), pp. 445–50.

B., A. [J. S. Hertz]. "Tsurikgeshmust." *Unzer tsayt* 7–8 (1959), pp. 28–34.

Barkai, A. "The Austrian Social Democrats and the Jews." *The Wiener Library Bulletin* XXIV, 1 (new series 18) (1970), pp. 31–40; 2 (new series 19) (1970), pp. 16–21.

Ben-Adir [Avrom Rozin]. "Tsum oyfkum fun der 'yidisher sotsialistisher arbeter partay' (y s)." In *Sotsialistisher teritorializm. zikhroynes un materialn tsu der geshikhte fun di partayen s"s, y"s, un "fareynikte."* I. Paris: Arkhiv komisie fun di partayen s"s, y"s, un fareynikte, 1934, pp. 9–56.

Berlau, Abraham Joseph. *The German Social Democratic Party 1914–1921.* New York: Octagon Books, 1975.

Bick, Abraham [Avrom Bik]. *In baginen.* New York: 1952.

———. *Merosh Tsurim.* Jerusalem: Pedut, 1972.

Binder, Dieter A. "Der 'reiche Jude': Zur sozialdemokratischen Kapitalismuskritik und zu deren antisemitischen Feindbildern in der Ersten Republik." *Geschichte und Gegenwart* IV, 1 (1985), pp. 43–55.

Birman, B. P., G. I. Kramol'nikov, and L. Sennikovski, eds. *Sotsialdemokraticheskie listovki 1894–1917 gg. Bibliograficheskii ukazatel'.* I. Gosydarstvennoe Sotsialno-Ekonomicheskoye Izdatel'stvo, 1931.

Bloom, Bernard H. "Yiddish-Speaking Socialists in America: 1892–1905." In *Critical Studies in American Jewish History* III. Cincinnati, Ohio: American Jewish Archives, 1971, pp. 1–33.

Bloom, Soloman F. "Kh. zhitlovski un karl marks vegn anti-semitizm." *Afn shvel* 3 (19) (April-May 1944), p. 11.

Blumenberg, Werner. *Karl Kautskys literarisches Werk.* The Hague: Mouton and Co., 1960.

Borochov, Ber [Borokhov]. "Arn liberman—der foter funem yidishn sotsializm un di ershte hebreish-sotsialistishe tsaytshrift 'haemes.' " In *Shprakh-
forshung un literaturgeshikhte.* Tel Aviv: I. l. peretz farlag, 1966, pp.
71–280.
Bottomore, Tom and Patrick Goode, eds. *Austro-Marxism.* Oxford: Clarendon Press, 1978.
Braunthal, Julius. *Victor und Friedrich Adler. Zwei Generationen Arbeiterbewegung.* Vienna: Verlag der Wiener Volksbuchhandlung, 1965.
Bronner, Stephen Eric. *A Revolutionary For Our Times: Rosa Luxemburg.*
London: Pluto Press, 1981.
Bros, Iakov. "Tsu der geshikhte fun der i.s.d.p. in galitsie." In *Royter
pinkes. tsu der geshikhte fun der yidisher arbeter-bavegung un sotsialistishe shtremungen bay yidn.* II. Warsaw: Farlag "kultur-lige," 1924.
Bruegel, J. W. "The Antisemitism of the Austrian Socialists, a Reassess-
ment." *The Wiener Library Bulletin* XXV, 3–4, New Series 24–25 (1972),
pp. 39–45.
Brügel, Ludwig. *Geschichte der österreichischen Sozialdemokratie.* III. Vi-
enna: Wiener Volksbuchhandlung, 1922.
Buchbinder, N. A. [Bukhbinder]. *Di geshikhte fun der yidisher arbeter-
bavegung in rusland loyt nit-gedrukte arkhiv-materialn.* Translated by
Dovid Roykhel. Vilna: Farlag "tomor," 1931.
Bunzl, John. "Arbeiterbewegung, 'Judenfrage' und Antisemitismus. Am
Beispiel des Wiener Bezirks Leopoldstadt." In *Bewegung und Klasse.*
Edited by G. Botz, H. Hautmann, H. Konrad, and J. Weidenholzer.
Vienna: Europa Verlag, 1978, pp. 743–63.
———. "Arbeiterbewegung und Antisemitismus in Österreich vor und nach
dem Ersten Weltkrieg." *Zeitgeschichte* IV, 5 (February 1977), pp. 161–
71.
———. *Klassenkampf in der Diaspora. Zur Geschichte der jüdischen Arbeiterbewegung.* Schriftenreihe des Ludwig-Boltzmann-Instituts für Geschichte der Arbeiterbewegung, 5. Vienna: Europa Verlag, 1975.
Bunzl, John and Marin, Bernd. *Antisemitismus in Österreich. Sozialhisto-
rische und soziologische Studien.* Vergleichende Gesellschaftsgeschichte
und politische Ideengeschichte der Neuzeit, III. Innsbruck: Inn-Verlag,
1983.
Burgin, Herts. *Di geshikhte fun der yidisher arbeyter bavegung in amerika,
rusland un england.* New York: Fareynigte yidishe geverkshaften, 1915.
Carlebach, Julius. *Karl Marx and the Radical Critique of Judaism.* The
Littman Library of Jewish Civilization. London, Henley, and Boston:
Routledge & Kegan Paul, 1978.
Chernov, Victor [Viktor Tshernov]. *Yidishe tuer in der partay sotsialistn
revolutsionern. biografishe eseyen.* Translated by Viktor Shulman. New
York: Grigori gershuni brentsh 247, arbeter ring, 1948.
Citron, S. L. [Sh. L. Tsitron]. *Dray literarishe doyres.* II. Vilna: Farlag sh.
shreberk, 1921.

Cohen, Mitchell. "Ber Borochov. Towards a Portrait of a Socialist Zionist." *Response* 34 (Fall 1977), pp. 5–28.

Cohen, Muriel. "Presenting her Past." *The Boston Globe Magazine* (May 31, 1987).

Dubnov, Simon. *History of the Jews.* Translated by Moishe Spiegel. V. South Brunswick, New York, London: Thomas Yoseloff, 1973.

Dubnow-Erlich, Sofia [Dubnov-erlikh]. *Dos lebn un shafn fun shimen dubnov.* Translated by Moisés [Moyshe] Ferdman. Mexico City: Shloyme mendelson fond bay der gezelshaft far kultur un hilf, 1952.

Duker, Abraham G. "Introduction. The Theories of Ber Borochov and Their Place in the History of the Jewish Labor Movement." In Ber Borochov, *Nationalism and the Class Struggle. A Marxian Approach to the Jewish Problem.* New York: Poale Zion—Zeire Zion of America, and Young Poale Zion Alliance of America, 1937.

Dziewanoski, M. K. *The Communist Party of Poland. An Outline of History,* 2d ed. Cambridge, Mass., and London: Harvard University Press, 1976.

Edelheim-Muehsam, Margaret T. "The Jewish Press in Germany." *Leo Baeck Institute Year Book* I (1956), pp. 163–76.

Eloni, Jehuda. "Die zionistische Bewegung in Deutschland und die SPD 1897–1918." In *Juden und jüdische Aspekte in der deutschen Arbeiterbewegung 1848–1918.* Edited by Walter Grab. Jahrbuch des Instituts für deutsche Geschichte, Beiheft II. Tel Aviv: Universität Tel Aviv, 1977, pp. 85–112.

———. "The Zionist Movement and the German Social Democratic Party, 1897–1918." *Studies in Zionism* V, 2 (Autumn 1984), pp. 181–99.

Epstein, Melech. *Jewish Labor in the U.S.A. An Industrial, Political and Cultural History of the Jewish Labor Movement.* 2 Volumes. N.p.: KTAV, 1969.

*Die Ergebnisse der eidgenössischen Volkszählung vom 1. Dezember 1900 in der Stadt Zürich.* 1. Heft. Zürich: Kommissionsverlag Ed. Rascher's Erben (Meyer & Zeller's Nachfolger), 1905.

Ermers, Max. *Victor Adler. Aufstieg und Grösse einer sozialistischen Partei.* Vienna and Leipzig: Verlag Dr. Hans Epstein, 1932.

Ettinger, Elżbieta. *Rosa Luxemburg. A Life.* Boston: Beacon Press, 1986.

Everett, Leila P. "The Rise of Jewish National Politics in Galicia, 1905–1907." In *Nationbuilding and the Politics of Nationalism. Essays on Austrian Galicia.* Edited by Andrei S. Markovits and Frank E. Sysyn. Harvard Ukrainian Research Institute Monograph Series. Cambridge, Mass.: Distributed by Harvard University Press for the Harvard Ukrainian Research Institute, 1982, pp. 149–77.

Feder, Ernst. "Paul Nathan and His Work for East European and Palestinian Jewry." *Historia Judaica* XIV, part 1 (April 1952), pp. 3–26.

———. "Paul Nathan, the Man and His Work." *Leo Baeck Institute Year Book* III (1958), pp. 60–80.

————. *Politik und Humanität. Paul Nathan, ein Lebensbild.* Berlin: Deutsche Verlagsgesellschaft für Politik und Geschichte m.b.H., 1929.

Fetscher, Iring, ed. *Marxisten gegen Antisemitismus.* Hamburg: Hoffmann und Campe, 1974.

Fishman, William J. *Jewish Radicals. From Czarist Stetl to London Ghetto.* New York: Pantheon, 1974.

Fletcher, Roger. "Revisionism and Empire: Joseph Bloch, the *Sozialistische Monatshefte* and German Nationalism, 1907–14." *European Studies Review* X, 4 (1980), pp. 459–85.

————. "Revisionism and Nationalism: Eduard Bernstein's Views on the National Question, 1900–1914." *Canadian Review of Studies in Nationalism* XI, I (Spring 1984), pp. 103–17.

Frankel, Jonathan. *Prophecy and Politics. Socialism, Nationalism and the Russian Jews, 1862–1917.* Cambridge: Cambridge University Press, 1981.

Frei, Bruno. "Marxist Interpretations of the Jewish Question." *The Wiener Library Bulletin* XXVIII, new series 35–36 (1975), pp. 2–8.

————. *Sozialismus und Antisemitismus.* Vienna: Europa Verlag, 1978.

————. *Rosa Luxemburg: Her Life and Work.* New York: Monthly Review Press, 1972.

Gaisbauer, Adolf. *Davidstern und Doppeladler. Zionismus und jüdischer Nationalismus in Österreich 1882–1918.* Veröffentlichungen der Kommission für neuere Geschichte Österreichs, LXXVIII. Vienna, Cologne, Graz: Böhlau Verlag, 1988.

Gartner, Lloyd P. *The Jewish Immigrant in England, 1870–1914.* London: Ruskin House, George Allen and Unwin, 1960.

Gay, Peter. *The Dilemma of Democratic Socialism. Eduard Bernstein's Challenge to Marx.* New York: Collier Books; London: Collier-Macmillan, 1962.

Geary, Dick. *Karl Kautsky.* New York: St. Martin's Press, 1987.

Gilcher-Holtey, Ingrid. *Das Mandat der Intellektuellen. Karl Kautsky und die Sozialdemokratie.* Berlin: Siedler Verlag, 1986.

Gitelman, Zvi Y. *Jewish Nationality and Soviet Politics. The Jewish Sections of the CPSU, 1917–1930.* Princeton, N.J.: Princeton University Press, 1972.

Glasneck, Johannes. "Die internationale Sozialdemokratie und die zionistische Palästina-Kolonisation in den Jahren 1929–30." *Wissenschaftliche Zeitschrift der Martin-Luther Universität Halle-Wittenberg.* Gesellschafts- und Sprachwissenschaftliche Reihe XXVI, 4 (1977), pp. 39–50.

Glickson, Paul. "Jacob Lestchinsky: A Bibliographical Survey." *The Jewish Journal of Sociology* IX, 1 (June 1967), pp. 48–57.

Görschler, H. "Die revolutionäre Arbeiterbewegung und ihr Verhältnis zum Antisemitismus." *Wissenschaftliche Zeitschrift der Karl-Marx Universität Leipzig.* Gesellschafts- und Sprachwissenschaftliche Reihe XIV, 3 (1965), pp. 539–51.

Gold, Hugo. *Geschichte der Juden in Wien. Ein Gedenkbuch*. Tel Aviv: Edition "Olamenu," 1966.

Goldberg, Harvey. "Jean Jaurès and the Jewish Question: The Evolution of a Position." *Jewish Social Studies* XX, 2 (April 1958), pp. 67–94.

————. *The Life of Jean Jaurès*. Madison: University of Wisconsin Press, 1968.

Goldhagen, Erich. "The Ethnic Consciousness of Early Russian Jewish Socialists." *Judaism* XXIII, 4 (Fall 1974), pp. 479–96.

Goldsmith, Emanuel S. *Architects of Yiddishism at the Beginning of the Twentieth Century*. Rutherford, N.J.: Fairleigh Dickinson University Press, 1976.

Gordin, Yitshok. "Roza luksemburg—odler fun revolutsie." *Morgn frayhayt* (December 31, 1967), p. 11.

Gorman, Robert. A. *Biographical Dictionary of Neo-Marxism*. Westport, Conn: Greenwood Press, 1985.

Grab, Walter, ed. *Juden und jüdische Aspekte in der deutschen Arbeiterbewegung 1848–1918*. Jahrbuch des Instituts für deutsche Geschichte, Beiheft II. Tel-Aviv: Universität Tel-Aviv, 1977.

Greenberg, Louis. *The Jews in Russia. The Struggle for Emancipation*. 2 vols. New York: Schocken Books, 1976.

"Grigori gurevitch (biografishe yedies)." In *Di yidishe sotsialistishe bavegung biz der grindung fun "bund." forshungen, zikhroynes, materialn*. Edited by E. Tscherikower [Tsherikover], A. Menes, F. Kursky [Kurski], and A. Rosin (Ben-Adir) [Rozin]. Historishe shriftn, III; Shriftn fun yidishn visnshaftlekhn institut, XI. Vilna, Paris: Historishe sektsie fun yivo, 1939, pp. 252–55.

Gutman, M. "Tsu der forgeshikhte fun 's.s.'." In *Royter pinkes. tsu der geshikhte fun der yidisher arbeter-bavegung un sotsialistishe shtremungen bay yidn*. I. Warsaw: Farlag kultur-lige, 1921, pp. 152–73.

Hamburger, E. *Juden im öffentlichen Leben Deutschlands. Regierungsmitglieder, Beamte und Parlamentarier in der monarchischen Zeit 1848–1918*. Schriftenreihe wissenschaftlicher Abhandlungen des Leo Baeck Instituts, XIX. Tübingen: J. C. B. Mohr, 1968.

Hamburger, Ernst and Pulzer, Peter. "Jews as Voters in the Weimar Republic." *Leo Baeck Institute Year Book* XXX (1985), pp. 3–66.

Hareven, Tamara K. "Unamerican America and the 'Jewish Daily Forward.'" *YIVO Annual of Jewish Social Science* XIV (1969), pp. 234–50.

Haupt, G. and P. Korzec. "Les socialistes et la campagne antisémite en Pologne en 1910." *Revue du Nord* LVII, 225 (April-June 1975), pp. 185–94.

Heimann, Horst and Thomas Meyer, eds. *Bernstein und der demokratische Sozialismus. Bericht über den wissenschaftlichen Kongreß "Die historische Leistung und aktuelle Bedeutung Eduard Bernsteins."* Internationale Bibliothek, CXIV. Berlin: Verlag J. H. W. Dietz Nachf. GmbH, 1978.

Hentze, Jürgen. *Nationalismus und Internationalismus bei Rosa Luxemburg.* Beiträge zur Politikwissenschaft, IV. Bern: Herbert Lang; Frankfurt/M.: Peter Lang, 1975.

Hertz, Jacob S. "The Bund's Nationality Program and its Critics in the Russian, Polish and Austrian Socialist Movements." *YIVO Annual of Jewish Social Science* XIV (1969), pp. 53–67.

Hertz, Jacob S., ed. [I. Sh. Herts]. *Doyres bundistn.* 3 vols. New York: Farlag unzer tsayt, 1956–68.

Hertz, Jacob S. [I. Sh. Herts]. "Di ershte ruslander revolutsie." In *Di geshikhte fun bund.* II. Edited by G. Aronson, S. Dubnow-Erlich [Dubnov-erlikh], J. S. Hertz [I. Sh. Herts], E. Nowogrudski [Novogrudski], Kh. Sh. Kazdan, and E. Scherer [Sherer]. New York: Farlag unzer tsayt, 1962, pp. 7–482.

———. *Fuftsik yor arbeter-ring in yidishn lebn.* New York: Natsionaler ekzekutiv komitet fun arbeter-ring, 1950.

———. "M. dragomanov un der oyfruf fun der 'grupe sotsialistn-yidn' (tsu zayt 53)." In *Di geshikhte fun bund.* I. Edited by G. Aronson, S. Dubnow-Erlich [Dubnov-erlikh], J. S. Hertz [I. Sh. Herts], E. Nowogrudski [Novogrudski], Kh. Sh. Kazdan, and E. Scherer [Sherer]. New York: Farlag unzer tsayt, 1960, pp. 359–60.

———. *Di yidishe sotsialistishe bavegung in amerika.* New York: Farlag der veker, 1954.

Herzig, Arno. "The Role of Antisemitism in the Early Years of the German Workers' Movement." *Leo Baeck Institute Year Book* XXVI (1981), pp. 243–59.

Hesselbarth, Hellmut. *Revolutionäre Sozialdemokraten, Opportunisten und die Bauern am Vorabend des Imperialismus.* Berlin: Dietz, 1968.

Hirsch, Helmut. *Der Fabier Eduard Bernstein.* Berlin, Bonn-Bad Godesberg: Dietz, 1977.

———. *Rosa Luxemburg in Selbstzeugnissen und Bilddokumenten.* Reinbek bei Hamburg: Rowohlt, 1969.

Holzer, Jerzy. "Relations between Polish and Jewish left wing groups in interwar Poland." In *The Jews in Poland.* Edited by Chimen Abramsky, Maciej Jachimczyk, and Anthony Polonsky. Oxford: Basil Blackwell, 1986, pp. 140–46.

Holzheuer, Walter. *Karl Kautskys Werk als Weltanschauung.* Münchener Studien zur Politik, XXI. Munich: C. H. Beck, 1972.

Hünlich, Reinhold. *Karl Kautsky und der Marxismus der II. Internationale.* Schriftenreihe für Sozialgeschichte und Arbeiterbewegung, 22. Marburg: Verlag Arbeiterbewegung und Gesellschaftswissenschaft GmbH, 1981.

Hulse, James W. *Revolutionists in London.* Oxford: Clarendon Press, 1970.

J., M. "Un inédit de Jaurès sur L'antisémitisme." *Bulletin de la société d'etudes jauressienes* III, 4 (January-February 1962), pp. 7–9.

Jacobs, Jack. "Austrian Social Democracy and the Jewish Question during the First Republic." In *The Austrian Socialist Experiment: Social Democracy and Austro-Marxism, 1918–1934*. Edited by Anson Rabinbach. Boulder and London: Westview Press, 1985, pp. 157–68.

———. "Marxism and Anti-Semitism. Kautsky's Perspective." *International Review of Social History* XXX, part 3 (1985), pp. 400–430.

———. "On German Socialists and German Jews: Kautsky, Bernstein and Their Reception, 1914–22." In *Studies in Contemporary Jewry. An Annual. IV. The Jews and the European Crisis, 1914–21*. Edited by Jonathan Frankel. New York, Oxford: Published for the Institute of Contemporary Jewry, The Hebrew University of Jerusalem, by Oxford University Press, 1988, pp. 67–83.

Janowsky, Oscar I. *The Jews and Minority Rights (1898–1919)*. Studies in History, Economics and Public Law, 384. New York: Columbia University Press; London: P. S. King & Son, 1933.

Jarblum, Marc. *The Socialist International and Zionism*. Translated by Maximilian Hurwitz. New York: Poale Zion–Zeire Zion of America, 1933.

Jeshurin, Ephim H. "Vilner frayhayts kemfer." In *Vilna. a zamlbukh gevidmet der shtot vilna*. Edited by Ephim H. Jeshurin. New York: Vilner brentsh 367 arbeter ring, 1935, p. 716–24.

"The Jewish Background of Victor and Friedrich Adler." *Leo Baeck Institute Year Book* X (1965), pp. 66–276.

Jochmann, Werner. "Die Ausbreitung des Antisemitismus." In *Deutsches Judentum in Krieg und Revolution 1916–1923*. Edited by Werner E. Mosse and Arnold Paucker. Schriftenreihe Wissenschaftlicher Abhandlungen des Leo Baeck Instituts, XXV. Tübingen: J. C. B. Mohr (Paul Siebeck), 1971, pp. 409–510.

———. "Die deutsche Arbeiterbewegung und der Zionismus 1897–1918." In *Juden und jüdische Aspekte in der deutschen Arbeiterbewegung 1848–1918*. Edited by Walter Grab. Jahrbuch des Instituts für deutsche Geschichte, Beiheft II. Tel Aviv: Universität Tel Aviv, 1977, pp. 113–26.

Joll, James. *The Second International 1889–1914*. London and Boston: Routledge & Kegan Paul, 1974.

Kane, Leon. *Robert Danneberg. Ein pragmatischer Idealist*. Vienna, Munich, Zurich: Europa Verlag, 1980.

Kapp, Yvonne. *Eleanor Marx*. 2 vols. New York: Pantheon, 1972–1976.

Karbach, Oscar. "The Founder of Modern Political Antisemitism: Georg von Schoenerer." *Jewish Social Studies* VII, 1 (January 1945), pp. 3–30.

Kazdan, Kh. Sh. "Der 'bund'—biz dem finftn tsuzamenfor." In *Di geshikhte fun bund. I*. Edited by G. Aronson, S. Dubnow-Erlich [Dubnoverlikh], J. S. Hertz [I. Sh. Herts], E. Nowogrudski [Novogrudski], Kh. Sh. Kazdan, and E. Scherer [Sherer]. New York: Farlag unzer tsayt, 1960, pp. 107–279.

Kaznelson, Siegmund. "Deutsche Juden im Pälastina-Aufbau." In *Juden im deutschen Kulturbereich. Ein Sammelwerk*. Edited by Siegmund Kaznelson. Berlin: Jüdischer Verlag, 1959, pp. 989–1002.

Kisman, Yoysef. "Di yidishe sotsial-demokratishe bavegung in galitsie un bukovine." In *Di geshikhte fun bund* III. Edited by G. Aronson, S. Dubnow-Erlich [Dubnov-erlikh], J. S. Hertz [I. Sh. Herts], E. Nowogrudski [Novogrudski], Kh. Sh. Kazdan, and E. Scherer [Sherer]. New York: Farlag unzer tsayt, 1966, pp. 337–482.

Klein, Dennis B. *Jewish Origins of the Psychoanalytic Movement*. Chicago & London: University of Chicago Press, 1985.

Knütter, Hans-Ulrich. *Die Juden und die deutsche Linke in der Weimarer Republik 1918–1933*. Bonner Schriften zur Politik und Zeitgeschichte, IV. Düsseldorf: Droste Verlag, 1971.

Kogan, Arthur. "The Social Democrats and the Conflict of Nationalities in the Habsburg Monarchy." *The Journal of Modern History* XXI, 3 (September 1949), pp. 204–17.

Kolakowski, Leszek. *Main Currents of Marxism*, I and II. Oxford, New York: Oxford University Press, 1978.

Korsch, Karl. "Die materialistische Geschichtsauffassung: Eine Auseinandersetzung mit Karl Kautsky." *Archiv für die Geschichte des Sozialismus und der Arbeiterbewegung* IV, 2 (1929), pp. 179–279.

Kupfer, Efrim. "Tsu der frage fun kamf fun SDKPL far der klasn-aynhayt fun di poylishe un yidishe arbeter." *Bleter far geshikhte* VII, 2–3 (April-August 1954), pp. 169–81.

*Kürschners deutscher Gelehrten-Kalender. 1931*. Berlin: Walter de Grunter, 1931.

Kursky, F. [Kurski]. "Di zhenever 'grupe sotsialistn-yidn' un ir oyfruf (1880)." In *Di yidishe sotsialistishe bavegung biz der grindung fun "bund." forshungen, zikhroynes, materialn*. Edited by E. Tscherikower [Tsherikover], A. Menes, F. Kursky [Kurski], and A. Rosin (Ben-Adir) [Rozin]. Historishe shriftn, III; Shriftn fun yidishn visnshaftlekhn institut, XI. Vilna, Paris: Historishe sektsie fun yivo, 1939, pp. 557–62.

Lamberti, Marjorie. *Jewish Activism in Imperial Germany: The Struggle for Civil Equality*. Yale Historical Publications, Miscellany, 119. New Haven and London: Yale University Press, 1978.

———. "Liberals, Socialists and the Defense against Antisemitism in the Wilhelminian Period." *Leo Baeck Institute Year Book* XXV (1980), pp. 147–62.

Laqueur, Walter. *A History of Zionism*. New York, London: Holt, Rinehart and Winston, 1972.

———. "Zionism, the Marxist Critique, and the Left." *Dissent* (December 1971), pp. 560–74.

Laschitza, Annelies. "Karl Kautsky und der Zentrismus." *Beiträge zur Geschichte der deutschen Arbeiterbewegung* 5 (1968), pp. 798–832.

Lee, Eric. "A Special Corner: Rosa Luxemburg and the Jewish Question." *The New International Review* II, 2 (Summer 1979), pp. 22–36.

Leser, Norbert and Richard Berczeller. *Als Zaungäste der Politik. Österreichische Zeitgeschichte in Konfrontationen.* Vienna, Munich: Jugend und Volk, 1977.

Lesky, Erna. *The Vienna Medical School of the 19th Century.* Baltimore and London: Johns Hopkins University Press, 1976.

Leuschen-Seppel, Rosemarie. *Sozialdemokratie und Antisemitismus im Kaiserreich. Die Auseinandersetzungen der Partei mit den konservativen und völkischen Strömungen des antisemitismus 1871–1914.* Reihe: Politik- und Gesellschaftsgeschichte. Bonn: Verlag Neue Gesellschaft GmbH, 1978.

Levine, Norman. "Lenin on Jewish Nationalism." *The Wiener Library Bulletin* XXXIII, n.s. 51–52 (1980), pp. 42–55.

Levy, Richard S. *The Downfall of the Anti-Semitic Political Parties in Imperial Germany.* Yale Historical Publications, Miscellany, 106. New Haven and London: Yale University Press, 1975.

Lidtke, Vernon L. *The Outlawed Party. Social Democracy in Germany, 1878–1890.* Princeton, N.J.: Princeton University Press, 1966.

Liebman, Arthur. *Jews and the Left.* New York: John Wiley and Sons, 1979.

Loewenberg, Peter. *Decoding the Past. The Psychohistorical Approach.* Berkeley, Los Angeles, London: University of California Press, 1985.

Löw, Raimund. *Der Zerfall der "Kleinen Internationale." Nationalitätenkonflikte in der Arbeiterbewegung des alten Österreich (1889–1914).* Ludwig Boltzmann Institut für Geschichte der Arbeiterbewegung, Materialien zur Arbeiterbewegung, 34. Vienna: Europa Verlag, 1984.

Löwy, Michael, "Marxists and the National Question." *New Left Review* 96, (March-April 1976), pp. 81–100.

MacDonald, H. Malcolm. "Karl Marx, Friedrich Engels, and the South Slavic Problem in 1848–9." *University of Toronto Quarterly* VIII (July 1939), pp. 452–60.

McCagg, William O., Jr. *A History of Habsburg Jews, 1670–1918.* Bloomington and Indianapolis: Indiana University Press, 1989.

———. "The Assimilation of Jews in Austria." In *Jewish Assimilation in Modern Times.* Edited by Bela Vago. Boulder, Col.: Westview Press, 1981, pp. 127–40.

McGrath, William J. *Dionysian Art and Populist Politics in Austria.* New Haven and London: Yale University Press, 1974.

Mahler, Raphael. *Hasidism and the Jewish Enlightenment. Their Confrontation in Galicia and Poland in the First Half of the Nineteenth Century.* Translated from the Yiddish by Eugene Orenstein. Translated from the Hebrew by Aaron Klein and Jenny Machlowitz Klein. Philadelphia, New York, Jerusalem: Jewish Publication Society of America, 1985.

Maitron, Jean and Haupt, Georges, eds. *Dictionnaire biographique du mouvement ouvrier international*. I. Paris: Les éditions ouvrières, 1971.

Massing, Paul W. *Rehearsal for Destruction. A Study of Political Anti-Semitism in Imperial Germany*. Studies in Prejudice. New York: Harper & Brothers, 1949.

Matthias, Erich. "Kautsky und der Kautskyanismus: Die Funktion der Ideologie in der deutschen Sozialdemokratie vor dem ersten Weltkriege." *Marxismusstudien* 2d series (1957), pp. 151–97.

Meisel, Nachman [Nakhman Mayzil]. *I. l. perets. zayn lebn un shafn. ophandlungen un materialn*. New York: Ikuf farlag, 1945.

———. "Leyzer tsukerman." In *Royter pinkes. tsu der geshikhte fun der yidisher arbeter-bavegung un sotsialistishe shtremungen bay yidn*. I. Warsaw: Farlag kultur-lige, 1921, pp. 92–112

Menachowski, Moyshe [Menakhovski]. *Ber borochov—zayn lebn un zayn shafn*. Buenos Aires: Farlag 'unzer vort,' 1959.

Mendelsohn, Ezra. "A Note on Jewish Assimilation in the Polish Lands." In *Jewish Assimilation in Modern Times*. Edited by Bela Vago. Boulder, Col.: Westview Press, 1981, pp. 141–49.

———. *Class Struggle in the Pale: The Formative Years of the Jewish Workers' Movement in Tsarist Russia*. Cambridge: Cambridge University Press, 1970.

———. "The Jewish Socialist Movement and the Second International, 1889–1914: The Struggle for Recognition." *Jewish Social Studies* XXVI (1964), pp. 131–45.

Menes, Abraham. "The Jewish Socialist Movement in Russia and Poland. (From the 1870s to the Founding of the Bund in 1897.)" In *The Jewish People, Past and Present*. II. New York: Jewish Encyclopedic Handbooks. Central Yiddish Culture Organization (CYCO), 1948, pp. 355–68.

Menes, Abraham, ed. *Der yidisher gedank in der nayer tsayt*. I. New York: Alveltlekher yidisher kultur-kongres, 1957.

Merchav, Peretz. "Jüdische Aspekte in der Einschätzung von Rosa Luxemburg." In *Juden und jüdische Aspekte in der deutschen Arbeiterbewegung 1848–1918*. Edited by Walter Grab. Jahrbuch des Instituts für deutsche Geschichte, Beiheft II. Tel Aviv: Universität Tel Aviv, 1977, pp. 185–201.

Meyer, Gustav. "Early German Socialism and Jewish Emancipation." *Jewish Social Studies* I, (1939), pp. 409–22.

Meyer, Thomas. *Bernsteins konstruktiver Sozialismus. Eduard Bernsteins Beitrag zur Theorie des Sozialismus*. Internationale Bibliothek, CIV. Berlin, Bonn-Bad Godesburg: Verlag J. H. W. Dietz Nachf. GmbH, 1977.

Misch, Carl. "Geschichtswissenschaft." In *Juden im deutschen Kulturbereich. Ein Sammelwerk*. Edited by Siegmund Kaznelson. Berlin: Jüdischer Verlag, 1959, pp. 349–82.

Mishkinsky, Moshe. "The Jewish Labor Movement and European Socialism." *Cahiers d' Histoire Mondiale* XI (1968–69), pp. 284–96.

Mohrmann, Walter. *Antisemitismus. Ideologie und Geschichte im Kaiserreich und in der Weimarer Republik*. Berlin: VEB Deutscher Verlag der Wissenschaften, 1972.

Mommsen, Hans. *Arbeiterbewegung und Nationale Frage. Ausgewählte Aufsätze*. Kritische Studien zur Geschichtswissenschaft, XXXIV. Göttingen: Vadenhoeck & Ruprecht, 1979.

———. *Die Sozialdemokratie und die Nationalitätenfrage im habsburgischen Vielvolkerstaat. I. Das Ringen um die supernationale Integration der zisleithanischen Arbeiterbewegung. 1867–1907*. Vienna: Europa Verlag, 1963.

Morton, Frederic. *Thunder at Twilight. Vienna 1913–1914*. New York: Charles Scribner's Sons, 1989.

Mosse, George L. "German Socialists and the Jewish Question in the Weimar Republic." *Leo Baeck Institute Year Book* XVI (1971), pp. 123–51.

Mosse, Werner, assisted by Arnold Paucker, eds. *Deutsches Judentum in Krieg und Revolution 1916–1923*. Schriftenreihe Wissenschaftlicher Abhandlungen des Leo Baeck Instituts, XXV. Tübingen: J. C. B. Mohr (Paul Siebeck), 1971.

Mosse, Werner and Arnold Paucker, eds. *Juden im Wilhelminischen Deutschland 1890–1914*. Schriftenreihe Wissenschaftlicher Abhandlungen des Leo Baeck Instituts, XXXIII. Tübingen: J. C. B. Mohr, 1976.

Nedava, Joseph. *Trotsky and the Jews*. Philadelphia: The Jewish Publication Society of America, 1972.

Nettl, [J.] Peter. "The German Social Democratic Party 1890–1914 as a Political Model." *Past and Present* 30 (1965), pp. 65–95.

———. *Rosa Luxemburg*. 2 vols. London, New York, Toronto: Oxford University Press, 1966.

Neumann, Daniela. *Studentinnen aus dem Russischen Reich in der Schweiz (1867–1914)*. Die Schweiz und der Osten Europas, I. Zurich: Verlag Hans Rohr, 1987.

Niewyk, Donald L. *The Jews in Weimar Germany*. Baton Rouge and London: Louisiana State University Press, 1980.

———. *Socialist, Anti-Semite and Jew. German Social Democracy Confronts the Problem of Anti-Semitism 1918–1933*. Baton Rouge: Louisiana State University Press, 1971.

Niger, Sh. *I. l. perets. zayn lebn, zayn firndike perzenlekhkeyt, zayne hebreishe un yidishe shriftn, zayn virkung*. Buenos Aires: Argentiner opteyl fun alveltlekhn yidishn kultur-kongres, 1952.

Niger, Shmuel, Yankev Shatski, et al., eds. *Leksikon fun der nayer yidisher literatur*. 8 vols. New York: Alveltlekher yidisher kultur-kongres, 1956–1981.

Novick, Paul. "Lumer vs. Lenin on the Jewish Question." *Jewish Currents* (July-August 1977), pp. 22–28.

Noy, Melekh. "Berl loker. etopn fun a rumful lebn." *Unzer vort* (May 13, 1957).

Osterroth, F., ed. *Biographisches Lexicon des Sozialismus*. I. Hannover: Verlag J. H. W. Dietz Nachf. GmbH, 1960.

Oxaal, Ivar, Michael Pollak, and Gerhard Botz, eds. *Jews, Antisemitism and Culture in Vienna*. London and New York: Routledge & Kegan Paul, 1987.

Patkin, Aaron L. *The Origins of the Russian-Jewish Labour Movement*. Melbourne and London: F. W. Cheshire Pty., 1947.

Paucker, Arnold. "Die Abwehr des Antisemitismus in den Jahren 1893–1933." In *Antisemitismus. Von der Judenfeindschaft zum Holocaust*. Edited by Herbert A. Strauss and Norbert Kampe. Schriftenreihe der Bundeszentrale für politische Bildung, CCXIII. Bonn: Bundeszentrale für politische Bildung, 1985, pp. 143–71.

———. "Jewish Defence Against Nazism in the Weimar Republic." *The Wiener Library Bulletin* XXVI, 1–2, n.s. 26–7 (1972), pp. 21–31.

———. "The Jewish Defense against Antisemitism in Germany, 1893–1933." In *Living With Antisemitism. Modern Jewish Responses*. Edited by Jehuda Reinharz. Hanover and London: Brandeis University Press, University Press of New England, 1987, pp. 104–32.

———. *Der jüdische Abwehrkampf gegen Antisemitismus und Nationalsozialismus in den letzten Jahren der Weimarer Republik*. Hamburger Beiträge zur Zeitgeschichte, IV. Hamburg: Leibniz-Verlag, 1968.

Paumgartten, Karl. *Judentum und Sozialdemokratie*. Graz: Heimatverlag Leopold Stocker, n.d.

Pavloff, Vladimir Nikolaevich. "Revolutionary Populism in Imperial Russia and the National Question in the 1870s and 1880s." In *Socialism and Nationalism*. I. Edited by Eric Cahm and Vladimir Claude Fisera. Nottingham: Spokesman, 1978, pp. 69–95.

Peled, Yoav. *Class and Ethnicity in the Pale. The Political Economy of Jewish Workers' Nationalism in late Imperial Russia*. New York: St. Martin's Press, 1989.

Peretz, I. L. [Perets]. *In mayn vinkele. mayne zikhroynes*. Di verk fun itskhok leybush perets, XIII. Edited by Dovid Pinski. New York: Farlag "yidish," 1920.

*Perspectives of German-Jewish History in the 19th and 20th Century*. Jerusalem: Leo Baeck Institute, Jerusalem Academic Press, 1971.

Petrus, Joseph A. "The Theory and Practice of Internationalism: Rosa Luxemburg's Solution to the National Question." *East European Quarterly* IV, 4 (January 1971), pp. 442–56.

Piasecki, Henryk. *Sekcja Żydowska PPSD i Żydowska Partia Socjalno-Demokratyczna 1892–1919/20*. Wrocław, Warsaw, Cracow, Gdańsk, Lodz: Zakład Narodowy im. Ossolińskich wydawnictwo Polskiej Akademii Nauk, 1982.

Pinson, Koppel S. "Arkady Kremer, Vladimr Medem, and the Ideology of the Jewish 'Bund.' " *Jewish Social Studies* VII (1945), pp. 233–64.

Poppel, Stephen N. *Zionism in Germany 1897–1933*. Philadelphia: Jewish Publication Society of America, 1977.

Pulzer, P. G. J. *The Rise of Political Anti-Semitism in Germany and Austria*. New York: John Wiley and Sons, 1964.

Radek, Karl. *Portraits and Pamphlets*. London: Wishart Books, 1935.

Ran, Leyzer. *Yerushalayim de-lite*. I. New York: Vilner farlag, 1974.

Reinharz, Jehuda. *Fatherland or Promised Land: The Dilemma of the German Jew, 1893–1914*. Ann Arbor: University of Michigan Press, 1975.

Reissner, H. G. "Rebellious Dilemma: The Case Histories of Eduard Gans and Some of his Partisans." *Leo Baeck Institute Year Book* II (1957), pp. 179–93.

Reyzen, Zalmen. "L. jogiches-tishka un der beginen fun der yidisher arbeter-bavegung." *Yivo bleter* I, 5 (1931), pp. 432–48.

————. *Leksikon fun der yidisher literatur*. 4 vols. Vilna: Farlag fun b. kletskin, 1926–1929.

————. *Leksikon fun der yudisher literatur un prese*. Edited by Sh. Niger. Warsaw: Farlags-gezelshaft "tsentral," 1914.

Rosdolsky, Roman. "Friedrich Engels und das Problem der 'geschichtslosen' Völker (Die Nationalitätenfrage in der Revolution 1848–1849 im Lichte der 'Neuen Rheinischen Zeitung')." *Archiv für Sozialgeschichte* IV (1964), pp. 87–282.

Rozenblit, Marsha L. *The Jews of Vienna, 1867–1914: Assimilation and Identity*. SUNY Series in Modern Jewish History. Albany: State University of New York Press, 1983.

Salvadori, Massimo. *Karl Kautsky and the Socialist Revolution 1880–1938*. London: NLB, 1979.

Sapir, Boris. "Jewish Socialists around 'Vpered.' " *International Review of Social History* X, (1965), pp. 365–84.

————. "Lieberman et le socialisme russe." *International Review for Social History* III (1938), pp. 25–88.

Sawicki, Aron. "Szkoła rabinów w warszawie (1826–1863)." *Miesięcznik Żydowski* 3 (1933), pp. 244–74.

Schappes, Morris U. "The Jewish Question and the Left—Old and New." *Jewish Currents* (June 1970), pp. 4–37.

Scheichl, Sigurd Paul. "The Contexts and Nuances of Anti-Jewish Language: Were All the 'Antisemites' Antisemites?" In *Jews, Antisemitism and Culture in Vienna*. Edited by Ivar Oxaal, Michael Pollak, and Gerhard Botz. London and New York: Routledge & Kegan Paul, 1987, pp. 89–110.

Schorsch, Ismar. *Jewish Reactions to German Anti-Semitism, 1870–1914*. Columbia University Studies in Jewish History, Culture, and Institutions, III. New York and London: Columbia University Press; Philadelphia: Jewish Publication Society of America, 1972.

Schorske, Carl E. *German Social Democracy 1905–1917. The Development of the Great Schism.* New York: John Wiley and Sons, 1955.

Schwarz, Robert. "Antisemitism and Socialism in Austria, 1918–1962." In *The Jews of Austria.* Edited by Josef Fraenkel. London: Vallentine Mitchell, 1967, pp. 445–66.

Shafir, Shlomo. "Julius Braunthal and his Postwar Mediation Efforts between German and Israeli Socialists." *Jewish Social Studies* XLVII (1985), pp. 267–80.

Shapiro, Judah J. *The Friendly Society: A History of the Workmen's Circle.* New York: Media Judaica, 1970.

Shtayn, Aleksander. "Di barimte roza luksemburg iz geven a 'landsfroy' fun dem barimten i. l. perets." *Forverts* (January 16, 1949), Second section, p. 4.

Shatzky, Jacob [Shatski, Yankev]. "Der bilbul oyf zamoshtsher yidn in 1870 in likht fun peretses zikhroynes." *Yivo bleter* XXXVI (1952), pp. 329–31.

———. *Geshikhte fun yidn in varshe.* 2 vols. New York: Yidisher visnshaftlekher institut, historishe sektsye, 1948.

———. "Haskole in zamoshtsh." *Yivo bleter* XXXVI (1952), pp. 24–62.

———. "Perets-shtudies." *Yivo bleter* XXVIII, 1 (Fall 1946), pp. 40–80.

———. Review of *Dr. shloyme etingers ksovim,* edited by Max Weinreich. *Pinkes. a fertlyoriker zshurnal far yidisher literaturgeshikhte, shprakhforshung, folklor, un bibliografie* I (1927–28), pp. 281–83.

———. *Yidishe bildungs-politik in poyln fun 1806 biz 1866.* New York: Yidisher visnshaftlekher institut, historishe sektsye, 1943.

Shelton, Anita K. "Rosa Luxemburg and the National Question." *East European Quarterly* XXI, 3 (September 1987), pp. 297–303.

Shub, Dovid. *Sotsiale denker un kemfer.* II. Mexico City: Farlag shloyme mendelson fond, gezelshaft "kultur un hilf," 1968.

Shukman, Harold. "Lenin's Nationalities Policy and the Jewish Question." *Bulletin on Soviet and East European Affairs* 5 (May 1970), pp. 43–50.

———. Review of *Rosa Luxemburg* by J. P. Nettl. *Jewish Journal of Sociology* IX (1967), pp. 126–29.

Silberner, Edmund. "Anti-Semitism and Philo-Semitism in the Socialist International." *Judaism* II (1953), pp. 117–22.

———. "Austrian Social Democracy and the Jewish Problem." *Historia Judaica* XIII, part 2 (October 1951), pp. 121–40.

———. "British Socialism and the Jews." *Historia Judaica* XIV (1952), pp. 27–52.

———. "Ein unbekannter Brief Simon Dubnows an Eduard Bernstein." *Jahrbuch des Instituts für deutsche Geschichte* VI (1977), pp. 525–26.

———. "Eleanor Marx. Ein Beitrag zu ihrer Biographie und zum Problem der jüdischen Identität." *Jahrbuch des Instituts für deutsche Geschichte* VI (1977), pp. 259–95.

———. "French Socialism and the Jewish Question, 1865–1914." *Historia Judaica* XVI (1954), pp. 3–38.

———. "Friedrich Engels and the Jews." *Jewish Social Studies* XI (1949), pp. 323–42.

———. "Friedrich Engels' Geschenk an eine jüdische Bibliothek in London." *Jahrbuch des Institut für deutsche Geschichte* IX (1980), pp. 493–96.

———. "German Social Democracy and the Jewish Problem Prior to World War I." *Historia Judaica* XV, part 1 (April 1953), pp. 3–48.

———. "The Jew-Hatred of Mikhail Aleksandrovich Bakunin." *Historia Judaica* XIV (1952), pp. 93–106.

———. *Kommunisten zur Judenfrage. Zur Geschichte von Theorie und Praxis des Kommunismus.* Opladen: Westdeutscher Verlag, 1983.

———. "Die Kommunistische Partei Deutschlands zur Judnfrage." *Jahrbuch des Instituts für deutsche Geschichte* VIII (1979), pp. 283–334.

———. "Rosa Luxemburg, ihre Partei und die Judenfrage." *Jahrbuch des Instituts für deutsche Geschichte* VII (1978), pp. 299–327.

———. *Sozialisten zur Judenfrage.* Berlin: Colloquium Verlag, 1962.

———. "Was Marx an Anti-Semite?" *Historia Judaica* XI (1949), pp. 3–52.

———. *Western European Socialism and the Jewish Problem (1800–1918). A Selective Bibliography.* Jerusalem: The Hebrew University—The Eliezer Kaplan School of Economic and Social Science, 1955.

Simon, Walter B. "The Jewish Vote in Austria." *Leo Baeck Institute Year Book* XVI (1971), pp. 97–121.

Socolow, Nahum [Sokolov, Nakhum]. *Perzenlekhkeytn.* Translated by Moises Senderey [Moyshe Shenderey]. Buenos Aires: Tsentral-farband fun poylishe yidn in argentine, 1948.

Šolle, Zdeněk. "Die Sozialdemokratie in der Habsburger Monarchie und die tschechische Frage." *Archiv für Sozialgeschichte* VI/VII (1966–1967), pp. 315–80.

———. "Die tschechische Sozialdemokratie zwischen Nationalismus und Internationalismus." *Archiv für Sozialgeschichte* IX (1969), pp. 181–266.

———. "Vzpomínka Karla Kautského na břevnovský sjezd československé sociální demokracie." *Československý časopis historický* XIII, 2 (1965), pp. 269–79.

Spira, Leopold. *Feinbild "Jud'." 100 Jahre politischer Antisemitismus in Österreich.* Vienna and Munich: Löcker Verlag, 1981.

Stadler-Labhart, Verena. *Rosa Luxemburg an der Universität Zürich 1889–1897.* Schriften zur Zürcher Universitäts- und Gelehrtengeschichte, II. Zurich: Verlag Hans Rohr, 1978.

Steenson, Gary P. *Karl Kautsky, 1854–1938. Marxism in the Classical Years.* Pittsburgh: University of Pittsburgh Press, 1978.

Sterling, Eleonore. "Jewish Reactions to Jew-Hatred in the First Half of the Nineteenth Century." *Leo Baeck Institute Year Book* III (1958), pp. 103–21.

Strobel, Georg W. *Die Partei Rosa Luxemburgs, Lenin und die S.P.D. Der polnische "europäische" Internationalismus in der russischen Sozialde-mokratie.* Wiesbaden: Franz Steiner Verlag, GmbH, 1974.

Tal, Uriel. *Christians and Jews in Germany: Religion, Politics, and Ideology in the Second Reich, 1870–1914.* Translated by Noah Jonathan Jacobs. Ithaca, N.Y., and London: Cornell University Press, 1975.

Talmon, J. L. *The Myth of the Nation and the Vision of Revolution: The Origins of Ideological Polarisation in the Twentieth Century.* London: Secker & Warburg; Berkeley and Los Angeles: University of California Press, 1980.

Teller, Judd L. *Scapegoat of Revolution.* New York: Charles Scribner's Sons, 1954.

Tennstedt, Florian. "Arbeiterbewegung und Familiengeschichte bei Eduard Bernstein und Ignaz Zadek. Hilfwissenschaftliche Mitteilungen zu persönlichen Aspekten von Revisionismus und Sozialreform bei deutschen Sozialdemokraten." *IWK. Internationale wissenschaftliche Korrespondenz zur Geschichte der deutschen Arbeiterbewegung* XVIII, 4 (December 1982), pp. 451–81.

Theilhaber, Felix A. "Die sozialistisch-zionistische Arbeiterpartei Poalei-Zion." In *Das deutsche Judentum. Seine Parteien und Organisationen. Eine Sammelschrift.* Berlin, Munich: Verlag der neuen jüdischen Monatshefte, 1919, pp. 38–43.

Tobias, Henry J. *The Jewish Bund in Russia. From Its Origins to 1905.* Stanford, Calif.: Stanford University Press, 1972.

Toury, Jacob. "Defense Activities of the Österreichisch-Israelitische Union before 1914." In *Living with Anti-Semitism: Modern Jewish Responses.* Edited by Jehuda Reinharz. The Tauber Institute for the Study of European Jewry Series, VI. Hanover and London: Brandeis University Press, University Press of New England, 1987, pp. 167–92.

―――. *Die politischen Orientierungen der Juden in Deutschland. Von Jena bis Weimar.* Schriftenreihe Wissenschaftlicher Abhandlungen des Leo Baeck Instituts, XV. Tübingen: J. C. B. Mohr, 1966.

Tscherikower, E. [Tsherikover]. "Bamerkungen un derklerungen tsu di zikhroynes fun grigori gurevitch." In *Di yidishe sotsialistishe bavegung biz der grindung fun "bund." forshungen, zikhroynes, materialn.* Edited by E. Tscherikower [Tsherikover], A. Menes, F. Kursky [Kurski], and A. Rosin (Ben-Adir) [Rozin]. *Historishe shriftn,* III; Shriftn fun yidishn visnshaftlekhn institut, XI. Vilna, Paris: Historishe sektsie fun yivo, 1939, pp. 244–52.

―――. "London un ir pionerishe role in der bavegung." In *Geshikhte fun der yidisher arbeter-bavegung in di fareynikte shtatn.* II. Edited by E. T[s]cherikower [Tsherikover]. New York: Yidisher visnshaftlekher institut—yivo, 1945, pp. 76–137.

―――. "Nokh vegn der zhenever 'grupe sotsialistn-yidn.' " In *Di yidishe sotsialistishe bavegung biz der grindung fun "bund." forshungen, zikhroynes, materialn.* Edited by E. Tscherikower [Tsherikover], A. Menes,

F. Kursky [Kurski], and A. Rosin (Ben-Adir) [Rozin]. Historishe shriftn, III; Shriftn fun yidishn visnshaftlekhn institut, XI. Vilna, Paris: Historishe sektsie fun yivo, 1939, pp. 563–67.

———. "Der onhoyb fun der yidisher sotsialistisher bavegung." In *Historishe shriftn* I. Edited by E. Tscherikower [Tsherikover]. Yidisher visnshaftlekher institut, historishe sektsie. Warsaw: Kooperativer farlag "kultur-lige," 1929, pp. 469–532.

———. "Yidn-revolutsionern in rusland in di zekhtsiker un zibtsiker yorn." In *Di yidishe sotsialistishe bavegung biz der grindung fun "bund." forshungen, zikhroynes, materialn.* Edited by E. Tscherikower [Tsherikover], A. Menes, F. Kursky [Kurski], and A. Rosin (Ben-Adir) [Rozin]. Historishe shriftn, III; Shriftn fun yidishn visnshaftlekhn institut, XI. Vilna, Paris: Historishe sektsie fun yivo, 1939, pp. 156–57.

Tsudiker, I. "Di odlerin vos iz aroysgefloygn fun zamoshtsh." In *Pinkes zamoshtsh.* Edited by Mordekhai V. Bernshtayn. Buenos Aires: Tsentral komitet far pinkes zamoshtsh, 1957, pp. 534–44.

*Tsum ondenk fun m. b. ratner. zamlbukh.* Edited by the Ratner fond. [Kiev]: Kiever farlag, 1919.

Tsuzuki, Chushichi. *The Life of Eleanor Marx, 1855–1898: A Socialist Tragedy.* Oxford: Clarendon, 1967.

Vettes, William George. "The German Social Democrats and the Eastern Question 1848–1900." *The American Slavic and East European Review* XVII, 1 (February 1958), pp. 86–100.

Volkov, Shulamit. "The Immunization of Social Democracy against Anti-Semitism in Imperial Germany." In *Juden und jüdische Aspekte in der deutschen Arbeiterbewegung 1848–1918.* Edited by Walter Grab. Jahrbuch des Instituts für deutsche Geschichte, Beiheft II. Tel Aviv: Universität Tel Aviv, 1977, pp. 63–83.

Walicki, A. "Rosa Luxemburg and the Question of Nationalism in Polish Marxism (1893–1914)." *The Slavonic and East European Review* LXI, 4 (October 1983), pp. 565–82.

Weltsch, Robert. "Introduction." *Leo Baeck Institute Year Book* XV (1970), pp. VII-XVIII.

Wendel, Hermann. "Marxism and the Southern Slav Question." *The Slavonic Review* II (December 1923), pp. 289–307.

Wininger, S. *Große jüdische National-Biographie.* Cernăuţi: Buchdruckerei "Arta," n.d.

Wistrich, Robert S. "[A]n Austrian variation on socialist antisemitism." *Patterns of Prejudice* VIII, 4 (July-August 1974), pp. 1–10.

———. "Anti-Capitalism or Antisemitism? The Case of Franz Mehring." *Leo Baeck Institute Year Book* XXII (1977), pp. 35–51.

———. "Austrian Social Democracy and the Problem of Galician Jewry 1890–1914." *Leo Baeck Institute Year Book* XXVI (1981), pp. 89–124.

———. "Back to Bernstein? A Neo-Revisionist Renaissance." *Encounter* L, 6 (June 1978), pp. 75–80.

————. "Eduard Bernstein and the Jewish Problem." *Jahrbuch des Instituts für deutsche Geschichte* VIII (1979), pp. 243–56.

————. "Eduard Bernstein on the Jewish Problem." *Midstream* (December 1979), pp. 8–13.

————. "Eduard Bernstein und das Judentum." In *Bernstein und der Demokratische Sozialismus. Bericht über den wissenschaftlichen Kongreß "Die historische Leistung und aktuelle Bedeutung Eduard Bernsteins."* Edited by Horst Heimann and Thomas Meyer. Internationale Bibliothek CXIV. Berlin, Bonn: Verlag J. H. W. Dietz Nachf. GmbH, 1978, pp. 149–65.

————. "French Socialism and the Dreyfus Affair." *The Wiener Library Bulletin* XXVIII, n.s. 35–36 (1975), pp. 9–20.

————. "German Social Democracy and the Berlin Movement." *IWK. Internationale wissenschaftliche Korrespondenz zur Geshichte der deutschen Arbeiterbewegung* XII, 4 (December 1976), pp. 433–42.

————. "German Social Democracy and the Problem of Jewish Nationalism 1897–1917." *Leo Baeck Institute Year Book* XXI (1976), pp. 109–42.

————. "The Jewish Origins of Rosa Luxemburg." *Olam* 3 (Winter-Spring 1977), pp. 3–10.

————. *The Jews of Vienna in the Age of Franz Joseph.* Oxford: Littman Library, Oxford University Press, 1989.

————. "Karl Marx, German Socialists and the Jewish Question, 1880–1914." *Soviet Jewish Affairs* III, 1 (1973), pp. 92–97.

————. "Marxism and Jewish Nationalism: The Theoretical Roots of Confrontation." *The Jewish Journal of Sociology* XVII (June 1975), pp. 43–54.

————. "The Marxist Concern with Judaism." *Patterns of Prejudice* IX, 4 (July-August 1975), pp. 1–6.

————. *Revolutionary Jews from Marx to Trotsky.* London: Harrap, 1976.

————. "Social Democracy, the Jews, and Antisemitism in *Fin-de-Siècle* Vienna." In *Living With Antisemitism. Modern Jewish Responses.* Edited by Jehuda Reinharz. Hanover and London: Brandeis University Press, University Press of New England, 1987, pp. 193–209.

————. "Socialism and Antisemitism in Austria before 1914." *Jewish Social Studies* XXXVII, 3–4 (Summer-Fall 1975), pp. 323–32.

————. *Socialism and the Jews. The Dilemmas of Assimilation in Germany and Austria-Hungary.* Rutherford, Madison, Teaneck, N.J.: Fairleigh Dickinson University Press; London and Toronto: Associated University Presses, 1982.

————. "The SPD and Antisemitism in the 1890s." *European Studies Review* VII, 2 (April 1977), pp. 177–97.

————. "Victor Adler: A Viennese Socialist against Philosemitism." *The Wiener Library Bulletin* XXVII, n.s. 32 (1974), pp. 26–33.

Yaari, Arieh. "Rosa Luxemburg ou le nihilisme national." *Les nouveaux cahiers* 39 (Winter 1974–1975), pp. 27–31.

*Yitshok nakhman shtaynberg—der mentsh. zayn vort. zayn oyftu. 1888–1957.* New York: Dr. y. n. shtaynberg bukh komitet, 1961.

Zadek, Walter, ed. *Sie flohen vor dem Hakenkreuz.* Reinbek bei Hamburg: Rowohlt Taschenbuch Verlag GmbH, 1981.

Zaks, A. S. *Di geshikhte fun arbeter ring 1892–1925.* 2 vols. N.p.: Nationaler ekzekutiv fun arbeter ring, 1925.

Zerubawel [Zerubavel] [Yakov Vitkin]. *Ber borokhov. zayn leben un shafen.* I. Warsaw: Arbeter-heim [heym], 1926.

———. "Leon khazanovitsh." In *Yidisher arbeter pinkes (tsu der geshikhte fun der poyle-tsien bavegung).* Edited by Zerubawel [Zerubavel]. I. Warsaw: Kooperativer farlag "naye kultur," 1927, pp. 579–89.

———. "Der grindungs-period fun der i.s.d.a.p. poyle-tsien in rusland." In *Royter pinkes. tsu der geshikhte fun der yidisher arbeter-bavegung un sotsialistishe shtremungen bay yidn.* I. Warsaw: Farlag kultur-lige, 1921, pp. 131–51

Zilberfarb, M. "Di grupe 'vozrozhdenie.' (vi zi iz antshtanen un zikh antviklt)." In *Royter pinkes. tsu der geshikhte fun der yidisher arbeter-bavegung un sotsialistishe shtremungen bay yidn.* I. Warsaw: Farlag kultur-lige, 1921, pp. 113–30.

Zivion [Dr. B. Hoffman] [Tsivyon (Dr. b. hofman)]. *Far fuftsik yor. geklibene shriftn.* New York: E. laub farlag ko., 1948.

# Index